FREUD, ADLER, AND JUNG

Discovering the Mind

Walter Kaufmann

with new introductory essays by Ivan Soll

Volume I *Goethe, Kant, and Hegel*

Volume II *Nietzsche, Heidegger, and Buber*

Volume III *Freud, Adler, and Jung*

FREUD, ADLER, AND JUNG

Discovering the Mind

Volume 3

Walter Kaufmann
With a New Introduction by Ivan Soll

Routledge
Taylor & Francis Group
LONDON AND NEW YORK

Originally published in 1980 by McGraw-Hill Book Company

Published 1992 by Transaction Publishers

Published 2017 by Routledge
2 Park Square, Milton Park, Abingdon, Oxon OX14 4RN
711 Third Avenue, New York, NY 10017, USA

Routledge is an imprint of the Taylor & Francis Group, an informa business

New material this edition copyright © Taylor & Francis

Library of Congress Catalog Number: 90-11108

Library of Congress Cataloging-in-Publication Data
(Revised for volume 3)

Kaufmann, Walter Arnold
    Discovering the mind.

Originally published: New York: McGraw-Hill, 1980.
Includes bibliographical references and indexes.
Contents: v. 1. Goethe, Kant, and Hegel—v. 3. Freud, Adler, and Jung.
        1. Philosophy of mind—History. 2. Self-knowledge, Theory of—
History. 3. Psychoanalysis—History. 4. Philosophy, German. I. Title.

BD418.3.K38 1990 193[B]   90-11108

ISBN 13: 978-0-88738-395-3 (pbk)

Freud in 1938.

Jung in New York in 1912.

Adler in 1910.

Contents ▶▶▶

V. Mind and Mask

ILLUSTRATIONS

Introduction
to the
Transaction Edition*

Ivan Soll

A Personal Approach to the Knowledge of Persons

Toward the end of an unflaggingly vital and productive life that was to be tragically truncated in an abrupt and unanticipated way, Walter Kaufmann wrote *Discovering the Mind*. Erudite but animated, monumental but not at all ponderous, it is, among other things, Kaufmann's final reconsideration of an intellectual tradition that had been the abiding source and focus of his own prolific writing.

---

*This introduction to volume 3 of *Discovering the Mind* contains, somewhat revised and recast, most of my introduction to volume 1 as its beginning and end (pp. xvii-xxxiv, lv-lvii in this text) and a brief mention of some of the themes of volume 2, derived from my introduction to that volume (pp. xxxiv-xxxv). I have done this for two reasons: First, because a great part of the material in my introduction to volume 1 addresses this three volume work as a whole. Second, because my discussion of the figures in the first and second volumes may provide a helpful orientation to those readers who are unfamiliar with those volumes. To this I have added a substantial amount of new material specifically focussed upon volume 3 (pp. xxxv-lv).

The subject of the work is explicitly defined not in terms of a historical tradition, however, but of an enterprise, "discovering the mind." Kaufmann conceives this broadly, using "mind" as "an inclusive term for feeling and intelligence, reason and emotion, perception and will."[1] And Kaufmann's avowed "central aim throughout" is "to contribute to the discovery of the mind."[2] But he also claims that "It should be one of the compensations of this study that it leads to a new and better understanding of a good deal of the intellectual history of the past two hundred years."[3]

What he in fact deals with historically is an intellectual tradition developed principally by thinkers who wrote in German. Since Kaufmann defines his subject matter in terms of its intellectual aim rather than its historical period, we are confronted by his implicit suggestion that in the last two hundred years most of the interesting developments in the discovery of the mind have, in fact, taken place among those who have written in German. Given the list of thinkers who are included in his discussion, this provocative suggestion is not without some plausibility.

The work is divided into three volumes. Each deals with three major figures: the first with Goethe, Kant, and Hegel; the second with Nietzsche, Heidegger, and Buber; the third with Freud, Adler, and Jung. There are also a number of other figures, like Lessing, Schiller, Kierkegaard and Schopenhauer, who are treated far more briefly, often by way of illuminating the writers receiving fuller analysis.

Each volume has a hero. A case is made that Goethe, Nietzsche, and Freud were in significant ways admirable human beings who made important contributions to the discovery of the mind. The other six do not come off nearly as well. Hegel and Buber receive mixed reviews. The rest are severely criticized as being both of unadmirable character and as having contributed little to the discovery of the mind, indeed, as having seriously impeded it. We are presented with an intellectual landscape in which what is not a help is usually a hindrance, in which an author's character is usually relevant to his contribution, and in which intellectual interventions are rarely ever impersonal.

Kaufmann makes no attempt to depict this landscape in muted tones, as he allows both his enthusiasms and distastes full expression.

Whether one always agrees with him is beside the point. His judgments are generally supported with cogent argumentation, and the passion with which he embraces and rejects thinkers and their thought seems appropriate to the importance of the issues at stake. Kaufmann's extremely frank and personal expression of his passions and preferences is unusual in academic writing. This should not be taken as a ground for criticism but rather as an essential part of his unique contribution to the discussion of these matters.

Kaufmann closely links the process of discovering the mind with the attainment of self-knowledge. He insists on this linkage not only in the case of our coming to know our own minds but also where it less obviously obtains, in the process of discovering the nature of the human mind in general. In closely connecting all knowledge of the mind with self-knowledge, Kaufmann is doing more than recalling Socrates's injunction, "Know thyself!," and allying his enterprise with it. He is calling attention to often overlooked or suppressed links between knowing one's own mind in particular and the human mind in general, between self-deception and the misunderstanding of others, between self-knowledge and the knowledge of selves. Kaufmann argues with reference to a number of thinkers, that flaws in one's understanding of oneself are usually obstacles to one's understanding of others, that the failure of a theory about the human mind often mirrors a failure of the theorist to come to terms with himself.

This consideration of theories about the human mind in conjunction with an examination of the personalities of the theorists constitutes another salient feature of Kaufmann's method, and one which again puts him at odds with standard academic practice. Kaufmann unabashedly breaches the prevalent prohibition against any *ad hominem* approach to philosophers, explicitly calling this taboo into question. Starting with the reasonable assumption that "the ideas of these men are not totally unrelated to their mentalities," he repeatedly offers evidence specifically linking their particular theories to their personalities. He thinks it enlightening and imperative to discover the minds of those who discovered the mind.

In entering upon this terrain, Kaufmann is careful and quick to distance himself from "reductionism," which he defines, with admirable and delightful concision as "the claim that something is 'nothing but' something else." In the context of exploring the relation between the personalities and theories of those who wrote about the mind, reductionism consists in the claim that conceptions of the human mind are nothing but reflections of the personalities of their authors.

Although Kaufmann does not spell out the reasons for rejecting reductionism, they are not difficult to locate. The kind of reductionism here at issue tends to have disastrous methodological consequences. If this type of reductionism were accepted, tracing the way in which any conception of the human mind is anchored in the personality of its author would become the central or even the sole question to be investigated. And it would tend to be pursued to the neglect or even exclusion of other issues, particularly those concerning the intrinsic plausibility and merit of the conceptions under investigation. I think that the widespread and tenaciously rooted resistance to any analysis of conceptions and theories as reflections of the character of their authors stems from a fear that the legitimation of such investigations would undermine the traditional assessment of the intrinsic value of the ideas themselves.

Kaufmann does not, however, intend his analyses of the relation between a writer's ideas and his personality to be a replacement for traditional investigations of the intrinsic merit of the ideas, but as a supplement to them. Having explicitly rejected reductionism, he is not inclined to replacing the assessment of the ideas themselves by accounts of their genesis out of the personalities of their authors. His program entails only enriching the accounts and assessments of the works themselves with considerations of the authors' personalities. And indeed, such considerations do sometimes help to explain otherwise puzzling adherences to implausible ideas and unpromising intellectual practices, to account for opinions rigidly held and curiously impervious to the claims of competing views, and to illuminate strong intellectual commitments made in the absence of decisive evidence.

Discovering the Mind as a whole constitutes a plea as well as a paradigm for the introduction of such considerations into the standard repertoire of historians and interpreters of philosophical and psychological theories. This program is certainly not without precedents, but they are not usually to be found among philosophers, and even more rarely among those of repute, like Kaufmann.

The most notable exception to this tendency and the principal inspiration of this and several other of the book's remarkable qualities is Friedrich Nietzsche. It was Nietzsche who argued that a philosophical theory was best understood primarily as the expression of the philospher's basic personality, rather than as the result of his impersonal consideration of data and arguments. Though Nietzsche was not as careful as Kaufmann to avoid the reefs of reductionism, his analyses of the relation between the character of various thinkers and their thought clearly constitute the model for Kaufmann's own excursions into this area. Kaufmann, in venturing hypotheses about various ideas and theories as *reflections of* as well as *reflections by* the minds that produced them, is reviving a promising type of Nietzschean analysis, generally neglected and taboo.

Nietzsche's influence can also be discerned in Kaufmann's masterfully rapid but penetrating approach, his refusal to get bogged down in the morass of his material, his deliberate decision not to attempt to offer an overly comprehensive account of the subject matter, whereby his major theses and insights would lose a great deal of their force and profile in a sea of related but not essential detail. This is a quality that Nietzsche had himself displayed and that he had singled out for discussion as the all-important "tempo" of a work. Though *Discovering the Mind,* like all of Kaufmann's work, is remarkably well informed and informative, it aspires neither to be complete nor compendious. In fact, it is one of Kaufmann's theses that the ideal of offering complete accounts of intellectual developments owes much of its influence to Hegel and has been an unfortunate development, an unrealizable requirement that creates pressure to mask the inevitable incompleteness of the narratives of intellectual history by recourse to obscurity.

Nietzsche's influence is also clear in Kaufmann's deliberate rejection of a dispassionate tone. Nietzsche was not only the subject of Kaufmann's first book, *Nietzsche: Philosopher, Psychologist, Antichrist* (1950), the philosopher much of whose work Kaufmann translated into English, and one of the three acknowledged heroes of *Discovering the Mind*. He, more than anyone, influenced Walter Kaufmann's entire philosophic work, and his imprint on the conception and style of Kaufmann's last book is unmistakable.

Breaking the Barriers

The tradition that Kaufmann reconsiders, that of "discovering the mind" in German letters of the last two hundred years, clearly crosses or ignores the boundaries among the disciplines as they have come to be defined and established in the academy. Some of the figures he discusses, such as Kant, Hegel, and Heidegger, have been clearly defined, by themselves and the tradition, as philosophers. Others, such as Goethe and Schiller, despite their historically influential and intrinsically valuable theoretical writings, have been usually categorized as being essentially writers of "literature," that is of "imaginative literature," whose works are studied primarily in departments of literature and written about by people who consider themselves literary critics and historians. Others, such as Freud, Adler, and Jung, find their niche in our established order of the disciplines among the "psychologists," even though not all of their neighbors in this edifice are particularly happy about the proximity.

Still others, like Nietzsche and Buber, have been harder to place. Nietzsche, who preferred to identify himself as a "good European" rather than as a German, led a life in which he had no fixed abode in any one country or academic discipline, a life in which he continually moved across borders, both geographic and intellectual. His work has suffered and enjoyed a similar fate. Because of its highly literary, metaphorical, and aphoristic style, its lack and avoidance of fully spelled out argumentation for its positions, its vehement and personal tone, its unorthodox set of concerns; it was long rejected by a majority of the philosophical establishment in the English-speaking world—not as being bad philosophy, but as not being philosophy at all. And not even Nietzsche's recent prominence has dissolved the problem of his marginality. In the English-speaking world, his new popularity still finds its center of gravity on the periphery of the discipline of philosophy or in other disciplines, in those, for example, that concern themselves with the theory of literature and art.

Buber's position in the world of academic philosophy is surely even more marginal and obscure than Nietzsche's. As in the case of Kierkegaard, there remains uncertainty as to whether he belongs to philosophy or theology.

Walter Kaufmann's *Discovering the Mind* speaks in an important way to these issues of disciplinary identity. As is usually the case in Kaufmann's work, the discussion has both a historical and a philosophical dimension. The historical dimension concerns the two-hundred-year tradition of German letters taken up for consideration in this book. The interdependence of philosophy, literature, and psychology in this tradition is so obvious and well documented, that one is tempted to say that it cannot be ignored, except that it has been ignored, particularly, though not exclusively, in the English-speaking world.

In this German tradition, those who produced literary works and those who produced philosophical works regularly read each other and drew inspiration from this cross-disciplinary reading. (Kant is perhaps the one notable exception: though he was widely read by literary figures in the tradition, he did not read them.) Some of the central figures in the tradition, notably Goethe, Schiller, and Nietzsche, produced significant theoretical and literary work. The literary work of Goethe and Schiller, as well as their theoretical work, importantly influenced the development of German philosophy. Most importantly, there was a strongly sensed community of purpose that transcended the barriers of genre and discipline. "Discovering the mind," Kaufmann argues, was an important aspect of what was viewed as a common enterprise, to which literature, philosophy, and psychology all contributed. We should not forget that psychology only gradually emerged as a separate discipline in the course of this period.

Though there has been some awareness and acknowledgment of the organic cohesiveness and interdependence of literature, philosophy, and psychology in this tradition, it remains for the most part superficial, undetailed, and without consequence in our approach to the period. Professional philosophers still tend to study the philosophical texts in abstraction from those literary works that often inspired them or to which they are a response. Although some literary critics do acknowledge the influence of philosophical works upon literary ones, they rarely analyze the philosophic texts in sufficient detail and almost never incorporate careful *philosophic* assessment of these texts into their accounts. Among psychologists, who are typically concerned with the legitimation of their discipline as a "science" on the basis of its similarities with the paradigmatic physical sciences, psychology's common origin with philosophy and literature and its long intermingling with them tend to be deemphasized, depreciated, and suppressed. Their enduring and intimate association tends to be viewed as a primitive and unproductive confusion, which we have fortunately now overcome by finally separating out what are essentially distinct enterprises.

This tendency toward fragmentation is the reflection of a general trend toward deeper and more numerous institutional divisions among the disciplines. Without taking a stand on the purported advantages and inevitabilty of this intellectual Balkanization, one cannot help but see how our present state of academic division tends to warp our understanding of a tradition in which what is now dispersed among different disciplines existed as an intermingled whole.

Kaufmann's *Discovering the Mind* has the merit of refocussing our attention upon the remarkable integration of philosophical, literary, and psychological work in the tradition of German letters from the Enlightenment to the Second World War. In our recent treatment of this period, we have tended to overlook or ignore its remarkably high degree of organic unity, in part because this sort of integration has been lost in our own literary culture. *Discovering the Mind* should make it harder for us to continue approaching with good conscience this literary-philosophical-psychological tradition from the exclusive perspective of a particular discipline. It impedes the facility and narrowness of approach that is the consequence of our own cultural fragmentation. Kaufmann has achieved with respect to our study of this period in German intellectual history what Kierkegaard wanted to achieve with respect to our embracing religious faith: he has made things more difficult for us—but also more rewarding. And we are in his debt for this difficulty.

The philosophical dimension of Kaufmann's emphasis on the integration of philosophy, literature, and psychology transcends the question of the interpretation of a particular period of intellectual history—or that of the appropriate methodology for intellectual history in general. It also consists in the implicit thesis that this former integration of what is currently separated furnishes the most fruitful context for discovering the mind. It suggests that it is in the interplay of literature, philosophy, and psychology that the best insights concerning mind have been, and are likely to be, obtained. His historical interpretation also furnishes the basis of an intellectual program, in as much as the period interpreted is presented as paradigmatic.

Discovering the mind is too important and central a human concern, Kaufmann implies, to be left exclusively to the "psychologists," that is, to those who have come to carry this institutionally and narrowly defined title of relatively recent origin—the professional psychologists. The major insights into the nature of the mind have often come, he argues, from thinkers who were not professional psychologists, and the greatest of the professional psychologists have drawn heavily on the insights of those who were not in the profession.

The refusal to abandon the discovery of the mind to the guild of professional psychologists is not just an insistence on the rights of writers and philosophers to address themselves to this task, justified by their traditional presence on this turf and their considerable contributions. It is also a reminder to philosophers and writers that involvment in this enterprise has been and should remain a central aspect of their vocation—a duty as well as a right. The lamentable tendency to relinquish psychology to the psychologists is not just the result of their presumptuous and aggressive appropriation of what is by nature an intellectual and existential concern common to all human beings. There has been complicity on the part of philosophers and writers who wanted to rid themselves of the burden of having to work at discovering the mind. In addition to the effective pursuit of prerogatives by a guild, there has been an all too willing retreat from this former common ground by those who found it easier not to maintain a presence there. We should chastise and lament the retreat as well as the aggression.

The Dual Legacy of Goethe and Kant

In the first of the three volumes, Kaufmann provides a bold historical hypothesis about intellectual life in the German-speaking world during the last two centuries: the development of philosophy in general and of theories and conceptions of the mind in particular is presented as having taken place in an intellectual space defined overwhelmingly by those two giants of German letters, Johann Wolfgang von Goethe (1749–1832) and Immanuel Kant (1724–1804). Other figures of the period are discussed and, in some cases, even allowed to have had considerable influence and intellectual virtue—Lessing, Schiller, and Hegel, for example. But Kaufmann is unwavering in his insistence that no other figure of the period even remotely compared in influence to Kant and Goethe. Some who have been put forward as major influences, like Herder, are argued to have had less influence than has been supposed. Still others, like Schiller and Hegel, are presented as themselves recipients and transmitters of the two major influences.

It is to be predicted that such a stark structuring of a complex subject will generate the protest that these matters cannot not be so simply viewed. No doubt the proponents of various other figures in this tradition (particularly those scholars who have written about them) will feel that the importance of these figures has not been fully appreciated. Confronted with these misgivings, one should not forget that Kaufmann's picture of Goethe and Kant as by far the two most important influences on subsequent intellectual life in Germany was not created by presenting the other leading contenders as pygmies. We should also keep in mind that the thesis concerns subsequent influence, not intrinsic merit.

Lessing, Schiller, and Hegel are all treated with enormous respect. And Kant, despite and because of his great influence, is presented as the source of much that went wrong in German intellectual life. We should also not forget that the thesis is clearly offered as a hypothesis, as an interesting proposal of considerable plausibility, to be pushed as far as it will go. It is a hypothesis of great synthetic power, supplying a well-defined perspective from which a bewildering amount of historical material can be systematically viewed. Whatever one decides about its ultimate adequacy, it furnishes a valuable focus for the further study of this rich chapter of intellectual history. The thesis is certainly both arguable and debatable. That it has been so forcefully argued by Kaufmann and will be heatedly debated by others is all to the good.

It would be well to remember that this eagle's-eye view of an extensive period in intellectual history was preceded by two substantial studies of major figures in the period (Hegel and Nietzsche) and a number of essays on related topics. Only those acquainted with Kaufmann's earlier contributions will fully appreciate the effort and power of synthesis, the admirable abbreviation, the simplicity and austerity of presentation arising from what had to be complex considerations and hard choices. Kaufmann's last, long-ranging look at his cultural heritage is a masterful distillation of an extensive erudition, effectively brought to bear upon specific and important issues, but never flaunted.

Kaufmann's conception of the place of Kant and Goethe in German culture is remarkable and provocative, not only because of the extraordinary influence he attributes to them, but also because of his evaluation of their respective influences. That Goethe is praised, not only as an enormous, but also as an enormously positive influence, is not at all unusual. But that a substantial part of Goethe's importance and merit is located in his contribution to the discovery of the mind and in his development of an alternative model for science in his *Theory of Colors,* written as a critique of Newton, is a significant hypothesis. Unlike the Newtonian conception of science, in which quantification and measurement occupy a central position, Goethe offers us an alternative model for "science" in which these are not essential, and which Kaufmann finds to be preferable in some contexts of inquiry, like that of discovering the mind. Kaufmann is using "science," in the broad way in which the Germans use "*Wissenschaft*," which includes humanistic disciplines as well as the natural and social sciences, and which applies to anything which is a *rational inquiry*. The crucial issue raised by Kaufmann's championing of a Goethean model of science is not, however, whether one should or should not extend the word "science" to these other disciplines and inquiries. It is rather whether or not the discovery of the mind (and by extension—the discovery of other human truths) is best pursued by adhering to quantitative methods.

Kaufmann's dismissal of the results of quantitative methodology in psychology as being insignificant is simply stated, not argued. This dismissal and the accompanying lack of argument are sure to raise the hackles and voices of the proponents of quantitative methods in psychology. Of course, the bold claim that quantitative studies have not substantially contributed to the discovery of the mind calls for a lot of further consideration and argument. Kaufmann does not make any pretense of argument; he advances this as a radical hypothesis, worthy of further consideration and argument, and worthy of enunciating because it calls into question prevalent and largely unquestioned beliefs. He devotes his energies rather to arguing for the correlative thesis that some of the greatest contibutions to the discovery of the mind have come from thinkers, like Goethe, Nietzsche and Freud, who did not use quantitative methods. The convincingly argued claim that Goethe's importance and influence flowed as much from his person as from his works is put forward as being generally instructive. Kaufmann makes a plausible case that it is not uncommon in the history of philosophy for one's influence to depend upon personal charisma or upon conveying the impression that one is in some way an exemplary human being. He adduces Socrates, Wittgenstein, and J. L. Austin as prominent examples of this phenomenon. Kaufmann wants to use the case of Goethe as exemplary to move us away from the prevalent idea that the history of ideas is only the history of ideas. It is also the history of individuals, whose manner of living or being, at least as it is publicly perceived, is to a great extent responsible for their influence.

This insistence upon the importance of the person of the writer, as perceived through and apart from his writings, for determining his influence upon the history of thought contributes to a larger and more important issue. It opens the way to a discussion of what constitutes not just the influence of a thinker but his actual merit, contribution, and greatness. It opens the way, moreover, to a discussion liberated from the narrowing constraints of the prevalent notion that philosophical merit is primarily, or even exclusively, a matter of the excellence of the argumentation, of impeccable logic, and the marshalling of all the relevant evidence.

By pointing out that Socrates and Wittgenstein do not offer complete and rigorous demonstrations for their views, Kaufmann is not suggesting that their reputation for greatness is undeserved, but rather that excellence and greatness in philosophy (and in discovering the mind) does not depend exclusively upon the definitiveness of the demonstrations for one's views. But he is not suggesting that rigor and adequacy of argumentation are irrelevant considerations. In calling attention to an astounding lack of rigor in both Kant and Hegel, he not only tries to correct common misconceptions about them, but also to suggest that they were great philosophers *despite* this lack of rigor, which he clearly considers a serious flaw, though one not incompatible with philosophic greatness. Kaufmann does not attempt to develop a positive and systematic account of what constitutes excellence or greatness in philosophy, but by rejecting an overly narrow conception of the matter that enjoys considerable currency, he implicitly encourages his readers to explore the question from a richer and more varied perspective than they might have otherwise adopted.

Kaufmann's treatment of Kant is far more startling than his treatment of Goethe. Kant, who has enjoyed respect and praise almost universally, and from the most diverse philosophical directions, is here astonishingly and unqualifiedly branded as a disastrous influence upon the subsequent development of German thought. It has been common enough to call attention to some of the obvious failings of Kant's writing style and even of the content of his philosophy. But this has usually occurred as a series of marginal comments in the context of an overwhelming reverence for his achievement, in an atmosphere of overall admiration that remains in no way challenged by these critical marginalia. Kaufmann makes no bones about his opinion of Kant as having been on the whole a catastrophe for German philosophy. His critique of Kant is radical and unorthodox, yet another philosophical heresy from the author of *The Faith of a Heretic* (1961), a book in which he locates the central virtue of our philosophical tradition in its ever renewed criticism of whatever has become generally accepted as true, authoritative, and canonical.

His case against Kant involves not so much new revelations of hidden flaws, but a clear-eyed assessment of fairly obvious failings and unfortunate influences, relatively unburdened and unblurred by the conventional pieties concerning Kant's unquestionable overall greatness and positive contribution to philosophy. Once again the value of Kaufmann's thesis lies primarily in the raising of an important issue that has rarely, if ever, been raised, and in the consideration of a plausible hypothesis that has rarely, if ever, been seriously considered.

Kant is blamed for a being the major source of at least two disastrous traditions in German philosophy. First, he is seen of the source of a continuing tradition of obscurity and obscurantism. He is also faulted as the fountainhead of an inappropriate insistence on certainty in our investigations and theories and, correspondingly, of unfounded claims to have achieved such rigor. One of Kaufmann's most intriguing ideas is that the two tendencies are actually connected. Having accepted the unrealizable requirement of certainty, one naturally resorts to obscurity to conceal from oneself and others one's failure to fulfill it.

Kant is blamed for yet another misguided requirement: that philosophy should endeavor to attain completeness. The requirement of completeness, like the demand for certainty, it is suggested, being gratuitous and unattainable, naturally produces a tradition characterized by the pretentious counterfeit of the misguided ideal and the attempt to conceal the failure and fakery by willful, though not necessarily conscious, obscurantism.

Some will no doubt want to question whether Kant is really the primary source of all these subsequent ills in German intellectual life. The quest for certainty can be easily traced back to Descartes and perhaps Newton, and, despite some foreshadowings in Kant, the ideal of completeness seems to have emerged in full force only with Hegel's *Phenomenology of Spirit* (1807). But such disputes about the exact origins of these false ideals are much less important than the crucial thesis that they have indeed proven to be counterproductive requirements, indeed pernicious and enduring afflictions of our intellectual life.

With respect to these flaws, so fateful for the subsesquent course of German philosophy, Goethe is presented as Kant's antipode. If Kant began the process of teaching the German language to speak philosophically (his notable German predecessors had used Latin and French), he taught it to speak badly—that is, obscurely. Goethe, on the contrary, used, and indeed himself developed, a German in which one could express one's ideas clearly. While Kant carried on the unfortunate tradition of Descartes, misguidedly seeking an absolutely certain foundation for our knowledge, Goethe emphasized that the true mark of a fruitful scientific procedure was the formulation and testing of hypotheses, which always remain open to further questioning.

The subsequent development of German philosophy can be viewed, argues Kaufmann, as largely determined by these polar opposites and the tension between them. Hegel can be understood as having acquired his notoriously obscure style and his unjustified claims to have achieved necessity and completeness in his "dialectical demonstrations" in imitation of Kant. Hegel's developmental approach, which so influenced the intellectual methodology of the nineteenth century, is argued to have derived from Goethe. Heidegger's obscurity and apodictic tone are also seen as part of the unfortunate legacy of Kant. The admirable writing styles of Schopenhauer, Nietzsche, and Freud, as well as the experimental spirit and constant questioning of one's own beliefs that Kaufmann finds characteristic of Nietzsche and Freud, is attributed to Goethe's influence. One may find this somewhat Manichean conception of the development German thought problematic or simplistic, but it is an original and not implausible hypothesis. And like a number of Kaufmann's central claims in this work, it is *fruitful* in the crucial sense, that critically considering it, independently of whether we ultimately accept, reject, or modify it, will deepen our understanding of the subject matter to which it pertains.

Considerable space is devoted to a recounting of the story of the composition and publication of Kant's *Critique of Pure Reason* and Hegel's *Phenomenology of Spirit*. Here as elsewhere in Kaufmann's work the erudition and information is not an end in itself. Although his account of these matters appears at first to be overly detailed and even gratuitous, it actually turns out to serve an important purpose. He presents ample evidence that Kant's *Critique* and Hegel's *Phenomenology* were both, though the products of long reflection, written in extreme haste and published pretty much without revision. Kaufmann thinks it important to emphasize that these works were hurriedly produced and never carefully vetted or reworked, for he wants to overcome the awe in which these texts have traditionally been treated. He wants to prepare us to accept his appraisal of them as severely flawed masterpieces, rich in ideas but very badly written and badly organized, and remarkably lacking in rigor.

This is meant to be a liberating corrective to the prevalent practice of approaching these (and other philosophical masterpieces) as if the failure to find an interpretation that reveals rigor of argumentation, deep aptness of organization, and truth in the conclusions, or at least an impressive plausibility in these matters, must be a failure of the reader and not of the text. It is an attempt to free us from the oppressive tradition of having to treat what are admitted to be great philosophical works as *authoritative texts*. It is meant to relieve us of the obligation to persist in prodigious hermeneutic exertions, even when they promise to be futile. These obligatory and often interminable efforts at interpretation are aimed at revealing supposedly hidden virtues of these texts, virtues whose veiled presence is often assumed in an act of unfounded and implausible faith. In denying these two books some of their generally presumed virtues Kaufmann is clearly not denying them all virtue or greatness. Nor is he suggesting that they are not worth studying. He is rather calling attention to the complexity and variation of what makes philosophical works great and addressing the related existential question of how we should approach those texts that merit our attention and respect.

Transmitters of the Tradition:
Nietzsche, Heidegger and Buber

In the second of the three volumes, themes established in the first are further developed. Nietzsche, its hero, is presented as the heir of Goethe and as the first German philosopher of the nineteenth century to free himself fully of the baneful influence of Kant. Moreover, he is argued to have been a great psychologist, one of the founders of depth psychology and forerunners of psychoanalysis.

Heidegger, its villain, appears as the bearer of the unfortunate Kantian tradition. Kaufmann claims that Heidegger, like Kant, claims not just to offer tentative hypotheses, but to have achieved apodictic certainty. And consequently, Heidegger has to conceal in the obscurity of his prose the inevitable failure to have reached this impossible goal. It is also argued that he had a large and disastrous influence upon subsequent intellectual life. Kaufmann charges him with having actually impeded the discovery of the mind through his disparagement of empirical investigation and disdain for the tentativeness empirical hypothesis, his dubious method of seeking enlightenment through quirky and unsound etymological analyses, and his pernicious theory of interpretation that disregards the intentions of the creator of a text in favor of forcing the text to mean what the reader wants it to mean.

Buber is viewed as a transmitter of both good and bad influences. Kaufmann criticizes his best-known book, *I and Thou*, whose central idea is that one can treat another person either as an object or as a subject like oneself (in Buber's terms, as an *"it"* or a *"thou"*). He sees this scheme as too Manichean and rigid—and as part of the negative legacy of Kant. On the other hand, Kaufmann praises Buber as the propounder of a humane and psychologically fruitful program for the interpretation of texts (and people), which seeks to locate and comprehend "the distinct voice of the original," that is, to understand others in their otherness, to comprehend their uniqueness. Kaufmann obviously sees in Buber's program an antidote to Heidegger's high-handed hermeneutics that disregards the voice and wishes of the one who is interpreted.

In Defense of Freud

As in the preceding two volumes of *Discovering the Mind*, there are in this third and last volume three major figures discussed, its hero, Sigmund Freud, and its villains, Alfred Adler and Carl Gustav Jung. Although each of the preceding volumes has a central hero and villain, this volume differs not only in having two villains instead of one, but in presenting their villainy as consisting largely in sins against the hero. Whereas Kaufmann faulted Kant and Heidegger for their generally disastrous influence upon our intellectual life, he criticizes Adler and Jung primarily for having treated Freud in a despicable manner. And he presents his negative assessment of their character and their work by constantly comparing them unfavorably to Freud's superior achievement and person. Kaufmann undertakes his criticism of Adler and Jung in the context of his homage to Freud. In this volume, Kaufmann sets out to mount a general defense of Freud against his critics in order to "set the record straight." Adler's and Jung's criticisms of Freud's person and work have formed an important part of the case against Freud, particularly because of their close association with him, and because of the claim of each to have developed a psychology that is superior to Freud's. But their influential attacks are still only a part of a much more widely shared rejection of Freud that Kaufmann sets out to combat.

Psychoanalysis and Science

An important and recurring criticism of Freud's psychoanalysis has been that it is a pseudoscience, an unscientific study with scientific pretensions. Kaufmann defends the claims of psychoanalysis to be a science, and he does this by challenging the conception of science that underlies the criticism. Relying upon the distinction traced in the first volume of this work between a conception of science championed by Kant and Newton and one defended by Goethe, he argues that Freud's work is clearly scientific in the Goethean sense, that is, in being nondogmatic. Freud's work, like that of Goethe and Nietzsche, is scientific in that it is always open to the consideration of new evidence, alternative explanations, and further revision. Kaufmann emphasizes the importance of considering rival accounts, holding this to be a crucial criterion of whether or not a person's work is scientific.

He claims that it is this consideration of alternatives that renders any investigation nondogmatic. Considering alternative accounts and rejecting them, persisting in a position while refuting competing conceptions, is, he insists, *not at all dogmatic*. It is the reluctance to seriously consider alternative accounts, not the refusal to accept them, that characterizes dogmatic procedure. Thus, Kaufmann defends Freud against the common charge that he was dogmatic because he strongly rejected emendations to his theory proposed by associates such as Adler and Jung.

By arguing in this way Kaufmann is, no doubt, also justifying his own literary and philosophic practices. Here, as in his other books, Kaufmann typically develops his positions in contrast to competing views, opposing them with strong criticism.

Kaufmann is surely right in insisting that it is the failure to consider alternative accounts rather than the considered refusal to accept them that consitutes dogmatism. From this it does not follow, however, that the consideration of alternatives alone protects Freud—or anyone else—from being dogmatic. One can be dogmatic in considering and rejecting competing views as well in ignoring them; it all depends, of course, upon the way in which one considers and rejects the rival theories. Kaufmann's claim, that Freud was, despite criticisms to the contrary, nondogmatic, ultimately depends upon his showing that Freud *objectively* and *openly* considered the virtues of alternative accounts—not simply that he considered them.

The debate concerning the scientific status of psychoanalysis has developed, for the most part, among philosophers of science who share a strong tendency to take the physical sciences as the paradigm for all science. They have consequently taken those features that have seemed typical of the physical sciences to be the defining criteria of science in general, notably the formulation of general laws that generate predictions concerning all those cases that fall under these laws. The fulfillment or nonfulfillment of these predictions provides, in turn, confirmation or disconfirmation of the laws that generate the predictions. Discussions of whether psychoanalysis is really a science have often amounted to little more than discussions of whether it really generates laws and predictions that can be confirmed or disconfirmed through experiment. Some, such as Karl Popper, have argued that it does not and that psychoanalysis is thus a pseudoscience like astrology. Others, such as Adolph Grünbaum, have argued, on the contrary, that psychoanalysis does generate some testable laws, predictions, and hypotheses.

Kaufmann's merit consists in his relocating the focus of the debate. While favoring the view that psychoanalysis has in fact produced hypotheses and even some general laws that are testable, he argues that this is really not the most important issue. It is rather whether Freud's work helps us better to understand our own minds and the minds of others. Kaufmann argues that it has significantly enlightened us, perhaps more than the work of any other individual, and that this illumination does not depend upon whether it generates general and testable laws. Kaufmann maintains more broadly that psychological analyses can in general be explanatory and enlightening without making reference to mechanisms and laws that lay claim to universal validity. For example, he argues that many cases of neurosis might be illuminated by reference to the Oedipus complex even if not all people suffer from unresolved Oedipal conflicts.[4]

This idea flies in the face of some standard doctrines about the nature of scientific explanation. It has been widely held that to explain an event is always to show that there are certain general laws that are true, which, given the factual conditions that obtained, would have predicted the event. For example, an explanation of why a particular sample of water vaporized consists, on this view, of the law that water vaporizes when a certain temperature is reached and the fact that this temperature was indeed reached. Kaufmann explicitly rejects this "covering-law model of explanation" as inappropriate for psychology. His argument ultimately rests on an appeal to what he takes to be the incontrovertible fact that some of Freud's analyses are obviously and importantly illuminating—and yet do not fulfill the requirements of the model.

A predictable response to Kaufmann's position by defenders of the covering-law model is that the apparent illumination supplied by Freud's analyses of human behavior is only apparent, only the mirage of an explanation. Another slightly more generous response commonly made is that, though Freud's analyses do supply some sort of illumination, they do not constitute "explanations" or at least not "scientific explanations."

How is one to decide these issues? One may approach them, as many have, committed to the doctrine that the physical sciences should serve as the paradigm of science in general, and that to count as a scientific explanation the conditions of the covering-law model must be met. If approached with these preconceptions, whether or not psychoanalysis will be found to be scientific, and to really offer explanations, depends upon how like the physical sciences it turns out to be and to what extent its analyses can be assimilated to the covering-law model. If one rejects these preconceptions, however, as Kaufmann does, the critical examination of the illumination and explanation provided by psychoanalysis undergoes a radical transformation in perspective and purpose. We need no longer ask only whether or not they meet certain immutable criteria for admission into the realm of science. If they furnish true understanding without meeting the standard criteria of scientific explanation, perhaps the criteria themselves should be called into question. In this way psychoanalysis may become a test case for the adequacy of certain common theories about the nature of science.

The question as to whether psychoanalysis is finally considered to be a "science," and whether its analyses are considered to be "explanations," might be regarded as shallow terminological and taxonomic issues of little real import. It may seem to concern only the possible extension of terms traditionally applied to the physical sciences to psychoanalysis. As long as Freud's contribution to our understanding of the mind is established and clearly delineated, one might ask why it is at all important to quibble about whether it is really "scientific" or "explanatory," particularly when these terms are so often used in narrow, problematic, tendentious, and question-begging ways. Kaufmann occasionally allows us a brief glimpse of his impatience with these issues, indicating that his major concern is to argue for the importance and worth of Freud's work, no matter how it is described. Yet he devotes considerable space to defending the scientific status of psychoanalysis—and with good reason. Disputes about which studies and theories are "scientific" involve more than value-neutral, taxonomic issues. Those characterized as nonscientific are often viewed as producing understanding or explanation that is less significant than the accounts supplied by those studies that are scientific. "Science" and "scientific" are honorific, not just descriptive terms. It is difficult to separate the issue of the scientific status of a body of work from the issue of its cognitive value. With respect to certain bodies of theoretical work, like Freud's, we may be inclined to endorse enthusiastically the understanding and enlightenment they offer, while waiving, or at least suspending, any claims to their status as science. But the failure to defend their "scientific" status in some reasonable sense of that word, often has the unwanted result of undermining the claim that they offer real understanding.

The question of what makes any study scientific appears at first to be simply a theoretical issue in the philosophy of science, but it has practical and programmatic implications as well. If a study of the mind must resemble the physical sciences for it to be a science of the mind, then pressure is created for those who study the mind to emulate the physical sciences to gain for their work the status, respect, and support reserved for scientific investigation. This has led to the prevalence in psychology of quantitative studies that explore the correlations of a limited number of isolated variables in controlled situations. Kaufmann repeatedly states that such work, though more "scientific" than Freud's in the sense of the term derived from Kant and Newton, is much less significant and enlightening. And to the extent practitioners of quantitative psychology are not open to questioning their fundamental presuppositions and considering alternative approaches, they are not scientific in the crucial sense developed and exemplified by Goethe, Nietzsche, and Freud.

Kaufmann clearly feels that the emulation of the physical sciences by those studying the mind has been a mistake and has produced much insignificant work. He sees a good part of Freud's accomplishment to consist in his development of a science of the mind unencumbered by this common and misguided zeal to approximate the physical sciences. Kaufmann praises Freud for having produced a "poetic science of the mind," stressing Freud's continuity with the those "poets and novelists, Sophocles, Shakespeare, and Dostoevsky—and Goethe," who he feels were, along with Nietzsche and Freud, "the people who contributed most to the discovery of the mind."[5]

Although Kaufmann defends Freud's work as a kind of science that, though scientific in a perfectly legitimate sense, is unlike the physical sciences in important ways, he then surprisingly concedes that psychoanalysis is not primarily a theory at all. He does not mean by this that it consists in a set of practices rather than doctrines but that its insights are not, for the most part, formulated as a series of general laws. But, in Kaufmann's view, this lack of law-like pronouncements is a virtue rather, not a defect.

Since "theory," as Kaufmann understands the term, is constituted by general laws and psychoanalysis is not, psychoanalysis, it turns out, is not really a theory. Despite the initial strangeness of Kaufmann's claim, its sense is readily comprehensible, and its philosophic implications considerable. Still, the issue of whether psychoanalysis is a "theory" or not does not really affect Kaufmann's most significant thesis. This is the claim that the scientific status of Freud's and other accounts of human behavior—and the contribution they make to our understanding of the mind—do not at all depend on their developing universally valid laws.

One might be in sympathy with the general intent of this provocative claim and choose to support it in a somewhat different way. Instead of denying that Freud's psychoanalysis is a theory because it is not essentially constituted by laws, one could maintain it is indeed a theory, but not one constructed of laws. If the lack of laws does not prevent psychoanalysis from being a science, why should this lack prevent it from being a theory? Why should the defender of psychoanalysis, who argues that it is scientific, concede that it is not a theory when the criteria for qualifying as a theory are usually less stringent than the criteria for qualifying as a science? Do we not think that there are some theories that are not scientific? Having expanded our view of what may legitimately count as a science, why constrict our conception of what counts as a theory? Furthermore, there is good reason why a defender of psychoanalysis, like Kaufmann, would be well advised not to concede that it is untheoretical. Like the terms "scientific" and "explanatory," the term "theoretical" has an honorific aspect. The corresponding negations, "unscientific," "nonexplanatory," and "untheoretical" all have a pejorative cast. Conceding that psychoanalysis is not a theory, like conceding it is not a science or does not provide explanations, is likely to be understood or misunderstood as an admission of a serious deficiency. And this is certainly not Kaufmann's intent.

Kaufmann claims that Freud's conceptions of "overdetermination" and "overinterpretation" play a crucial role in establishing the difference between the human and physical sciences. Freud maintained that human behavior always "issues from more than one motive and stimulus and permits more than one interpretation."[6] Freud's claim that in explaining behavior there is always more than one *legitimate* interpretation and that this multiplicity of interpretations should be present in any full explanation of behavior certainly promises important implications for our theories of explanation. And it does seem to entail, if true, profound structural differences between a science of physical events, presumably not overdetermined, and a science of overdetermined human behavior. Although Kaufmann offers no arguments for the truth of Freud's thesis of overdetermination and no detailed analysis of its implications, he has located a fascinating and neglected issue. Still, it is not at all clear that where overdetermination prevails explanation cannot rely on laws. It might be argued that overdetermination allows a plurality of explanations each constructed on the covering law model. We need a closer analysis of the consequences of overdetermination for psychological theory. While Kaufmann has not worked this out, he has provided impetus for others to undertake this important task.

Materialism and the Mind

Since Kaufmann defends Freud's work against charges that it is not really scientific by locating it in a scientific tradition different from the one that has emphasized quantification and taken the physical sciences as its paradigm, he is understandably eager to show that Freud deliberately distanced himself from this quantitative and physicalist tradition. But it is well known that Freud, who began his career as a neurophysiologist, was, at least in his earler years, very much taken with the idea of grounding psychology in physiology, that is, with the idea of explaining the life of the mind as a reflection of physical processes.

Freud has been, in fact, often criticized for adhering to a *"materialistic"* and *"reductionistic"* picture of mental life, that is, to the idea that mental events are nothing but the epiphenomenal reflection of certain physical (or *material*) processes, and that the ideal account of mental events would be to trace them back (or *reduce* them) to the physical events that really constitute them. To this is often added the related charge that his view is *mechanistic* in that Freud supposedly seeks to explain human behavior by establishing its causes rather than by understanding it in terms of its goals and purposes. It is objected that explaining something solely through its causes as opposed to its purposes is inappropriately appropriated from the physical science of *mechanics.*

Kaufmann defends Freud against such charges. He claims that Freud's adherence to a program of mechanistic and materialistic reductionism was true only of the young Freud, who was still under the spell of scientific ideals that were prevalent in the neurophysiological circles from which he had just emerged. In the course of developing his psychoanalytic theories, Freud is, on the common interpretation that Kaufmann favors, supposed to have rejected his earlier materialist, mechanistic, and reductionistic tendencies. In support of this not uncommon picture of Freud's development, Kaufmann rightly points out that the properly psychoanalytic accounts that Freud later developed were not physical, but clearly psychological and relied upon reference to the intentions, wishes, desires and purposes of the persons analyzed—and not primarily upon mechanistic or material causation. He also cites a number of statements that suggest Freud viewed himself as having abandoned the reductionistic materialism of his youth.

Kaufmann makes a fairly compelling case that from the *The Interpretation of Dreams* (1899) onward Freud did not attempt any materialistic reduction of psychological phenomena and spoke of his own adherence to such a program as a thing of the past. But Freud's rejection of materialism may have been less clear-cut than his theoretical practices and disclaimers suggest.

Freud's fullest expression of a materialistic view and program is to be found in his "Project for a Scientific Psychology" (1895), a long essay published posthumously, which he called "a psychology for physiologists." In this essay he began to work out a theory of mental functioning that drew heavily upon concepts from neurophysiology and that mirrored in its structure current physiological theories of neural activity. The incentive for developing such a theory seems to have been that it would facilitate the eventual drawing of psychophysical correlations. According to the account given by Kaufmann and others, Freud had fully abandoned this project by the turn of the century. But what was the nature of this abandonment?

Freud clearly gave up trying to discover psycho-physical correlations. The question remains, however, as to whether he rejected this program as totally misguided or as simply unattainable at that time. There is much to suggest that it was the latter, that he rejected the project of materialistic reductionism as unrealizable—at least given the state of our scientific development—but not its ideals and underlying assumptions. One might well be convinced that what we refer to as the mind and mental life are completely constituted by physical processes whose complexity and obscurity make us unable to say much about them as such.

If we view Freud as having simply and totally rejected his initial materialist program, we are likely to overlook the ways in which scientific ideals that he felt were distant and inaccessible continued to haunt and subtly influence his thinking. It is instructive to consider Freud's *Beyond the Pleasure Principle* (1920) with these possibilities in mind. Though written about a quarter of a century after "The Project for a Scientific Psychology," it relies upon many of the concepts and hypotheses found in the earlier work and derived from neurophysiology. For example, pleasure and pain are still equated with the reduction and increase of tension or energy in the organism. One might view the unmistakable appearance in this late work of Freud's of ideas such as this, which are clearly derived from biology, as a puzzling return to a long abandoned quasimaterialistic approach. It is more likely the re-emergence of ideas that were never really rejected but rather held in abeyance until Freud returned to the discussion of certain topics concerning the basic nature of mental functioning, to which these ideas are relevant.

Although Kaufmann is certainly right in objecting to the simplistic characterizations and criticisms of Freud as a materialist, the influence of materialistic thinking upon Freud seems to have persisted, though in an attenuated and indirect way, throughout most, if not all, of his career and manifested itself in complex and subtle ways. To regard Freud as primarily a materialist, as some have done, is a gross distortion. Kaufmann's major concern is to correct this distortion, not to pursue those aspects of materialism that continue to haunt and influence Freud's thought.

Freud's Contribution

Kaufmann lists point by point, with a remarkable absence of any beating around the bush, what he takes to be Freud's contributions to the discovery of the mind. Along with Freud's development of a poetic science of the mind, Kaufmann mentions, Freud's discovery of the importance of childhood experiences, his discovery of the importance of sex, his interpretation of dreams, his psychopathology of everyday life, his interpretation of mental illness, his new method of psychotherapy, and his interpretation of literature, art and religion. Concerning the comprehensiveness of this list, the aptness of this way of dividing Freud's accomplishment, and Kaufmann's evaluation of the originality and significance of Freud's achievement in each of these areas, questions are bound to arise—and are meant to be provoked. Though these questions are important, Kaufmann's own contribution is to some extent independent of their outcome. It consists in part in having the temerity to offer such a list, which serves us well as a starting point for the reassessment of Freud's achievement. Though many have paid homage to Freud, seldom, if ever, has anyone grounded his praise in such a clear and comprehensive way. Like so much else in Kaufmann's *Discovering the Mind*, his contribution consists in presenting hypotheses that are designed to enable and enhance discussion and debate rather than bring them to a close.

His list notably does not include as separate items Freud's development of theories about the existence and importance of unconscious mental processes or the activities of repression and defense that help account for them. Of course, these subjects appear in Kaufmann's account as recurrent elements of Freud's discussions of other matters, such as dreams and parapraxes ("Freudian slips"). But since the phenomena of unconscious mental processes and repression are not separately focussed upon, they are somewhat de-emphasized. Kaufmann constructs the case for Freud's achievement more in terms of the areas of mental life he illuminated rather than in terms of the general principles and mechanisms of mental life he revealed. While this approach is enlightening, it presents Freud's work as a rich mosaic in which the unifying structures and principles are not always apparent. A fuller case for Freud's contribution to the discovery of the mind might emerge from the supplementation of Kaufmann's presentation with one that traced the general principles and mechanisms that Freud discovered and developed in the course of his work. These principles and mechanisms of general mental function cut across the various areas of Freud's work and reveal its unity.[7]

When Kaufmann does briefly discuss Freud's advocacy of unconscious mental states and processes, he mentions that this idea, far from being obvious and trivial, has met continued resistance among philosophers. He cites the prominent American philosopher C.I. Lewis and the famous French existentialist, Jean-Paul Sartre as opponents of the idea that there are unconscious mental processes. Their opposition is adduced to show that Freud was correct when he accused philosophers of dogmatic resistance to the idea of the unconscious. It should be added that Franz Brentano, a professor of philosophy in Vienna, several of whose courses Freud attended as a student, was a prominent advocate of the view that consciousness was a defining characteristic of all that is mental. No doubt it was Brentano, whom Freud had in mind when he complained about the recalcitrance of philosophers with respect to the idea of the unconscious mind.

Kaufmann defends Freud only against the criticisms of the unconscious developed by Jean-Paul Sartre in his *Being and Nothingness,* published in 1943, soon after Freud's death in 1939.

This focus can be justified in as much as Sartre's attack is much more widely read than Brentano's. Kaufmann is not trying to trace the history of philosophic opposition to the the idea of unconscious mental processes in any full way. Instead, following his own recipe for an intellectual procedure that is nondogmatic, which he finds admirably exemplified by Goethe, Nietzsche, and Freud; he critically confronts the most prominent proponent of this opposition in order to defend and develop Freud's idea of the unconscious.

Freud's Ungrateful Progeny: Adler and Jung

Freud's difficulties with his followers, particularly his break with his two most distinguished disciples, Alfred Adler and Carl Gustav Jung, have been written about extensively. Kaufmann feels it important to enter into this debate for at least two reasons. First, he thinks that Freud has in general been unfairly treated in this discussion. He tries to show that, contrary to a popular view, Freud actually behaved in an exemplary way with respect to these two younger colleagues and that they behaved in an altogether despicable manner toward him. Second, given Kaufmann's thesis that one's contribution to the discovery of the mind cannot be separated from one's own character, he thinks it important to establish what kind of human beings Freud, Adler, and Jung were in order to arrive at an assessment of their achievement.

Kaufmann's portrayal of Adler and Jung is unrelentingly critical and devastating. He finds almost nothing good to say about them as human beings or as contributors to the discovery of the mind. And he compares them repeatedly and unfavorably to Freud on both counts. Anyone looking for a "balanced" or "evenhanded" account of these figures, one which contains their virtues as well as their vices, will not find it here. But one should not assume that this sort of a balanced or evenhanded account is always what is wanted. If, in fact, the work of Adler and Jung and their treatment of Freud was as bad as Kaufmann claims—and their weaknesses and transgressions not widely recognized—then what is wanted is rather a forceful exposé and a convincing indictment. Kaufmann's intent is to offer just that. Devastating criticisms of human beings can and should be balanced by an appreciation of their significant positive qualities and contributions—where they exist. But Kaufmann's radical and vigorously argued thesis is that Adler and Jung did not have significant redeeming qualities and that they did not make contributions of real value.

This thesis will, of course, be hotly disputed by the many admirers of Adler and Jung. As in the case of Kaufmann's strong indictments of Kant and Heidegger in the first two volumes of this work, his radical attack on Adler and Jung is designed to open a debate in which the standard pieties are no longer sacred.

Some will no doubt object that Kaufmann presents Freud as one-sidedly wonderful and Adler and Jung as one-sidedly deficient. Admittedly, the picture that he constructs of these figures is, to use one of his own favorite critical terms, somewhat "Manichean." But, the real issue confronting any literary savaging of others is not whether the critic also says something good about the figures he criticizes, but whether he has treated them fairly and accurately. And this issue, as Kaufmann realized, remains open to further discussion and disagreement.

One does not have to agree with Kaufmann's overall assessments to appreciate the force of his arguments concerning the particular strengths and weaknesses of the figures treated. He makes a persuasive case for the meanspiritedness, envy, and self-deception of both Adler and Jung in their dealings with Freud and their dishonesty in reporting these dealings. He also offers compelling evidence for Jung's opportunistic anti-Semitism. Perhaps because it has been less publicized than Heidegger's anti-Semitism, Jung's is all the more shocking and distressing.

Kaufmann argues tenaciously that neither Adler or Jung, produced writings that make a significant contribution to the discovery of the mind. He maintains that Adler was an extremely weak theoretician and writer. He argues that Adler could not coherently synthesize or clearly articulate his ideas; that he never gave anything like adequate elucidation and development to concepts, like "the inferiority complex," for which he is famous; and that his work is accessible, if at all, mainly through the reconstructions and accounts of others. Even those who were followers of Adler and undertook these reconstructions readily admit that Adler never was able to work out his ideas and theories coherently and fully.

Having argued that Adler was "neither much of a writer or a profound thinker," Kaufmann classifies him as "the first of a new breed of gurus," in whose number he also includes Jung along with Wilhelm Reich, Erich Fromm, Fritz Perls, and Werner Erhard.[8] It is doubtful whether Kaufmann's redescription of Adler and Jung as "gurus" rather than thinkers is meant to locate their true genius and contribution. Even if they were essentially gurus, it is crucial to know whether they were helpful rather than harmful ones. And Kaufmann remains silent on this issue.

Jung, in contrast to Adler, did produce a considerable corpus of work. But Kaufmann denies that either produced a superior alternative to Freud's work or even an important enhancement of it. He argues that both relied heavily upon Freud's work without giving him adequate credit, and that where they deviated from him, it was not for the better.

He questions the motivation, purported theoretical gain, and the sources of the popularity of Jung's well-known desexualization of the Freudian concept of the libido and of Freud's psychology in general. He accuses Jung of having generally modified Freud's theories to make them less offensive to widespread taboos against openly discussing sexuality, prejudices that Jung, unlike Freud, shared. Kaufmann attributes a good part of Jung's popularity to his having transformed Freud's insights into more conventionally acceptable, but less illuminating variants. Freud's achievement consists precisely in having had the courage to advocate ideas and express himself in terms that were not *salonfähig*, because they were too direct and clear to be acceptable to a prudish society.

Kaufmann also takes a dim view of the highly touted and influential Jungian investigation of "archetypes," that is, of the meanings of symbols that appear across a wide range of cultures. He sees it as "full of undigested and undigestible erudition that seems to have no other function than distraction from the central task of depth psychology: a better understanding of ourselves and our fellow men."[9] Kaufmann gives an extremely unflattering account of its fascination: "Jung's rather loose talk of archetypes opened up a new game for scholars that one could play without being very scholarly—that is, without self discipline—and *that* is a gift for which many people are always grateful."[10]

It should not be overlooked, however, that Jung's work on archetypes is an extension of ideas espoused by Freud concerning the existence of a universal symbolic language valid for all human beings. Freud had argued that the meaning of certain dream symbols does not vary from one individual or culture to another, and he speculated that this universal symbol system was transmitted by some sort of memory or consciousness that belonged to the human race as a whole. It may be that the way in which these ideas were later developed and used by Jung and his followers is particularly objectionable. But we should not forget that Freud was an important source of ideas and hypotheses that are the foundation for the Jungian enterprise—ideas that are intrinsically problematic and which easily lend themselves to further abuse.

Freud and Nietzsche

Nietzsche, the hero of the second volume of *Discovering the Mind*, also plays a major role in this volume. Since he was a pioneer of depth psychology and forerunner of psychoanalysis, the question naturally arises concerning his influence upon Freud. Kaufmann turns his attention to the question of Freud's relation to Nietzsche, raising interesting issues and shedding considerable light upon the topic. He gathers and presents a substantial amount of illuminating material from a variety of sources: passages from the minutes of the meetings of Freud's circle in Vienna at which Nietzsche was discussed; Freud's own statements about Nietzsche in his books and essays, letters, and recorded conversations; and statements by Freud's associates (some of them addressed directly to Freud) concerning the importance of Nietzsche's psychology as a precursor, complement or even as a theoretical alternative to Freud's.

Kaufmann's material reveals that Freud's relation to Nietzsche was an extremely peculiar mixture of admiration and avoidance. Freud, who had heard enough about Nietzsche from friends to suspect that he was a kindred spirit with similar ideas, an important thinker, and an admirable human being, nevertheless tenaciously resisted reading him. While Kaufmann furnishes ample evidence for Freud's lifelong avoidance of a direct and full confrontation with Nietzsche's work, he treats Freud's behavior toward Nietzsche in an extremely gentle and sympathetic manner. Some will no doubt find his treatment somewhat apologetic.

Kaufmann argues that Freud's insistently repeated claim that he had hardly read any of Nietzsche's work is plausible. He argues that Freud's knowledge and admiration of Nietzsche was based for the most part on the hearsay of associates. One may agree with Kaufmann concerning Freud's veracity but find this not to be the crucial question. Assuming that Freud is telling the truth, why did he refuse and resist reading a writer whose works he believed were extremely valuable and particularly relevant to his own concerns? And what are the implications of this behavior for our assessment of Freud's greatness as a thinker and as a human being?

Freud's public explanation of his motives for avoiding Nietzsche , whom he considered a "philosopher whose intimations and insights often coincide in the most amazing way with the laborious results of psychoanalysis," was that he "was less concerned about priority than about the preservation of [his] open-mindedness."[11] Kaufmann finds this explanation to be "credible" and Freud's desire to remain "open-minded" creditable. Kaufmann analyzes this desire as the admirable wish "to work out his own themes in his own way, at his own speed," and "not to be influenced by Nietzsche's formulations one way or another—either to accept them or to change them to show his own independence."[12]

Kaufmann seems to find this strategy much less problematic than Freud himself did. As Kaufmann points out, Freud betrayed feelings of guilt about the way he had treated Nietzsche. Kaufmann insightfully accounts for Freud's occasional hyperbolic praise of Nietzsche as a compensation for not having given him his due in a more consistent and public manner.[13] Nevertheless, Kaufmann, intent upon reaffirming Freud's reputation against what he takes to be a host of envious and unjust critics, does not pursue the dark side of Freud's treatment of Nietzsche or the incoherence of Freud's rationalizations of this treatment. But the material Kaufmann marshalls will point the way for others.

What are we to think of someone, like Freud, who not only keeps himself ignorant of the work of a reputedly important predecessor to preserve his open-mindedness at the outset of his investigations, but also neglects to consult and credit this prior work after his initial ideas have been developed? Does one really preserve one's "originality," as Freud repeatedly suggests, by cultivating an artificial innocence of what has already been accomplished? And does such "originality" maintained by artificially cultivated ignorance deserve to be honored by our society? Should we praise and thus encourage such reinventing of the wheel?

Why does Freud single out Nietzsche for avoidance? Freud certainly makes reference to the work of many other thinkers. He claimed that he could not read Nietzsche because the wealth of ideas encountered there gave him too much to think about to read any further.[14] Is this rather perverse rationalization at all acceptable? (In other contexts it would naturally be construed as a joke.) Finding a rich density of ideas in Nietzsche's work should have induced Freud to read it in smaller doses but with greater interest and tenacity—not to abandon it. And what is one to make of Freud's similarly incoherent claim that "an occasional attempt to read [Nietzsche] was smothered by an excess of interest."[15]

Already at the turn of the century, Freud wrote his friend, Wilhelm Fliess, that he had purchased Nietzsche's works, but could not bring himself to read them: "I finally treated myself to Nietzsche, in whom I hope to find words for a great deal that remains mute in me, but have not opened him yet. Too inert so far."[16] This curious inertia, atypical of the young Freud, who was generally a dynamo of almost endless intellectual energy, was never overcome. In physics, inertia needs no further explanation; with respect to human behavior it often does. Freud's treatment of Nietzsche cries out for an analysis in depth—using the methods Freud himself advocated.

The unmistakable peculiarity of Freud's behavior toward Nietzsche and the feebleness of his rationalizations for it demand a critical investigation of the real, unstated motives of this behavior. And this investigation promises (and threatens) to have substantial implications for our appraisal the father of psychoanalysis.

Such investigations of the motivations of a person's behavior, which do not confine themselves to the conscious and declared motivations, constitute "depth psychology." Both Nietzsche and Freud were, as Kaufmann argues, pioneers of depth psychology. Nietzsche tended to find the deep motivation of all human behavior in a "will to power," that is, in an omnipresent desire to experience one's own power and its increase. Freud has been commonly interpreted as having found the deep motivation of human behavior in "the pleasure principle," the supposedly universal human desire for pleasure and the avoidance of pain—and particularly in the desire for sexual satisfaction. Kaufmann argues that this way of opposing Nietzsche and Freud is crude and misleading. He maintains that the notion that Freud "tried to explain as much as possible in terms of sex" is a "caricature."[17] He points out that even early on Freud had posited two basic drives, contrasting the pleasure principle to an often opposed "reality principle." Later, notably in *Beyond the Pleasure Principle,* Freud radically revised his theories of the basic drives, replacing the pleasure and reality principles with a new duality of drives: *Eros,* a drive that strives for the synthesis and preservation of ever larger unities, and an opposing drive for destruction and death, that is, for the dissolution of such unities.

Kaufmann is certainly right in challenging the simplistic notion that Freud thought sex to be the basic motivation of all human behavior. It should be remembered, however, that in Freud's earlier theory the reality principle is presented as a modification of the pleasure principle and as serving the interests of the pleasure principle. Whereas the pleasure principle aims only at a reduction of tension or displeasure in the organism, the reality principle deals with the exigencies of the external world, avoiding its dangers and enduring it difficulties. The adaptive behavior initiated by the reality principle regularly involves the renunciation of immediate but fleeting pleasures in order to secure delayed but more substantial ones. It also involves the rejection of satisfactions based upon pleasurable hallucinations for those based upon reality. But these procedures of the reality principle are still conceived as strategies for the long-term maximization of pleasure. Freud's introduction of a reality principle into his theory of motivation does not in any way undermine the fundamentally hedonistic nature of his theory.

Moreover, the question of whether Freud thought all behavior is ultimately motivated by a desire for *pleasure* must be separated from the question of whether he thought all behavior is ultimately motivated by *sexual pleasure*. The thesis that Freud's early theory is basically hedonistic is left untouched by any attempted refutation of the more dubious thesis that Freud held all motivation to be sexual.

Kaufmann rightly calls attention to the importance of the shift in Freud's theory of motivation that occurs in *Beyond the Pleasure Principle* and its resemblance at certain points to "a synthesis of Nietzsche and the early Freud." Kaufmann's discussion is too brief to do more than call into question certain overly simplistic and unfortunately widespread ways of viewing Freud, though it does this with admirable succinctness. But his suggestive comments should encourage us to take a closer look at this crucial Freudian text with Nietzsche in mind. A careful reading will reveal, I believe, something more complex than a simple attempt at synthesis; it will show the essay to be a mirror and microcosm of the entire complex of not entirely coherent attitudes, of the admiration and avoidance, with which Freud confronted and failed to confront Nietzsche.

Kaufmann, who is concerned to show continuity and similarity in the work of Freud and Nietzsche, attacks common and all-too-shallow ways of contrasting them. He shows at least that their relationship has been misunderstood, that the connection is important, and that it deserves further scrutiny.

The Continental Divide: Traditions within the Tradition

Kaufmann's project across the three volumes of this work has involved tracing in continental European thought a tradition of "discovering the mind" that transcends the currently drawn boundaries among philosophy, literature, and psychology, between art and science, and between imagination and intellect. And it involves showing that there are villains as well as heroes among the major figures in this tradition, that there are some who have obscured our understanding of the mind and obstructed its discovery as well as some who have uncovered and illuminated it. In this last volume Kaufmann argues that what divides the heroes from the villains is not merely the quality of their contribution and influence. The villains not only all have vices but to a great extent the same vices, for they acquire them from their villainous predecessors. Correspondingly the heroes' virtues are acquired to a considerable degree from the example and teachings of admirable predecessors. To the extent that a set of methodological conceptions and practices has been passed along from one to another of a group of thinkers, and, correspondingly, a different set of conceptions and practices has been passed along among another group of thinkers, one can claim that there exist two distinguishable intellectual traditions. Indeed, Kaufmann argues that there are really two traditions within continental European thought of the last two hundred years. There is a pernicious one, whose major source is Kant and which is carried on by Heidegger, Adler, and Jung among others. And there is a fruitful one, whose major source and model is Goethe and which was further developed by Nietzsche and Freud.[18]

The division of continental thought that Kaufmann proposes is original and enlightening, and it constitutes one of his major contributions to the study of the history of ideas. One should keep in mind that various taxonomic schemes for dividing the history of thought are like a series of lenses or filters for a camera that allow the same material to be seen in a variety of ways. They are incompatible with one another only as the lenses and filters are. One cannot view the same material through all filters or taxonomic schemes at once, but one can try one after another, and each may produce its own revelations and obscurities, its own peculiar delights and dissatisfactions. To ask whether such a scheme is true or false may be simplistic and inappropriate. Still some schemes—and filters—are particularly revealing and satisfying. Kaufmann's should prove to be one of these.

What could be thought of as Kaufmann's *continental divide*, his division of continental thought into two traditions, like the American continental divide, the imaginary line that divides those waters that flow toward the Pacific Ocean from those which flow toward the Atlantic, has not been obvious to the uninstructed eye or mind. There exist no labels that name the two traditions Kaufmann delineates, nor does he coin any. If his proposed division really marks an important distinction between two divergent intellectual traditions that have been generally muddled together, particularly in the English-speaking world, as "continental philosophy," he has performed an invaluable service. He has redrawn the map of an important and much studied, but confusing and much misunderstood area of human thought so as to make its contours more perspicuous.

The Will to Obscurity

The question of style, particularly of the clarity of style, is a central and abiding aspect of Kaufmann's program. And it is a crucial point of difference between the two intellectual traditions he distinguishes. Goethe, Nietzsche, and Freud are praised for their clarity; Kant, Heidegger, Adler, and Jung are criticized for their obscurity. Implicit in the discussion of the writing styles of the various figures considered is the rejection of the idea that clarity or obscurity of style is something with which one is blessed or cursed, something that is a given. Kaufmann approaches the style of a writer as Freud approached dreams, parapraxes, and neurotic symptoms, with the fundamental suspicion that it is something willed, that obscure writing is usually also obscurantist. He suspects obscure philosophical writers, like Kant, Hegel, and Heidegger, of wanting to hide something from themselves as well as from others—presumably the unsoundness or triviality of their positions. Obscure writing, he suspects, is a tool of deception, the deception of others and ourselves. And those who deceive themselves, not knowing their own minds, usually are in a bad position to know and write about the human mind in general. For Kaufmann, there is an intrinsic connection between the failure of style and the failure to know the mind. It is no mere coincidence that Kaufmann finds that those who write badly usually do not have much of value to say. With the exception of Hegel, he finds those who have written unclearly not to have made significant contributions to the discovery of the mind. Correspondingly, those who, in his opinion, have made major contributions tend to be masterful writers.

This attack on obscure writing is particularly significant with respect to a tradition, like that of German philosophy, in which there is not only a great deal of obscure writing, some of it *extremely* obscure, but also a remarkable toleration of obscurity and even a perverse tendency to find some virtue in it. How often complaints about the grotesque syntax and seemingly insurmountable opacity of these authors is met with lame excuses and hackneyed justifications: "The text may indeed be ferociously difficult, but the effort will be repaid by the excellence of the ideas it contains"; "Keep reading! If you are tenacious and intelligent, you shall be rewarded. If you are not rewarded by hard-won but important revelations, you were obviously not tenacious and intelligent enough"; "Given the complexity of the ideas, there is no simpler way to express them"; "Given the *depth* of the ideas, there is no way to express them more clearly"; "Considering the recondite content of the text, this is, despite all appearances to the contrary, the best of all possible prose."

Kaufmann is not buying any of this. What seems to be bad writing, he suggests, usually is bad writing—and should not be tolerated or justified. Convolutedness and obscurity in writing are hardly ever the ineluctable reflections of corresponding complexities of content and of depths beyond the reach of direct illumination. They are more often subterfuges. The depths may appear dark when viewed from the surface, but not everything dark is deep. The job of the thinker is to bring deep treasures to the surface for illumination or return to the surface with illuminating reports of what he has seen below. Often the prolonged study of devilishly difficult texts does not repay the effort. It is high time someone confronted, as Kaufmann does, the existential issues raised by this body of almost impenetrable classics.

This concentration on writing style is a significant part of an attempt to capture the overall style of the thinkers discussed, a unifying style that includes the way they wrote, thought, and lived. To this admirable end, the analysis of specific texts almost always serves to reveal more general textures. The microscope is almost always a prelude to the telescope. The aim is always the large view, in which the trees do not obscure the forest. In this way, Walter Kaufmann made his last and grandest attempt to appropriate—and contribute to—his cultural heritage. *Discovering the Mind* was for Kaufmann, though in a much more modern and modest manner, what *The Phenomenology of the Spirit* had been for Hegel. Following the advice of Goethe's *Faust,* he too "took what he had inherited from his fathers and made it his own."

Ivan Soll
Madison, Wisconsin

Notes

1. Discovering the Mind, vol. 1,"Prologue," sec. 1, p. 4.
2. Ibid., p. 7.
3. Ibid., pp. 6-7.
4. Defenders of the view that explanation is always constituted by general, law-like statements would, no doubt, reply that Kaufmann's example shows only that the relevant laws are different from what was supposed. Perhaps it is not true that everyone suffers from an oedipal conflict, but that all those who do tend to exhibit certain sorts of neurosis. Moreover, they would warn that the laws are always asserted *ceteris paribus*, that is, given that standard conditions apply and nothing interferes with the production of the effects predicted by the law. That other factors can and sometimes do interfere with developments predicted by a law *ceteris paribus*, does not show that the law in question fails to obtain nor that the world is not governed by laws. The interfering factors may themselves be law-like. Such rejoinders call into question any suggestion that there are no laws governing the behavior being explained, or, more generally, that there are no laws governing the psyche. But the main thrust of Kaufmann's position can be stated independently of these dubious theses. The real issue is not whether the world of psychology is governed by laws, nor whether there exist laws that govern the behavior under examination. The question is rather whether one need to refer to the relevant laws, directly or indirectly, in furnishing illuminating explanations of human behavior. And this question is intriguing precisely because its answer is not so obvious.
5. Ibid., v. 3, sec. 84, p. 465.
6. Quoted by Kaufmann from a footnote in Freud's footnote to his section on Hamlet in the *Interpretation of Dreams. Discovering the Mind*, vol. 3, sec. 20, pp. 96-8.
7. That Kaufmann does not focus upon the general principles of mental life propounded by Freud is not surprising given Kaufmann's contention that general principles do not play an essential role in Freud's work. The critical question is whether Kaufmann's manner of inventorying Freud's achievements does not serve to obscure those general principles whose importance Kaufmann is trying to deny.
8. Ibid., vol. 3, sec. 48, pp. 257-58.
9. Ibid., vol. 3, sec. 63, p. 370.
10. Ibid., p. 369.
11. From Freud's autobiographical sketch of 1925, quoted in *Discovering the Mind*, v. 3, sec. 50, p. 264.
12. Ibid.
13. In particular, he points out that Freud's remarkable tribute, that Nietzsche had achieved a degree of self-knowledge unequalled and unlikely to be equalled by any other human being, involves an acknowledgement of Nietzsche's superiority with respect to the central ideal of psychoanalysis.
14. In the *Minutes* of Freud's psychoanalytic discussion group meeting of October 28, 1908, at which Nietzsche's *Ecce Homo* was discussed. Cited by Kaufmann, *Discovering the Mind*, v. 3, sec. 50, p. 265. Freud said that the wealth of ideas in Nietzsche kept him from ever reading more than half a page.
15. *Minutes*, meeting of 1 April 1908, at which Nietzsche's *Genealogy of Morals* was discussed. Cited by Kaufmann, v. 3, sec. 50, p. 264.
16. Cited in *Discovering the Mind*, v. 3, p. 271.

17. *Discovering the Mind*, vol. 3, sec. 51, p. 274.
18. Though content of Kaufmann's position will be clear enough those who read only volume 3 of this work, the full force of his vision of this period of intellectual history naturally emerges only through a reading of all three volumes.

Prologue ▶▶▶

1 ▶▶▶ Nobody has contributed more to the discovery of the mind than Freud, but we must go beyond him. Adler and Jung tried to go beyond Freud while he was still living, but slowly and reluctantly, I have arrived at the conclusion that they have obstructed rather than advanced our understanding of ourselves and others. Adler and Jung were singularly lacking in self-understanding, and their images of Freud were caricatures.

Today the real Freud is obscured by all sorts of legends. He is widely seen as a dogmatist who excommunicated disciples who dared to dissent. He is also portrayed again and again as a thinker who was rooted in nineteenth-century reductive materialism. Others believe that the clue to his thought must be sought in the city in which he lived at the turn of the century: Vienna.

These legends, as well as others, this book strips away and shows both Freud and his contributions in a different light. It deals with the man and his ideas before it turns Adler and Jung to establish new readings of their personalities and ideas.

For scholars, the destruction of widely shared errors can be an end in itself, the more so because it sometimes has all the fascination of detective work. Gradually, as the clues accumulate, a radically new picture emerges, and there is immense satisfaction in finally getting a story straight. Seeing that Freud, Adler, and Jung were among the most fascinating men of our time, I found it exciting to discover what they were really like, how their minds worked, how they grated on one another, and why they parted ways. Recently published documents, like Freud's and Jung's correspondence and the minutes of the Vienna Psychoanalytical Society, allow us to see how many supposedly scholarly books have spread false stories, and I aim to set the record straight.

2 ▶▶▶ This historical dimension, however, is only one facet of what follows. Why not let the dead bury the dead? Why bother with three psychologists who wrote in German some decades ago, when there are thousands of psychologists writing in many different languages today?

One reason for writing about these three men is that much of the work done by psychologists today is busy-work, while Freud's contributions can still help us, once we get them straight, to understand ourselves and others better. Of course, it is not only in psychology that an excess of noise drowns out great music. Exactly the same is true in other fields, including philosophy and literature, history and literary criticism. In fact, in some academic disciplines there may be only busy-work and no music at all.

Freud's, Adler's and Jung's ideas are appraised critically in the following pages, and I argue that some of Freud's theories as well as the therapy he developed may well be dated. Nevertheless, he made immense contributions that can be stated crisply. An attempt to sort out what actually advances and what in fact impedes the discovery of the mind may well contribute something to our understanding of ourselves and others.

3 ▶▶▶ What has fascinated me the most in writing this book is a third dimension. If we want to show how to discover the minds of others, there is no better way than to demonstrate it concretely in a few cases. And that is what I have attempted here. As it happens, my procedure is quite different from Freud's as well as Jung's or Adler's. Clearly, I am no Freudian, much less an Adlerian or Jungian.

Instead of first defending my method, I have plunged *in medias res*, hoping that the pictures that emerge of the three men and of their parting of the ways will speak for themselves. If the new account is as plausible as I think, then the question arises where precisely my assumptions differ from those of my subjects. This question is tackled briefly in the final chapter.

4 ▶▶▶ The book can easily be read without knowledge of Volumes I and II of this trilogy. But the final chapter is meant to conclude the trilogy no less than the present volume.

This book tells a story about three men. One of the most striking points of this story is that Adler and Jung understood Freud and themselves so badly. Their misunderstandings of Freud was due in part to their failure to see whose spiritual child he was. They mistook his ancestry. One might suppose that this would not matter much, but in fact it makes all the difference.

They saw him as a dogmatist when he actually was a skeptic, and they assumed that he was rooted in nineteenth-century materialism, when in fact he stood in an altogether different tradition. The high points of this tradition were Goethe and Nietzsche, the heroes of Volumes I and II.

To place Freud in this tradition is the burden of the opening sections of this book. At times it may seem as if the details did not matter all that much and were perhaps of interest only to historians. But even as details in a detective story may appear to be of doubtful relevance until one finds much later that they really were crucial, much of the material in these early sections turns out to be crucial when we get to Adler and to Jung.

Looking back, I feel impatient with myself and ask if one could not eliminate a great many quotations, footnotes, and discussions of alternative interpretations. Why not simply state my own conclusions?

For anyone who merely wants to tell an interesting story for the entertainment and diversion of the public, that is clearly good advice. But if one wants to make one's story stick, this recipe won't do. And it is my hope that future studies of these three men and their relationships will have to take into account the material presented here.

Moreover, there is an interesting parallel here to psychotherapy. One often feels like exclaiming: Why does it have to take so long? Why not simply tell the patient what is what? There are at least two answers to that. First, it is important for the patients to discover some things for themselves; otherwise they cannot really accept the conclusion. Second, for the reader of the case history, getting there is half the fun.

If these two answers do not justify the time and money spent by ever so many patients in an attempt to get well, a scholar, too, must ask himself whether the length and detail of his study are excessive. I hope that the reader will agree that they are not.

Finally, it should be mentioned that all translations from the German are my own. That may seem odd in this case, because it is widely assumed that the official translations of Freud and Jung are perfectly adequate. Indeed, most of the work done on these two men is now done in English, and most writers consider it quite unnecessary to check the original texts. That, as we shall see, is one of the reasons why the legends have survived so long.

PART I

Freud and
His Poetic Science ▶▶▶

5 ▶▶▶ I know that it was the recitation of *Goethe's* beautiful essay "Nature" in a popular lecture shortly before my graduation that decided me to study medicine.

Thus ends the paragraph that begins with Freud's birth, in a short autobiography he wrote in 1925.[1] Much earlier, in *The Interpretation of Dreams* (1900), Freud had referred to "the incomparably beautiful essay by Goethe, for it was the recitation of this essay in a popular lecture that pushed me into the study of natural science when I was irresolute as I faced graduation."[2]

Recently scholarship has come to the conclusion that the essay was not really by Goethe but by Georg Christoph Tobler.[3] But when Goethe himself was shown this essay in his old age and asked whether he had written it, he said that he did not remember for sure but that he

[1] *Werke*, XIV, p. 34.

[2] *Werke*, II/III, p. 443 = 1900, p. 254.

[3] See, e.g., the Hamburg edition of Goethe's *Werke*, XIII (3rd ed., 1960), p. 571f.

Freud in 1891.

could have written it (his exact words will be considered in Section 11); and so it was included in his collected works. One of Goethe's biographers says that the young Goethe expressed his view of nature "poetically in verse and prose, as well as in conversation. A young Swiss visitor to Weimar, Tobler, noted down a fragment of such a conversation—,'On nature' . . . ."[4] In Freud's time "Nature" was quite generally credited to Goethe, and it is noteworthy that he himself felt that he was following Goethe's direction when he choose his profession. Not only that, but he wanted his readers to know this. Goethe had been a scientist as well as a poet, he had made a biological discovery (the intermaxillary bone), and he had written about the metamorphosis of plants. Beyond that he had championed a distinctive, non-Newtonian conception of science.[5]

That Freud loved Goethe and was steeped in his writings should be obvious to all who study Freud. Goethe is cited and quoted constantly—on about two dozen pages of *The Interpretation of Dreams* alone, and on more than a hundred in the collected works. Kant, Goethe's great antipode, and Newton, who was for Kant and ever so many others the quintessential scientist, meant nothing to Freud. Kant is mentioned a few times, Newton only once in passing.

Freud's extraordinary style should be seen in this perspective. It cannot be praised too highly. No other man of science was such a great writer. Freud was not always pleased when people praised his style because the compliment was often two-edged—a way of putting him down as a scientist and a form of resistance to his psychology. It was very much like praise of Nietzsche as, of course, a great *stylist*. It was felt that anyone who

---

[4] Friedenthal, *Goethe* (1965), p. 280.
[5] See section 11ff. of the first volume of this trilogy.

wrote that well could not be a serious philosopher or scientist.

Freud's style, like Nietzsche's, breathed defiance of the German academic establishment. It was experienced as a provocation though it was born of love of literature and a clarity of thought not equaled by any major German philosopher, except for Nietzsche. Yet Freud's prose was much more rational and patient than Nietzsche's and hence clearer in the long run. Nietzsche could formulate a thought as lucidly as possible but then delighted in sudden reversals, in startling us by not staying with a train of thought and asking us instead to reconsider not only our own position but also his. And Nietzsche's wit was unruly and refused to stay in harness, while Freud was always able to employ his sense of humor to his purpose.

I shall quote Freud a great deal in this chapter, not so much to illustrate his style, which is bound to suffer in translation, but simply because I cannot sum up what he said better than he did. With other writers who are known for their good style it is usually possible at least to tighten the argument and state some points more briefly. What is impressive about Freud's writing is not ornamentation; he was about as far from the art nouveau of fin-de-siècle Vienna as a writer could be. Rather he did not waste words but managed to state and explain even the most outrageous ideas tersely, clearly, and persuasively.

Asked about his style, Freud once said: "My conscious and deliberate model was Lessing."[6] In an extremely informative study of Freud's style, Walter Schönau has explained this statement very plausibly: "It will have been above all the clarity, honesty, and sobriety of his polemical scholarly treatises that Freud felt to be exemplary"; also the fact "that Lessing presents his

---

[6] Wortis (1954), p. 109.

thoughts not as the finished products of an act of thought but instead presents the process of thinking itself."[7]

Freud also loved Heine, of whom Nietzsche had said in *Ecce Homo;* "It will be said one day that Heine and I have been by far the foremost artists of the German language."[8] In 1908, when *Ecce Homo* was published posthumously, Thomas Mann did say in "A Note on Heine"[9] that Heine's polemic against Ludwig Börne "contains the most inspired [*genialste*] German prose before Nietzsche." It would be pointless to argue at length about who wrote the best German prose after Luther, but the following list of six writers may at least point to a very un-Kantian, antiacademic tradition in German thought: Lessing and Goethe, Heine and Nietzsche, Freud and Kafka. What these writers share is a profound feeling for human suffering coupled with extraordinary lucidity and wit—qualities that have not distinguished the mainstream of German prose. But there is this tradition, too, and it is important to see how Freud stands in it.

6 ▶▶▶ Awareness of both traditions helps us to understand Freud's otherwise puzzling attitude toward philosophy. When he was almost forty, he wrote his friend Wilhelm Fliess, on January 1, 1896:

> I see how, via the detour of being a physician, you are reaching your first ideal of understanding human beings as a physiologist, even as I most secretly nourish the hope of arriving on these same paths at my original goal of philosophy. For that is what I originally wanted when it

[7] Schönau (1968), p. 42f. Muschg (1956) also contains a fine essay on Freud as a master of German prose as well as a devastating chapter on Heidegger.

[8] Chapter II, section 4.

[9] "Notiz über Heine" (1908) in (1922), p. 382.

was not yet at all clear to me for what I might be in the world.

The letter of April 2 is even more explicit:

> If both of us are still granted a few years for quiet work, we shall surely leave behind something that can justify our existence. In this consciousness I feel strong against all daily cares and troubles. As a young person I knew no other longing than that for philosophical knowledge [!], and now I am about to fulfill it as I move from medicine to psychology. I became a therapist against my will . . .

From Freud's books one occasionally gains the impression that he did not care for philosophy. Perhaps an unpublished letter of November 4, 1937, contains the most extreme formulation:

> Dear Sir,
>
> Unfortunately you have sent your, no doubt, valuable work to a man to whom nature has denied not only all understanding of music but also all philosophical talent. Hence I am really in no position to follow your thoughts, not to speak of judging them. What, then, is to be done with your manuscript? In case you want it back I request a clearly written address as I am not sure I can read it.[10]

Of course, it was generous of Freud to even acknowledge this unsolicited manuscript, and one might suppose that any excuse for not reading it would have served him. But he was a man of extraordinary honesty and would not have said what he believed to be wrong. Surely he felt that he really lacked all talent—and patience—for the kind of philosophy that was cultivated at the universities; and that feeling was shared by Goethe and Nietzsche, as well as Lessing, Heine, and Kafka.

[10] Seen in the autograph department of Goodspeed's Book Shop in Boston, in November 1978.

Specifically, we can distinguish at least three characteristics that Freud associated with academic philosophy and disliked. First, its abstractness, which had repelled Goethe, too. Freud had no mind to stray that far from real life.

The second point is subtle but profound and important. We find it in the chapter on misspeaking in *The Psychopathology of Everyday Life*. While Freud did not mention philosophy in this connection, the passage is wonderfully applicable to Kant and Hegel, not to speak of the philosophers who were teaching at the German and Austrian universities in Freud's time:

> A clear and unambiguous way of writing shows us that the author is here at one with himself, and where we find forced and tortuous expressions that, as an [*Austrian*] idiom puts it very well, squint in more than one direction, we recognize either an insufficiently worked out and complicated thought or the stifled voice of the author's self-criticism.[11]

Elsewhere he noted his admiration for two epigrams he found in Ludwig Börne:[12] "What most authors would need to become better than they are is not spirit but character," and "Honesty is the source of all genius, and men would be more ingenious [*geistreicher*] if they were more ethical." Similar sentiments have been voiced by other rebels. Einstein said: "Scientific greatness is essentially a question of character. The main thing is to refuse to make rotten compromises."[13] And Nietzsche: "Error is cowardice."[14]

Freud's third objection to the kind of philosophy for which he did not care was formulated by Heine in a

[11] *Werke*, IV, p. 112.
[12] *Werke*, XII, p. 312.
[13] Seelig (1956), p. 72.
[14] *Ecce Homo*, Preface, section 3.

poem that Freud admired. He liked to cite the last two lines,[15] but the whole is worth quoting:

> *Too fragmentary are world and life—*
> *But the German professor produces a knife*
> *And knows how to patch up life till it turns*
> *Into an intelligible system one learns;*
> *With his bathrobe rags and long nightcaps*
> *He mends the world and plugs all the gaps.*[16]

Kant actually wrote his books "in his bathrobe and slippers, wearing a nightcap,"[17] and there is a well-known lithograph by L. Sebbers showing Hegel in his study, in 1828, in similar attire.[18] This critique of the German professor of philosophy is widely associated with Kierkegaard and existentialism, but Heine wrote this poem before Kierkegaard was ten years old, and Kierkegaard, who admired Heine, may have known it. The German existentialist professors, Jaspers and Heidegger, were far from pressing any such criticism against Kant and Hegel. Not only did it remain for Freud to quote Heine, but in many ways Freud stayed far closer to the problems of human existence than any of the major existentialists. Much of what many readers look for in vain in the philosophical works of the existentialists is actually to be found in Freud's books. Jaspers and Heidegger and even Kierkegaard and Sartre made "rotten compromises" with academic philosophy, while

---

[15] *Werke,* II/III, p. 494, and XV, p. 173; also in a letter of 1883 quoted by Jones, I, p. 196.

[16] *Die Heimkehr,* section 58:
    Zu fragmentarisch ist Welt und Leben—
    Ich will mich zum deutschen Professor begeben.
    Der weiss das Leben zusammenzusetzen,
    Und er macht ein verständlich System daraus;
    Mit seinen Nachtmützen und Schlafrockfetzen
    Stopft er die Lücken des Weltenbaus.

[17] See section 34 of Volume I of this trilogy, p. 180.

[18] Reproduced, e.g., on the cover and on p. 103 of Wiedmann (1965).

Freud aligned himself with Lessing, Goethe, and Nietzsche.

In the last lecture of what Freud himself considered his last major work (1933), the Heine quotation appears in the following context:

Of the three powers that can challenge the territory of science, religion is the only serious enemy. Art is almost always harmless and beneficent; it does not wish to be anything but illusion. . . . Philosophy is not opposed to science; it gives itself the airs of a science, works partly with the same methods, but parts company with it by clinging to the illusion that it can offer a gapless and coherent world picture which, however, must collapse every time our knowledge makes some new progress. In its method it is mistaken insofar as it overestimates the cognitive value of our logical operations and sometimes also acknowledges other sources of knowledge, like the intuition. And often enough one feels that the mockery of a poet (*H. Heine*) was not unjustified when he said of the philosopher:

With his bathrobe rags and long nightcaps
He mends the world and plugs all the gaps.

But philosophy has no influence on the vast majority of people; it is of interest only to a small number even in the thin upper crust of the intellectuals, and scarcely comprehensible for all others. Religion, however, is a tremendous power . . .[19]

What Freud here calls philosophy is the kind of philosophy that had kept him from approaching his "original goal" more directly, and he did not choose to call the fulfillment of his early aspirations his "philosophy." That name, he felt, had been preempted by others, and he wanted no part of it. Moreover, he considered religion a serious enemy, and philosophy, as practiced by the professors, inconsequential. He was eager to reach a

[19] *Werke*, XV, p. 173.

much wider audience than they did. Insofar as he eventually arrived at his "original goal of philosophy," it was not philosophy à la Kant but philosophy in another, more literary tradition.

7 ▶▶▶ It follows that Freud is not at all easy to translate. About scientific theories one may be able to write good books on the basis of translations, but not about Goethe or Heine. Their greatness is too closely tied to their language. Freud represents an intermediate case.

Since the Nazis proscribed psychoanalysis and Freud himself emigrated to England, most of the literature on him has been written in English, not in German. Gradually it has come to be considered quite respectable to write about him without checking the original German texts to find out what he actually said.

On the whole, the English-speaking world has done remarkably well by him. I remember how on arriving in the United States from Germany in 1939 I discovered the Modern Library Giant *The Basic Writings of Sigmund Freud* (1938), which contained six of his books in a single volume and cost only $1.25—and at Macy's was sold for 89 cents. Nothing remotely comparable had ever been available in Germany or Austria. But on closer inspection it turned out that the dreams, the "Freudian slips," and the jokes were not always those reported by Freud; they were often contributed by the translator because they depended on words that were similar in one language but not in the other. This practice had the master's approval. Thus he wrote Edoardo Weiss, who translated him into Italian:

> The way you translate dreams and mischievements by substituting your own examples for mine is obviously the only right way to do it. Unfortunately I have no guarantee

that this is also done in other translations, most of which are not made by analysts.[20]

What mattered to Freud was that his readers in other countries should find psychoanalysis plausible, and he did not want them to feel that it all depended on oddities of the German language that had to be explained in footnotes. Up to a point, of course, psychoanalysis could be understood and discussed on the basis of Dr. Abraham A. Brill's English versions. But as interest in Freud himself increased, it came to be felt that an entirely new effort was needed, which resulted in *The Standard Edition of the Complete Psychological Works of Sigmund Freud,* published in England in twenty-four volumes between 1953 and 1974. This was a heroic undertaking, supported, like Ernest Jones's indispensable three-volume *The Life and Work of Sigmund Freud,* published in England between 1953 and 1957, by Freud's daughter Anna.

Even as there is nothing like Jones's work in German, except a German translation of it, there is nothing like *The Standard Edition* in German. The German edition of Freud's collected works, also published in England but largely in the 1940s, much of it during the war, does not contain the rich editorial material, including hundreds of informative footnotes, that adds greatly to the value of the English version.

It is understandable then that Richard Wollheim, an analytical philosopher with broad interests, should have said at the beginning of the bibliography of his *Sigmund Freud* (1971):

> Anyone who sets out to write on Freud owes his primary debt to three important works. First, and most heavily, to the great *Standard Edition* . . . Secondly, to Ernest Jones, *Sigmund Freud* . . . Thirdly, to *The Origins of*

[20] *Sigmund Freud-Edoardo Weiss* (1973), p. 42: letter of November 7, 1920. "Mischievements" will be discussed below.

Psycho-analysis . . . which contains the greater number of Freud's letters to Wilhelm Fliess, along with numerous drafts and notes (including the *Scientific Project*) that formed part of the correspondence.

Yet there is also a sense in which this paragraph is stunning. There is no indication whatsoever that any of this material has been translated. Editors are mentioned in the lines omitted in the above quotation, but no translators. And this also goes for Freud's other letters, listed later in the bibliography, which incidentally contains only a single German title. Of course, one might suppose that this was merely due to the fact that the volume appeared in the popular Modern Masters series and that most readers were assumed not to have any German. But the last sentence of the bibliography suggests forcibly that students of Freud and even Freud scholars miss nothing if they have no German:

Otherwise there is a massive literature on Freud, most of which, insofar as it does not make a direct contribution to psychoanalysis itself, is of no great value.

In two crucial ways, however, familiarity with German can help us to understand Freud better. In the first place, his style is so colorful that the best translations often cannot be more adequate than black-and-white photographs of great paintings. When one has no access to the originals, one has reason to be grateful for good reproductions; but to write a whole book on a major artist on that basis would be going rather far. If one's interest were solely in iconography, one might even get away with that: Many art historians have no interest at all in quality or in the aesthetic dimension of the paintings they discuss. But then they also come nowhere near understanding the man or woman whose work they explore. For certain purposes it may be possible to make do with *The Standard Edition*, notably if one is interested only in the adequacy of an argument. And the general reader has certainly been served well and has every reason to be grateful that parts of this fine edition have been made available separately in paperback. But let us see for a moment what is lost in translation.

Peter Gay, the intellectual historian, has said, in *Freud, Jews and Other Germans* that the translators "have done a heroic job" but have made Freud "both more prolix and more genteel than he really was" (p. 41). To this one might add that Freud's ideas come across better in translation than his sense of humor or his personality. But in Freud, as in Nietzsche, it is often the tone that makes the music. His break with Adler and with Jung was by no means merely a consequence of different ideas; it had a great deal to do with their incompatible personalities. And if one gets the wrong picture of their mentalities and fails to see, for example, Freud's very distinctive sense of humor or Adler's or Jung's lack of a sense of humor, or the nuances of gentle irony and savage sarcasm, then one misunderstands some important chapters in intellectual history.

It follows from what has been said that Freud's letters are even harder to translate than his books, and the translations we have frequently offer mere paraphrases of the originals. That is true even in the important letters to Fliess and to Jung. Take a single seven-line paragraph in Freud's letter of December 5, 1912, to Jung. The English version says: "You yourself have no doubt become familiar while in America with the principle . . ." The German says: "You have surely adopted this principle yourself when you were in America . . ." The English goes on to say: "I have less sympathy than you with Bergmann; if he has been misled by Stekel, that is his affair. I too have suffered enough at his hands." The German: ". . . if he has allowed himself to be misled by Stekel that is his affair. He has done me enough harm, too." In Freud's next letter the English version speaks of "attacking Adler's book" while the original has "criticizing Adler's book." The translator also gets the tone of the all-important closing paragraph all wrong. But the translations of Jung's letters by his chief translator, R. F. C. Hull, are by far even freer and more inadequate. A few examples will be considered when we get to the Freud-Jung break.

Even as one has to read Goethe and Kant in the original German to realize how great a writer Goethe was and how dreadful Kant's style is, English versions also flatten out the immense differences between Freud's style and Jung's, not to speak of Adler's. This point is doubly important because Adler and Jung were keenly aware of Freud's superiority as a writer.

A special problem is posed by Freud's brilliant coinages. *Fehlleistungen* means literally, misachievements, like misspeaking, misreading, mislaying, forgetting or misremembering. Freud aims to show that such mistakes are not mere accidents but rather due to some unconscious motive that makes mischief. "Mischievement" seems to me an appropriate English coinage, though it does not sound very scientific. *The Standard Edition* offers us "parapraxis," exemplifying what Nietzsche called the spirit of gravity; but Freud was very far from that spirit. Ordinary people, of course, have not accepted this coinage; they speak of "Freudian errors" or "Freudian slips."

Where Freud has *das Ich, das Es,* and *das Überich,* the obvious translations would be: the I, the It, and the over-I. Again, that would not sound scientific enough. So we get the ego, id, and superego—Latin this time, not Greek. But Freud himself, though he read Latin and Greek and knew his Virgil well enough to notice instantly when someone quoted a Latin line and left out a word that made no difference whatsoever as far as the meaning was concerned, did not like pompous terms that made a show of his Latin or Greek.

Here are a few more examples that are discussed more fully in *The Language of Psycho-Analysis* by Laplanche and Pontalis. German *Anlehnung* (an ordinary work that suggests imitation or reliance) becomes anaclisis; *Besetzung* (occupation), cathexis; *Überbesetzung* (overoccupation), hypercathexis; *Erinnerungssymbol* (memory symbol), mnemonic symbol; *Ichgerecht* (I-compatible), ego-syntonic.

Surely, Freud was served better when his translators used vivid equivalents like day's residues, dream work, free association, oral stage, overinterpretation, penis envy, repression, and resistance. It is noteworthy that Freud wrote about the death instinct but never used *Thanatos* in his books even after that term was introduced into the literature by one of his disciples. *Eros* is a term he did use because, like Oedipus, it posed no stumbling block for readers who do not know Greek. It is revealing that Ernest Jones should have found it "a little odd that Freud himself never, except in conversation, used for the death instinct the term *Thanatos* . . ." (III, p. 273).

Of course, there is one Latin word that Freud did use prominently: libido. In the first paragraph of the first chapter of his *Three Essays on the Theory of Sexuality* (1905) he made clear that he needed a simple word like "hunger" to designate the sex drive, but the choice of this Latin term caused a great deal of trouble. In his wonderfully clear and concise manner Freud himself summed up later, in a letter to Edouard Claparède,[21] what happened:

> . . . . I made a distinction between the sexual instincts and the ego-instincts and . . . so far as I am concerned, "libido" means only the energy of the former, the sexual instincts. It is Jung, and not I, who makes the libido into

[21] Probably early in 1921. The original seems to be lost. An English translation of Claparède's French translation appears in a footnote in *The Standard Edition*, XI, pp. 214f.

the equivalent of the instinctual force of *all* the psychical faculties, and who combats the sexual nature of the libido. Your account fits neither my conception nor Jung's but is a mixture of the two. From me you borrow the sexual nature of the libido and from Jung its generalized meaning. And it is thus that there is created in the imagination of critics a pan-sexualism which exists neither in my view nor in Jung's. As far as I am concerned, I fully realize the existence of the group of ego-instincts as well as of all that mental life owes to them.

If Freud had spoken of the sex drive instead of libido, Jung could never have denied its sexual nature. But we shall consider Jung later.

By way of concluding this discussion of the transformation of Freud in the course of translation, let us return to "the incomparably beautiful essay by Goethe, for it was the recitation of this essay in a popular lecture that pushed me into the study of natural science." When we turn to *The Interpretation of Dreams* in *The Standard Edition*,[22] "incomparably beautiful" has become "exquisitely written," and *in einer populären Vorlesung* has become "read aloud at a public lecture." This last phrase matters less, but it helps to explain why Wollheim, in *Sigmund Freud*, tells us that Freud was "listening to a public reading of Goethe's 'Ode of Nature'" (p. 2). At public readings one is apt to know before what will be read unless the reading is given by a famous actor and one goes to hear *him*. But this was a lecture by a professor whose only claim to fame is that in the course of one lecture he once quoted two and a half pages—not an ode, incidentally—that led Freud, whose interests had been predominantly humanistic, to study medicine. There is some poignancy in that. And "exquisitely written" is on a level with saying the Freud or Nietzsche was a great *stylist*, while "incomparably beautiful" (*un-*

[22] V, p. 441.

vergleichlich schön) does not refer exclusively or even mainly to the style. That, as it happens, is so effusive that Freud might well have been put off by it if it had not been for the contents.

8 ▶▶▶ This leads us to the second way in which familiarity with German can help us to understand Freud better. He himself taught us not only that language is very significant and that nuances can be revealing, but also, following Goethe, that human beings need to be understood through their development. Authors writing books about Freud who disagree with this central contention should argue their case against him, while those who accept it should naturally apply it to him. But how can one do that if one is not familiar with the tradition out of which he came and the writers whose influence on him was formative?

This rhetorical question can actually be answered by seeing how two recent authors have dealt with Freud's development. Wollheim's exposition is roughly chronological but ignores the first thirty years of Freud's life and gives a good deal of attention to the so-called "Project," which is a draft that Freud sent to his friend Fliess in 1895, just before he himself turned forty and four years before he completed his *Interpretation of Dreams*. In the book of essays on Freud that Wollheim edited, this "Project" looms even larger, and it has won as much favor with analytical philosophers as Marx's early "Philosophical Manuscripts" have won with philosophers who teach Marx.

Frank Sulloway's *Freud, Biologist of the Mind: Beyond the Psychoanalytic Legend* (1979) one might well ignore here if this tome of more than six hundred pages had not entered the world to the din of such extravagant advance claims. Perhaps the oddest thing about this book is the author's notion that his conception of Freud as a biologist or, as he puts it in the Introduction and many times after that, a "crypto-biologist," is a revolutionary new discovery. In fact, it has been a commonplace for a very long time and is a misleading half-truth. To show that it is highly misleading is one of the burdens of this book. That the idea is not new could be documented easily by citing Lionel Trilling, who often remarked that Freud's pessimism about man was due to his biological orientation, which contrasted with the sociological orientation of the neo-Freudians; or by citing some of the neo-Freudians themselves; or Alfred Adler from whom they took so much without acknowledging their debts. Here it may suffice to quote one of the most eloquent Adlerians, who wrote a biography of Adler as early as 1926. In a more recent book on Adler (1970, English in 1974) Manes Sperber said:

> Under the influence of his teacher Brücke and the materialist ideas of the physiologists Du Bois-Reymond and Helmholtz, Sigmund Freud tried to establish a physiology of the mind (p. 21).

We can save ourselves Sperber's elaboration of this formulation which, unlike Trilling's way of putting the point, is more false than true. Hanns Sachs had put the point a little more judiciously when he said of Freud: "The texture of his thoughts was made up of a psychological warp and a biological woof" (p. 148; cf. p. 68f.).

Although Sulloway's claims for his book are more ambitious than those made by any previous scholar for a work on Freud, its serious limitations have been pointed out first in a long review by Wollheim in *The New York Review of Books* (November 8, 1979) and then in a very different but also very perceptive review by Peter Brooks in *The New York Times Book Review* (February 10, 1980). Indeed, for our purposes here it will do to quote Brooks:

Of Mr. Sulloway's "principal ambitions," as he calls them, the ambition to "produce a comprehensive intellectual biography of Freud" must be judged mostly a failure. . . .

From the considerations that the reviewer adduces in support of this judgment it will suffice to quote a single sentence:

> There is much here about 19th-century scientists but precious little about philosophers and nothing on the poets, though Goethe must be cited by Freud more than any other writer.

Sulloway's sole reference to Goethe only makes matters worse. The index lists "Goethe, Wolfgang: Freud and, 146;" and the text says:

> It is thus in the writings of adherents to *Naturphilosophie* and Romantic medicine (among other figures, Galdston specifically cites Leibnitz, Kant, Fichte, Schelling, Goethe, Carus, Oken, Novalis, and Bachofen) that one discovers important anticipations of Freud's theories . . .

The author goes on to regret that Galdston "has had surprisingly little impact"; yet this list of nine names is a hopeless chronological jumble, and the notion that Leibniz and Kant were "adherents to *Naturphilosophie* and Romantic medicine" is grotesque. Moreover, it makes a mockery of "intellectual biography" to ignore totally how important Goethe was to Freud and how he took little or no interest in the other eight men.

Of course, each interpreter tends to stress what is of special interest to him. One dwells on Freud's early "Project;" another makes much of Charles Darwin's, Wilhelm Fliess's, and Albert Moll's influence on Freud; and a third finds Goethe more congenial. It does not follow that each of these approaches is as good as any other. While one can learn a good deal from the books under discussion here, they are very seriously misleading.

Sulloway assumes that Freud's developmental approach is derived from Darwin, quite unaware of the fact that this approach had become quite widespread in Germany in the wake of Goethe and Hegel, long before Darwin. And he speaks again and again of "Ernst Haeckel's *biogenetic law*—better known as the theory that 'ontogeny is the short and rapid recapitulation of philogeny'" (p. 199). In the index there are more than two dozen subheads under "biogenetic law," and the eighteen entries under one of them, "Freud's endorsement of," include several that refer to a number of consecutive pages. Hegel is not mentioned in the index, but in 1807, before Darwin and Haeckel were born, Hegel proclaimed in his *Phenomenology*:

> The individual must also pass through the contents of the educational stages of the general spirit, but as forms that have long been outgrown by the spirit, as stages of a way that has been prepared and evened for him.[23]

Geist, here translated as "spirit," could also be rendered by "mind." Freud, of course, preferred to speak of the soul.

In sum, familiarity with the German language and intellectual currents in Germany can add a great deal to our understanding of Freud. It would be foolish to claim that this is all we need to know. Obviously, the present book makes no claim to being "a comprehensive intellectual biography of Freud," but it is intended to contribute something to our understanding of Freud's mind as well as Adler's and Jung's.

---

[23] 1807 editions, p. xxxiv = section II.3 of my translation of the Preface.

Freud's desk in London. (Photograph by the author, 1952.)

9 ▶▶▶ Given the erudition of so many of the people who have written about Freud, one might suppose that the essay on nature that led Freud to study natural science must have been discussed again and again to determine what it was that appealed so much to him. After all, the letter in which Freud was informed that the city of Frankfurt had decided to award him the Goethe Prize in 1930—the only major prize he ever received—referred to his praise of this essay, and both *The Interpretation of Dreams* and the autobiography of 1925 are very well known. Yet the question of why this essay impressed him so much has been almost totally ignored in the vast Freud literature. Why?

Obviously, interpretations are heavily influenced by the interests of the interpreter. Ernest Jones, whose three-volume biography of Freud is a gold mine, had no feeling for Goethe, least of all for the young Goethe. British and American writers who came later and had not known Freud personally took even less interest in German literature. We also have to take into account the antihistorical bias of the new critics, analytical philosophers, and structuralists who have done so much to mold recent thought.

The one biographer who quoted the essay at length and tried to explain what had impressed Freud so much was Fritz Wittels, one of Freud's early followers who later left him and then returned to the fold for a while. Before we consider Wittels's explanation, however, we must consider the essay itself. Since it is quite short, it seems best to quote the whole of it. It is divided into very short paragraphs, but no single paragraph seems to account for Freud's admiration.

NATURE
Fragment
[1783]

Nature! We are surrounded and embraced by her—unable to step out of her and unable to penetrate her more deeply. Unasked and unwarned, she accepts us into the circulation of her dance and propels herself with us until, tired out, we fall out of her arm.

She creates eternally new forms; what is there has never been; what has been does not recur—everything is new and yet always the [same] old [thing].

We live in her midst and are strangers to her. She speaks with us unceasingly without betraying her secret to us. We affect her continually but have no power over her.

She seems to have designed everything for the sake of individuality, but does not care for individuals. She always builds and always destroys, and her studio is inaccessible.

She lives in lots of children, but the mother—where is she? She is the only artist: from the simplest material to the greatest contrasts; without any appearance of exertion to the greatest perfection—to the most exact determination, always covered by something soft. Every one of her works has its own character, every one of her manifestations the most isolated concept, and yet everything constitutes a unity.

She puts on a play: whether she sees it herself we do not know, and yet she plays it for us who stand in a corner.

Eternal living, becoming, and motion are in her, and yet she does not move on. She transforms herself eternally, and there is not a moment's standing still in her. For staying she has no concept, and she has placed her curse on standing still. She is firm, her step is measured, her exceptions rare, her laws immutable.

She has been thinking and muses continually, yet not as a human being but as nature. She has reserved for herself a sense that is her own and all-embracing, but nobody can see it by looking at her.

All human beings are in her, and she is in all of them. With all of them she plays a friendly game and rejoices the more one wins from her. With many she does it so secretly that she finishes the game before they notice it.

Even what is most unnatural, *even the plumpest Philistinism, has something of her genius.* Whoever does not see her everywhere does not see her correctly anywhere.

She loves herself and always clings to herself with eyes and hearts without number. She has spelled herself out in order to enjoy herself. Always she lets new enjoyers grow forth because she desires insatiably to communicate herself.

She delights in illusion. Those who destroy that in themselves and others she punishes as the most severe tyrant. Those who follow her trustingly she clasps to her bosom like a child.

Her children are without number. To none is she stingy everywhere, but she has favorites on whom she squanders much and to whom she sacrifices much. She has reserved her protection for what is great.

She squirts her creatures out of nothing and does not tell them whence they come and whither they are going. They are to run; the course is known to *her.*

She has few mainsprings that are never used up, always effective, always manifold.

Her play is always new because she always creates new audiences. Life is her most beautiful invention, and death is her artifice for having much life.

She shrouds man in dimness and eternally spurs him toward the light. She makes him dependent on earth, indolent and heavy, and shakes him up again and again.

She implants needs because she loves movement. A wonder that she achieves all movement with so little. Every need is a benefit, quickly satisfied, quickly grown back again. When she implants one more it is another source of pleasure; but soon she achieves a balance.

Every moment she gets ready for the longest race, and every moment she is at her goal.

She is vanity itself but not for us for whom she has made herself the most important thing.

She allows every child to fuss over her, every fool to pass judgment on her, thousands to walk obtusely over her without seeing anything, and rejoices in all of them and always comes out well.

One obeys her laws even when one resists them; one works *with her* even when one wishes to work *against* her.

She turns all she gives into a benefit, for she first makes it indispensable. She delays to be desired; she hurries lest one grow tired of her.

She has neither language nor speech, but she creates tongues and hearts through which she feels and speaks.

Her crown is love. Through that alone can one come close to her. She creates clefts between all beings, and everything wants to become entangled. She has isolated everything in order to pull everything together. With a few drafts from the beaker of love she compensates us for a life of trouble.

She is everything. She rewards herself and punishes herself, rejoices and torments herself. She is rough and gentle, lovely and terrible, without strength and all-powerful. Everything is always present in her. Past and future she does not know. The present is for her eternity. She is gracious. I praise her with all her works. She is wise and silent. One cannot tear any explanation from her body, nor force any present from her that she does not give of her own free will. She is cunning, but for a good end, and it is best not to notice her cunning.

She is whole, yet always unfinished. The way she carries on she can always carry on.

To each she appears in a distinctive form. She conceals herself in a thousand names and terms, and is always the same.

She has placed me inside, she will also lead me out. I entrust myself to her. She may dispose of me. She will not hate her work. I did not speak about her. No, what is true and what is false, everything she has spoken. Everything is her fault, everything to her credit.

10 ▶▶▶ It is by no means immediately obvious what led Freud to emphasize in 1900 and again in 1925 that it was this essay that had led him to study medicine. Freud's own style was so very different that one can perhaps sympathize with all the writers on Freud who have simply ignored the problem. Fritz Wittels, the one great exception, represents an interesting case. Having left Freud's circle in 1920,[24] he published a book on Freud in 1924 and was able to send Freud an advance copy in December 1923. Freud's response to that book is of considerable interest and easily accessible in his published *Letters*. It should suffice here to quote a little from it.

> . . . I naturally would never have wished or asked for such a book. It seems to me that the public has no claim to my person and also cannot learn from it as long as my case—for ever so many reasons—cannot be made fully transparent. You think differently about this and have therefore been able to write this book. Your personal distance from me, which you definitely consider an advantage, also has great disadvantages. You know too little about your subject . . . .
>
> On the other hand, I gladly concede that your acuity has guessed quite right a few things about me that are well known to me; for example, that it is necessary for me to go my own way, often a roundabout way, and that I can't do anything with the ideas of others when they are called out to me at the wrong time. . . .
>
> It does not seem impossible to me that you may be in a position to revise this book for a second edition. For that eventuality I put at your disposal the enclosed list of corrections. These are entirely reliable data, quite independent of my subjective opinions . . . Consider this information a sign that I do not by any means hold your work, which I cannot approve, in low esteem.[25]

[24] Jones, II, p. 8.

[25] In a footnote in *The Standard Edition*, XIX, pp. 286–88, the final sentence of this letter of December 18, 1923, is turned into a cliché: "The fact that I send you these corrections is a token that I value your work though I cannot wholly approve it." The word "wholly" is made up of whole cloth.

A few months later, August 15, 1924, Freud wrote Wittels about the English translation of the book; he could not compare it with the original, "which after all I did not take along on my vacation (any more than Nietzsche). Evidently you have made use of my corrections." We do not know what Wittels had said about Nietzsche, but Freud's attitude toward the book

> has not become friendlier. I still insist that if one knows as little about somebody as you do about me, one has no right to write a biography about him. One waits until he is dead; then he has to submit to everything, and it is fortunately also a matter of total indifference to him. . . .
>
> If you cannot prove this or have misunderstood or confused something, you cannot spare yourself the reproach of a serious infraction of an ethical duty. It won't do to say: "You are in my eyes a great man and a genius; consequently you have to put up with any way I compromise you. I have flattered you so outrageously that I may count on your absolute tolerance."

This did not keep Freud from adding a footnote to *The Interpretation of Dreams:* "The motive of the mischievement . . . was probably guessed correctly by *Wittels.*"[26] Nor did it keep "the uninvited biographer"[27] from publishing a second book about Freud that displays the same mixture of perceptiveness and outright mistakes. He entitled the first chapter of the second book (1931) "Goethe and Freud" and quoted the "Fragment upon Nature" in its entirety (pp. 31–34), although he inadvertently omitted the sentence emphasized in the original. Moreover, a section in Chapter II, "Freud the Antiphilosopher," bears the title "Artistic Science," and here Wittels says of Freud: "He pursues—as I believe—an artistic natural science in Goethe's sense" (p. 74).

[26] *Werke,* II/III, p. 425.
[27] *Ibid.,* p. 219.

I discovered Wittels's books long after I had decided to call the present chapter "Freud's Poetic Science" and felt half delighted by the confirmation and half disappointed that someone else should have got there first. It was a relief to find that Wittels really did not anticipate my account. Nor can I agree with this two central points.

About the essay on nature Wittels says: "The imperishable value of the essay rests, however, in the recognition that nature has meaning. This thought inspired the youthful Freud and illuminated his investigations" (p. 36). Yet the notion that nature has meaning was a commonplace that came under widespread attack only in the nineteenth century; it does not set apart this essay; and it is not even stated forcefully in the essay.

Wittels's other central contention is that Goethe had the rare ability to make scientific discoveries—"of the metamorphosis of plants, of the vertebrate cranium, and of the human intermaxillary"—through prolonged contemplation of a single case, and that Freud made his discoveries in the same way. In 1790, for example, Goethe picked up

> a split sheep's skull . . . gazed at it for a long time, and found . . . that the skull bones were greatly altered vertebrae. "At first sight," says Helmholtz, "nothing can be more dissimilar than the broad, cranial cavities of mammals bounded by flat bones and the narrow cylindrical tube of the vertebral column, composed of short, compact, and irregularly notched bones. It requires keen vision to recognize in the skull of vertebrates the enlarged and transformed vertebral ring . . ." Instead of "keen vision" we prefer to say: It requires an idea or . . . a preconceived opinion. This is just what happened with Goethe in regard to the metamorphosis of plants. He already bore the idea within him when in Padua he saw a fan palm which seemed to him to show clearly the transition from the first very simple radical leaflets to the complex pinnules (p. 91f.).

According to Wittels, Freud also made his discoveries after bearing the crucial idea within him and then contemplating for a long time a single case. But this is as implausible as the first contention.

What Wittels calls "a preconceived opinion," although this "might sound somewhat disreputable to many scientists," is no more than an intuition or at most a hypothesis, and there is nothing at all disreputable about having intuitions and formulating hypotheses. But the claim that Freud approached a single case with a preconceived opinion or a hypothesis and then reflected on that case until his opinion or hypothesis could be seen to be right is simply false.

So far from approaching a single case with the notion of the Oedipus complex in his mind, Freud was led by case after case to assume that many of his female patients had been seduced in childhood by their own fathers. Eventually it struck him how improbable this was; and the idea that this might be a fantasy shared by many women, and that men might harbor similar feelings for their mothers, occurred to him in the complicated interplay between ever so many cases on the one hand and his self-analysis on the other. This interplay was typical for Freud. There were generally large numbers of cases in addition to his own.

11 ▶▶▶ What impressed Freud so much in the essay on nature was an idea that can be stated very simply and briefly but is nonetheless crucial for understanding Freud's mentality. Both Adler and Jung misrepresented Freud in this matter, and neither Jones nor Wittels, not to speak of authors who had never known Freud, grasped what was at issue.

The essay transcends the dualisms that have plagued European thought from the time of Parmenides and Plato through Descartes and Kant down to our own time. All of these dualisms have issued from a division of man into body and soul (or mind) and the claim that the body belonged to one world and the soul (or mind) to another. Around 1900, Heinrich Rickert and Wilhelm Dilthey, who profoundly influenced Martin Buber and Martin Heidegger, argued that the humanities or mental sciences (*die Geisteswissenschaften*) required a method altogether different from the methods appropriate for the natural sciences.[28]

Sartre misrepresented Heidegger when he called him an atheist like himself.[29] Heidegger's dualism of human Being (*Dasein*) and all other beings or, as he also put the point, of the Who and What, was based on and appealed to religious ideas: Man is supposed to have a unique position in the cosmos, and the growth of science and technology is perceived as a dire threat. Sartre himself lacked Heidegger's religious background but was still an avowed dualist, insisting on the basic distinction between the being of things and bodies, which he called the in-itself (*en soi*), and the being of human selves, which he called the for-itself (*pour soi*). Buber's dualism of the I-It and the I-You goes back to the same tradition that is rooted in the contrast of body and soul.

The essay that impressed Freud so much said, in effect, as Goethe did his life long: Spirit or mind or soul is also nature. But it did not say this in a reductionist or materialist sense; it did not deprive the world of soul, beauty, or mystery. Neither did the essay oppose determinism or espouse some form of metaphysical idealism, denying the reality of matter.

Goethe's collected works contain a page and a half he wrote about the "Fragment on Nature" on May 24, 1828:

[28] Rickert, *Die Grenzen der naturwissenschaftlichen Begriffsbildung* (1896–1902); Dilthey, *Einleitung in die Geisteswissenschaften* (1883, reprinted in Vol. I of his *Gesammelte Schriften*, 1922).

[29] *L'existentialisme est un humanisme* (1946), p. 17.

This essay has recently been communicated to me from the epistolary estate of. . . . It has been written down by a familiar hand that I used to employ in the eighties for my business. That I am the author I cannot actually remember, but these observations agree entirely with the ideas that my mind had then reached in its education. . . .

In the years to which this essay probably belongs I was occupied above all with comparative anatomy, and in 1784 tried terribly hard to get others to take an interest in my conviction that *man should not be denied the intermaxillary* [a bone found in animals]. Even very bright people refused to recognize the significance of this claim; the best observers denied its correctness; and I, as so often, had to proceed quietly on my own way by myself.[30]

Goethe went on to speak of his studies of the metamorphosis of plants, and then also of animals, and he also mentioned how in 1790 in Venice the origin of the skull from vertebrae became clear to him. He had followed up this discovery, "dictated the scheme in the year 1795 to Max Jacobi in Jena, and soon had the great pleasure of seeing how in this area German scientists carried on my work." But what was the significance of these discoveries? They established development as a characteristic not only of mind but also of matter, and they did their share "to translate man back into nature," to use a fine phrase found in Nietzsche.[31] Man was closer to other animals than people liked to believe seventy years before Darwin published *The Origin of Species*, and the human mind is part of nature.

The essay that Freud admired so much was the credo of a comparative anatomist who stood alone against "the compact majority,"[32] a scientist with a poetic imagination second to none, a man who never belonged to any

[30] *Werke*, XL, p. 281f.

[31] *Beyond*, section 230.

[32] Freud liked this phrase from Ibsen's *An Enemy of the People*. See *Werke*, XIV, p. 35.

guild but followed his own path, writing magnificent books. He refused to turn his back on nature in order to concentrate on the mind, or to turn his back on the mind to immerse himself in the study of matter.

Freud's deeply humanistic bent and his love of art and literature were striking. His archaeological collection of figurines met the eye in his waiting room and on his desk no less than his feeling for the great poets meets the eye in his books. Science must have held some attraction for him even before he encountered the essay on nature, but it was this essay that convinced him that one could be a scientist without renouncing one's humanistic bent. He chose biology as the natural science in which man and nature meet, as it were, and studied medicine. But he also became a great writer. And before long he created a new literary genre: the case history that can be as fascinating as any short story or novel.

12 ▶▶▶ In the first volume of this trilogy Goethe was credited with four major contributions to the discovery of the mind: He provided a new model of autonomy; he insisted that man is his deeds; he showed how the mind has to be understood in terms of development; and, refusing to accept the equation of science with Newtonian science, he insisted on the importance of bold hypotheses and envisaged a nonmathematical science. All of these contributions were accepted and developed by Freud.

I also tried to show how

Kant impeded the discovery of the mind by (1) establishing a misguided "transcendental" method, by (2) providing an untenable model of the mind as well as (3) a grotesque notion of autonomy, by (4) persuading generations of philosophers that serious and important studies must be written like the *Critique of Pure Reason,* and finally (5) by insisting that in philosophical analyses of the mind hypotheses are illegitimate and certainty and necessity are requirements (section 33).

It was philosophy in this mold that never interested Freud and led him to avow his lack of talent for philosophy.

Finally, we saw how Hegel advanced the discovery of the mind by developing Goethe's ideas, but also how he was impeded by Kant's legacy. This legacy meets the eye as soon as one opens one of Hegel's books. It is doubly remarkable that Nietzsche, whose style could scarcely have been more different from Hegel's, took to task Schopenhauer, by whom he had been influenced in his youth, for his "unintelligent wrath against Hegel."[33] A year after doing that, Nietzsche praised the "Hegelian innovation that first introduced the decisive concept of 'development' into science"; and then Nietzsche went on to say:

> We Germans are Hegelians, even if there had never been any Hegel, insofar as we (unlike all Latins) instinctively attribute a deeper meaning and a greater value to becoming and development than to what "is"; we hardly believe in the justification of the concept of "being"—and also insofar as we are not inclined to concede that our human logic is logic as such or the only kind of logic . . .

This generalization about the Germans is highly questionable. It does not apply to Kant and to more recent thinkers who were not greatly influenced by Goethe—for example, Husserl and Heidegger. Instead of juxtaposing Germans and Latins we should understand the crucial difference historically—in terms of development. Goethe's developmental approach was developed by Hegel, Nietzsche, and Freud, while the unhistorical

---

[33] *Beyond Good and Evil,* section 204. For the wrath see section 37 of the first volume of this trilogy.

structuralism of Kant conquered academic philosophy in the guise of neo-Kantianism.[34] Husserl's quest for absolute certainty and his attempt to establish "phenomenology as strict science,"[35] as well as Heidegger's attempt to lay a new foundation (*Grundlegung*) by creating a "fundamental ontology," stand in this Kantian or neo-Kantian tradition.

The popular conceit that there are two major twentieth-century philosophies, Anglo-American analytical philosophy and "Continental philosophy," which is thought to consist of phenomenology and existentialism, is blind. These two kinds of philosophy are variations on a single academic philosophy that goes back to Kant, and the radical alternative to both of them is the tradition whose high points are Goethe, Hegel (who tried to reconcile Goethe with Kant), Nietzsche, and Freud. In the so-called existentialists, to be sure, one finds something of Nietzsche, but these radical elements are always overshadowed by the heritage of Kant and—in Heidegger and Sartre— also by Husserl. What is wanted is taken to preclude hypotheses and empirical psychology.

Freud, of course, was put off by the Kantian cloak of Hegel's philosophy and did not learn anything directly from Hegel. Yet he did accept several of the contributions that I ascribed to Hegel in the final section of the first volume of this trilogy. He tried to show "how each view must be seen in relation to the person holding it"; also "that every position should be seen as a stage in a

---

[34] The critique of Kant in Richard Rorty (1979), which appeared as I was making final revisions in this manuscript, supplements mine, and his critical remarks about the neo-Kantians and their immense influence provide a most welcome addition to the picture I have drawn. Yet our starting points as well as our ideas about Heidegger are very different.

[35] This is the title of the essay he contributed to *Logos*, Vol. I (1900/01). See also my article "Existentialism (and Phenomenology)."

development"; and he followed Hegel's example in applying these ideas to literature, art, and religion. As for Hegel's systems approach, Freud remarked (March 2, 1910, according to the *Minutes of the Vienna Psychoanalytic Society*) that he "personally never made an effort to construct a complete system: He was instead focused on the gaps"—a comment that brings to mind the lines from Heine that he liked so much. But he agreed with the view I ascribed to Hegel:

> that views and positions have to be seen as a whole, that the theoretical and moral belong together as aspects of a single standpoint, and that, in effect, atomism and microscopism miss the spirit that holds everything together.

One thing that he might have learned from Hegel but didn't is that "a position needs to be seen in relation to opposing views that help us to see not only its motivation but also the partiality and inadequacy of both sides." Jung tried to do just that with Freud and Adler, in *Psychological Types,* and we shall examine this attempt in due time, but even Jung did not apply this difficult lesson to his own position. Nor had Hegel done that. It had remained for Eduard von Hartmann to try to concoct a synthesis of Hegel and Schopenhauer. The reason why Freud did not try harder to see his own position in relation to Adler's or Jung's has already been cited in his own words from a letter he wrote to his unsolicited biographer: "It is necessary for me to go my own way, often a roundabout way"—like Goethe, one might add— and "I can't do anything with the ideas of others when they are called out to me at the wrong time." He had to develop organically in his own way, like an artist or a poet. It was important for him not to be deflected by the views of others. That was the reverse side of Goethe's model of autonomy.

A letter to his fiancée, written in Paris on February 2, 1886, shows beautifully what was at issue.

13 ▶▶▶ . . . The little bit of cocaine
that I have taken makes me garrulous . . .

. . . I have known long since that I am no genius and I no longer understand how I could ever have wished to be one. I am not even very gifted; my whole talent for work probably lies in my character traits and in the lack of preeminent intellectual weaknesses. But I know that this mixture is very favorable for slow success, and that under favorable circumstances I could achieve more than Nothnagel, to whom I think I am far superior, and that perhaps I could catch up with Charcot. That does not mean that I'll do it, for these favorable circumstances I do not find any more; and the genius, the strength to compel them, I do not have. But the way I chatter! I had meant to say something quite different. Namely, explain the source of my inaccessibility and abrasiveness against strangers of which you speak. It is merely the consequence of mistrust after I have experienced often that ordinary or bad people treat me badly, and will disappear proportionately as I no longer have to fear anything from them, as I become more powerful and independent. I always console myself with the fact that subordinates or persons whose position equals my own have never found me disagreeable, only superiors or people otherwise superior. One would scarcely be able to tell this from looking at me, and yet I was in school already a bold opposition man who always stood where an extreme had to be avowed and as a rule also paid for afterwards. When I finally obtained a privileged position since I had been the first in my class for many years and I enjoyed general confidence, one did not have any grounds for further complaints about me. Do you know what Breuer said to me one evening? I was so moved by it that I then told him the secret of our engagement. He said that he had found out that there was concealed in me under the shroud of shyness an immeasurably bold and fearless human being. But I have always believed that and merely never dared to tell anybody. I often felt as if I had inherited all the stubborn defiance and all the passion of our ancestors when they defended their temple, as if for the sake of one great moment I could throw down my life joyously. And all the time I was always so powerless and could not even give expression to my ardent passions in a word or a poem. So I have always suppressed myself, and that, I think, must show.

Such stupid confessions I make to you, sweet treasure, really for no good reason, unless it is the cocaine that makes me talk. . . .

When he wrote this letter he was not quite thirty. He had published a dozen scientific papers with such titles as "On the Spinal Ganglia and Spinal Cord of the Petromyzon" and "On the Construction of the Nerve Fibers and Nerve Cells in the Crayfish," mostly in the annals of the Imperial Academy of the Sciences; a series of papers on cocaine; one paper written in English, "A New Histological Method for the Study of Nerve-Tracts in the Brain and Spinal Cord" (in *Brain*, 1884); and one book: For the last (12th) volume of John Stuart Mill's collected works in German, edited by Theodor Gomperz, Freud had translated Mill's *Ueber Frauenemancipation. Plato. Arbeiterfrage. Socialismus* (1880) and his name, spelled Siegmund Freud,[36] had appeared on the title page.

We do not think of Nietzsche as having read Freud, and he collapsed before psychoanalysis was born, but his knowledge of Mill was actually based in large measure on Freud's translation, which he owned. His copy is still in the Nietzsche archive in Weimar.

In 1886, the year Freud wrote the letter just quoted—and Nietzsche published *Beyond Good and Evil*—Freud published four more scientific papers as well as a volume containing a German translation of a book by Charcot. In 1888–89 he published a German

[36] In the annals of the academy his name appears as "Sigm. Freud," as it later did on the title pages of his own books.

Ueber Frauenemancipation.
Plato.
Arbeiterfrage. Socialismus.

Von

John Stuart Mill.

———

Ueberſetzt

von

Siegmund Freud.

———

Leipzig, 1880.

Fues's Verlag (R. Reisland).

Freud's first book: Translation of John Stuart Mill.

translation of a book by H. Bernheim, on hypnosis, and in 1892–94 another translation of a book by Characot. His very own first book, on aphasia, appeared in 1891. Nothnagel, whom Freud mentions in his letter, was Professor of Medicine at the University of Vienna.

The most interesting theme in that letter is surely that Freud felt sure that he was not a genius—and he never came to think of himself as a genius or "a great man"—but thought that his achievements would have to depend—and later felt they did depend—on certain "character traits," above all boldness and stubborn defiance. To inquire in the face of opposition to his ideas whether they were not perhaps one-sided and whether he might not be able to accommodate the views of his critics would have opened the way for accommodation, "rotten compromises," and the loss of his integrity.

It may seem odd how much this letter, written before he turned thirty, anticipates the ethos that he manifested a quarter of a century later. The oddity evaporates when we recall Freud's great admiration for two quotations he had encountered in a set of Ludwig Börne's works that he received, presumably for his Bar mitzvah,[37] when he was thirteen. These passages have already been quoted (in section 6) along with Einstein's "The main thing is to refuse to make rotten compromises."

The little essay of not quite four pages in which Freud quoted Börne is actually worth another look. Havelock Ellis had suggested that psychoanalysis should not be evaluated as a science but as Freud's artistic achievement. In support of this view he claimed that Dr. J. J. Garth Wilkinson, who was better known as a poet and a Swedenborgian mystic than as a doctor, had anticipated in some measure Freud's technique of free association as early as 1857. Freud countered in "On the

[37] See Ernst Simon (1957).

Prehistory of the Analytical Technique" (1920) that Otto Rank had found a passage in which Friedrich Schiller, in 1788, had made much the same point as Wilkinson. He continued:

> One may suppose that the allegedly new Wilkensonian [sic] technique has occurred to many others before, and its systematic application in psychoanalysis appears to us less as a proof of *Freud's* artistic bent than as a consequence of his conviction, to which he clung as to a prejudice, that all psychic events without exception are determined. That whatever freely comes to mind should belong to the fixed topic was then the nearest and most probable possibility that is also confirmed by experience in analysis . . .[38]

While neither Wilkinson nor Schiller had influenced the development of his technique, Freud went on to point out that an essay by Börne that a doctor in Budapest had brought to the attention of one of Freud's associates was in some ways more remarkable. "The Art of Becoming an Original Writer in Three Days" (1823), a mere four and a half pages long, was included in the first volume of Börne's works, which Freud was given at thirteen, and fifty years later it was the only book of those days that he still owned. Börne had been the first writer whom he had studied intensively and, while he could not recall this essay, in the course of all those years he had frequently recalled, for no apparent reason, several other pieces in the same volume. Yet it was in the essay on becoming an original writer, which he could not remember reading, that he found with surprise some ideas that he himself had always prized and championed, including the two already cited in section 6 as well as:

> A disgraceful and cowardly fear of thinking restrains us all. More oppressive than the censorship of governments

[38] *Werke*, XII, pp. 309–12.

is the censorship that public opinion exerts over the works of our minds.

Here, finally, is Börne's recipe for becoming a writer:

Take a few sheets of paper and write down for three consecutive days, without falseness or hypocrisy, what passes through your mind . . . . and at the end of the three days you will be beside yourselves with amazement . . .

To rebut the insinuation that psychoanalysis was unscientific and close to such a minor poet and mystic as Wilkinson, Freud could insist on his conviction "that all psychic events without exception are determined." But no sooner had he done that than he quoted not some nineteenth-century materialistic scientists but Börne. For he did not associate his own determinism with mechanism and materialism, nor did he derive it from the scientists of that period. He knew his sources and considered "the incomparably beautiful essay" on nature the most important among them. But for that he might never have become a scientist.

14 ▶▶▶ We are now ready to reconstruct Freud's intellectual development. Jones says (I, p. 43):

Freud himself, inspired by Goethe . . . passed through a brief period of the pantheistic *Naturphilosophie*. Then, in his enthusiasm for the rival physiology, he swung to the opposite extreme and became for a while a radical materialist.

Later in the same volume (p. 367) he picks up the story:

In his early student days Freud passed through a phase of

radical materialism, but this could not have survived his attendance at Brentano's and Meynert's lectures.

Jones explains further that for Meynert force, not matter, was basic.

In the autobiographical sketch in which Freud speaks of the "beautiful essay 'Nature'" he does not mention Brentano, but he stresses the impression made on him by Ernst Brücke and Theodor Meynert. Jones tells us (p. 65) that "Freud agreed with the general opinion that Meynert was the greatest brain anatomist of his time, but he had only a moderate opinion of him as a psychiatrist." In his autobiography he speaks of "Meynert, whose work and personality had enthralled me even as a student," and in *The Interpretation of Dreams*[39] he speaks of his "veneration" for him. Actually, both Meynert and Brücke are encountered a number of times in the dream book, and at one point Freud remarks how "the dear name of Brücke" (*der teure Name* Brücke) serves "to remind me of the same institute in which I spent my happiest hours as a student."[40] In his autobiography he puts the crucial point as clearly as possible:

> In the physiological laboratory of *Ernst Brücke* I finally found rest and full satisfaction as well as persons whom I could respect and make my models.

And a few lines later Freud speaks of him as "my boundlessly revered teacher." Incidentally, he named one of his sons Ernst.

In other words, the personalities of Brücke and Meynert made a powerful and enduring impression on him and, we may add, influenced his conception of science. He worked in Brücke's institute "from 1876 to

[39] *Werke*, II/III, p. 439.
[40] *Werke*, II/III, p. 212f. See also pp. 424ff., 455–58, 481, 485f., and 488.

1882, with short intervals, and was quite generally expected to be appointed to the next assistantship." During these years he published several histological papers and was in no hurry to become a doctor of medicine, though he received his degree in 1881. In 1882 Brücke advised him to give up pure science and make use of his medical degree, "considering my poor economic condition."[41]

Two years after this autobiography, Freud returned to this point:

> After forty-one years as a doctor, my self-knowledge tells me that I really was no proper doctor. I became a doctor through being forcibly deflected from my original purpose, and the triumph of my life consists in the fact that after a long detour I have recovered my original direction. . . . During my youth the need to understand something of the riddles of this world and perhaps to contribute something myself to their solution was preponderant. The study of medicine seemed the best way to this end, but then I tried it, without success, with zoology and chemistry until, under the influence of *von Brücke*, the greatest authority that ever influenced me, I got stuck in physiology, which in those days limited itself too largely to histology.[42]

Freud's statements add up to a coherent and thoroughly plausible picture. The original goal had been philosophy in the sense of making some contribution to the solution of great problems. Academic philosophy, of course, never attracted Freud, while medicine was an art as well as a science and a place where man and nature meet.

It is amusing and instructive to note also that in his autobiography Freud quotes Goethe's Mephistopheles directly before he introduces Brücke. The short speech

---

[41] *Werke*, XIV, p. 35.
[42] *Werke*, XIV, p. 290.

about medicine from which he quotes also contains this quatrain, which he does not quote:

And give the women special care;
Their everlasting sighs and groans
In thousand tones
Are cured at *one* point everywhere.[43]

15 ▶▶▶ In one respect Jones's summary is misleading. It suggests that the phase inspired by Goethe was as brief as the radical materialism that Freud passed through afterward. Yet Freud went out of his way to tell the world both in *The Interpretation of Dreams* and, twenty-five years later, in his autobiography, that it was Goethe's influence that led him to study medicine. The remarks he made about materialism in his books are uniformly negative.

In the dream book he recalled a scene near the beginning of his student days when

I, a green boy, full of the materialist doctrine, refused to wait my turn and immodestly championed a most one-sided point of view. Then an older fellow student who was superior . . . dressed us down; he, too, had fed the swine in his youth before returning, repentant to his father's house.

The allusion here is to the parable of the prodigal son in Luke 15. Freud went on to recall how he then insulted the older student who "was too sensible to accept the advice given him that he should challenge me to a duel and allowed the matter to rest."[44] By 1899, then, Freud looked back on his adoption of materialism as an episode that belonged to his distant past, and he sympathized

---

[43] *Faust*, lines 2023–26.
[44] II/III, p. 218 = 1900, p. 146.

with the student who had perceived that this was merely a phase through which many youngsters passed.

Freud's explicit references to materialism and mechanism are few in number and almost all late. Discussing forms of resistance to psychoanalysis, in 1925, he remarks:

> If anybody succeeded in isolating and demonstrating the hypothetical material entity or entities that might relate to the neuroses, this discovery would not have to fear any objections from physicians. But as yet there is no way of doing that. For now we can only proceed from the picture of the neurotic symptoms which, for example in the case of hysteria, consist of physical as well as psychic disturbances. Now the experiments of *Charcot* as well as *Breuer's* observations of patients have taught us that the physical symptoms of hysteria, too, are *psychogenic* . . .
>
> This new insight was taken up by psychoanalysis, which thus began to ask what might be the nature of these psychical processes which produce such unusual consequences. But this direction of research was not congenial to the contemporary generation of physicians. The medical profession had been educated to esteem highly only anatomical, physical, and chemical factors. . . . They clearly doubted that psychic things admit of any exact scientific treatment. . . . In this materialistic—or better: mechanistic—period medicine made magnificent advances, but also failed myopically to recognize the noblest and most difficult problems of life.[45]

In 1925 Freud still distinguished his own position sharply from materialism, stressing that much of the resistance to psychoanalysis was due to the materialistic-mechanistic training of the medical establishment. His opponents found it hard to believe that physical symptoms could be psychogenic— and curable by dealing

[45] *Werke,* XIV, p. 101f.

with the patient's mind. Freud never ruled out the possibility that some day one might be able to isolate the physical factors "that might deserve consideration in connection with the neuroses." If only that could be done, the medical establishment might be satisfied. In the long draft he had sent to Wilhelm Fliess in 1895 he had tried unsuccessfully to explore this path, and to the end of his life he would have been glad if someone could have done this to round out the picture. Nietzsche, too, had spoken more than once of his high hopes for physiology, but willy-nilly both men had to settle for psychology.

The resistance of the *philosophers,* Freud goes on to note in the same paper of 1925, is due to the fact that "the overwhelming majority of them call psychic only what is a phenomenon of consciousness." For them something that is unconscious but psychic is "an un-thing, a *contradictio in adjecto.*" One might also translate *Unding* as something unthinkable. But the philosopher "does not want to note that this judgment merely repeats his own, perhaps too narrow, definition of what is psychic." In the 1940s Professor C. I. Lewis at Harvard, one of the most outstanding American philosophers of his time, who taught generations of students Kant, epistemology, and ethics, still argued like that, and so did Sartre. But as Freud goes on to say,

> For the philosopher it is easy to be so certain, for he does not know the material whose study compelled the analyst to believe in unconscious acts of the soul. He has not paid attention to hypnosis nor exerted himself to interpret dreams.

The discovery of physical factors would help on this front also. It would allow philosophers to say that some physical processes are accompanied by consciousness, others not. But Freud's discoveries and therapy did not have to wait for the discovery of physical factors.

On one occasion, however, Freud did call himself a mechanist and materialist—in a manuscript on psychoanalysis and telepathy, written in 1921 for a lecture at a small gathering of leading analysts; but he never published it, and when he incorporated one whole section from it in his *New Introductory Lectures* (1933) and used a good deal more in altered form, he did not include this passage. On the contrary, in print he referred to a view he had held "more than ten years ago" as a view he no longer held. Still, as long as this manuscript was included in the collected works, we might as well consider this passage also. Freud's attitudes toward occult phenomena are of considerable interest in any case because Jung came to feel that they contributed to the break between the two men, which will be considered at length in Chapter III, where we shall round out the picture by also considering Freud's feelings about occult phenomena before the First World War.

In the 1921 manuscript "Psychoanalysis and Telepathy," Freud said:

> The vast majority of occultists are not impelled by the thirst for knowledge, nor by the sense of shame that science should have failed so long to take notice of undeniable problems and by the desire to subjugate to science new realms of phenomena. Rather are they people who are already convinced and look for confirmation . . . The faith, however, that they first want to prove to themselves and then press upon others is the old religious faith . . . The analysts, on the other hand, cannot deny their descent from the outlook of rigorous science [*von der exakten Wissenschaftlichkeit*].

Here most of those interested in the occult are seen as seeking to satisfy religious needs, even to justify a preconceived religious faith, while Freud was trained by men like Meynert and Brücke and had written painstaking papers on histology. The analysts, he continues, are prepared to forgo "the blinding splendor of a theory without gaps" (we recall Heine's poem about plugging all the gaps with bathrobe rags and long nightcaps).

> They are satisfied with fragmentary crumbs of knowledge and with unsharp basic assumptions that are ready for any modification. Instead of lying in wait for the moment that might allow them to escape from the coercion of known physical and chemical laws, they hope for the appearance of expanded natural laws that reach deeper and are prepared to submit to them. The analysts are at bottom incorrigible mechanists and materialists, even though they want to guard against robbing the psychic and spiritual of their as yet unknown distinctive characteristics. They enter into examination of occult things only because they expect that in this way they will exclude once and for all from material reality the wishful fantasies of humanity.[46]

If we accepted Heidegger's principle that a man's books can be safely discounted and that his authentic views are to be found in snippets carved from drafts that he never published,[47] we could rest satisfied with Freud's nine-word admission that he was an incorrigible mechanist and materialist. Except for that one rhetorical flourish, the position adopted in this draft is wholly consistent with what we find elsewhere. The central contrast of a basically religious approach that needs to buttress a faith and is, at bottom, antiscientific, with the scientific approach is drawn beautifully and might almost have come from Nietzsche's pen. Nor should we overlook the clause that immediately follows upon "mechanists and materialists," for it disavows reductionism. Freud would not be at all averse to finding the material factors or energy charges, but he is far from

---

[46] *Werke*, XVII, p. 28f.

[47] See Section 32 of the second volume of this trilogy.

claiming that the psychic or spiritual is "nothing but" matter or energy.

The lecture "Dream and Occultism" in the *New Introductory Lectures* returns to the subject of telepathy.

> I think it does not show any great confidence in science if one does not trust here to assimilate and digest whatever may turn out to be true among occult claims. And as for telepathy in particular, it actually seems to favor the extension of the scientific—opponents say: mechanistic— way of thinking to include the mental [*Geistige*] which is so hard to grasp. . . . What lies between the two psychic acts could easily be a physical process into which the psychic transforms itself at one end and that at the other end transforms itself again into the same psychic act. Then the analogy to other transformations, like speaking and listening at the telephone, could not be missed. And just think what it would mean if we could get hold of this physical equivalent of the psychic act! I feel like saying that, by inserting the unconscious between the physical and that which until then had been called "psychic," psychoanalysis has prepared us for the acceptance of such processes as telepathy.[48]

Freud goes on to speculate that the general will in large insect societies may perhaps be produced by some such psychic transference. This could have been the archaic form of communication that has gradually been pushed into the background

> by the better method of communication by means of signs that are perceived through the sense organs. But the older method might have been preserved in the back- ground and could still come through under certain condi- tions . . .

It may be instructive to contrast Freud once more with Kant. Kant contradicts himself frequently even in

[48] *Werke*, XV, p. 59.

such short works as his 1785 book on ethics; he operates with a terminology that he cannot keep straight in his own head and keeps forgetting; he works with mutually opposed basic conceptions; and he writes so obscurely that he himself fails to notice all this. At the same time he insists that in the philosophy of mind a philosopher ought to achieve, and he himself has attained, absolute certainty, and that it would be illegitimate to entertain mere hypotheses.

Freud's clarity and consistency are two sides of the same coin. When he changes his mind about something, he calls attention to it. He constantly admits hypotheses into his work and points out that this is all they are; he distinguishes between bold speculations for which there is as yet no evidence and hypotheses that have been confirmed again and again; and he tells us precisely what speaks for them.

16 ▶▶▶ Freud's attitude toward one particular form of materialism, namely dialectical materialism, or Marxism, is of special interest because Freud has often been linked with Marx and Nietzsche as one of the three great revolutionary thinkers who have molded the mind of modern man, and attempts to synthesize Freud and Marx have become quite popular. Freud, like Nietzsche, always considered it a point of honor to swim against the stream, but there are writers whose claim to fame rests precisely on their virtuosity in swimming with many streams at once. After Freud became intellectually fashionable, writers of this type tried to show how one could accept Freud as well as Marx, Christianity, and existentialism (Paul Tillich), or the same mix without Christianity (Herbert Marcuse), or Freud, Marx, and analytical philosophy (Jürgen Habermas).

Any really serious effort to synthesize Freud and Marx would have to begin by exploring the deep contradictions between their doctrines. Anything less than that could not be called "dialectical," nor need it be taken seriously. That there is a large market for shallow eclecticism that offers everything and perhaps heaven on earth, too, proves that this sort of thing *is* taken seriously by many people, not that it *should* be.

Until he was in his seventies, Freud ignored Marx and Marxism, which is really remarkable. He lived in a world in which thousands of intellectuals were hotly debating Marxism, but even the Russian Revolution did not lead him to say anything about Marx or Marxism in any of his books. This is even more astonishing than Nietzsche's silence on the same subject. Unlike Shaw, Russell, and Gide, to name only a few of his illustrious contemporaries, Freud evidently found Marxism totally uncongenial. The two late works in which he finally broke his silence on this subject leave no doubt about this. In *Civilization and Its Discontents* (1930) he did not discuss Marxism at length; but speaking of aggression in Section V, Freud referred to "the extreme intolerance of Christianity" and then continued:

> Nor was it an unintelligible accident that the dream of Germanic world dominion called upon anti-Semitism to complement it, and one sees how it is comprehensible that the attempt to construct a new Communist culture in Russia should find psychological support in the persecution of the bourgeois. One merely asks oneself with apprehension what the Soviets will do once they have exterminated their bourgeois.[49]

Long before the Moscow trials, Freud was totally out of sympathy with the Soviet policy of persecution and extermination and far from considering it merely an accidental perversion of a basically humanitarian idea by one or two monsters. To understand Freud's view of

[49] *Werke*, XIV, p. 474.

humanity, one also needs to consider at least parts of the immediately preceding paragraph:

> The communists believe that they have found the way to redemption from evil. Man is unequivocally good, well disposed toward his neighbor, but the institution of private property has corrupted his nature. Possession of private goods gives some the power and thus the temptation to maltreat their neighbor; those excluded from possessions must rebel in hostility against their oppressors. When private property is abolished and all goods are made common and their enjoyment accessible to all men, ill will and hostility among men will vanish. Since all needs are satisfied, no one will have any reason to consider anyone else his enemy; and then everyone will do the necessary work voluntarily. I have no business with the economic critique of the communist system . . . But I am able to recognize its psychological presupposition as a baseless illusion.[50] With the abolition of private property one deprives the human lust for aggression of one of its instruments, certainly a strong one and certainly not the strongest. The differences in power and influence that aggression abuses for its purposes remain as unchanged as the nature of aggression itself. Aggression has not been created by property; it prevailed almost without barriers in primeval times when property was still pretty wretched, manifests itself already in the nursery . . . and furnishes the grounds of all tender and loving relationships between human beings, possibly with the sole exception of those between a mother and her male child. If one removed the personal right to the possession of things, there would still be the privileges in sexual relations which are bound to become the source of the strongest ill will and the most violent hostility among human beings placed on a footing of equality in other ways. If one abolished this also by achieving the total liberation of sexual life, abolishing the family, which is the germ cell of culture, then we cannot predict, to be

[50] See also *Werke*, XVI, p. 23, and Wortis (1954, 1975), p. 108f.

sure, what new paths the development of culture might be able to take, but one thing one may count on: that the indestructible trait of human nature would follow it there also.

This paragraph almost reads as if it came from a critical review of Herbert Marcuse's *Eros and Civilization* (1955). It does not follow that Freud was right and Marcuse wrong, but it is remarkable that Marcuse simply ignored Freud's opposition to Marxism. Marcuse had learned the art of exegetical reading from Heidegger, his teacher, to whom he dedicated his first book. In *Eros and Civilization* ideas are proved by being found in Freud, and if they can also be called radical then it is taken to follow that all who do not accept them are reactionary. At the same time Freud is reinterpreted, and Marcuse seems to assume that if his reinterpretations are radical in both senses he must be right. While Marcuse could have learned these techniques from generations of theologians who read Scripture in this fashion, he actually did learn it from Heidegger, of whom he said in conversation that he was the best teacher he had ever had.

Near the end of *Civilization and Its Discontents* Freud accused "the socialists" of "a modern idealistic misjudgment of human nature."[51] But that was not the only reason for his rejection of socialism as well as communism. He was also an unrepentant individualist who felt that the kind of character he admired depended on alienation. Elsewhere I have contrasted his attitude with that of Marx and various twentieth-century apostles of the notion that alienation is an evil that ought to be abolished.[52] Here it will be quite sufficient to illustrate this point from Freud's postscript (1927) to *The Question of Lay Analysis:*

[51] *Werke*, XIV, p. 504.
[52] Chapter 6, "The Need for Alienation," in Kaufmann, *Without Guilt and Justice* (1973).

We analysts aim at an analysis of patients that should be as complete and reach as deep as possible; we do not wish to unburden them by admission to a Catholic, Protestant, or socialist community but wish to enrich them from their own inner resources by making accessible to the ego the energies that through repression are tied up in their unconscious as well as those others that the ego must squander in an unfruitful way to maintain the repression.[53]

The ideal is, as in Nietzsche, Goethean autonomy, and much of what has been quoted in this section is very close to Nietzsche indeed.

Freud's most extensive attack on Marxism is to be found on the last six pages of his *New Introductory Lectures*. These lectures were conceived as his last major work,[54] and he began the numbering with XXIX to mark them as the continuation of his earlier introductory lectures. The intention was plainly that the old and the new lectures together should henceforth serve as the best guide to psychoanalysis and the one text that nobody interested in the subject could well ignore.

Of "Russian Bolshevism" Freud said, years before the Moscow trials that finally opened the eyes of many other intellectuals, not to speak of Stalin's pact with Hitler, that it had

created a prohibition of thought that is quite as inexorable as that formerly imposed by religions. Critical examination of the Marxist theory is forbidden; doubts about its correctness are punished as heresy once was by the Catholic Church. The works of *Marx* have assumed the place of the Bible and the Koran as a source of revelation although they are hardly freer of contradictions and obscurities than these older holy books.

[53] *Werke*, XIV, p. 293.

[54] When Freud decided to publish *Moses and Monotheism* (1939), he included another attack on the Soviet Union: *Werke*, XVI, p. 156f.

rischen Entwicklung zu überlassen, sondern sie durch
revolutionären Eingriff selbst durchzusetzen. In seiner
Verwirklichung im russischen Bolschewismus hat nun der
theoretische Marxismus die Energie, Geschlossenheit
und Ausschließlichkeit einer Weltanschauung gewonnen,
gleichzeitig aber auch eine unheimliche Ähnlichkeit mit
dem, was er bekämpft. Ursprünglich selbst ein Stück
Wissenschaft, in seiner Durchführung auf Wissenschaft
und Technik aufgebaut, hat er doch ein Denkverbot geschaffen, das eben so unerbittlich ist wie seinerzeit das
der Religion. Eine kritische Untersuchung der marxisti-
schen Theorie ist untersagt, Zweifel an ihrer Richtigkeit
werden so geahndet wie einst die Ketzerei von der katholischen Kirche. Die Werke von M a r x haben als
Quelle einer Offenbarung die Stelle der Bibel und des
Korans eingenommen, obwohl sie nicht freier von Wider-
sprüchen und Dunkelheiten sein sollen als diese älteren
heiligen Bücher.

Und obwohl der praktische Marxismus mit allen
idealistischen Systemen und Illusionen erbarmungslos
aufgeräumt hat, hat er doch selbst Illusionen entwickelt,
die nicht weniger fragwürdig und unbeweisbar sind als
die früheren. Er hofft im Laufe weniger Generationen
die menschliche Natur so zu verändern, daß sich ein
fast reibungsloses Zusammenleben der Menschen in der
neuen Gesellschaftsordnung ergibt und daß sie die Auf-
gaben der Arbeit zwangsfrei auf sich nehmen. Unterdes
verlegt er die in der Gesellschaft unerläßlichen Trieb-
einschränkungen an andere Stellen und lenkt die aggres-
siven Neigungen, die jede menschliche Gemeinschaft be-

Freud on Marx, in his *New Introductory Lectures*, 1933.

And although practical Marxism has done away mercilessly with all idealistic systems and illusions, it nevertheless has developed illusions of its own that are no less questionable and unprovable than those that preceded it. It hopes to alter human nature within a few generations so that human beings can live together almost without friction in the new order of society and take upon themselves without compulsion the tasks of labor.

What follows is similar to the long quotation from *Civilization and Its Discontents* and easily accessible, so there is no need to quote more. But it is noteworthy that Freud's critique is not limited to Stalin; it is no less applicable to Mao's China, to the Soviet Union and China after the eras of Stalin and Mao, and to such neo-Freudians as Marcuse. A synthesis of Marx and Freud is a wooden iron.

Seeing how widely Marcuse has been read, it may be worth while to point out that Paul Robinson was right when he said in *The Freudian Left* (1969) that Marx

> was clearly the unacknowledged hero of *Eros and Civilization*. That Marcuse never mentioned Marx's name in the book was an extraordinary feat of legerdemain. It is my contention that the underlying tactic of *Eros and Civilization* was to bring Freudian theory into line with the categories of Marxism. (p. 201)

Perhaps Marx was not mentioned because when the book was written McCarthyism was at its height. However that may be, the synthesis of Freud, Marx, and existentialism that was to prove so popular was accomplished by a sleight of hand, and the trick was exegetical thinking of the kind I have described in the Heidegger chapter of this trilogy.

It should be obvious by now why this trilogy does not contain a chapter on Marx. I do not believe that he made any great contribution to the discovery of the mind;

nor do I believe that many people would think of him as a great philosopher if Lenin had not succeeded in imposing Marxism on the Soviet Union. Since then Marxism has spread, of course, and millions who have never read a single book by Marx proclaim their allegiance to Marxism and their hatred and contempt not only for non-Marxists but also for all those who allegedly misinterpret Marx. This would be ridiculous if it had not led to so much bloodshed, torture, terror, and oppression. It certainly comes nowhere near creating a presumption that Marx made any major contributions to the discovery of the mind.

17 ▶▶▶ In one of his many interesting letters to the novelist Arnold Zweig (November 26, 1930), Freud explained that he would gladly sign a manifesto sent to him if only it did not contain a certain remark about capitalism.

> For that would amount to taking sides with the communist ideal, and I am far from that. For all of my dissatisfaction with our present economic orders I nevertheless lack any hope that the path chosen by the Soviets will lead to improvements. Indeed, any such hopes I might ever have nourished have perished during the decade of Soviet rule. I remain an old-style liberal.

By that he evidently meant that he was a thoroughgoing individualist to whom freedom was a supreme value. For he certainly did not share the optimism so often associated with liberalism, nor the belief in human equality.

In the long passage quoted above from *Civilization and Its Discontents* there is a footnote omitted so far. But it is important if we would understand Freud:

> Whoever has tasted the misery of poverty when young and has experienced the indifference and haughtiness of the well-to-do, ought to be protected against the suspi-

cion that he lacks understanding and sympathy for the aspirations of those who want to fight the inequality of possessions among human beings and what follows from that. To be sure, when this fight relies on the abstract demand of justice in the name of the equality of all human beings, the objection is too obvious that nature, by means of the highly unequal physical equipment and intellectual-spiritual [geistige] gifts of individuals, has established injustices against which there is no redress.[55]

Indeed, there is a remark Freud made repeatedly that goes even more against the grain of modern liberalism. In a letter to Lou Andreas-Salomé, July 28, 1929, he said: "Deep down I am convinced after all that my dear fellow men—with individual exceptions—are rabble." Having been Nietzsche's friend in 1882, she must have noticed the echo of Nietzsche's *Zarathustra:* Part II contains a chapter "On the Rabble," *Vom Gesindel.*

On December 2, 1927, Freud had written Arnold Zweig:

Regarding the question of anti-Semitism, I have little desire to seek explanations but feel a strong inclination to surrender to my emotions and feel confirmed in my entirely unscientific attitude that human beings are after all on the average and on the whole a miserable rabble.

Much earlier, on October 9, 1918, Freud wrote to Oskar Pfister:

I do not rack my brains very much about good and evil, but on the average I have not found much "good" in human beings. Most of them are, according to my experiences, rabble, whether they loudly admit to this, that, or no ethical doctrine. . . . If we must speak of ethics, I admit to a high ideal from which the ideals that I have

[55] *Werke,* XIV, p. 472.

become acquainted with deviate very sadly for the most part.[56]

Yet Freud was almost as far from thinking of himself as a great man as he had been in 1886 (see Section 13). Here is what he said about *Civilization and Its Discontents* in the letter of July 28, 1929, in which he told Lou Andreas-Salomé that he had just completed it—and it should be kept in mind that the book is widely considered a masterpiece:

> It deals with culture, guilt feelings, happiness, and similar elevated things and seems to me to be, surely justifiably, very superfluous, as distinguished from earlier works behind which there always was some urge. But what was I to do? One cannot smoke and play cards all day; walking, I no longer have much endurance, and most of what one can read no longer interests me. I wrote, and that way the time passed quite agreeably. In the course of this work I have newly discovered the most banal truths.
>
> The essay by Th. Mann [on the occasion of Freud's seventieth birthday] is certainly honorific. It gave me the impression as if he just had an essay on romanticism ready when the invitation came to write about me, and so he fixed up this half essay with psychoanalysis in front and behind . . .

Freud had few illusions either about himself or about others, except for a few men who were close to him for a while and of whom he was extremely fond. But in this respect, too, he had no illusions about himself and "always insisted that he was not a *Menschenkenner*," meaning that he was not a good judge of men. Hanns

---

[56] Jones, who has often been criticized very unfairly in recent years, did not try at all to tone down this side of Freud. He printed this letter (II, p. 457f.). It is of little consequence that he did not get the last half-sentence above quite right: The original cannot mean "from which most people I know sadly deviate."

Sachs, who reports this in *Freud: Master and Friend* (p. 58), and renders the German word rather infelicitously as "mind-reader," does not fail to record his initial surprise, even shock, when he first heard Freud say that.

> Once or twice the force of circumstances had compelled me to disclose to him a part of my life which hitherto I had strictly kept secret. I found regularly to my surprise, and sometimes to my consternation, that he had known my secret all the time. He had drawn his conclusions from the observation of smallest signs, in the spirit of his *Psychopathology of Everyday Life.*[57] In spite of all that he was not quite wrong in accusing himself . . . He saw every single trait and hidden factor correctly, but elevated the whole personality to a higher plane than that on which ordinary minds usually move. He saw passionate zeal, strength, endurance, and highminded motives, where only a trace of these fine things existed.

One must add: in the cases of a few men who were very close to him. Or did he give the benefit of the doubt also to others of whom we simply do not know? Edoardo Weiss, who also knew Freud personally though not as closely as Sachs did, says:

> The great honesty and integrity in Freud's character often blinded him to the unreliability and falseness of persons who approached him. A friend who admired Freud once said to me: "A horsetrader is a better judge of men than Freud."
> It is understandable that Freud could be seduced by people who seemed to be well disposed toward psychoanalysis, and at times his judgments of them were wrong.[58]

No doubt, when he was subsequently disappointed by these people, he felt confirmed in his view that by and

[57] In this spirit one might ask how "regularly" and "sometimes" can be applied to what happened only "once or twice."

[58] Freud/Weiss p. 30 (see Bibliography).

large, with individual exceptions, people were rabble. He brings to mind "Oedipus, who solved the riddle of the Sphinx by perceiving that it portrayed the human condition and that the answer was 'man'—Oedipus, who was 'the first of men' and able to deliver Thebes from the Sphinx when even Teiresias, the seer and prophet, failed, [but] comes to grief because he does not comprehend his relationship to those he loves most dearly."[59] Although Freud identified with Oedipus, the riddle-solver, he failed to notice Oedipus's tragic blindness as well as Sophocles' theme that honesty, though utterly admirable, has a curse attached to it and does not necessarily make for happiness. There was a lot about Sophocles' Oedipus that Freud did not see.[60]

Among the crucial differences between Freud and Oedipus is that Oedipus not only was, according to the poet, "the first of men," but also knew it and expected others to recognize it. Freud honestly believed that he was not a great man. He realized very clearly, as few people do, that "one must distinguish greatness of achievement from greatness of personality"[61]; and he was convinced that he had no claim to the latter.

"Not because I am modest, not at all. I have a high opinion of what I have discovered, but not of myself. Great discoverers are not necessarily *grosse Geister*,"[62] which one might translate as "great minds" or, perhaps better, "noble spirits." "Who changed the world more than Columbus?" Freud continued to Marie Bonaparte. "What was he? An adventurer. He had character, it is true, but he was not a great man."

Marie Bonaparte was not convinced and brought up the subject another time when she called him a genius.

[59] Kaufmann, *Tragedy and Philosophy* (1968), Section 24.
[60] *Ibid.*, the whole Chapter IV, "The Riddle of Oedipus."
[61] Binswanger, p. 54. Letter of April 14, 1912. Also in *Briefe*. See also Section 13 above.
[62] Jones, II, p. 415.

Freud replied: "Geniuses are unbearable people. You have only to ask my family to learn how easy I am to live with, so I certainly cannot be a genius."

The evidence is ample that Freud was utterly candid in all of this. He was quite sure, as Jones says,[63] "that he had a poor intellectual capacity. There were so many things, e.g. in mathematics and physics, he knew he should never be able to understand where so many others easily could."

To round out this picture, here is what Freud said in June 1926, to George Sylvester Viereck:

> Fame comes to us only after we are dead, and frankly what comes afterwards does not concern me. I have no aspirations to posthumous glory.

When Viereck asked him whether it meant nothing to him that his name should live, he answered:

> Nothing whatsoever, even if it should live, which is by no means certain. I am far more interested in the fate of my children.

Freud also had a deep feeling for plants and animals. "'I am far more interested in this blossom,' he said, 'than in anything that may happen to me after I am dead.'" Viereck asked him whether he was a profound pessimist. "I am not. I permit no philosophic reflection to spoil my enjoyment of the simple things of life." Asked if he believed in some sort of persistence of the human personality after death, he replied: "I give no thought to the matter. Everything that lives perishes. Why should I survive?" Would he like to come back in some form?

> Frankly, no. If one recognizes the selfish motives which underlie all human conduct, one has not the slightest desire to return. Life, moving in a circle, would still be the same.

[63] *Ibid.*

Freud in 1922.

Moreover, even if the eternal recurrence of things, to use Nietzsche's phrase, were to reinvest us with our fleshly habiliments, of what avail would this be without memory? There would be no link between past and future.

So far as I am concerned, I am perfectly content that the eternal nuisance of living will be finally done with. . . . The wish to prolong life unduly, strikes me as absurd.[64]

Summing up Freud's attitude toward himself and others, one might say that he was utterly disillusioned and considered it a point of principle to be free of illusions, but never felt that this entailed discouragement or resignation. He demanded a great deal of himself and at least sometimes measured others by the same high standards. Even when he did not actually do this, people who knew him well often assumed that he did and felt defensive. Above all, Freud's standards of honesty were very high; in fact, psychoanalysis gave honesty a new dimension. Few people before Freud had realized how difficult it was to be really honest with oneself. Freud not only realized it but refused to derive from this insight any license for self-deception. Far from feeling that his own honesty was extraordinary and made him a great man, he felt that he was a man of limited gifts and that nobody deserved any great credit for being honest: That was, after all, a matter of course.

> You really should know about me that I have always been dissatisfied with my mental endowments and can give myself a precise account of my deficiencies, but that I consider myself a very moral person who can subscribe to the good saying of Th. Vischer: "Morality is always a matter of course." I believe that in respect for right and consideration for one's fellow human beings, in displeasure at making others suffer or taking advantage of them, I can vie with the best people I have got to know. I really

[64] G. S. Viereck, *Glimpses of the Great* (1930), p. 26f.

have never done anything mean or malicious and also do not feel any temptation in that direction, and hence feel no pride at all on that score. I understand the kind of ethics we are talking about in a social sense, not sexually. Sexual morality, as defined by society, in its most extreme form in America, appears to me utterly contemptible. I stand for an incomparably freer sexual life, although I myself have made very little use of such freedom. Only to the extent that I have believed in myself in defining the limits of what is permitted in this area.

Jones deserves our gratitude for having included almost all of this letter in his biography.[65] It may seem ungracious to call attention to two errors in his translation, but they concern really crucial points, and the English translation of *The Letters of Sigmund Freud* took over both mistakes. It also seems worthwhile to show how important it is for Freud scholars to go back to the original German texts.

To begin with, Jones rendered the final sentence: "only in so far as I myself judged it to be allowable."[66] Even if one has no German, one may note that this makes very little sense after the immediately preceding sentence. But on reading the original one finds that it says the opposite.

Freud is admittedly very difficult to translate, and I am far from fancying that my translations of the many quotations in this volume capture the full flavor of Freud's German. No translation could do that, and it may be arguable whether *Rechtsinn* should be rendered as "respect for right." But the more or less official versions

[65] II, pp. 416–18. My rendering is based on *Briefe*, July 8, 1915, to James J. Putnam.

[66] *Letters:* "Only so far as I considered myself entitled to." Original: *Gerade nur soweit, dass ich mir selbst bei der Begrenzung des auf diesem Gebiet Erlaubten geglaubt habe.* In other words: I was fully autonomous in theory, but only in theory.

of the last sentence seriously misrepresent Freud's position; and so does their rendering of Vischer's saying as "What is moral is self-evident." In effect, they ascribe to Freud an epistemological position—as if Freud had meant that all of us know intuitively what is right and wrong. But what he said and meant was altogether different: *Das Moralische versteht sich immer von selbst* means "Morality is always a matter of course," or, in other words, it is not worth making a fuss about, as if one deserved points for being decent or was entitled to feel proud for never having done anything mean. His uncompromising honesty did not strike Freud as something that made him a superior person. It was only the other side of the same coin when he felt that most people were rabble.

All of this is as relevant as can be for understanding Freud as well as the break between him and Adler and later also between him and Jung. Yet Freud himself would have preferred less attention to his own person and more to his new science.

18 ▶▶▶ That Freud was a scientist before he created psychoanalysis is undeniable, but not everybody would agree that psychoanalysis is a science. Whether it is or not obviously depends on what is meant by "science."

Freud himself repeatedly called psychoanalysis an art of interpretation,[67] but occasionally he also called it a science. What he meant was first of all that it was not merely a kind of therapy but also and above all a sustained exploration of the human mind. Sometimes he also explained how psychoanalysis was scientific rather than dogmatic, and in a few particularly interesting passages he developed his conception of science. Any-

[67] *Werke*, V, p. 7; XIII, pp. 215–17, 411; XIV, pp. 66f., 69, 250.

one who speaks of "Freud's poetic science" naturally must examine what Freud had to say about these questions:

> . . . the word psychoanalysis has acquired more than one meaning. Originally the designation of a particular therapeutic procedure, it has now also become the name of a science, that of the unconscious-psychical. This science can rarely complete work on a problem all by itself, but it seems to have a calling to furnish important contributions to the most various areas of knowledge. The region of application of psychoanalysis extends just as far as that of psychology to which it adds a supplement of powerful import.[68]

Implicitly, Freud rejected Hegel's conception of science as, by definition, a complete system. It is a way of dealing with problems, but in most of the passages that call psychoanalysis a science the point is that it is not merely or mainly a form of therapy.

> The future will probably judge that the significance of psychoanalysis as science of the unconscious far excels its therapeutic significance.[69]

But psychoanalysis was not a science à la Kant or Newton. It never refused admission to hypotheses, and it did not claim to offer timeless certainties. As Freud put it in 1926:

> I present it to you dogmatically as if it were a finished doctrinal edifice. But don't suppose that it immediately came into being that way like a philosophical system. We have developed it very slowly, wrestled for a long time for every little piece, modified it continually in constant touch with observation until it finally gained a form in which it seems adequate to us for our purposes. Only a few years ago I should have had to clothe this doctrine in

[68] *Werke*, XIV, p. 96.
[69] *Werke*, XIV, p. 301; see also p. 283f.

different expressions. Of course, I cannot promise you that today's form of expression will remain definitive. You know, science is not revelation; it lacks, long beyond its origins, the characteristics of certainty [*Bestimmtheit*], unchangeableness, and infallibility which human thought craves so much.[70]

Goethe has been reproached often for having failed to appreciate the immense importance of mathematics for science; but for the discovery of the mind his disparagement of mathematical certainty and his notion that development, not timeless certainty, was the key to the understanding of at least a great many phenomena spelled liberation. It may be helpful to pose a few rhetorical antitheses: fruitfulness versus certainty, illumination versus eternal truths, a new way of looking at things versus entrenched dogmatism, a shock that restores life versus ossification. These antitheses breathe Goethe's spirit and throw light on Freud's work. For Goethe, moreover, the paradigm for the understanding of nature was his own creative development; he rejected the dualism that sees man as a subject and nature as an object and assumes that they belong to two different worlds.

Some writers who claim to have learned this lesson from existentialism and especially from Heidegger have criticized Freud for seeing his patients as mere objects and for failing to note how patient and analyst are in a way in the same boat. This critique of Freud is as implausible as the tribute to Heidegger. In fact, it was one of Freud's most important discoveries that patients whom society considered more or less mad were not essentially different from himself, and that by studying them he could learn to understand himself better, just as by analyzing himself he could comprehend them better. Far from seeing them as objects and himself as subject,

[70] *Werke*, XIV, p. 217f. Cf. Weiss, p. 85: Freud's letter of December 4, 1933.

them as nature and himself as mind, he broke through these dichotomies. The goal for the patient no less than the therapist was Goethean autonomy—not to live according to rules or maxims à la Kant, not to break through determinism by performing uncaused acts that sprang solely from respect for reason, à la Kant, but to become self-reliant and to live independent and creative lives.

> We can easily show society that what it likes to call its morality exacts more sacrifices than it is worth and that its procedure is neither based on truthfulness nor gives evidence of prudence. We do not spare our patients the experience of listening to this criticism, we accustom them to consider sexual matters no less than other questions without prejudice, and when after the completion of their cure they have become self-reliant and decide on their own for an intermediate position between libertinism and unconditional asceticism, we do not experience any such outcome as a burden for our conscience. We say to ourselves that those who have absolved successfully an education for being truthful with themselves will be protected permanently against the danger of immorality, even if their standard of morality should deviate in some ways from what is customary in society.[71]

The most beautiful formulation of Freud's Goethean and deeply anti-Kantian conception of science is to be found near the end of what he himself considered his last major work (1933):

> This is the way of science: slow, groping, laborious. That cannot be denied or changed. No wonder that the gentlemen on the other side are dissatisfied; they have been spoiled; revelation made everything easier. Progress in scientific work is very similar to that in analysis. One brings some expectations to one's work, one has to push them back. Through observation one learns something

[71] *Werke*, XI, p. 451.

new, now here, now there, and at first the pieces do not fit together. One formulates surmises and makes auxiliary constructions that one takes back when they are not confirmed; one requires a lot of patience, readiness for all possibilities, renounces early convictions lest under their compulsion one should overlook new and unexpected factors; and in the end all this exertion proves worthwhile, the scattered finds do fit together, one gains an insight into an altogether new piece of psychic processes, is done with the task and ready for the next one. Only the help that experiments provide for research has to be dispensed with in analysis.

This [religious] critique of science also contains a goodly piece of exaggeration. It is not true that it reels blindly from one attempt to the next, exchanging one error for another. As a rule it works like an artist with his clay model when he makes changes indefatigably in his rough design, adding and subtracting until he has attained a degree of similarity to the object he sees or imagines that satisfies him.[72]

An innovative scientist requires imagination, and his work is not altogether different from that of an artist or poet, as Goethe well knew. Not surprisingly, Nietzsche knew it, too; and his contrast of religion and science in *The Antichrist* is strikingly similar to Freud's. While most interpreters of Nietzsche have overlooked his disparagement of certainty, faith, and convictions, and his insistence that "great spirits are skeptics," these themes have been documented and discussed in Section 23 of the second volume in this trilogy. There I have also argued that "the essence of critical thinking is the consideration of objections and alternatives, while dogmatism ignores both."

Jung liked to accuse Freud of dogmatism, though it meets the eye of any open-minded reader that what

[72] *Werke*, XV, p. 188f.

makes Freud's books so exciting is precisely that he constantly considers objections and alternatives. In this respect Freud differs remarkably from some of his disciples and ex-disciples, notably including Jung. Nor did Jung make any such effort as Freud did to impress this critical ethos on his readers and his leading disciples.[73] Jung and the Jungians were closer to religion in this respect also. They impart all sorts of secret lore to their readers without projecting the laborious struggle to get some things straight, as Freud often did.

What is and what is not dogmatic is frequently misunderstood. What is truly dogmatic is the failure to consider objections and alternatives, as if one's own point of view were the only one that needed to be taken seriously. Yet those who simply tell their own story, ignoring all that speaks against it as well as rival accounts, make things easy for their readers by making no demands on them; and the readers tend to be grateful for being entertained and told how things are, without being called upon to exert themselves and to make a strenuous decision. Authors of that kind are apt to seem self-effacing. Since their own views are the only ones they mention, there is no need to speak of themselves or of their rivals.

On the other hand, the writer who takes account of objections to his story and indicates how he proposes to meet them, and who discusses rival views and shows why he cannot accept them and why, in effect, his own story is the best he has been able to come up with, is often experienced as egoistic, threatening—and dogmatic. The problem created by the English translations of Freud furnishes a good example.

Writing on Freud in English, one can, first of all, rely on the official English versions without so much as

[73] Regarding Freud, see, e.g., Sachs (1944), pp. 49 and 63; regarding Jung, Section 61 below.

checking the originals. This is what most scholars have done for some time now, and they have met with no criticism although on reflection it seems obvious that this procedure is not particularly critical or scientific. Probably one could also get away with taking a second path: offering one's own translations without ever referring to rival versions. After all, most readers could not care less, and scholars generally hesitate to criticize other scholars for mistranslations, although they occur constantly in scholarly works and are often of some importance. There is a third alternative. One can offer one's own translations and say something about the limitations of the official versions. But that makes the reader feel insecure and threatened; foundations that had seemed firm begin to totter; and one is apt to fight back by considering the writer who has chosen this way egoistic and dogmatic. To live and let live without being critical is so much more comfortable. But it may be objected that it *is* conceited to suppose that one's own translation is better than the official one. It is indeed, unless one has proof that there really are a great many cases in which the official translations are very free or misleading or downright wrong. And to claim that one has proof but not to produce it brings to mind Senator Joe McCarthy's saying that he held in his hand a list of Communists in the U.S. Department of State: the number of people he claimed to be on that list changed, and eventually it became clear that he had no list at all. But isn't criticism of other translators and scholars motivated by the need to put down the work of others? Isn't it nasty?

Socrates, according to Plato's *Apology*, loved to be nasty in this way, enjoyed putting down his fellow Athenians, especially those who were regarded as authorities and who thought well of themselves; and when he was brought to court and charged with impiety and corrupting youths, he delivered an "apology" in which biting sarcasm was fused with incomparable dignity. He was sentenced to death and died well, and the critical ethos that does not shrink from nastiness was a central part of his legacy.

Ludwig Wittgenstein said in a remarkable letter:

> You see, I know that it's difficult to think *well* about "certainty," "probability," "perception," etc. But it is, if possible, still more difficult to think, or *try* to think, really honestly about your life & other people's lives. And the trouble is that thinking about these things is *not thrilling*, but often downright nasty. And when it's nasty, then it's most important.[74]

Actually this letter to one of his students and friends is rather singular; as a philosopher Wittgenstein made little effort to teach people how to think honestly about their lives.

Of Freud, on the other hand, one might say that precisely this was his central concern, and as a writer he proved that thinking about these things *can* be thrilling. Of course, his discoveries struck many of his contemporaries as nasty, but it is extraordinary how Freud managed not to be nasty, as Socrates had been, about individuals who were widely regarded as authorities. In his books he refrained almost completely from polemics and almost never gave vent to anger or resentment. In his letters and in conversation he occasionally expressed his personal feelings with vigor and humor, but when he wrote for publication he always addressed the reader as a friend who might be willing to embark with him on a fascinating voyage. He liked to be a considerate travel companion who made it a point to discern any hint of impatience or incredulity, and he kept asking himself what objections he might have to meet.

In *The Interpretation of Dreams* he surveys alternative approaches to dreams in the first chapter (65 pages in

---

[74] Norman Malcolm (1958), p. 39.

the first edition, 99 in the final version in the German collected works), and then explains, giving some attention to alternatives and objections, why he will use his own dreams as examples. In the course of his interpretation of his first dream, which comprises the whole second chapter, he does not spare himself but repeatedly lays his character and conduct open to objections, the point being patently not to build up himself and to show how great he is but rather to demonstrate how dreams can be interpreted. It is precisely the opposite of all dogmatism and self-righteousness that hooks the reader, namely the author's extraordinary honesty. In the final paragraph of Chapter II Freud says:

> I myself know the places from which one might begin to pursue further thought connections; but considerations that come into play with any dream of one's own deter me from the work of interpretation. Whoever is quick to reproach such reserve should really try to be more honest than I.

Here, too, Freud is mindful of a possible objection, and the way he meets it is, in effect, to repeat his invitation to embark on a voyage of discovery. No scientist has ever been more courteous in his writings than Freud, who is always mindful of the reader.

Hanns Sachs, one of Freud's most devoted disciples, a member of his innermost circle who eventually taught at Harvard Medical School, relates in *Freud: Master and Friend:*

> Freud communicated to us his new ideas and theories; of these, some have been incorporated in his books, many others were abandoned when they did not stand up well enough under further scrutiny. Behind every discovery he showed us a long row of new question marks. (p. 62f.)

Obviously, Freud did not include in his books all the objections and alternatives that had occurred to him; he made a selection, omitting some of his own false starts to avoid needless confusion. But Sachs exaggerates, of course, when he says:

> before he undertook the next step forward he surveyed all possible objections [!], formulated these clearly and answered them fully, so that when he moved on in an unexpected direction it seemed the most natural thing to do. (p. 49)

While it is true that Freud's exposition is so masterly that even very bold steps forward seem quite natural, nobody can survey all possible objections, and Freud neither dealt at length with the views of Adler and Jung and the later writings of Otto Rank, nor did he anticipate all of the objections raised against psychoanalysis in recent years. His reactions to the men mentioned will be considered in subsequent chapters, but one objection that is heard frequently needs to be noted now.

19 ▶▶▶ Karl Popper, the most outstanding and influential philospher of science of his time, has charged repeatedly that

> Marx's theory of history, Freud's psycho-analysis, and Alfred Adler's so-called 'individual psychology . . . though posing as sciences, had in fact more in common with primitive myths than with science; that they resembled astrology rather than astronomy.

While ignoring Jung, Popper has spoken of Freud and Adler as if they were equals and assured us:

> I personally do not doubt that much of what they say is of considerable importance, and may well play its part one day in a psychological science which is testable. But . . . those "clinical observations" which analysts naively believe confirm their theory cannot do this any more than

the daily confirmations which astrologers find in their practice.[75]

One might suppose that a distinguished philosopher of science who claims that what Freud had to offer was as far from science as that would make out his case very conscientiously, giving us an example of rational procedure. But this is not what Popper has done. He has said:

> every conceivable case could be interpreted in the light of Adler's theory, or equally of Freud's. I may illustrate this by two very different examples of human behaviour: that of a man who pushes a child into the water with the intent of drowning it; and that of a man who sacrifices his life in an attempt to save the child. Each of these two cases can be explained with equal ease in Freudian and in Adlerian terms. According to Freud the first man suffered from repression (say, of some component of his Oedipus complex), while the second man had achieved sublimation. (p. 35)

Of course, this is not how Freud actually explained behavior of interpreted dreams. What he did in his books could not be done with such ease. Specifically, he did not simply offer *ad hoc* postulates of one or another repression in order to "explain" what somebody had done, dispensing with any demand for evidence. This is no mere caricature of Freud; the attack is "uninformed as well as unfair."[76]

[75] 1965, pp. 34, 37f. These charges are repeated more than once in Sir Karl's "Autobiography" and "Replies to My Critics" (in P. A. Schilpp, 1974).

[76] Adolf Grünbaum, who has criticized Popper's treatment of Freud at length in several articles (including this passage, in 1979), used these words—and worse—in reference to Popper's long footnote on p. 38 (1980, IV.2). Since Grünbaum has dealt repeatedly with Popper's rather casual charges and with the question "How Scientific is Psychoanalysis?" (1977), giving ample references to the vast literature on this subject, it would serve little purpose for me to go over the same ground at length, the less so because he is about to publish a big book on these questions.

Almost every book of Freud's will show this, but it seems convenient to refer to an essay published in 1937 in which Freud dealt at length with an accusation that he considered "as insulting as it is unjust":

> He said, when we present our interpretations to a patient we treat him according to the notorious principle: Heads I win, tails you lose. That is, if he agrees with us, we are right; but if he contradicts us, that is merely a sign of his resistance and therefore also proves us right.

The essay is entitled "Construction in Analysis"[77] but could also have had the Popperian title "Conjectures and Refutations."

Freud compares the analyst's "work of construction or, if one should prefer that term, of reconstruction" to the work of an archaeologist. Here it will suffice to quote a few of the most important points from his essay:

> It does no harm if we make a mistake for once and present to the patient an incorrect construction as the probable historical truth. It means a loss of time, of course; and anyone who always relates to the patient nothing but erroneous combinations will not make a good impression and will not get far in his treatment; but a single error of that kind is harmless. What happens in such cases is rather that the patient remains, as it were, untouched and reacts with neither Yes nor No.

Freud deals specifically with the charge that the patient's consent to the analyst's interpretations may be vitiated by suggestion.

> The danger of leading the patient astray by means of suggestion, by talking him into things that one believes oneself but which he ought not to accept, has certainly

---

[77] *Werke*, XVI, pp. 43–56. I quote from pp. 43, 45 48f., and 52.

been exaggerated immeasurably. An analyst would have to have behaved very improperly if such a misfortune could occur to him; above all he would have to reproach himself for not allowing the patient to speak. I can claim without vainglory that such an abuse of "suggestion" has never occurred in my practice.

In the summary that concludes the second section of the essay Freud points out that the responses of the patient to the analyst's constructions often furnish valuable clues and rarely consist of a simple Yes or No. They are usually ambiguous and do not permit any final decision about the truth of the matter.

> We do not pass off a single construction as anything more than a conjecture that awaits testing, confirmation, or rejection. We claim no authority for it, do not demand from the patient any immediate agreement, and do not debate with him if initially he contradicts it. In short, we follow the example of a well-known character in [a play by] *Nestroy,* the servant who has but one answer for all questions and objections: *In the course of events everything will become clear.*

Freud depends on a wealth of intuitions of highly educated guesses, of which many are rejected before they ever pass his lips, while a few are tried out on the patient. There is no quick way to establish that a single proposition corresponds to reality; what is needed is a detailed reconstruction that takes into account all the clues we have without disregarding any inconvenient bits and pieces. The patient's acceptance of a conjecture is no substitute for such a reconstruction, nor is his improvement. But in Freud's experience a successful reconstruction was accompanied by drastic improvement.

All of this leaves open the question whether every case could be brought to a successful conclusion both by a Freudian and an Adlerian analyst. This is surely not so; many cases seem to resist *both* even as far as cures are concerned. But that occasional cases might allow for more than one coherent and detailed reconstruction, one Freudian and one Adlerian, cannot be ruled out in principle as simply impossible. In specific cases it certainly seemed to Freud that Adler was leaving out a great many data that did not fit his theories; but cases in which neither of two rival theories or explanations can be ruled out are found in other fields, such as history and even physics and astronomy, and in his own field Freud could have made room for such cases by invoking a concept that we shall examine soon: overinterpretation.

Returning to the passage quoted from Popper's "Science: Conjectures and Refutations," we can skip Adler for the present, but not the point at which Popper is trying to get.

> I could not think of any human behavior which could not be interpreted in terms of either theory. It was precisely this fact—that they always fitted, that they were always confirmed—which in the eyes of their admirers constituted the strongest argument in favour of these theories. It began to dawn on me that this apparent strength was in fact their greatest weakness.

That was in 1919 when Popper was seventeen. And if he had not returned to the charge in 1953 and then printed his speech and persuaded many others that Freud was indeed totally unscientific, one might let it go at that. But these three sentences are surely very strange. If saying that a "man had achieved sublimation" really counted as an explanation of his sacrificing his life to save a child, then it would seem that anything goes and that, of course, one cannot think of any human behavior that cannot be explained in some such equally implausible and inadequate way. But where is the theory? What is it that always fits and is always confirmed? What is "this apparent strength"? Surely, one feels like protesting, the objection to that sort of explanation is not that it allows us to explain *all* of human behavior but rather that the explanation is *ad hoc*, arbitrary, unsupported by independent evidence, and utterly implausible and lacking in explanatory power.

When Popper goes on to say, "With Einstein's theory the situation was strikingly different," it turns out that "the impressive thing about this case is the *risk* involved in a prediction . . ." In other words, Popper supposes, as do many others under his influence, that psychoanalysis does not and cannot make risky predictions. "A theory which is not refutable by any conceivable event is nonscientific. Irrefutability is not a virtue of a theory (as people often think) but a vice."

Now we need to sort out several distinct points. First, there is the question: "Is Freudian Psychoanalytic Theory Pseudo-Scientific by Karl Popper's Criterion of Demarcation?" In a paper with that title (1979) Adolf Grünbaum has argued that it is not. Instead of trying to evaluate his arguments, I should like to proceed in my own way and stress a few points that strike me as especially interesting and important. I shall confine myself to Freud and ignore the Freudians.

Freud repeatedly modified his theories in the light of negative evidence and, what is more, told his readers what considerations had led him to do this. Hegel, Heidegger, Buber, and Sartre published major books that were conceived as the first volumes of larger works, then found themselves unable to build on the foundations they had laid, but never gave the public or themselves any account of what had gone wrong. Heidegger's style in *Being and Time* is very different from that of Buber's *I and Thou*, but these books share a systematic failure to consider objections and alternatives. In a crucial sense these books are uncritical and unscientific while Freud's are critical and scientific.

Instead of simply ignoring objections, one could also patch up old theories indefinitely, as Goethe pointed out in 1810, until they become ossified. One could keep adding epicycles to the ancient Ptolemaic theory. This procedure might be called scholastic to distinguish it from the oracular air of those who prefer to ignore objections. Freud eschewed both of these alternatives.

At the end of Section 10 we saw how he gave up his belief that many of his female patients had been seduced in childhood by their fathers. He did not hide behind the fact that this belief could not be falsified conclusively. That the fathers would have denied these accusations, which could have brought them to the penitentiary, would not have sufficed to refute the belief. But Freud weighed the improbability of this belief against an alternative explanation and concluded that it was much more probable that "memories" of this sort were prompted by wishful thinking; and this line of thought lent support to the theory of the Oedipus complex.

Beyond the Pleasure Principle (1920) involved a public change of mind of major proportions. After the First World War many psychotherapists encountered cases that did not seem explicable in terms of psychoanalytical theory as it had been developed up to that point. Freud discussed the evidence and showed why he had decided to postulate a death instinct as well as life instincts and precisely what modifications in his theories this involved.

Six years later, when he was seventy, he revised his theory of anxiety. At that time Ludwig Binswanger, one of the pioneers of existential psychotherapy, wrote him:

> That in fundamental questions I reach views that deviate from those of the psychoanalytical "school" you will not hold against me after you have shown once again in your book on anxiety how inexorably you "expose" the prog-

eny of your own mind when they do not get along any
more with your advanced insights.[78]

Binswanger was right that Freud did not hold it against
him. The two men were always honest and forthright
with each other and remained loyal friends whose deep
affection was not clouded by their disagreements. Nor,
incidentally, did Freud's extensive disagreements with
Oskar Pfister, who was a Swiss pastor and psychotherapist, interfere with their cordial feelings for each other.
Their correspondence, from 1909 until 1939, was published in 1963 and further illustrates Freud's scientific
attitude.

Freud, like Nietzsche, had "the courage for an attack
on [his] own convictions."[79] Popper, who has preached
such courage, perhaps without being aware of
Nietzsche's formulation or example, seems to have
lacked it in the case before us. Proud of what he claimed
to have discovered at the age of seventeen, he did not put
his discovery to the test by risking a confrontation with
Freud's works but simply repeated and reprinted his
early notions about psychoanalysis.[80] The gap between
preachment and example, theory and practice, is so
striking in Popper's case that it may help to account for
the very considerable animus that so many philosophers,
including philosophers of science, feel against him.

[78] Binswanger (1956), p. 92.

[79] Nietzsche, *Werke*, XVI, p. 318.

[80] His reaction to severe criticisms of the Hegel chapter in *The Open
Society and Its Enemies* (revised ed., 1950) in the "Addendum" to a
later edition (e.g., 1963, pp. 393–95) is even more embarrassing.
Popper retained and reprinted the chapter while admitting that it
contained errors that he did not specify; he misled his readers about
the nature of these errors by mentioning only one utterly trivial one,
giving the impression of great scrupulousness by admitting to that
one; and then he said that *one* critic "has told me that there are, in his
opinion, a number of more serious—if less clear-cut—historical errors
. . ."

We still have to confront Popper's complaint that psychoanalysis does not make risky predictions. This point calls for several comments. First, there are many occasions on which Freud or any one of us could make a risky prediction based on psychoanalysis—and it is part of the excitement of reading Freud that his readers find themselves making such predictions. We shall return to this point when discussing *The Psychopathology of Everyday Life*. Still, it must be admitted that these predictions are rather different from astronomical predictions: They are not mathematical, not exact. But is it really regrettable and surprising that Freud could not predict human behavior the way astronomers chart the orbits of celestial bodies? Is it not a fact that human beings are importantly different from stars and comets—and that our knowledge of human beings is incomparably richer? Moreover, biologists who study elephants or lions also do not make exact predictions about the behavior of individual animals.

Since Freud's death, growing numbers of psychologists have tried to devise tests with control groups to see whether predictions entailed by Freud's theory of repression, to give a single example, were borne out by the facts. Quite a number of research scientists reported "findings supporting the concept of repression," but critics have claimed again and again that other explanations of the test results could not be ruled out or that the

He also had recourse to an immunization strategy that is wildly implausible for a fifty-page chapter which is supported by another nineteen large pages of closely printed notes that give the appearance of scholarship: "I wrote about Hegel in a manner which assumed that few would take him seriously. And although this manner was lost on my Hegelian critics"—actually the best-known critique of this chapter was not written by a Hegelian—some others got "the joke."

On page 253 of the 1950 edition Popper had said that "intellectual honesty is fundamental for everything we cherish." Freud would have agreed, and never strayed as far from it as Popper did both in the Hegel chapter and in this "Addendum."

tests were deficient in some other way.[81] Many of these tests are surprisingly remote from what Freud himself actually said. Like much of the work done by professors and their graduate students in the social sciences, including countless projects funded by the government and various foundations, a lot of the tests are busy-work that may be more "scientific" than Freud's books but adds nothing much to human knowledge or self-understanding.

20 ▶▶▶ In the social sciences and humanities "scientific" procedures that introduce quantification or elaborate tests are not directly proportionate to advances in human knowledge or self-understanding. On the contrary, they are often, if not usually, a waste of time, money, and energy, prompted by a lack of imagination and insight. The notion that in these areas we need to approximate astronomy if we wish to escape the stigma of being compared with astrologers is extremely crude and Manichaean.

There are two camps, Popper implies, the one occupied by astrology and primitive myths, the other by astronomy and Albert Einstein, and Freud's psychoanalysis is closer to the former. In the absence of any discussion of astrology and primitive myth, this comes close to name-calling.

In fact, astrology is not at all compatible with, or confirmed by, absolutely any set of facts. Large parts of astrology are clearly refutable in principle, and in an article in *Encounter* (December 1979) H. J. Eysenck has tried to show at length how astrology passes "the Popperian test. It makes many quite firm predictions, and these can certainly be tested."

Ironically, Eysenck is well known for his view that

[81] D. S. Holmes, "Investigations of Repression: Differential Recall of Material Experimentally or Naturally Associated with Ego Threat," *Psychological Bulletin* (1974), pp. 632–53.

psychoanalysis "can in fact be made to generate predictions, and these predictions have in general been disconfirmed." He has been in the forefront of those who have tried to derive testable predictions from psychoanalysis, and he complains that "what usually happens is that followers of a prophet come up with some rather lame excuse for the failure, and thus try to argue it away." Astrology, on the other hand, does not have to "be *made* to generate predictions"; it deals in predictions. Eysenck was surprised to find that "Vernon Clark, an American psychologist working in the early 1950s," had made "three experiments, each of them apparently fool-proof . . . and each giving positive results affirming the validity of the astrological method." But "there have been no replications, so that we still do not know whether the results are trustworthy." Eysenck then reports on the work done by Michel and Françoise Gauquelin, "French psychologists who have been working in this field for over 20 years" with large samples. Their work strongly suggests that personality is influenced by the position of the planets at birth, rather along the lines long claimed by astrologers. The Gauquelins, however, point out that orthodox astrologers would not have predicted precisely the results they got, and they see their own work as "the beginnings of a new science of cosmobiology, which they define as the relationship between planetary positions and psychological and physical events on the earth."

In the present context the details do not matter much. Long before Eysenck's article appeared, Thomas Kuhn had pointed out that although "Astrology is Sir Karl's most frequently cited example of a 'pseudo-science'"—in a note he adds that the index of *Conjectures and Refutations* alone "has eight entries under the heading 'astrology as a typical pseudo-science'"—it really "cannot be barred from the sciences because of the form in which its predictions were cast. Nor can it be barred because of the way its practitioners explained failure."[82]

Kuhn does not consider astrology a science but rejects Popper's criteria, and I have no wish to enter into controversies about astrology at this point. I do mean to impugn the neat Manichaean scheme in which Freud's psychoanalysis is said to resemble "astrology rather than astronomy." It seems obvious to me—and I should think that any careful reader of Freud's books would agree— that what he offers us does not greatly resemble either astronomy or astrology, any more than it resembles either black magic or white magic, or either food or drink.

Psychoanalysis is not a theory that formulates general laws with the help of mathematics and then makes precise predictions. It is more like history, archaeology, and evolutionary biology: an attempt to reconstruct the past and tell the most likely story about what happened. To be sure, Freud also offered causal explanations and tried to discover typical sequences or patterns, but when he did all this he was much more modest and tentative than is widely supposed. Nor can we afford to overlook his crucial concept of overinterpretation.

He introduced this concept in what may well be the most exciting footnote in world literature. It is found in the first edition of his dream book but was eventually moved into the text.[83] After discussing the story of Oedipus, Freud showed in the footnote how the same motifs appear also in *Hamlet,* but how Shakespeare used them quite differently:

> Hamlet can do anything but carry out his revenge against the man who has done away with his father and taken his place with his mother, the man who shows him the

[82] In *The Philosophy of Karl Popper,* ed. P. A. Schilpp, Vol. II (1974), p. 803.

[83] 1900, p. 183f.; *Werke,* II/III, p. 271–73. The discussion that follows re the text above is preliminary and will be completed in Section 51.

das Ergänzungsstück zum Traum vom Tod des Vaters. Die Oedipus-fabel ist die Reaction der Phantasie auf diese beiden typischen Träume, und wie die Träume vom Erwachsenen mit Ablehnungs-gefühlen erlebt werden, so muss die Sage Schreck und Selbst-bestrafung in ihren Inhalt mit aufnehmen. Ihre weitere Gestaltung rührt wiederum von einer missverständlichen secundären Bearbeitung des Stoffes her, welche ihn einer theologisirenden Absicht dienstbar zu machen sucht. (Vergleiche den Traumstoff von der Exhibition Seite 168.) Der Versuch die göttliche Allmacht mit der menschlichen Verantwort-lichkeit zu vereinigen, muss natürlich an diesem Material wie an jedem anderen misslingen.*)

---

*) Auf demselben Boden wie „König Oedipus" wurzelt eine andere der grossen tragischen Dichterschöpfungen, der Hamlet Shakespeare's. Aber in der ver-änderten Behandlung des nämlichen Stoffes offenbart sich der ganze Unterschied im Seelenleben der beiden weit auseinander liegenden Culturperioden, das saeculare Fortschreiten der Verdrängung im Gemüthsleben der Menschheit. Im Oedipus wird die zu Grunde liegende Wunschphantasie des Kindes wie im Traum an's Licht gezogen und realisirt; im Hamlet bleibt sie verdrängt, und wir erfahren von ihrer Existenz — dem Sachverhalt bei einer Neurose ähnlich — nur durch die von ihr ausgehenden Hemmungswirkungen. Mit der überwältigenden Wirkung des moderneren Dramas hat es sich eigenthümlicher Weise als vereinbar gezeigt, dass man über den Charakter des Helden in voller Unklarheit verbleiben könne. Das Stück ist auf die Zögerung Hamlet's gebaut, die ihm zugetheilte Aufgabe der Rache zu erfüllen; welches die Gründe oder Motive dieser Zögerung sind, gesteht der Text nicht ein; die vielfältigsten Deutungsversuche haben es nicht anzugeben vermocht. Nach der heute noch herrschenden, durch Goethe begründeten Auffassung stellt Hamlet den Typus des Menschen dar, dessen Thatkraft durch die überwuchernde Ent-wickelung der Gedankenthätigkeit gelähmt wird („Von des Gedankens Blässe angekränkelt"). Nach Anderen hat der Dichter einen krankhaften, unentschlossenen, in das Bereich der Neurasthenie fallenden Charakter zu schildern versucht. Allein die Fabel des Stückes lehrt, dass Hamlet uns keineswegs als eine Person erscheinen soll, die des Handelns überhaupt unfähig ist. Wir sehen ihn zweimal handelnd auf-treten, das eine Mal in rasch auffahrender Leidenschaft, wie er den Lauscher hinter der Tapete niederstösst, ein anderes Mal planmässig, ja selbst arglistig, indem er mit der vollen Unbedenklichkeit des Renaissance-Prinzen die zwei Höflinge in den ihm selbst zugedachten Tod schickt. Was hemmt ihn also bei der Erfüllung der Aufgabe, die der Geist seines Vaters ihm gestellt hat? Hier bietet sich wieder die Auskunft, dass es die besondere Natur dieser Aufgabe ist. Hamlet kann alles, nur nicht die Rache an dem Mann vollziehen, der seinen Vater beseitigt und bei seiner Mutter dessen Stelle eingenommen hat, an dem Mann, der ihm die Realisirung seiner ver-drängten Kinderwünsche zeigt. Der Abscheu, der ihn zur Rache drängen sollte, ersetzt sich so bei ihm durch Selbstvorwürfe, durch Gewissensscrupel, die ihm vor-halten, dass er, wörtlich verstanden, selbst nicht besser sei als der von ihm zu strafende Sünder. Ich habe dabei in's Bewusste übersetzt, was in der Seele des Helden unbewusst bleiben muss; wenn Jemand Hamlet einen Hysteriker nennen will, kann ich es nur als Folgerung aus meiner Deutung anerkennen. Die Sexualabneigung stimmt sehr wohl dazu, die Hamlet dann im Gespräch mit Ophelia äussert, die nämliche Sexualabneigung, die von der Seele des Dichters in den nächsten Jahren immer mehr Besitz nehmen sollte, bis zu ihren Gipfeläusserungen im Timon von Athen. Es kann natürlich nur das eigene Seelenleben des Dichters gewesen sein, das uns im Hamlet entgegentritt; ich entnehme dem Werk von Georg Brandes über Shakespeare (1896) die Notiz, dass das Drama unmittelbar nach dem Tod von Shakespeare's Vater (1601). also in der frischen Trauer um ihn, in der Wiederbelebung, dürfen wir annehmen, der auf den Vater bezüglichen Kindheitsempfindungen gedichtet

The footnote on *Hamlet* and overinterpretation, in *The Interpretation of Dreams*, 1900.

realization of his repressed childhood wishes. The revulsion that ought to propel him toward revenge is thus replaced by self-reproaches . . . .

But Freud was far from being a reductionist. He claimed neither that his interpretation diminished Shakespeare in any way nor that he had explained Hamlet's behavior or the tragedy. The footnote ends:

> Just as, incidentally, every neurotic symptom and even a dream is capable of overinterpretation and actually demands nothing less for its full understanding, every genuine poetic creation will also have issued from more than one motive and one stimulus in the poet's soul and will permit more than one interpretation. What I have attempted here is merely an interpretation of the deepest layer of impulses in the creative poet's soul.

In the chapter "The Riddle of Oedipus" in my *Tragedy and Philosophy* I have taken issue with Freud's analysis of Sophocles' play and his attempts to explain why the play moves us so much, and I have offered a different reading. It would be futile to argue at length about whether the layer Freud interpreted is indeed the deepest layer in Shakespeare's soul, but it seems clear enough that Freud has deepened our understanding of both tragedies without saying, or claiming to say, the last word about them. The final two sentences of the footnote, which introduce the concept of overinterpretation, should be borne in mind by Freud's interpreters and critics. They point to a profound difference not only between psychoanalysis and astronomy but between the study of humanity and the study of celestial bodies.

About celestial bodies and the phenomena studied in physics and chemistry we know next to nothing until science comes along and offers us some knowledge. In these areas scientists have scored momentous advances over next to nothing.[84] Their achievements rise from a level of almost zero and some of them look as stupendous as Mount Rainier or Fujiyama when one views them from sea level. When the clouds lift and we suddenly behold them in their solitary splendor, we are overawed by their beauty, elegance, simplicity, and majesty.

From Gulmarg in Kashmir you can see Nanga Parbat, a mountain more than twice as high as Fujiyama. Mount Fuji rises to a height of just under 3,800 meters, while Nanga Parbat reaches 8,126 meters. And yet the sight of the Himalayan peak from Gulmarg is apt to be disappointing because it seems to be part of a long chain of mountains and looks only a little higher than the others. One may actually be in doubt for a moment which point in this squiggle is the highest, though in the end there is no doubt about it. Still, one could never tell from such a distance that Nanga Parbat is one of the very highest mountains in the world, or that its steep south wall rises 4,500 meters above the valley immediately below, while the north side drops 7,000 meters to the Indus River. From a great distance Freud's achievement may not seem all that much greater than that of any number of others. One must get closer and study him to appreciate his stature. But there is also another point that these images may help to get across.

The interpretation of *Hamlet* furnishes a splendid paradigm. Everybody who has read or seen the play, not to speak of those who have done neither, knows a good deal about it. People do not merely think they know a lot about it, but much of their information is correct, and large numbers of people have long had an understanding of the play that is nowhere near the zero base. To add to the understanding that intelligent and sensitive people

[84] Frithjof Bergmann has developed this idea very fruitfully in an unpublished paper, "Epistemology and Social Science." Much of what he says, including his critique of the social sciences, supplements the above comments.

have long had of this play is difficult. Writing about Sophocles or about Freud himself, one faces the same predicament. In the discovery of the mind there is no Fujiyama. We never start from sea level or zero. But there may be a Nanga Parbat.

If it should be the case that nobody else has added as much to our understanding of human behavior as Freud has, it seems odd to charge that because he did not offer predictions comparable to Einstein's that made possible a crucial experiment, he should be condemned as more like an astrologer than an astronomer. The intended slur of the comparison with astrology is less important than the misleading implication that psychology ought to emulate astronomy if it wants to come of age. This is the wrong prescription for the discovery of the mind.

Thousands of psychologists have been following this prescription for several decades now, and there is neither a Fujiyama nor a Nanga Parbat among them. Not only are most of their squiggles near the zero base, but they add up to noise that drowns out music and insight and impedes the discovery of the mind. What is needed for that discovery is sensitivity and imagination as well as intelligence, or, to be succinct, a poetic science.

21 ▶▶▶ Freud once said:

Mediocre spirits demand of science a kind of certainty which it cannot give, a sort of religious satisfaction. Only the real, rare, true scientific minds can endure doubt, which is attached to all our knowledge. I always envy the physicists and mathematicians who can stand on firm ground. I hover, so to speak, in the air. Mental events seem to be immeasurable and probably always will be so.[85]

---

[85] Jones, II, p. 419.

By now we are familiar with this theme, which is as central in Freud as it was in Nietzsche. What may seem to be new, however, is the suggestion that the demand for measurement in psychology may be prompted by the weakness that craves certainty and cannot endure doubt. But this motif, too, had been sounded by Nietzsche in *The Gay Science*, in Section 347, which is entitled "Believers and their need to believe":

> How much one needs a *faith* [86] in order to flourish, how much that is "firm" . . . that is a measure of the degree of one's strength (or, to put the point more clearly, of one's weakness). . . .
>
> Metaphysics is still needed by some; but so is that impetuous *demand for certainty* that today discharges itself among large numbers of people in a scientific-positivistic form. . . .

At the end of this section, which is, like many of Nietzsche's so-called aphorisms, more than two pages long and closely related to what is said before and after, Nietzsche envisages a state of autonomy in which the mind or spirit

> would take leave of all faith and every wish for certainty, being practiced in maintaining itself on insubstantial ropes and possibilities and dancing even near abysses.

Freud speaks very similarly of hovering in the air.

Once again we see Nietzsche's "gay science" as the major link between Goethe's non-Newtonian, nonmathematical science and Freud's psychoanalysis. Hanns Sachs reports: "One of Freud's favorite sayings was: 'Man muss ein Stück Unsicherheit ertragen können.' "[87] That means: "One must be able to endure some uncertainty." In Freud's works we find the remark: "*Sie haben*

[86] In German there is only one word for faith and belief: *Glaube*. And *glauben* means "to believe."
[87] 1944, p. 147.

gelernt, ein Stück Wahrheit zu ertragen."[88] "They have learned to endure some of the truth." Freud said that in 1911. And Nietzsche had said in *Ecce Homo,* which Freud had read as soon as it had appeared, in 1908:[89]

> How much truth does a spirit *endure, how much truth does it dare?* More and more that became for me the real measure of value.[90]

And in *The Antichrist* (Section 54): "Great spirits are skeptics."

Some of these ideas have become more or less fashionable, however untimely they were in Nietzsche's day. Fallibilism, the view that all empirical knowledge is fallible, is widely held, but the idea that the demand for mathematical exactness is born of weakness that cannot endure doubt is likely to sound as strange to most social scientists today as ever. Yet coming from Freud (or Nietzsche, for that matter) it did not signify a relaxation of standards and a lack of rigor. The crux is that those who employ mathematics, compile statistics, or use computers have no monopoly on rigor. Freud had extraordinarily high standards of honesty, and I know of no man or woman who was more honest than Freud. Compared to him, most of his critics seem somewhat lax.

While psychoanalysis is not the kind of science astronomy is, it is science as opposed to religion and dogmatism, and Freud's own way of thinking was exceptionally scrupulous, tentative, and mindful of possible

---

[88] *Werke,* X, p. 87.

[89] The book was discussed by the Vienna Psychoanalytical Society on October 28, 1908, and Freud participated in the discussion.

[90] Preface, Section 3. See also *Beyond,* Section 39: "The strength of a spirit should be measured according to how much of the 'truth' one could still barely endure—or to put it more clearly, to what degree one would *require* it to be thinned down, shrouded, sweetened, blunted, falsified."

objections and alternatives. It was that way in his first great psychoanalytical book, *The Interpretation of Dreams*, which he completed in 1899, and it was still that way forty years later when, in his eighties, dying of cancer, he wrote but did not live to finish his startlingly brilliant, vigorous, and terse *Outline of Psychoanalysis*. Even in that last work one finds no rigidity, no ossification or calcification, but the stubborn critical bent, the clarity, and the scrupulous skepticism that distinguished all the works of his maturity.

22 ▶▶▶ Now it may be asked what is poetic about Freud's science. What I mean is not mainly that Freud had, almost as much as Nietzsche, a great artistic gift and might have become "a major writer if he had not opted (under the impression of the . . . hymn 'Nature') for the study of medicine and the career of a doctor."[91] But it has been one of the themes of this trilogy that style is the mirror of the mind and that it is important to see how a major thinker's work is of one piece.

Hermann Hesse understated the case when he said in 1925 that Freud's "work carries conviction outside the guild, too, through its extraordinary human as well as literary qualities."[92] It carried conviction outside the guild—and outside Vienna—long before it was acclaimed closer to home. And many of the foremost writers of his time were among those who recognized Freud's genius while he was still living. Why?

Freud's coinages are not only singularly literate and elegant but are also literary. The Oedipus complex is merely the most famous example of a conception derived from literature that is overcharged with associations and

[91] Schönau, p. 12.
[92] *Gesammelte Werke*, XII (1970), p. 365.

suggestions. Although Freud tried to be scientific and made clear what precisely his terms meant, his terms immediately came to life and quickly entered the German language, and those which were not mutilated in translation entered other languages as well and became part of the human imagination. Unlike some of Nietzsche's dazzling coinages, Freud's do not conjure up meanings that are diametrically opposed to the author's avowed intentions, but, like Nietzsche's, they have the power of poetry to set the mind in motion and to stimulate interesting thoughts and new perspectives.

Freud accepted Darwin's blow to human self-esteem no less than Copernicus's and, for good measure, realized that psychoanalysis was a third such blow.[93] His attitude was scientific and he tried to explain dreams and mental illnesses rationally. Nevertheless he did not contribute to what Max Weber called *die Entzauberung der Welt. Zauber* means magic or charm. Instead of helping to deprive the world of its magic, charm, and poetry, Freud made our psychic life more poetic—more poetic and more rational at the same time.

This feat did as much as anything to gain for him the admiration of so many poets, novelists, and artists. No other scientist has ever had a comparable influence on art and literature. But the more he influenced creative men and women outside the guild and won their love, the more were many scientists persuaded that he could not be a scientist. While the greatest scientists have always had a powerful imagination, Freud's was exceptionally poetic, and what he did was incomparably more accessible to nonspecialists.

He taught us, as it were, to snorkel and discover a whole new world under the surface—an unsuspected, utterly fascinating realm that was there all along though few swimmers and sailors had any inkling of it. Now and

[93] *Werke*, XI, p. 294f., XII, p. 7f., and XIV, p. 109.

then something from the depths is washed ashore or caught by a fisherman, but Freud explored the depths and taught us how to get glimpses of these regions for ourselves.

He himself, of course, was not a snorkeler enjoying a new diversion but rather a deep-sea diver in search of archaeological finds that might illuminate the past. The diving he did required courage and took him far beyond the reef fish and corals that look enchanting in the sun, into regions that are so dark that one cannot always be sure that things are what they seem to be.

Oddly, despite his love of Greek myths, Freud nowhere in his works compares himself to Odysseus, who descended into the underworld. But the Latin motto, from Virgil, that Freud placed both on the cover and on the title page of the original edition of *The Interpretation of Dreams* suggests that since the heavens do not help us we had better do something about the underworld.

Psychoanalysis does have something "in common with primitive myths," as a previously quoted critic charged, but not more than with science. It does allow for the possibility that men may be disturbed by the ghosts or spirits of their dead fathers. Instead of joining in the then still modern contempt for myth, Freud was interested in recovering its wisdom. Unlike many romantics, however, he was never satisfied with allegedly profound intimations and grandiloquent talk about mysteries; he always wrote with a brilliant clarity far surpassing that of most social "scientists."

If Adler and Jung have succeeded in anything it was in leading so many people to overlook all this. It has been said so often that Freud's explanations were causal and Adler's teleological, and that Freud was a mechanist, materialist, and reductionist with no sense for anything that is of the spirit, that large numbers of people have come to believe all this without as much as asking whether this is really a likely story, given Freud's un-equaled impact on the arts and on literature.

That Freud's explanations are causal is, of course, true; but the Adlerians' dichotomy of causal and teleo-logical actually brings to mind the old contrast between scientific and religious explanations. Modern science came of age when it abandoned teleological explana-tions. Surely, the followers of Adler and Jung do not really wish to insist that in terms of this old contrast their own explanations are teleological. But if "teleological" is redefined to indicate a particular kind of causal explana-tion that takes into account the agent's unconscious intentions or propensities, then it is obviously ridiculous to claim that this was either Adler's or Jung's innovation.

In his reminiscences of Freud, Binswanger refers to a manuscript on Freud's psychology that he wrote in 1924 and says he began

> with the *definition* of the psychic in Freud, that is with its "meaningfulness" [*Sinnhaftigkeit*], and what Freud means by meaning [*Sinn*] is, as everybody knows [!], significance [*Bedeutung*], intention, tendency, and place in a series of psychic contexts. (p. 86)

What is wrong with this brief statement is only the author's confidence that everybody knows this.

Later on Binswanger says:

> Here I must note that today I no longer adopt a wholly negative attitude toward Freud's naturalism; in other words, I have learned to distinguish between the ephem-eral naturalistic clothing of the doctrine and its "eternal contents." (p. 111)

Freud would not have applauded that formulation, and it is part of the point of Binswanger's book to show how their important theoretical differences never affected their profound friendship (pp. 68, 103, etc.).

His report of his visit with Freud in September 1927 is of special interest:

> I hardly believed my ears when I heard the answer [from Freud], "Yes, the spirit is everything" [*Ja, der Geist ist alles*], although I was inclined to suppose that what he meant by *Geist* here was something like intelligence. But then Freud continued: "*After all, humanity knew that it had spirit; I had to show them that there are drives, too. But human beings are always dissatisfied, they can't wait and always want something whole and finished; but one makes a beginning somewhere and advances only slowly.*" (p. 98)

This encouraged Binswanger to break a lance for religiousness, but Freud would have none of that, and his last words on that occasion were: "Unfortunately I cannot satisfy your religious needs." Still, some readers may wonder why Freud did not say in his books that the spirit is everything. No doubt, that was partly because this formulation is excessively imprecise and misleading and also for the same reason that led him to say "sexual" rather than "erotic." He agreed with Nietzsche's dictum in the third essay in *On the Genealogy of Morals*—an essay that was discussed by the Vienna Psychoanalytical Society April 1, 1908:

> If a psychologist today has *good taste* (others might say, integrity) it consists in resistance to the shamefully *moralized* way of speaking which has gradually made all modern judgments of men and things slimy. (Section 19)

Of course, the point Freud himself made should not be underestimated. In the study of humanity or, as we might say, the discovery of the mind so much is known before we set sail to discover more that one can rarely give a perfectly balanced and fully rounded picture. All we can do is correct and supplement existing maps. When we find that some deeply entrenched prejudices obstruct the advance of knowledge, we are almost bound to stress especially what is not gladly heard. If we merely mentioned it more or less in passing, we would stand no chance at all of breaching the walls of prejudice. Need I add that this also applies to my picture of Freud?

23 ▶▶▶ So far I have concentrated on discovering Freud's mind and advancing our understanding of the man and the tradition in which he stands. Apart from that, his break with Adler and Jung really cannot be understood very well. But we still have to ask what, specifically, Freud contributed to the discovery of the mind or to human self-understanding. To answer this question briefly is very difficult, for two reasons.

First, Freud himself was asked again and again to furnish neat summaries and did it in all kinds of formats, ranging from less than ten pages to the two books containing his thirty-five introductory lectures.[94] It hardly makes sense to try to compete with him. Second, to limit oneself to roughly half a dozen contributions is as difficult in his case as confining oneself to six theses against Heidegger.

Nevertheless, if one wants to facilitate fruitful discussion it is probably essential to suggest briefly and very undogmatically what I take to be, say, his ten major contributions. Obviously, it would be easy to come up with a different list, and this way of seeing his contributions is, for better or worse, somewhat original or, if you prefer, unusual. Listing some of Freud's concepts or theories would immediately invite controversies that tend to obscure some of Freud's greatest achievements. But enough of preliminaries! Whether my list of ten is fruitful cannot be settled without presenting it.

[94] See *Werke*, V, pp. 1–10; VIII, pp. 1–60; X, pp. 43–113; XI, entire; XIII, pp. 209–33 and 403–27; XIV, pp. 31–96 and 297–307; XV, entire; and XVII, pp. 63–138.

Freud's creation of a poetic science of the mind constitutes his first major contribution to the discovery of the mind. In the preceding sections I have tried to show what precisely I mean by a poetic science. The point is not mainly that with his case histories he created a new genre, and that they were contributions to imaginative literature that are true. Nor is it merely that in his other writings, too, Freud created a new style, as Plato and Nietzsche had done before him. Yet these accomplishments are relevant. The crux is that Freud pioneered a new approach, a new way of studying and understanding ourselves and others. That his style was closer to literature than to ordinary scientific prose is incidental, though revealing. What is decisive is that he managed to fuse the sensitivity of a poet with the rigor and self-discipline of a scientist. He was not afraid of very bold and imaginative hypotheses or conjectures but intent on not permitting himself, or his readers, illusions. He spurned the security of obscurity à la Kant or à la Hegel, à la Heidegger or à la Buber, as well as the safety of laboratory psychology, quantification, and statistics. He had the courage to create not only a new science but a new kind of science.

Whether this really was a major contribution or rather a *Holzweg*, a path that eventually gets lost in the woods and does not lead anywhere,[95] depends on the other contributions Freud made. What I mean to suggest is that no unpoetic psychologist has contributed half as much to human self-understanding as did Goethe, Nietzsche, and Freud. Most of them, like most philoso-

[95] *Holzwege* is the title of one of Heidegger's books—it could be the title of all of his works—and Heidegger went to some lengths to assure us that the peasants in the area from which he came knew the meaning of this term, suggesting how close he was to what the Nazis called "blood and soil." Roughly forty years earlier (February 25, 1913), Freud had used the term casually in a letter to Binswanger; he considered it probable at that time that Jung with his innovations might be on a *Holzweg*.

phers and academicians in other fields, are engaged in busy-work that, whether "scientific" or not, contributes nothing much of enduring importance.[96]

24 ▶▶▶ *Freud's discovery of the importance of childhood experiences for character development is his second major contribution.* In fact, if this were his only contribution, it would still amount to a revolution in human self-understanding. Literature and pedagogy as well as our whole way of thinking about human beings and our attitudes toward children have been altered profoundly. It is important to realize this before one moves on to appraise some of Freud's particular theories.

Like no one before him, Freud called attention to the formative influence of sibling relationships, to the problems created by the birth of a younger sibling, and to the common admixture of hatred in sibling love. Before Freud, most people would have denied that they had ever felt hatred for their brothers and sisters or parents, and insofar as they realized that they had such feelings, or even that at one time long ago they had felt a deep resentment of that kind, they would have felt guilty on that account. Since Freud, "ambivalence" is a commonplace, and very large numbers of people recognize that it is quite normal to have mixed feelings—especially for those who are closest to us.

No other idea of Freud's about childhood, and perhaps no Freudian concept of any kind, has gained as much attention as the Oedipus complex. Few people know how modestly Freud himself introduced this idea.

[96] At least one anthropologist has recently developed a view that seems to point in the same direction as my suggestion. Clifford Geertz in "A Wary Reasoning: Humanities, Analogies, and Social Theory."

It is first encountered in a letter he wrote to his friend Wilhelm Fliess, October 15, 1897:

> To be totally honest with oneself is a good exercise. A single idea of general value has occurred to me. I have found the phenomenon of being in love with the mother and jealous of the father in myself, too, and now consider it a general event in early childhood . . . If that should be so, then one could understand the gripping power of *Oedipus Rex* . . . Everyone in the audience was once in germ and in fantasy such an Oedipus . . .
>
> Fleetingly the idea passed through my mind whether the same motif might not also be at the bottom of *Hamlet*. I am not thinking of Shakespeare's conscious intention . . .

In *The Interpretation of Dreams* these ideas are broached even more tentatively, with Freud's characteristic consideration for the reader. But it is no mere matter of courtesy or strategy. It is one thing to share an exciting speculation with a friend and quite another to proclaim a discovery to the public. Freud's manner is wholly undogmatic:

> According to my experiences, which are by now quite numerous, the parents play the main roles in the childhood psychic life of all later psychoneurotics, and being in love with one parent and feeling hatred for the other one are always part of the material of psychic impulses formed at this time that is so crucial for the symptoms of the later neurosis. But I do not believe that in this respect the psychoneurotics are sharply different from other human beings who remain normal . . . It is far more probable and is supported by occasional observations of normal children that with these loving and hostile wishes against their parents, too, they merely show us on a magnified scale what happens less clearly and not so intensively in the souls of most children. Antiquity supports this realization with a traditional myth . . .
>
> I mean the myth of King *Oedipus* and the drama with the same name by *Sophocles*. . . .

As noted earlier (in Section 20), the interpretation of *Hamlet* followed in a long footnote that ended with the demand for "overinterpretation."

While suspending judgment about *all* neurotics, I see no reason for taking exception to these cautious remarks. The introduction of Sophocles' and Shakespear's tragedies is important because it helps to establish the thesis that what Freud had observed in Vienna in the 1890s is not confined to one place or period. That the theme is also central in Dostoevsky's *The Brothers Karamazov,* where Ivan actually asks,[97] "Who doesn't desire his father's death?" is doubly significant. Not only does it add support from yet another culture, but it gives us food for thought that this motif should be present in some of the very greatest and most haunting works of world literature. And Ivan's "Liars! They all desire the death of their fathers" invites comparison with Sophocles' Jocasta when she says: "Many men have in their dreams/lain on their mothers" (line 981f.). Of course, she is trying to reassure Oedipus, and Ivan is half mad; yet the poets are telling us that such desires are by no means as exceptional as one might like to think. Again, Oedipus' cry of triumph when he hears that the man he considers his father has died is consciously motivated by his relief that, despite the prophecy, the old man died all by himself, "and I stand here/and never raised my spear against him" (968f.). Yet it is an extremely unsentimental reaction, and the fact that not one reader in a thousand seems to have been offended by it also makes one think.

It may still be objected that three works do not prove much even if they are among the most stupendous masterpieces of all time. But instead of adducing more examples here, it seems better to refer to Otto Rank's book, *Das Inzest-Motiv in Dichtung und Sage* (1912). A revised and enlarged edition of *The Incest Motif in*

---

[97] Near the beginning of Chapter V of Book XII.

Literature and Legend appeared in 1926, a French translation, again revised, in 1934.

The Oedipus complex is often misunderstood as if Freud had suggested that boys at about the age of four desired to have intercourse with their mothers. In fact, he said explicitly that children at that age have no clear understanding of sexual intercourse and that little boys do not have fantasies in which they see their own sexual organs inside their mothers'. What they want, according to Freud, is sole possession of their mothers, while they experience their fathers as rivals. When I said at the age of four or five—I remember the setting but not my exact age—"If Daddy goes to prison, I'll marry Mommy," I voiced the typical fantasy. I was fortunate to be able to express it so candidly in the presence of both parents instead of having to repress it; and thanks to Freud they did not make me feel guilty about it.

One aspect of Freud's ideas on this subject is that a boy's relationship to his mother is all-important for his whole development. It may be thought that we had always known that and did not need Freud to tell us about it. But that is not so. When writing *Without Guilt and Justice* (1973), I tried to find out how many great philosophers had lost father or mother very early in life. This turned out to be very difficult to establish.

> Even in *biographies* of philosophers their mothers are rarely more than mentioned! The fathers are mentioned more often—usually in connection with the sons' education. The character and attitudes of a mother or her death during a future philosopher's childhood are widely considered irrelevant. The tradition that shapes works of this sort has been molded by an absurd male chauvinism and a mixture of psychological obtuseness with hostility to any attempt at psychological understanding. (p. 247)

People are always tempted to say that, in the first place, Freud was wrong, and that, second, we had always known what he said. In fact, I am suggesting that he was right about a lot of things that we had not always known and that a great many intelligent people still do not know.

In this trilogy I have made no attempt to explain the ideas of philosophers by referring to their childhood experiences. Nor did I furnish their biographies. But it is surely startling that authors who *have* written biographies of the great philosophers have considered it unnecessary to speak of their mothers, or even to mention that Kant and Hegel lost their mothers at thirteen, or that Schopenhauer was seventeen when his father committed suicide after having shown signs of mental disturbance for some time. Nietzsche and Freud, of course, have told us about their parents, and at the end of his life Martin Buber told us about his loss of his mother and its importance for his thought. Some people think that Adler had a higher opinion of women than Freud did, but it is revealing, as we shall see, that Adler told his biographer about his father but not about his mother.

Freud was nothing if not bold, and his scientific training suggested to him that it was entirely appropriate to try to formulate general laws. Instead of opting for the safety of obscure intimations, he did offer many generalizations that go beyond the tentative tone of the quotation from the dream book. This fact calls for at least three comments.

First, such formulations are not by any means as common in his works as many people seem to suppose. The predominant impression one gains as one reads him is that of an extraordinarily fertile imagination that spins off ideas and speculations but is harnessed by a critical spirit that constantly brings up objections and alternatives. Yet the critical spirit is also nourished by the author's imagination, as if he delighted in inventing splendid lines for Mephistopheles no less than Faust.

Second, the occasionally sweeping generalizations that speak of what is *allgemein* (general or universal) are, of course, inspired by the wish to formulate laws, but they also make Freud's theories testable. They make it possible to make risky predictions and to prove Freud wrong.

Third, it is a common fallacy to suppose that the discovery of counterexamples, which naturally proves that a generalization does not hold, refutes more than the generalization. Counterexamples do not necessarily show that we are not dealing with a major contribution. We should keep in mind where we stood before Freud came along. It had occurred to hardly anybody that in childhood people might experience an Oedipal triangle. And when people first read Freud, most of them thought that such things either *could* not happen or at the very least must be utterly exceptional and extremely rare. If it should be found that such a triangle is not at the core of *every* neurosis, or that children raised without any visible father, or in nonpatriarchal societies, or without any family structure, should be importantly different, it would not follow at all that Freud's discovery of the Oedipus complex was not a major contribution.

While Freud had little faith in statistical tests, which have mushroomed during the second half of the twentieth century, he was not averse to having his ideas tested in other ways and wrote Pfister, for example, on September 14, 1926:

> I find interesting another objection: that among savages there is no period of latency at all, in which case this period would not be instituted by nature but a product of culture. I don't believe this, but the question can only be decided by new, extensive investigations (Malinowski).

The conception of a period of latency takes us to Freud's next contribution.

25 ▶▶▶ *Freud's discovery of the importance of sex is his third major contribution.* This statement invites two responses. First: Surely, the importance of sex did not have to wait for Freud in order to be discovered. Second: Surely, it is a commonplace that Freud overestimated the importance of sex. Neither of these responses is entirely unjustified, nor is the initial claim. We cannot settle the matter by deciding precisely how much importance sex was assigned before Freud, how much importance he gave it, and how much importance it actually has. Measurement fails us, but it is possible to be more precise by being more detailed.

Sexual attraction has been one of the central subjects of world literature and art from the earliest times; and religions, too, have taken an interest in it, if only to erect barriers and decide what is impermissible. But thoughtful, more or less analytical discussions of the sex drive and its significance in human life and culture, including its less overt manifestations, were almost nonexistent before Freud published *The Interpretation of Dreams.* In German there was not even any halfway adequate vocabulary for these matters, and when Schopenhauer spoke of the *Geschlechtstrieb* he actually meant the drive for the propagation of the species *(Geschlecht)* as much as the sex drive. (This point has been discussed in some detail in Section 9 of the second volume of this trilogy.) Nietzsche's epigram "The degree and kind of the sexuality of a human being reach up into the ultimate pinnacle of his or her spirit [or mind]"[98] stands out as an exception—even in his books. As one reads that, one instantly thinks of Freud. But if one should also wonder whether what Nietzsche says here is true, or even what precisely he might mean, one finds that this is really an "aphorism" and not part of an intricate argument. Of course, there are many scattered remarks about sex in

[98] *Beyond Good and Evil,* Section 75.

Nietzsche's writings that one can assemble, having read Freud, to see what they might add up to; for example, later in the same book (Section 189), ". . . why it was . . . only under the pressure of Christian value judgments that the sex drive sublimated itself into love (amour-passion)." Here and in several other places Nietzsche actually used the word *sublimieren*. But Nietzsche certainly does not prove my initial statement about Freud and the importance of sex wrong.

Neither does Richard Freiherr von Krafft-Ebing (1840–1902), whose *Psychopathia Sexualis* appeared in 1886, like *Beyond Good and Evil;* or Havelock Ellis (1859–1939), whose *Man and Woman* appeared in 1894 and was followed by the seven volumes of his *Studies in the Psychology of Sex* 1897–1928); of Magnus Hirschfield (1868–1935), who in 1899 commenced publication of a yearbook "for intermediate sexual stages, special attention being given to homosexuality."[99] All of these men deserve credit for helping to make the unspeakable speakable and preparing the ground for dispassionate discussions of the significance of the sex drive in human life and culture, but it was Freud more than anyone else who opened up that subject. And if only by comparison with the way he did it, the writings of those pioneers of sexology seem to cater to some extent to a prurient interest. Freud's, it seems to me, never did, and that in itself was a remarkable achievement that was experienced as liberating by innumerable grateful readers. More than anyone else, Freud restored to sex its innocence. I shall return to this point at the end of this chapter.

A full discussion of Freud's thoughts about sex could easily fill a book. I shall confine myself to a few points. In an early paper, published in 1894, Freud reported:

[99] *Jahrbuch für sexuelle Zwischenstufen unter besonderer Berücksichtigung der Homosexualität.*

> In all the cases I have analyzed it was the *sex life* [*Sexualleben*] that had produced a painful [or embarrassing: *peinlichen*] emotion of precisely the same nature that attached to the obsession.[100]

It was the study of his patients that first led Freud to discover the importance of sex. That it really plays an incomparably more important role in the genesis of neuroses and some other forms of mental illness and disturbance than was known before Freud seems to be indisputable. Hence his discovery is of immense importance even if he should have overestimated the importance of sexual factors.

Second, Freud explored, like no one before him, child sexuality. This was widely considered a slander of innocent children because sex was somehow assumed to be dirty—under the influence of almost two thousand years of Christian teachings. It took some time before our culture began to absorb the opposite lesson: that sex is natural and innocent.

Specifically, Freud made the following claims:

> The sex drive, whose dynamic expression in psychic life will here be called *libido*, is composed of partial drives and can fall apart into these; and they join only gradually in various configurations. The sources of these partial drives are bodily organs, especially certain preeminent *erogenous zones* . . . The first (pregenital) configuration that can be recognized is the *oral* one in which, corresponding to the main interest of the infant, the *mouth zone* plays the main part. It is followed by the *sadistic-anal* configuration . . . The third and final configuration is the integration of most partial drives under the *primacy of the genital zones*. As a rule, one passes through this development quickly and inconspicuously . . .
>
> . . . Even in the first years of childhood (approximately from 2 to 5 years) an integration of the sexual aspirations

[100] *Werke*, I, p. 66.

takes place, and for boys the mother is the object. This choice of object together with the concomitant rivalry and hostility against the father is the content of the so-called *Oedipus complex,* which has for all human beings the greatest significance for the final form of their love life. It has been suggested that it is characteristic for those who are normal that they learn to cope with the Oedipus complex while the neurotic gets stuck in it.

. . . This early period of sex life normally comes to an end around the fifth year and is replaced by a period of more or less complete *latency* during which ethical restraints are built up as protective formations against the wishes associated with the Oedipus complex. In the following period of *puberty* the Oedipus complex is revived in the unconscious and begins its further transformations. Only during puberty do the sex drives develop to reach full intensity; but the direction of this development and all the dispositions that attach to it are determined by the prior infantile early blossoming of sexuality. These two periods in the development of the sexual functions, interrupted by a period of latency, seem to be a biological peculiarity of the human race and seem to contain the conditions for the origins of neuroses.[101]

If the tone of this exposition is somewhat dogmatic, that is because I have been quoting from Freud's article "Psychoanalysis," which was written for a concise encyclopedia *(Handwörterbuch der Sexualwissenschaften,* 1923). The reason for nevertheless citing these formulations is that no paraphrase could be briefer than, or half as authoritative as, this summary. But in fairness to Freud it should be added that the pioneering work in which these ideas were initially presented, *Three Contributions to the Theory of Sex* (1905), ended:

These investigations of disturbances in our sex life come to a conclusion that is not satisfying: We do not know

[101] *Werke,* XIII, 220–22.

nearly enough about the biological processes that constitute the nature of sexuality to be able to form from our scattered insights a theory that might be adequate for understanding what is normal as well as what is pathological.

What has been said here so tersely is obviously not the last word about the importance of sex—even in this chapter. It is interesting to recall what a reviewer of the *Three Contributions* said December 21, 1905, in *Die Fackel,* edited by Karl Kraus: "No *last* word, but on countless problems the *first* sober, valuable word." The whole review, written by Otto Soyka, was immensely appreciative and, I think, basically right in perceiving that Freud was opening up a new subject and striking a new, liberating tone.

Just as these reflections on sex continue the discussion of the importance of childhood, the contributions that remain to be considered here amplify the importance of sex. Freud's overestimation of the importance of sex will be considered in connection with the ninth contribution. But it should be kept in mind that Freud said repeatedly (for example, *Werke,* XII, p. 5) that he had "not forgotten or denied for a moment" that human beings "have other interests besides sexual ones. Our one-sidedness is like that of a chemist," who "does not deny gravity; he leaves its study to the physicist." I will present my most important criticism of Freud near the end of this chapter, before closing on a positive note.

26 ▶▶▶ *Freud's interpretation of dreams constitutes his fourth major contribution.* Again, his contribution cannot be reduced to one or another of his theories, nor does it stand or fall with his controversial—and, I think, false—claim that all dreams represent wish fulfillments. Freud himself considered *The Inter-*

DIE

TRAUMDEUTUNG

VON

DR. SIGM. FREUD.

›*FLECTERE SI NEQUEO SUPEROS, ACHERONTA MOVEBO.*‹

LEIPZIG UND WIEN.

FRANZ DEUTICKE.

1900.

The first edition of *The Interpretation of Dreams*, 1900.

pretation of Dreams his greatest book. While such value judgments cannot be proved to be true, it is reasonable to ask what precisely was the nature of Freud's achievement.

Once again, he opened up the subject for detailed discussion. He showed that dreams are worth taking seriously and, when approached intelligently and perceptively, reveal a great deal about those who dreamed them, their problems and preoccupations. Millions of intellectuals and writers as well as countless therapists—not by any means only psychoanalysts—have accepted these basic notions.

One could also say that Freud sought to show that dreams are meaningful; in fact, that there is no part of a dream that is not meaningful. It is here more than anywhere else that Freud is indebted to a rabbinical tradition that goes back roughly two thousand years. He approached our dreams (as well as our mischievements, which will be considered next) as the rabbis had approached Scripture: There must be some reason for everything. And I mean *reason*, not just some *cause*. Nowhere is it plainer that Freud was not rooted in nineteenth-century mechanism and materialism. He insisted on finding a reason, a purpose, an intention, a desire to communicate something—in the end, even a wish. Even as the rabbis had postulated that if a word is used twice, or if there seems to be a mistake, or if there is a little ornament on a letter, there must be some reason for that and it must be there to tell us something, Freud assumed doggedly that *nihil est sine ratione*, that nothing is without a reason in the sense that every little detail can tell us something.

If we do not remember something too well, that is significant also; indeed, precisely what at first we do not recall is often of special importance. After all, most of us forget our dreams as soon as we wake up, suggesting to Freud that we do not want to remember them. On reflection, he is surely right. If we did want to remember them, we could make an effort that we do not make. We could take a pencil or pen and start to write down what we do remember and try hard to recall more. Moreover, when we say before falling asleep, "I will remember my dreams tonight," that usually makes a big difference; but even after having found out that it does, we rarely do say that. Plainly, then, we prefer not to remember our dreams.

It does not follow that we are afraid of them. It could be that we grudge them the time; but we do seem to find time for all sorts of trivia. It could be because we really do not want to become so preoccupied with our dreams; our lives seem to function well enough, and we do not want to risk any upset. There is no end of reasons or excuses.

DREAMS

Dreams are so private we don't share
their magic with our probing minds
and when we wake we do not dare
to bring our iridescent finds

into the daylight lest the sun
should fade and dry their fragile splendor.
We can recall what we have done
but what we saw we don't surrender.

It really does not matter right now what our reasons may be. What is important is that for the most part we do not want to hear what our dreams may have to tell us. Now that is what Freud claimed, without approaching this claim in the manner in which I have argued for it here; and this claim has met with a great deal of resistance.

What Freud suggested was that even during the dream we do not want to hear what our dream is telling us. He put this point anthropomorphically by speaking of a censor. There is, he said, a censor in us who will not allow the "latent dream thoughts" to become manifest. "The manifest content of the dream" must be distinguished from our "latent dream thoughts," which have been transformed to get by the censor. This transformation Freud called *die Traumarbeit*, the dream work; and the labor of undoing it and getting back to the latent dream thoughts he called *die Deutungsarbeit*, the work of interpretation.

The dream work involves, according to Freud, condensation (*Verdichtung;* it should be noted that *Dichtung* means poetry), displacement (*Verschiebung;* but *Schiebung* also means skulduggery), and the translation of thoughts into visual images. Now one can question whether all this work is really done to get past the censor. I remain unconvinced. Just as poets do not write dramas or use symbols merely to get past a censor, I do not believe that all of the dream work needs to be explained that way.

All human beings need to be creative, as I have argued elsewhere,[102] and feel frustrated when they are not. Some people may deny this, saying that they lack the talent to be creative; and they may add, for example, that they simply cannot write. In our dreams, however, all of us are creative and invent the most fantastic stories and playlets. Recent research has established that people who are not allowed to dream, being waked up as soon as they begin to dream, become very disturbed. This may be partial evidence for my thesis that we need to be creative. Dreams deal creatively with psychic problems.

This objection to Freud's account does not involve any agreement with those who claim that the conception of the censor is nonsensical. I have no quarrel with that conception and claim only that Freud is unconvincing

[102] *Without Guilt and Justice* (1973), pp. 218–24. On pp. 131f. and 245f. I have also taken issue with Freud's interpretation of punishment dreams and offered a different interpretation.

when he argues that the dream work is motivated entirely by the need to get past the censor.

Freud's interpretation of dreams is obviously similar in some ways to ancient religious ideas. The dream is a message, but not from God or gods; it is part of what one might call, borrowing an image from Plato,[103] the soul's dialogue with itself. That dreams involve symbolism was known even in ancient times and is familiar to us, as it was to Freud, from the story of Joseph in Genesis, for example. Freud frequently stressed that interpreting dreams was an art, that symbols cannot be interpreted mechanically—as it were, by using a dictionary—and that it is essential to have the dreamers' associations with various parts of the dream as well as their reactions to the interpreter's questions and suggestions.

Those who take issue with Freud on a number of points and remain unpersuaded that every dream is best understood as a wish fulfillment, can still grant that it was Freud who conquered the continent even if he did not chart it definitively and left work for others. Friedrich Schiller's distich "Kant and His Interpreters" is eminently applicable to Freud but brings to mind not only Freud's interpreters but also all the testers who have contributed to *The Scientific Evaluation of Freud's Theories and Therapy*,[104] as well as those who interpret dreams but do not consider themselves Freudians:

> One who is opulent offers   legions of famishing beggars food. When the kings construct,   carters find plenty of work.

[103] *Theaetetus* 189e.

[104] *A Book of Readings,* edited by S. Fisher and R. P. Greenberg (1978). See also Fisher and Greenberg, *The Scientific Credibility of Freud's Theories and Therapy* (1977).

27 ▶▶▶ *Freud's psychopathology of everyday life constitutes his fifth major contribution.* In effect, he accepted Goethe's dictum that we are what we do, but credited us not only with our achievements but also with our mischievements. I have already explained why I prefer "mischievements" to "parapraxes" (Section 7). *Fehlleistungen* (literally, misachievements) has "light feet" and calls our attention to the element of mischief in misspeaking, misreading, mislaying, forgetting, and misremembering. Again, Freud's approach brings to mind that of the rabbis toward scripture: everything that is of the spirit or psyche must have a meaning; there must be some purpose that a skilled interpreter should be able to find.

The Psychopathology of Everyday Life is a singularly readable book that contains an immensely entertaining collection of anecdotes. Many are self-explanatory, while others become the occasion for intricate detective work. Freud kept adding material, including stories and analyses submitted to him by such colleagues as Adler and Jung, Ferenczi and Rank, Jones and Brill, until the tenth edition appeared in 1924, twenty-three years after the essay had first been published in a journal. From a purely literary point of view the book suffered a little from the piling up of more and more material, for the addition of so many more cases does not greatly strengthen the argument. Of course, some of the added material is beautiful and very quotable. In any case, the analysis of mischievements represents one of Freud's major contributions and furnishes an excellent introduction to psychoanalysis. Freud himself recognized this when he devoted the first of the three parts of his introductory lectures to this subject.

Let us begin with "The Forgetting of Resolutions" (VII.B).

Normal behavior in the case of a resolution coincides perfectly with the behavior that can be produced experimentally by giving people a so-called "post-hypnotic suggestion for later on." The phenomenon is usually described as follows: The suggested resolve slumbers in such people until the time of its execution approaches. Then it awakens and impels them to act.

In two kinds of situations, Freud continues, even people who know nothing of psychoanalysis adopt the same attitude as Freud: in love and in the military.

A lover who has forgotten a rendezvous will excuse himself in vain by saying that he unfortunately forgot it. She will not fail to answer him: "A year ago you would not have forgotten it. You just don't care for me any more." Even if he had recourse to the above mentioned psychological explanation, trying to excuse his forgetfulness by saying how much business had piled up, he would only succeed in having his lady—as keen by now as a psychoanalyst—reply: "How odd that such business matters never used to interfere."

In love and in the military, forgetting is not accepted as an excuse.

In many other cases as well, Freud's theory is very close to common sense. Three examples that appear in English even in the original German text may help to show this. The first comes from Charles Darwin's autobiography:

I had, during many years, followed a golden rule, namely, that whenever a published fact, a new observation or thought came across me, which was opposed to my general results, to make a memorandum of it without fail and at once; for I had found by experience that such facts and thoughts were far more apt to escape from the memory than favourable ones.[105]

[105] *Werke*, IV, p. 164.

As Freud notes expressly, this passage reflects Darwin's "scientific honesty" no less than "his psychological acuity." It also brings to mind some of Freud's critics. Karl Popper—despite all his talk of "refutations" and "falsification" (what a horrible and misleading coinage that is!)—has not followed this golden rule regarding material opposed to his views of Freud or Hegel. But what is one to say about "Investigations of Repression: Differential Recall of Material Experimentally or Naturally Associated with Ego Threat"? In an article with this title David S. Holmes reported on large numbers of tests by different researchers and concluded:

> Certainly, the lack of empirical support for the hypotheses derived from the theory of repression cannot be attributed to a lack of research interest in the topic. (p. 649)

What then can it be attributed to? Was Darwin right at most about his own experience and, if right about that, more dishonest by nature than lesser human beings who require no such golden rule? To be sure, this is not altogether impossible, but as one reads about one experiment after another one is struck again and again by a certain obtuseness. It would seem that the great majority of the psychologists had never read Freud's *Psychopathology of Everyday Life*, nor even the little quotation from Darwin. Certainly, it would raise standards in the academic world if more people adopted Darwin's rule.

Our second quotation is an epigram by A. A. Brill: "We are more apt to mislay letters containing bills than checks." I am not sure whether any research teams have obtained sizable grants to test this claim.

Freud also quotes a bon mot by Ernest Jones in the original English:

> One can almost measure the success with which a physician is practising psychotherapy . . . by the size of the

collection of umbrellas, handkerchiefs, purses and so on, that he could make in a month.

Again, I know of no experimental work, but the notion that forgetting something at somebody's home or office indicates a wish to return there and is thus a compliment of sorts has, no doubt, been tested by large numbers of Freud's readers, both when they themselves have forgotten something and when others have left things with them.

These three English quotations suggest how close to common sense much of Freud's theory is. He himself says:

Indeed, at times one cannot resist the impression that everything one could say about forgetting and mischievements is familiar to people anyway as a matter of course.[106]

Critics usually make things easy for themselves by claiming that there is no proof that *all* mischievements are, so to say, "Freudian"—as if that could possibly be proved, and as if Freud's contribution stood or fell with such a proof. One can hardly resist the impression that most of Freud's critics have never read *The Psychopathology of Everyday Life*. After analyzing half a dozen cases of mislaying, Freud says:

When one surveys the cases of mislaying it really becomes difficult to suppose that mislaying ever occurs without being a consequence of an unconscious intention.[107]

Analyzing ten or twenty more cases would not clinch this point, nor can one disprove Freud by citing a few examples of mislaying in which one cannot discover any

[106] *Ibid.*, p. 178.
[107] *Ibid.*, p. 159.

unconscious intention. Freud's contribution does not consist in establishing a general law but rather in illuminating a very large number of mischievements of various kinds and leading us to look at them in a new way.[108] It was in this spirit that he himself presented his material. One looks in vain for general laws or dogmas in *The Psychopathology of Everyday Life*. Freud specifically exempts "the simplest and most unobtrusive examples of misspeaking and miswriting in which, say, words are merely contracted or words and letters omitted"; in such cases he has no "complicated interpretations."

> From the point of view of psychoanalysis one must claim that in these cases some disturbance of an intention is indicated, but one cannot identify the source and intention of this disturbance. It did not accomplish anything more beyond making known its existence. In these cases one also sees at work something we never denied, namely that similar sounds and inviting psychological associations favor mischievements. But it is a fair scientific demand that such rudimentary cases of misspeaking and miswriting should be judged in accordance with the more fully developed cases whose interpretation yields such unambiguous disclosures about the causes of mischievements.[109]

These disclosures are summarized in the closing pages of the book.

> The analysis of examples of forgetting that seem to us to demand some special explanation shows in every case that the motive of forgetting was a displeasure at remembering something that could awaken painful [or embarrassing: *peinliche*] feelings.[110]

[108] See Section 22 of the second volume of this trilogy for some discussion of two different models for science, one associated with Newton and Kant, the other with Nietzsche.
[109] *Ibid.*, p. 301.
[110] *Ibid.*, p. 305.

It is striking how cautiously and undogmatically Freud proceeds. Regarding the question

> what the origin of the thoughts and impulses might be that find expression in mischievements, one can say that in a number of cases the origin of the disturbing thoughts can easily be shown to lie in suppressed impulses of psychic life. Egotistical, jealous, hostile feelings and impulses that are under pressure from our moral education, employ in healthy people not infrequently the path of mischievements to express somehow their undeniably existing power that is not recognized by the higher courts of the psyche. . . . Among these suppressed impulses the manifold sexual currents play no mean role. It is an accidental feature of the material that they appear so rarely in my examples among the thoughts uncovered by analysis.[111]

Later on the same page Freud adds:

> the more harmless the motivation of a mischievement is, the less offensive and hence less unfit for consciousness the thought is that finds expression in it, the easier is also the solution of the phenomenon once we devote some attention to it.

It will be noted that none of this involves an ego, id, and superego—concepts that Freud introduced only after the First World War—nor any cumbersome theoretical apparatus. Freud stays extremely close to the cases he relates and offers explanations that are recognized as obviously right by the mischievers. Indeed, in many of his examples the explanations are furnished by the person who committed or omitted the act.

[111] *Ibid.*, p. 306f.

28 ▶▶▶ In the last chapter Freud

says:

> When I had occasion recently to relate a few examples of the forgetting of names along with analyses to a philosophically educated colleague, he quickly replied: That is very nice, but in my case the forgetting of names is quite different. That is obviously making it too easy for oneself; I do not believe that my colleague had ever before as much as thought of an analysis of the forgetting of names, nor could he say how it was different in his case.[112]

Many of us have heard other philosophers and nonphilosophers explain in what way many cases are supposed to be different. Two points in particular are made frequently. First, it is said that forgetting, misspeaking, miswriting, mislaying, and the rest are due to distraction or tiredness. But that is like saying that dreams are due to some such disturbance as an alarm clock going off. The question remains why we dreamed what we did dream, or why we forgot this name or word rather than that, or why we made this mistake or mislaid that object.

Second, to quote a communication from Adolf Grünbaum: "If a biology professor in a lecture means to say 'organism' but says 'orgasm,' why is it unreasonable to postulate that word similarity and *slight* neurological failure explain such cases?" We are back to the alarm clock. Obviously, word similarity has a great deal to do with such a slip, but it does seem unreasonable to suppose that anybody would make that particular mistake if he did not have "orgasm" on his mind. In most cases, of course, small slips like that are of no great interest because they do not disclose anything very profound or significant.

The most widely read philosopher of our time, Jean-

[112] *Ibid.*, p. 298.

Paul Sartre, called one whole chapter of his philosophical *magnum opus, L'être et le néant* (1943), "Existential Psychoanalysis" and criticized Freud at length in the chapter on *mauvaise foi* ("bad faith," or "self-deception"). When he wrote that book, Sartre held what he himself came to consider by 1960 a rather exaggerated view of human freedom, and he felt that Freud had failed to recognize the full extent of our freedom. Freud, according to Sartre, had seen us, or at least had made it easy for us to see ourselves, as victims of our parents or others who had influenced our childhood. Worse yet, Sartre claimed, Freud had not realized that when we are in self-deception it is we who deceive ourselves, and thus we are responsible. Freud, according to Sartre, split up the self and allowed us to see ourselves as deceived by an internal censor. In other words, Sartre rejected Freud's account in the name of freedom, responsibility, and honesty, and he exhorted us in effect not to see ourselves as victims.

I find it easy to sympathize with Sartre's intentions, but his image of Freud bears little relation to what we find in Freud's books and seems to have been prompted either by a rather crass misunderstanding or by the uses to which Freud's ideas may perhaps have been put by some people who had never studied him. Certainly, Freud himself never declined responsibility for anything he did or said or wrote by claiming or implying that it was his parents' fault, or that he could not help it, seeing how he had been raised. Nor did he ever encourage his patients or his readers to see themselves as victims and decline responsibility. It meets the eye that he did just the opposite. Moreover, the whole thrust of *The Psychopathology of Everyday Life* is to enlarge the area of our responsibility by including in it not only our deliberate actions but even our mischievements. And by teaching us to understand them, Freud means to make us more honest and more autonomous.

Moreover, Sartre's argument is invalidated by two very serious errors. His approach to *mauvaise foi* is Kantian and deliberately unempirical. His basic question is modeled on Kant's "transcendental method": How is *mauvaise foi* possible? What must be the nature of the *pour-soi,* the for-itself, which is Sartre's name for the human mode of being, to make *mauvaise foi* possible?

Sartre's own answer, given at great length, is in brief that our being is different from the being of things, which he calls *en-soi,* "in itself." A man, to give Sartre's own examples, is not a waiter, a homosexual, or a coward in the same way in which objects have various characteristics. They are not free, we are. We can decide at any time to cease being waiters, homosexuals, or cowards and begin to behave differently. The man who claims to be a waiter, etc., in the way in which things have characteristics, as if he could not help being this or that and were a victim of his condition, is in bad faith. For that matter he is also in bad faith if he says that, although he has been a homosexual or a coward for years, he really is not a homosexual or coward. This interesting but relatively elementary point is inflated by Sartre into an allegedly profound paradox that calls into question whether sincerity is possible at all. Sartre suggests strongly that *mauvaise foi* is inescapable.

It takes a lot of obscure writing in the tradition of Kant, Hegel, and Heidegger to create this paradox. Yet Sartre's prose is punctuated by occasional insights, and he may have done his share to convince many students that they were not fated to be students but could choose at any time to drop out of school. On the other hand, he clearly misled his readers when he suggested that it was as easy to cease being a homosexual as it was to cease being a waiter.

My main concern here, however, is with the two major errors that destroy his argument against Freud. The first involves Sartre's analysis of the deception that is part of self-deception or bad faith. Liking to use rather strong language occasionally, which certainly enlivens his often turgid, Kantian prose, he called this deception a lie and said such things as the following:

"The essence of the lie implies, in fact, that the liar is in complete possession of the truth which he is hiding." This is obviously false but repeated again and again. Thus Sartre said, after a bow to Heidegger, that "the liar must make the project of the lie in entire clarity and that he must possess a complete comprehension of the lie and of the truth which he is altering." "There must be an original intention and a project of bad faith." Again:

> I must know in my capacity as deceiver the truth which is hidden from me in my capacity as the one deceived. Better yet I must know the truth very exactly in *order* to conceal it more carefully . . .

These assertions on the opening pages of the chapter on *mauvaise foi* provide the basis for what follows. They are wrong. I do *not* have to be in complete possession of the truth about, say, the date when Sartre wrote these passages to be able to lie about the date by saying, for example, that he wrote them in 1945 or in the fifteenth century.

Sartre is no less wrong when he postulates "the total translucency of consciousness." On the basis of this wholly unempirical assumption he then protests against Freud's "distinction between the 'id' and the 'ego,'" and says that "Freud has cut the psychic whole in two." He claims that "psychoanalysis substitutes for the notion of bad faith the fact of a lie without a liar." Against Freud, Sartre insists that "the censor, in order to apply its activity with discernment, must know what it is repressing." Again: "Thus the resistance of the patient implies on the level of the censor an awareness of the thing repressed." Sartre claims that the unconscious is a fiction, and that we really know all along what, according to Freud, is repressed.

If Sartre thought that this was a powerful argument against Freud, he deceived himself, but I am far from claiming that such self-deception requires that he must have possessed "a complete comprehension of the lie and of the truth which he is altering," or that "there must have been an original intention and a project of bad faith." All such claims are as ill conceived as the notion of "the total translucency of consciousness."

Instead of starting with the ego and the id, it makes far better sense to start, as Freud did, with mischievements. When I forget a name or a telephone number or have mislaid something, talk about "the total translucency of consciousness" does not help at all. On the contrary, mischievements help to show that consciousness is far from being totally translucent.

It *is* helpful, on the other hand, to return once more to *The Psychopathology of Everyday Life* and consider the fascinating case that Freud analyzed in detail in the second chapter. This may help us to see how far Sartre and many other critics are off the right track.

A man misquotes Virgil very slightly in the original Latin. The mistake is so trivial that one might suppose that only a Virgil scholar would have noticed it. The man has suffered from anti-Semitism and quotes Virgil's Dido as exclaiming: *"Exoriar(e) e nostris ossibus ultor!"*— "May an avenger rise from our bones!" Freud, who had used another line from Virgil's *Aeneid* as an epigraph for his dream book, showed by his facial expression that he had noticed this little mischievement and, upon being questioned, admitted that the line really reads: *"Exoriar(e) aliquis nostris ex ossibus ultor!"* The error does not seem to make any difference whatever. The forgotten word means "some," and in English as in German "an" really seems to be more idiomatic.

At this point the man who had made the mistake

tried to get even with Freud by challenging him to explain this mistake, and Freud accepted on condition that his partner should tell him honestly, and without any reservation, whatever associations came to his mind when he thought about the forgotten *aliquis*. These associations began with *a-Liquis*, relics, liquidation, liquid, fluid, Simon of Trent whose relics he had seen two years before in a church, blood accusations against the Jews, a newspaper article about what Saint Augustine had said about women, then Saint Januarius and his blood miracle, and "this just goes on and on mechanically." "Never mind," replied Freud; Saint *Januarius* and Saint *Augustine* both have some relation to the calendar. Couldn't you remind me of the blood miracle?"

In a church in Naples a vial is kept that is said to contain the dried blood of Saint Januarius, and on a certain holiday it becomes liquid again. The populace becomes excited when there is a delay, and on one such occasion a general took the priest of that church aside and told him, leaving no doubt about his meaning, "that he *hoped* the miracle would happen very soon."

At this point the man preferred not to go on because his next association was too intimate and in any case irrelevant. And now Freud could have made a risky prediction. But he still allowed the man to admit that he suddenly thought of a lady from whom he might easily receive some very disagreeable news. He was surprised when Freud replied: "That she has missed her period?"

How, the man asked, had Freud been able to guess that? Freud then reminded him of the calendar saints, the blood becoming liquid on a certain day, the distress when this event did not happen on time, and the hope that the miracle would happen very soon. Moreover, Dido's line expressed the wish for an heir, but as the man was about to voice this wish he asked himself, as it were: Do I really wish for an heir? Wouldn't it be most embarrassing if a little avenger were on his way? There was in him what Freud calls, later in the book (p. 171), "a *counterwill*." And when it came to the word *aliquis*, with which his very first association was *a-liquis*, nonliquid, he preferred not to think about that and dropped it.

When we reread Sartre in the light of such a case, we see how far he is out of touch with experience. It makes no sense to say that the man knew the correct wording of the line all along and that his consciousness was really totally translucent. Would telling him that have led him to say, "Of course, I left out *aliquis* and slightly rearranged the line to make up for that"? And was the correct wording clearly present to his mind before he said to himself, "*Aliquis* reminds me of something I would rather not think about, so I'd better omit that word"?

It makes far better sense to say that consciousness is far from being totally translucent, and that a censor does not have to be clearly aware of the significance of the things he censors. A censor may cut out a word or paragraph in a letter or a newspaper merely because it seems suspicious, or because it comes from a suspicious quarter. It is quite enough for the censor to feel apprehensive, and he does not have to give himself a detailed account of the matter and prove why something does not perhaps deserve the benefit of the doubt.

Moreover, much of the material that Freud found to be repressed had been repressed in early childhood when—as also in our dreams—our reason is not at its best and we often feel that there is something, we do not necessarily know what, with which we cannot cope, something that seems frightening enough for us to lack the courage to examine it closely. In such cases one may need help in later years to get at the repressed material.

A short poem may help to clinch the point:

Contra Sartre

The mind is a foggy beach
where shapes are hard to make out

What is near is still out of reach
and all is guesswork and doubt.

The threatening truths we hide
we cannot see too well
and weakness, fear, and pride
misread the signs of hell.

Sartre's conception of "the total translucency of consciousness" is utterly dogmatic. Consciousness is not like a room that is well and evenly lit. It is more like a cellar in which one area near a stairwell has enough light for us to see easily, while the regions that are farther away are quite dim, and beyond them almost everything seems to be dark. As one's eyes get used to the dark one is able to make out more and more, and it obviously helps if one has some idea of the sorts of things that usually are stored in cellars, if only in that part of the world. But children, as well as many grownups, are likely to be so frightened by some shapes that they refuse to take a close look—also at other things, later in life, that remind them of what frightened them in the cellar, if only because they suddenly perceive a similar musty smell or hear an ominous rustling.

Some other criticisms of Freud are also off the mark. It has been said often that "free associations" are not really free because if a person associates "freely" long enough, virtually anything will appear, and the analyst picks out what seems to suit his theory and then steers the associations. No doubt, this may happen, but it seems equally clear that Freud considered it important not to let it happen. In the case at hand, the man's first association with *aliquis* was *a-liquis,* then relics, liquid, etc. While I have omitted a couple of links that fit well into the same chain, it is plain that the process did not go on and on and on, allowing *Freud* to construct the chain.

Others take offense at the division of the self into separate agencies, such as the unconscious and the censor. Apart from the fact that Freud himself did not rely on any such explicit model in the case at hand, or in scores of other cases, it seems to me that the suggestion that our self is wholly one and undivided is as unempirical as the notion of the total translucency of consciousness. The man who forgot *aliquis* thought he wanted an heir who would avenge the wrongs done to his people, but he was also of another mind and rather frightened by the possibility that he might have an heir in much less than a year's time.

This is surely typical of the human condition: We have conflicting wishes, we love and hate the same persons, we are at odds with ourselves. In those who are neurotic, disturbed, or mentally ill, these strains often become very severe and disabling, while so-called normal people manage to cope with them and are much of the time quite unaware of them. In some mischievements such conflicts announce themselves so plainly that even people who have never heard of psychoanalysis have no trouble at all understanding what is going on, and Freud gave many examples of writers and poets who capitalized on this fact, inventing mischievements that are instantly grasped by the audience.

In Shaw's *Caesar and Cleopatra*, for example, Cleopatra appears as Caesar is about to leave Egypt and asks him whether he is not even going to say goodbye to her. He retorts: "Ah, I *knew* there was something. How could you let me forget her, Rufio?" One sees in an instant that Shaw's Caesar, unlike Shakespeare's Antony, is not going to lose an empire and his life for the sake of a woman.

Other mischievements baffle us and seem inexplicable. Freud aimed to show us how many of them can be assimilated to these easy cases; and having analyzed a large number, suggested that "it really becomes difficult to suppose that mislaying [for example] ever occurs without being a consequence of an unconscious intention."[113] At that point some philosophers bristle at the concept of "an unconscious intention," though all of us have many intentions of which for long periods of time we are not conscious; and if we made lists of all our intentions we would be sure to find that some of them conflict with each other. Moreover, the concept of "unconscious intention" is derived from posthypnotic suggestion, and philosophers inclined to reject this concept should tell us how they propose to deal with that.

I am not much of a typist but type my own manuscripts, mostly using only two fingers and my thumbs, and am pretty fast but keep making mistakes that I erase quickly, correct, and go on. Is everyone of these typos profoundly significant? I doubt it; but it is interesting and amusing that when it came to the seventh word of the present paragraph I wrote not "typist" but "typos." I do not type as fast as I think and am impatient to get to the point.

Freud's contribution in this area is that he has greatly enlarged our understanding of ourselves and others. In effect, he has enlarged the area of human responsibility, showing us how it extends to our mischievements, too, not only in love and in the military. In the process he has also enlarged our autonomy. To show this, I shall offer a final example of my own.

I kept forgetting the name of a man whom I disliked. This fitted in with Freud's theory, but I had no similar problems with the names of other people whom I liked no better. (Thinking this over once more as I write it down, I find that the other people I disliked were famous, and I heard and read their names frequently, while this man was not famous; and perhaps there was nobody who was not famous whom I disliked that much.) I looked for an additional reason and found it. His first and his last name were very similar to the first and last

[113] See note 107 above.

names of a recently deceased relative whom I had esteemed especially. She was as pure, gentle, and sensitive as he was not, and it was offensive to my mind that his name should be so similar to hers. Ever since I understood this, I have had no trouble remembering his name. What was once an impediment to memory has now become a mnemonic device. I conclude that Sartre's model of consciousness is wrong while Freud's theory of mischievements constitutes a major contribution and enlarges our self-understanding and autonomy.

29 ▶▶▶ *Freud's interpretation of mental illness constitutes his sixth major contribution.* If we proceeded chronologically, we might call it his first contribution. Moreover, one might suppose that this is the crux of psychoanalysis. Nevertheless, it does not require extensive discussion here. Only one point must be stressed, which owing to Freud's success, is often overlooked. Freud more than anyone else tore down the wall that had long divided the mentally ill from the supposedly normal human being. They were supposed to be basically different from the rest of us, and Freud emancipated them.

If he had done nothing else, this alone would make him memorable. But in our time this insight is widely taken for granted, and some critics actually reproach Freud for having sat on a chair while his patients were reclining on a sofa, thus accentuating the difference between therapist and patient. This criticism seems historically blind.

When Freud came along, it was generally felt that people who were mentally disturbed were crazy and quite unlike normal human beings; also that perhaps they could be healed through hypnosis. Freud took the crucial step toward seeing them as essentially like himself. The insights he derived from treating patients he used to analyze himself, and the insights he derived from his self-analysis he used in therapy.

The interpretation of dreams and the psychopathology of everyday life were further steps along the same path. In our dreams all of us are far from rational and sane, and in our waking hours, too, we do weird things that could be called pathological and point up the continuity between the mentally ill and the normal.

In another context one might now go on to discuss in detail Freud's understanding of hysteria and his theory of neuroses. In the present trilogy, however, that would be out of place. The best exposition is to be found in the third and last part of Freud's introductory lectures, which takes up almost half of the book. But here it may be more to the point to stress once more Freud's undogmatic bent and the difficulties that confront any very brief summary. To that end I shall quote two brief passages from his 1926 book on anxiety. Chapter VII begins with a discussion of phobias, and the second paragraph starts:

> It is almost humiliating that after so many years of work we still encounter difficulties in understanding the most basic relationships, but we have resolved not to simplify anything and not to hide anything. If we cannot see clearly, let us at least see clearly what is unclear.

And chapter IX ends:

> These small corrections cannot possibly be designed to call into question the fact discussed here—the fact that so many people remain infantile in their attitudes toward danger and do not overcome long-dated conditions of anxiety. To deny that would be to deny the fact of neurosis, for such people are simply called neurotics. But how is this possible? Why are not all neuroses episodes in a development that are concluded when the next stage is reached? What is the source of the enduring character in these reactions to danger? . . . In other words, . . . what is the source of neurosis, what is its ultimate and distinc-

tive motive? After whole decades of analytical exertions, this problem raises itself up before us, untouched, as in the beginning.

The final chapter deals with Otto Rank's *The Trauma of Birth* (1923), comparing Freud's approach with Rank's. And except for a number of "Postscripts" the book ends: "Further than that, I must believe, our insight into the nature and causes of neurosis has not got so far."

30 ▶▶▶ *Freud's new therapy constitutes his seventh major contribution.* This point needs to be seen in historical perspective; it can be granted without any suggestion that this therapy is the best and most efficient therapy available today. It was Freud who put aside hypnosis, which infringed upon the patient's autonomy, and developed a talking cure in which the patient did most of the talking. Physical symptoms were found to be amenable to this kind of therapy.

Here another word about the analytical couch is in order. The women whom Freud got to speak more or less freely about sex would never have done that in those days if they had had to look into his eyes. He had to get them to relax as much as possible while they related their free associations without constant feedback from his own facial expressions. Nor did he wish to be in a position that required him to respond continuously. He, too, needed to enter into a special state of consciousness in which his awareness was evenly distributed over the stream of talk, allowing him to pick up clues that from the speaker's point of view were peripheral and irrelevant.

Hanns Sachs reports that Freud once said:

"I cannot let myself be stared at for eight hours daily" (*Ich kann mich nicht acht Stunden täglich anstarren lassen*). It sounded too simple and a bit coarse. Later

PROF. DR FREUD   April 10th 1921

WIEN, IX., BERGGASSE 19.

Dear Miss Newton

I am glad to hear that you have been greatly benefitted by Psychoanalysis and have kept an interest for our science. Do not neglect to call at me when you are here in May. As regards the possibility of continuing analysis with me I see three points against it. first your not needing it being in excellent health secondly your expecting to be all taken up by your work and thirdly my having all my working-hours engaged just now. I may look forward to your visit every Monday Wednesday friday 3—4th. with kindest regards yours freud

Freud's letter to Caroline Newton. Not published before.

experience taught me that it conveyed everything essential. No man who feels himself under constant close
observation, and knows that his slightest movement will
be utilized as a signal, can give himself over to the "free
gliding attention" (*frei schwebende Aufmerksamkeit*)
which is needed for the assimilation of unconscious
material. (1944, p. 130)

Earlier (p. 101f.), Sachs reports:

Freud had the habit of taking one or another piece of his
collection from its place, and of examining it by sight and
touch while he was talking. He never did this however
when he was listening; then he sat still, his eyes looking
inwards, only now and then he played with his ring.
Neither the expression of his face nor a shift in his
position gave the slightest sign of whether he was pleased
or displeased by what he heard. His later comments left
no doubt how attentively he had listened.

One may wonder whether a man who could listen
like that could not have afforded to expose himself to
constant observation. On reflection, it would seem that
listening like that for eight hours a day would have been
far too exhausting and that listening for the still small
voice of the unconscious called for a different state of
mind. But it was at least equally important that the
patient should not feel stared at all the time.

Freud's therapy was not based on ordinary conversation but on an attempt to get at things that his patients
did not want to know. Even though they came to him and
paid him to get help, they still resisted finding out some
things. He had to create a special situation that would
make it a little easier to overcome this deep-seated
resistance.

It is at least worth asking whether therapists who
have given up the Freudian setting, preferring to con-
verse with their patients face to face, manage to get down
as deep into repressed materials as Freud did. It is

possible, of course, that even if they don't they manage to improve their patients just as much or even more. But it should also be kept in mind that going to a therapist nowadays is a very different and much less frightening experience than it was when Freud developed his new therapy. And there is nobody who deserves more credit for the fact that situations of that kind are much less threatening now than Freud.

At least a few features of Freudian therapy should be mentioned specifically: free associations, the interpretation of dreams, and transference. Dreams have been discussed earlier, and the technique of free associations has been illustrated in the context of the *aliquis* story (in Section 28). Transference is a phenomenon Freud discussed repeatedly at some length. In his introductory lectures he devoted to it the penultimate chapter, and then the final chapter to psychoanalytical therapy. He also dealt with it very charmingly in *The Question of Lay Analysis,* which is cast in the form of a dialogue.

The crux of the phenomenon is that the patient falls in love with the analyst, an event that alarmed Breuer when he was engaged in the first talking cure, and led him to break off the treatment. Freud discovered that the love did not involve any great compliment to the therapist, that it was, as it were, quite undeserved, but that it could become invaluable precisely because patients re-enact long-forgotten and repressed experiences. They reproduce them instead of remembering them. The patients transfer to the analyst emotions originally felt in childhood, usually in relation to one of their parents.

The transference develops in the context of therapy, and Freud discovered how the analyst can use it to advance the therapy. For the sake of the cure, he must never take advantage of the patients' feelings and have an affair, or all but an affair. It is essential, according to Freud, for the therapist to remain reserved. He tried to explain in his books why this was so, but in December

1931 his closest friend among the psychoanalysts, Sandor Ferenczi, wrote him that he had decided to kiss his patients. Freud's reply of December 13 throws a great deal of light on his character. He was by no means the intolerant authoritarian he is so widely thought to have been. Jones has printed the whole letter, which is quite long (II, pp. 163–65). Freud had already heard from a patient what Ferenczi was doing to comfort his patients. Now, he asks, what will you do when giving a full account of your technique and its results?

> Either you relate this or you conceal it. The latter, as you may well think, is dishonorable. What one does in one's technique one has to defend openly. Besides, . . . it will soon get known, just as I knew it before you told me.
> Now I am assuredly not one of those who from prudishness or from consideration of bourgeois convention would condemn little erotic gratifications of this kind.

But where will this end? Every revolutionary is supplanted by one who is more radical,

> and soon we shall have accepted in the technique of analysis the whole repertoire of demiviergeries and petting parties, resulting in an enormous increase of interest in psychoanalysis among both analysts and patients. . . .
> I do not expect to make any impression on you. . . . The need for definite independence seems to me to be stronger in you than you recognize. But at least I have done what I could in my father role. Now you must go on.

It should be noted that the mechanism of transference is not confined to therapy. Emotions are frequently displaced; anger occasioned by one person is vented on another; and love mixed with hostility that was originally felt for a parent is often transferred decades later to a man or woman for whom this specific mix is quite inappropriate. We are much more irrational than most of us suppose.

That large numbers of patients have been helped by Freudian therapy is clear and the suggestion that spontaneous remission might account for most of these cases need not be taken seriously. The question, on the other hand, whether it is really psychoanalytical theory that accounts for the improvement or whether therapists with different theories might not perhaps have done as well is, I think, serious. One may wonder whether the personality and wisdom of the therapist may not be more important than the therapist's theoretical orientation.

With hindsight one is apt to feel that seeing Sigmund Freud several times a week and being able to talk to him about one's troubles, being taken seriously, and having the benefit of his wise and humane responses, must have been an enviable boon. I have never been analyzed and do not feel tempted to go to an analyst, but I am surely not the only one who has felt often: If Sigmund Freud were still alive and willing to take me on, that would be a different matter!

Yet I am inclined to think that Freud's mode of therapy is somewhat dated, rather like great ocean steamers. When I came to the United States from Europe in 1939, when Freud was still living, that was just about the only way one could go. A few decades later only very well-to-do people with lots of time went that way, while everybody else went by plane. And now the great ocean liners that survive are used as cruise ships for the wealthy.

There is a demand now for techniques that take less time and cost less money than Freudian psychoanalysis. Moreover, Freud's new therapy cannot be fully understood apart from his personality and unusual talents.

Freud's therapy was plainly the creation of a man who loved language and was exceptionally sensitive to words, nuances, overtones. He loved to read—and read between the lines. He enjoyed therapy much less than his more creative scientific work, and he enjoyed difficult cases that did not show any quick improvement far more than easy ones that came closer to routine. So he created a form of therapy that was relatively remote from routine and that allowed him to be creative and do what he did exceptionally well: read (if only figuratively speaking), interpret, speculate, try out bold ideas, and attempt to construct a comprehensive theory of the mind.

This becomes more obvious as soon as we contrast Freud with Fritz Perls, the founder of Gestalt therapy. Perls had no great gift for language and could not write well at all. The book presenting the new approach, *Gestalt Therapy* (1951), had to be written largely by Ralph Hefferline and Paul Goodman, while Perls contributed the ideas and the title.[114] Perls's autobiography *In and Out the Garbage Pail* proves his inability to write well to the hilt. His gifts lay elsewhere, and the modifications he made in Freud's therapy were designed to allow him to use his own gifts to the full. In a nutshell, his therapy was less verbal.

Freud's contribution in this area does not stand or fall with the efficiency of orthodox psychoanalysis. Most forms of psychotherapy since Freud have built on his foundations and are profoundly indebted to him, even various forms of group therapy and even *est*, which is not really a form of therapy and more eclectic than most.

31 ▶▶▶ Should one say that *Freud's interpretation of jokes is his eighth major contribution?* It does not seem to me to be on a par with the other nine, but it does not greatly matter whether one ranks it as a major contribution or not. It is certainly worth mentioning, because it helps to indicate the range of Freud's theories. Moreover, the joke book, which is literally full of jokes, is very closely related to *The Interpretation of*

[114] Martin Shepard, *Fritz* (1975, 1976), p. 62.

Dreams. Although it was published only in 1905, the same year as the three essays on sex, five years later than the dream book, "It is nevertheless important to note that the three books just mentioned all belong together," as Jones said.[115] Indeed, Chapter VI bears the title "The Relation of Jokes to Dreams and to the Unconscious," and no halfway careful reader of *The Joke and Its Relation to the Unconscious* can miss the fact that Freud aims to show how the same mechanisms are at work in jokes and dreams. Above all, both involve "condensation." As even Shakespeare's Polonius knew, for all his verbosity, "brevity is the soul of wit,"[116] and Freud goes to considerable lengths to show how jokes depend on condensation as well as the other mechanisms that transform the latent dream thoughts into the manifest dream content. It is important for an evaluation of Freud's theories to see to what extent they are of one piece and support each other.

In this connection a point made briefly by Jones in his summary of the joke book is of special interest:

> As to the *aim* of jokes Freud distinguished between the harmless ones, where only the technique is concerned, and the tendentious ones. If the latter are analyzed it will be found that their main sources are either aggressive or erotic.[117]

This, if true—as it seems to be—would support Freud's later postulation of two basic drives. But it also invites a critical question that I have held back so far. Clearly, the aggressive joke cannot always be reduced to an erotic tendency; but it seems far from impossible to reduce erotic jokes to an aggressive tendency. To pursue this

[115] II, p. 336.
[116] *Hamlet,* II, ii, 90. Freud cites Polonius in the Introduction, *Werke,* VI, p. 10.
[117] II, p. 336.

question in the context of a theory of jokes would be a little frivolous, for the problem of how Nietzsche's theory of the will to power compares with Freud's theories extends far beyond jokes. We shall consider this problem in Section 51 of the next chapter, "Adler's Break with Freud."

32 ▶▶▶ *Freud's interpretations of literature, art, and religion constitute his ninth major contribution.* I think he was right in principle to try to do what he did although his results are often unacceptable and in one especially important case crucially wrong. At the end of the first volume of this trilogy we saw how it was Hegel who

> taught people to see history and art history as well as the history of religion and of philosophy as disciplines through which we can try to discover the human mind or spirit or, in one word, man. (p. 265)

This was a great insight that psychologists ignore at their peril; but most of them do ignore it, and Freud did not.

To understand humanity, including our own minds as well as those of others, it will not do to concentrate largely on rats or laboratory tests; it is important to take into account literature, art, and religion, as well as philosophy, psychology, and the human pursuit of other sciences. It is one of Freud's great merits that he felt this and, like no other psychologist before him, except Nietzsche, who was not a professional psychologist, constantly kept literature, art, and religion in mind.

For all that, his essays "A Childhood Memory of Leonardo" (1910), "The Moses of Michelangelo" (1914), "Dostoevsky and Parricide" (1928), and *The Future of an Illusion* (1927) do not stand up well, and his last book, *Moses and Monotheism* (1939), is, though beautifully written, probably his worst book.[118] What is wrong with these works is not Freud's alleged reductionism. Indeed, he was far from trying to debunk great men, nor did he try to reduce either their greatness or the works he discussed to sexual desires. The essay on Leonardo begins with an attempt to make this clear. The essay on Michelangelo's Moses actually aims to show how the sculptor was even greater than had been realized: His Moses is, according to Freud, "superior to the historical or traditional Moses." Michelangelo

> has reworked the motif of the broken tables of the law, he does not let them break owing to Moses' wrath but lets the threat that they might break assuage his wrath or at least inhibit it before it is translated into action. Thus he has brought into the figure of Moses something new and superhuman, and the powerful mass of his body and the musculature that is swelled with strength merely become a physical means of expression for the supreme psychic achievement that is possible for a human being, for the subduing of one's own passion for the sake of and in obedience to a vocation to which one has dedicated oneself.[119]

Here as elsewhere it is plain how much Freud admired some great men and how little desire he had to drag them down or prove that they were not really great. The Dostoevsky essay, originally published as "an introductory study" in the first German edition of "The Original Form of *The Brothers Karamazov*,"[120] begins:

[118] *Werke*, VIII, pp. 128–211; X, pp. 172–201; XIV, pp. 399–418 and pp. 323–80; and XVI, pp. 103–246.

[119] *Werke*, X, p. 198.

[120] F. M. Dostojewski, *Die Urgestalt der Brüder Karamasoff: Dostojewskis Quellen, Entwürfe und Fragmente*, Erläutert von W. Komarowitsch. Mit einer einleitenden Studie von Professor Dr. Sigm. Freud. Munich, 1928.

F. M. Doſtojewski

Die Urgeſtalt
der Brüder Karamaſoff

Doſtojewskis Quellen, Entwürfe und Fragmente
Erläutert von W. Komarowitſch

*

Mit einer einleitenden Studie von
Profeſſor Dr. Sigm. Freud

R. Piper & Co. Verlag / München

First edition of Freud's essay on Dostoevsky, 1928.

In the rich personality of Dostoevsky one may wish to distinguish four facets: the poet, the neurotic, the ethicist, and the sinner. . . .

The poet is subject to the least doubt; he has his place not far behind Shakespeare. *The Brothers Karamazov* is the most magnificent novel ever written; the episode of the Grand Inquisitor is one of the supreme achievements of world literature and can scarcely be overestimated. Unfortunately, analysis must lay down its arms before the problem of the poet.

What is wrong with these essays is simply that Freud was not well enough informed, and at least some of his speculations are not borne out by the facts. Of course, that may be taken as a warning that his speculative bent was rather powerful, but a critique of these monographs does not prove wrong either psychoanalysis or the desirability of applying hard-won psychological insights to art and literature. But this problem has already been discussed in the second volume of this trilogy (Section 24) in connection with psychohistory.

The Future of an Illusion is unlike the essays on art and literature. Its intent is plainly critical. Freud means to show that religion is "an illusion," meaning that it is born of wishful thinking and that it would be a most remarkable coincidence if it happened to be true. Elsewhere I have argued against the view

that all, or even most, religious beliefs should be prompted by a single psychological motive, as Freud contended in *The Future of an Illusion*. Wishful thinking is indeed characteristic of the diluted religion of William James and many others, but much less so of the religion of Jeremiah or the Buddha. And even the faith of James can be illuminated by the first principle of all genealogy of beliefs, that statements are believed if nothing speaks against them.[121]

[121] *Critique of Religion and Philosophy* (1958, 1979), Section 42.

There is no need here to recapitulate my own theory of seven causes of the acceptance of beliefs and to show how wishful thinking is merely one of them.[122] But one need not swallow the whole of Freud's theory of the origin of religion to see how in *The Future of an Illusion*, too, he added greatly to our understanding of what he discussed. Specifically, he illuminated the role of wishful thinking in religion, and the penultimate paragraph of Section VI is among the most brilliant passages ever written about religion:

> . . . Ignorance is ignorance; no right to believe anything is derived from it. No reasonable person will behave so frivolously in other matters or rest content with such wretched grounds for his opinions . . . Where questions of religion are concerned people are guilty of every possible kind of intellectual misdemeanor and lack of candor. Philosophers stretch the meanings of words until they scarcely retain anything of their original meaning, they call some nebulous abstraction they have created for themselves "God" and can then pose before all the world as deists, as believers in God, and can even boast that they have recognized a higher, purer concept of God, although their God is nothing but an insubstantial shadow and no longer the powerful personality of religious doctrine. Critics insist on calling "deeply religious" those who confess the smallness and powerlessness of man in the face of the universe, although it is not this feeling that constitutes the essence of religiousness but only the next step, the reaction to it which seeks a remedy against this feeling. Those who go no further but humbly resign themselves to the minute role of human beings in the vast world are really irreligious in the truest sense of the word.

Friedrich Schleiermacher's famous definition of a feeling of "absolute dependence" as "the essence of religiousness" has been repeated again and again, and

[122] *Ibid.*, Section 41.

dehnen die Bedeutung von Worten, bis diese kaum etwas von ihrem ursprünglichen Sinn übrig behalten, sie heißen irgendeine verschwommene Abstraktion, die sie sich geschaffen haben »Gott«, und sind nun auch Deisten, Gottesgläubige, vor aller Welt, können sich selbst rühmen, einen höheren, reineren Gottesbegriff erkannt zu haben, obwohl ihr Gott nur mehr ein wesenloser Schatten ist und nicht mehr die machtvolle Persönlichkeit der religiösen Lehre. Kritiker beharren darauf, einen Menschen, der sich zum Gefühl der menschlichen Kleinheit und Ohnmacht vor dem Ganzen der Welt bekannt, für »tief religiös« zu erklären, obwohl nicht dieses Gefühl das Wesen der Religiosität ausmacht, sondern erst der nächste Schritt, die Reaktion darauf, die gegen dies Gefühl eine Abhilfe sucht. Wer nicht weiter geht, wer sich demütig mit der geringfügigen Rolle des Menschen in der großen Welt bescheidet, der ist vielmehr irreligiös im wahrsten Sinne des Wortes.

Es liegt nicht im Plane dieser Untersuchung, zum Wahrheitswert der religiösen Lehren Stellung zu nehmen. Es genügt uns, sie in ihrer psychologischen Natur als Illusionen erkannt zu haben. Aber wir brauchen nicht zu verhehlen, daß diese Aufdeckung auch unsere Einstellung zu der Frage, die vielen als die wichtigste erscheinen muß, mächtig beeinflußt. Wir wissen ungefähr, zu welchen Zeiten die religiösen Lehren geschaffen worden sind und von was für Menschen. Erfahren wir noch, aus

52

Passage from *The Future of an Illusion*, 1927.

nobody has ever criticized it more poignantly. Of course, others had found fault with it in various ways, notably Schleiermacher's contemporary, Hegel, who retorted that in that case dogs would be the best Christians. But Freud's critique is no mere sarcastic jibe against a rival who is widely overestimated; it goes to the heart of an error that is still widely shared. At the same time Freud did not only say tersely what is wrong with ever so many discussions of religion, including the works of many celebrated writers, but he also defined beautifully his own stance.

Freud's other writings on religion include *Moses and Monotheism* and a four-page essay called "A Religious Experience" (1928). About the Moses book it seems best to quote what Freud himself wrote Arnold Zweig, September 30, 1934, before any of it had appeared in print: "My work received the title: The Man Moses, A Historical Novel." The style is remarkable, especially for a man close to eighty, but the content does not enhance Freud's stature. The little essay of 1928, on the other hand, deserves to be better known. It was written in response to a letter Freud had received from an American doctor:

> . . . I answered politely that I was happy to hear that such an experience had made it possible for him to keep his faith. For me God had not done that much, he had never let me hear such an inner voice, and if—considering my age—he should not hurry up, it would not be my fault if I remained until the end what I was now—*an infide jew* [sic, in English].

The colleague's "kind reply" contained the assurance that he was praying to God that he might grant Freud *"faith to believe."* Freud continued: "The success of this intervention is still outstanding. Meanwhile the religious experience of my colleague is food for thought." And he offered a brief analysis.

33 ▶▶▶ I have defended Freud against a number of unfair charges but must now offer a criticism that is crucial for the discovery of the mind. Long ago, in 1958, in my *Critique*, I sought to show in one of the last sections, called "Kant and Freud," how *both* had "inadequate images of man." Kant tried to account for our truths, Freud mainly for our errors. In the following section I argued that Freud, like Kant, had failed to give its due "to that aspiration which is central in art and religion, philosophy and science, and which gained such notable expression in his own work." While I would rather not go over the same ground again, it does not seem right to defend Freud while suppressing an objection that is vital for human self-understanding.

There are passages in which Freud suggested that art is a substitute gratification and science a diversion. At the end of the twenty-third introductory lecture, for example, Freud offered a brief psychology of art. "The artist," he said, "wants to attain honor, power, wealth, and the love of women; but he lacks the means to reach these satisfactions." He therefore turns his back on reality, but in the end the public may derive great pleasure from his fantasies. When that happens, "he has attained by means of his fantasy what initially he had attained only in his fantasy: honor, power, and the love of women."

Not many lectures come to such a striking conclusion, but we should reject the implication that art is a substitute gratification; that what human beings really want is honor, power, and the love of the other sex; and that if only the artist had been able to attain that in the first place he would never have created works of art. Freud leaves out of account the possibility that the creation of works of art may give one a greater sense of power than honor, the power *he* meant, and the love of women ever could.

Freud and His Poetic Science ▶ 159

In *Civilization and Its Discontents* Freud argues similarly that life is too hard for us and that we cannot dispense with "palliatives."

> Perhaps there are three such remedies: powerful diversions that make us esteem our miseries lightly, substitute gratifications that lessen them, and intoxicants that render us insensitive to them. Something or other of that sort is indispensable. . . . Scientific work is also such a diversion. Substitute gratifications, as art offers them, are illusions when compared with reality . . .[123]

Of course, all this is far from being totally mistaken. And it is moving to recall the previously quoted letter in which Freud explained to Lou Andreas-Salomé immediately after finishing this book that it was essentially a diversion.[124] Nevertheless, these passages are seriously misleading. To show this one could hardly do better than to quote Freud himself. On March 6, 1910, he wrote Oskar Pfister:

> I cannot imagine life without work as at all comfortable; giving my imagination free play and working coincide for me; nothing else amuses me.

Long before this correspondence was published in 1963, Jones, who deserves our gratitude for that, too, quoted this beautiful letter; his portrait of Freud took documents like this into account. As often, Freud is hard to translate, and Jones's version sounds a little more heroic than the original and misses the note of self-disparagement: "Creative imagination and work go together with me; I take no delight in anything else."[125] My version is inade-

[123] *Werke*, XIV, p. 432f.
[124] Above, after footnote 56.
[125] II, p. 396f.

quate, too. *"Phantasieren und Arbeiten fällt für mich zusammen, ich amüsiere mich bei nichts anderem."* *Amüsiere* does not sound at all heroic or grandiloquent; but the real trouble is that *phantasieren* means to fantasize, indulge in fancies, rave as in a delirium, as well as improvise or extemporize at the piano.

Jones also quoted what Freud said to Marie Bonaparte in 1925:

> No one writes to achieve fame, which anyhow is a very transitory matter, or the illusion of immortality. Surely we write first of all to satisfy something within ourselves, not for other people.[126]

"No one" may actually be a slight exaggeration. As Jones remarked, Freud was "evidently speaking for himself." But he might well have said, "No genuine writer . . ." And this refutes his theory of art as a "substitute gratification," at least as far as the artist is concerned. The theory has some plausibility regarding those who *enjoy* art, notably many readers of novels—especially novels that have little artistic merit. But it is misleading even regarding people who enjoy *art*.

Freud took insufficient note of the fact that a person enjoying fame, honor, and the love of women (or men) might nevertheless feel bored and desperate. What we seek in artistic and scientific work is not mainly a substitute or distraction but something that fame, honors, and a good sex life cannot give us. Indeed, the hunt for fame and honors, wealth or women (or men) can be, and often is, a quest for narcotics, diversions, or substitute gratifications—and typically fails to provide the satisfaction that was expected. Finding that wealth or sexual conquests are not really satisfying, the disappointed hunter often fails to get the point and seeks more

[126] II, p. 397.

wealth or more conquests, as if quantity might make the difference.

Freud compounds what I take to be his error when he concludes Section IV of *Civilization and Its Discontents:*

> Sometimes one thinks one recognizes that it is not only the pressure of civilizaiton but something in the nature of the sexual function itself that denies us full satisfaction and pushes us on to other paths. It may be an error; it is hard to decide.

If he meant that one can never gain full satisfaction even for a very short span of time, he was plainly wrong. But if he meant that even complete sexual satisfaction does not spell enduring satisfaction and cannot provide us with a sufficient meaning or content for our lives, the two sentences just quoted amount to an incredible understatement, and his attempts to support them in a long footnote are utterly beside the point. He offers three possible explanations:

> . . . [1] if we take it to be a fact that people want to satisfy male as well as female wishes in their sexual life, then we are prepared for the possibility that these demands are not satisfied by the same subject and that they interfere with each other . . . [2] Another difficulty arises from the fact that erotic relationships do not only have a sadistic component that is characteristic of them but are also frequently accompanied by a direct inclination to aggression. The object of our love will not always meet these complications with as much understanding and tolerance as the peasant woman did who complained that her husband did not love her any more because for a whole week now he had not beaten her.
>
> [3] Still greater depths, however, are reached by the surmise . . . that . . . the sexual function is accompanied by a reluctance . . . that prevents full satisfaction and pushes us away from the sexual goal to sublimation and shifts of libido. . . . The fact that *"Inter urinas et faeces*

nascimur" is offensive to all neurotics and many others besides. The genitals also produce strong sensations of smell that are intolerable for many human beings and spoil sexual intercourse for them.

In a much earlier paper (1912) Freud had used the same Latin quotation ("we are born between urine and feces") and introduced yet another oddly irrelevant explanation:

> I believe that, strange as it may sound, one has to consider the possibility that something in the very nature of the sex drive does not favor the attainment of full satisfaction. In the long and difficult history of the development of this drive one immediately notices two factors that one could hold responsible for this difficulty. In the first place, owing to . . . the barrier against incest, the final object of the sex drive is never the original one but only a surrogate for it. Psychoanalysis, however, has taught us: when the original object of a wish has been lost owing to repression, it is frequently supplanted by an unending series of substitute objects of which none satisfies fully.[127]

A page later Freud concludes that "the inability of the sex drive to give full satisfaction" has been

> the source of the most magnificent cultural achievements that are brought about by the ever advancing sublimation of its instinctual component. For what motive would human beings have to divert the energy of sexual drives to other uses if any distribution of these had resulted in full satisfaction of the lust?

It seems to me that Freud misses the obvious point that while the sex drive, no less than hunger, *can* attain complete satisfaction, this satisfaction is not enduring in either case. Soon the appetite awakens again, and satisfying it again and again does not satisfy all our other

[127] *Werke,* VIII, p. 89f.

appetites and aspirations and certainly cannot give sufficient content and meaning to our lives. It may be an illusion to suppose that anything can provide enduring satisfaction, but the attraction of art and religion, science and philosophy is inseparable from this hope, and that is true not only of creative artists, scientists, and philosophers but also of the far more numerous people who love art, science, or philosophy more passively.

Freud's speculations about the incest barrier seem to me to be as wide of the mark as his appeal to the Latin quotation. Ever since the days of the pharaohs of Egypt many men have cohabited with their sisters and some with their mothers, and there is no reason whatever to believe that they found the kind of complete satisfaction that is denied to the rest of us, and that they had less need for cultural achievements. Actually, Freud himself knew better and said only two pages earlier, in his essay of 1912:

> But unrestricted sexual freedom from the beginning does not lead to any better result. It is easy to show that the psychic value of the need for love goes down at once as soon as its satisfaction is made easy. It requires an obstacle to drive the libido up to a high point, and where the natural obstacles to satisfaction are not sufficient, men have at all times interposed conventional ones to be able to enjoy love.

That is to say that sexual satisfaction is not really purely sexual but depends on the sense of power that we feel when overcoming obstacles!

In the sex act both man and woman can attain a superlative sense of power—not mainly power over someone else but a vivid feeling of triumph over obstacles and limitations and a sense of intense well-being and fulfillment, of being, as it were, superior to the world and "in heaven"—but it does not last. It may well extend beyond the orgasm, but hardly by more than a few hours, if that.

Because this experience can be so satisfying and beautiful people are often willing to sacrifice a great deal for it. Hence all societies have tried to regulate sexual relations to keep them from tearing the society apart. But making rules and regulations also gives people a sense of power and tends to become a game that is played for the satisfaction it gives. Those who make rules make more rules than are needed for whatever purposes they may avow; and "as a rule" they curtail freedom beyond need and sense.

Unfortunately, there is abundant evidence that human beings have experienced ecstasies also when making others suffer. Here a frightening economy comes into play. The torture of a few or even of a single human being can provide intense delight for a large audience. All societies have also made rules to keep aggression within bounds and to direct it mainly toward the outside and some specified groups inside the society. These rules, too, are not distinguished by surpassing rationality. While regulations of sexual conduct are easy to fault for what they forbid, rules concerning cruelty are no less easy to fault for what they permit.

In society, then, neither sex nor aggression is allowed free play, and much of the frustration that goes with living in a society is due to this fact. But there is no alternative to living in a society; the human child would not survive left to its own devices, and we are, for better or for worse, social animals. Nevertheless, not all of our frustration is due to the excessive regulation of sex and aggression. Indeed, if aggression were curtailed still less, we would suffer still more. And those who manage to have a satisfying sex life do not necessarily live full and satisfying lives. We can even allow for the point that a satisfying sex life may involve some obstacles; that is not the point. What matters is, to put the matter crudely, that

Goethe, Kant, and Hegel, as well as Nietzsche and Freud could never have been content to spend most of their lives in bed, having sex, no matter who their partners might have been.

Of course, the men mentioned were exceptional in many ways, but in this respect they were not altogether unlike other human beings, who after all form a continuum. Art is no more a substitute gratification than sex or hunger. In fact, "it is only in some works of art that ecstasy endures."[128]

34 ▶▶▶ Any such list of ten major contributions as I have attempted to construct here is, of course, to be taken with a grain of salt. The contributions are bound to overlap, and it would not be difficult to cover much the same material either under fewer headings or under still more. It does not follow that this list is pointless. Not only does it facilitate discussion, it also places the discussion on a different plane. My approach to Freud is less abstract, conceptual, and remote from real life than much of the debate about him has been. I have placed him in an altogether different historical context and have concentrated on the advances he made in the understanding of men, women, and children, instead of getting hung up on "the unconscious" and "resistance," the ego and the superego, and other concepts that he used as tools. Still, one point remains.

Freud's personality may be seen as his final contribution. He was one of the most remarkable human beings of all time. The fact that he himself was far from sharing this opinion does not refute it, any more than Einstein's modesty and unpretentiousness disprove the

[128] Kaufmann, *From Shakespeare to Existentialism*, p. 261 (the conclusion of "Art, Tradition, and Truth").

same claim about him. On the contrary, the world is full of more or less mediocre people who think they are great or who have a great need for others to think of them as great; and Freud's wish that people should pay more attention to psychoanalysis and less to him is far from diminishing his stature.

It may well be felt that even if Freud was a great man in some sense, it does not follow that this constitutes a contribution to the discovery of the mind. But I believe that we learn about man and humanity very largely from examples—from exemplary human beings. Some of these never lived but are found in myths, in art, and in literature. The ceiling of the Sistine Chapel changes one's sense of what it might mean to be human. Some of Michelangelo's sculptures have a similar effect. So do the works of Rembrandt and of Vincent van Gogh, and Goethe's *Faust,* as well as Goethe himself.

In *What Is Man?* I have dealt with this problem at some length and devoted one chapter ("Ecce Homo") to "paradigmatic individuals." Now it seems appropriate to add that Freud was a paradigmatic individual who, as one gets to know him, enlarges one's sense of humanity. Actually, this theme has been present throughout this treatment of Freud and his poetic science. Freud constantly drew on his self-observation in his books, and I have also drawn on his letters, on Jones's *Life,* and on the recollections of Sachs, Binswanger, and Weiss.

If man is his deeds, and the mind, too, is what it does, then we know the human mind through the works of individual human beings. But some cases are more instructive than others, and few are as instructive as that of Freud.[129]

If that should sound just a little vague, it may be well to consider one of Freud's very greatest contributions

---

[129] See *ibid.,* Chapter 16, "Freud," and "Freud and the Tragic Virtues," in Kaufmann, *The Faith of a Heretic* (1961).

under this heading. He emancipated not only the mentally ill but all of us by restoring to us an innocence that we had lost thousands of years ago. Nietzsche blamed Christianity for this loss, but it may well go back much further—perhaps even to the origins of civilization. If that should be so, then Freud did not restore our innocence, he gave humanity something that it had never had.

He took away the sense of guilt that poisoned not only sexuality but also many other wishes. We owe it to Freud that we can recognize our hatred or resentment of our parents, siblings, and others whom we feel we ought to love. He taught us to see that while we love them we also feel hostility toward them, that this is normal, and that nothing is gained by denying it or hiding the facts from ourselves. On the contrary, much is lost when we are not honest with ourselves.

He remarked occasionally how important it was to be honest with oneself, but what changed the whole climate in which we live was Freud's example. He was a new Adam, and through his transformation we were transformed. In the end we are brought back once more to Freud's style. The *way* he discussed sexual and hostile wishes was no less important than the content. His totally unsensational and nonlascivious manner, his ability to speak quite naturally of what was natural instead of raising his voice or making us feel that it was, after all, deliciously naughty, ushered in a new era. In fact, the change he brought about was so great that one may ask whether it invalidates some of his findings. Could it be that some of them apply only to the *old* Adam?

In one way, this manner of speaking about Freud is misleading. I do not mean to suggest that he was a messiah or a religious figure. Indeed, one of the central points that I am trying to establish is that his mentality was more scientific than religious and more skeptical than dogmatic. Those who see him as a dogmatist have generally cited his alleged excommunication of Adler and Jung. Before turning to that it may be well to deal very briefly with Otto Rank's break with Freud. This case is pretty clear, and the letters quoted by Rank's disciple and biographer Jessie Taft speak for themselves. There is no need here to invoke Freud's disciple and biographer Ernest Jones. The record rounds out the picture given here of Freud's personality.

Taft introduces Freud's letter to Rank of August 25, 1924: "It would be hard to resist a letter so full of kindness and warm concern. One wonders if Rank would have been able to send his letter . . . if he had waited long enough to receive" it (p. 104). Rank, born in 1884, had come to Freud in 1906, and Freud had got him to finish secondary school and helped him to attend the University of Vienna and to get a Ph.D. Of all the disciples Freud ever had, none was more like a son. In 1923 Rank had given him the completed manuscript of *The Trauma of Birth,* with a dedication to Freud, for his birthday. The same year it became apparent that Freud had cancer, and Edoardo Weiss, among others, had the distinct impression that Rank began to grieve for Freud prematurely, and that his feelings changed when Freud continued to live (p. 31). By August 1924 Rank had ceased to be warm and friendly. It should suffice to quote two sentences from Freud's letter to Rank:

> The difference of opinion concerning *The Trauma of Birth* carries no weight with me. Either, in the run of time—if there is enough time left—you will convince and correct me or you will correct yourself and separate the lasting new gains from what the bias of the discoverer has added.[129]

---

[129] This letter appears also in *Briefe,* and Taft's translation is excellent. I have not seen the original German text of the second letter.

Of Rank's letter, which crossed Freud's in the mail, Taft says: "It was like a blow in the face from a supposedly loyal friend and adherent." Yet Freud did not strike back in his reply of August 27. The most interesting sentences are found in the middle of this long letter:

> Your experiences are different; do they therefore cancel mine? We both know that experiences permit of many different explanations; hence we have to wait for further experience.
>
> . . . I was not and I am not in agreement with Ferenczi's statements on homosexuality and with many points of his active therapy. In my opinion he puts a too great store on complete agreement with me; I do not. Suppose you had told me one day that you could not believe in the primordial horde and the primordial father, or thought the separation into ego and id to be inexpedient, do you really believe that I would not have invited you for meals or would have excluded you from my circle? . . . You seem shattered and offended that I refuse your *Trauma of Birth*, though you have my admission that it is never easy for me to follow a new train of thought that somehow does not go my way or to which my way has not yet led me.

There is no need here to go into the details of Freud's comments on Rank's book or of his response to Rank's letter. Near the end Freud said: "My feelings toward you have not been shaken by anything."

Rank really was deeply offended that Freud could not fully agree with his *Trauma of Birth*, yet within a few years Rank himself abandoned much of it. Exactly the same had happened earlier with Adler and Jung. Yet Freud is often criticized for not having been sufficiently receptive to ideas that the men who proposed them actually did not maintain for any length of time. In all three cases, the book was clearly a declaration of independence, and the independence mattered more to the author than the soundness of the ideas. Rank's *Trauma of*

The "Committee": Rank, Freud, Abraham, Eitingon, Ferenczi, Jones, and Sachs, in 1922.

Birth, Adler's *Nervous Character,* and Jung's *Transformations and Symbols of Libido* were meant to be provocative rather than tenable, and once the split with Freud was accomplished, the authors did not choose to stand by these books. In their eagerness to fault Freud, his critics have overlooked this. Jung did not even include *Transformations and Symbols of Libido* in his *Collected Works;* he included instead an extensively revised version with a different title, done forty years later!

In December 1924, after some sessions with Freud, Rank wrote a letter to the other members of the "Committee," apologized, and explained that he had been traumatized by Freud's "dangerous illness." He had been very close to Freud and had also depended heavily on patients referred to him by Freud, yet he also had expected Freud to die and found it difficult to adjust to his survival, the more so because he had thought that he would become Freud's successor. Soon after making his peace with Freud and his circle, he emigrated to the United States and broke with Freud for good. He was then forty.

The idea that Rank was mentally unbalanced has been ascribed to Jones but was accepted by Rank himself, and not only in a letter to the "Committee." Taft remarks that "from the time of the *Daybooks* [his journals, which antedate his acquaintance with Freud], Rank as in this letter has always understood his own manic-depressive swings" (p. 113). What is most moving is that, having learned that Freud had finally died on September 23, 1939, aged eighty-three, Rank, who had married for the second time in August, died October 31, 1939, in New York. Yet our concern here is not with Rank but with Freud's personality. It remains to be seen whether his attitude was essentially different and more dogmatic in the cases of Adler and Jung.

PART ▶

Adler's
Break with Freud ▶▶▶

35 ▶▶▶ Here are two riddles. When Freud died, *The Times of London* said: "Some of his terms have become part of everyday language, the inferiority complex, for example." When Jung died more than twenty years later, *The New York Times* misspelled his first name but more than made up for that by giving *him* credit in its headline for having coined "Inferiority Complex."[1] Actually, neither of them had coined that term, nor had Adler, but the concept was one of Adler's central contributions to psychology. Why is Adler not known better?

If Adler was unsuccessful in some ways, why is it that he was so successful in having large numbers of people accept *his* image of Freud as an intolerant dogmatist and reductionist? When one inquires why so many people feel so sure that Freud was that kind of a man, one finds that their view is based on Freud's alleged excommunication of Adler and Jung. Ironically, Adler

[1] London, September 25, 1939, and New York, June 7, 1961. See Ellenberger (1970), p. 645.

Adler in 1930.

did not claim to have been excommunicated. He insisted both that he had never been a disciple and that he himself decided to break with Freud, and not the other way around. Nevertheless, although Freud is incomparably better known, Adler bruised his heel.

Actually, the misleading picture of Freud is due to Jung much more than Adler, but Jung's break with Freud was by no means independent of Adler's. In Deuteronomy at least two witnesses were required in a capital case, and when it came to Freud's reputation there were two physicians who testified against him. Of course, very few people have bothered to examine their testimony, and hardly anyone has taken the trouble to determine whether their accusations were at least internally consistent. But reputations are fragile and easily damaged.

This study of "Adler's break with Freud" is meant not only to solve the two riddles mentioned but also to extend our study of Freud and to show how Freud actually behaved in this matter. Above all, we must ask whether his attitude was not unscientific after all insofar as he tried to immunize his theories against criticism by discounting Adler's and Jung's objections as due to "resistance."

The question why Adler is not known better requires some consideration of the kind of man he was as well as some consideration of his main ideas. Once again, the relation of the man's conception of the mind to his own mind will be of special interest to us.

On the face of it, Adler refurbished Nietzsche's theory of the will to power; and while Freud initially rejected Adler's version of that theory, he later went "beyond the pleasure principle" and allowed for aggression as a basic drive. A study of Freud versus Adler also requires some discussion of Freud's attitude toward Nietzsche.

Finally, seeing that Adler was born and raised in a suburb of Vienna, while Freud did not move to Vienna until he was four, we shall also ask whether there is any merit in the popular notion that it is somehow very significant that Freud was Viennese. Was he really more typically Viennese than Adler?

36 ▶▶▶ It seems best to begin with *Alfred Adler: A Biography,* which appeared in 1939, two years after his death. He had asked Phyllis Bottome (1884–1963), a minor novelist, to write "the story of his life in conjunction with himself" (p. vii). This in itself is interesting. Freud wrote Fritz Wittels, "the uninvited biographer," that he felt "the public has no claim to my person and also cannot learn from it as long as my case— for ever so many reasons—cannot be made fully transparent" (see Section 10 above). That was in 1923. Toward the end of his life, on May 31, 1936, he dissuaded one of the best-known German-speaking novelists, Arnold Zweig, from writing his biography:

> You, who have so many more beautiful and important things to do, being able to install kings and survey the violent follies of humanity from a superior vantage point! No, I love you far too much to permit such a thing. Whoever becomes a biographer takes on the obligation to lie, to cover up, to be hypocritical, to whitewash, and even to conceal his lack of understanding; for biographical truth cannot be had, and if one did have it one could not use it.
> Truth is not viable, human beings do not deserve it . . .

Adler felt differently; he wanted a biography (because he wanted to be considered a great man?) and agreed to collaborate on it.

Next, it is interesting that he gave up Judaism and had himself baptized, although he did not believe in

Christianity. Bottome does not mention the date; she even forgets to tell us when Adler was born. He was born in 1870 and baptized in 1904[2]—not "early in life," as Bottome says (p. 4), but at the age of thirty-four, while he was a member of Freud's circle. Freud, of course, did not believe in the Jewish religion, either, but never considered a step like that. In the same autobiographical sketch in which he paid tribute to the influence of the essay "Nature" he dealt with this matter in the very next sentences:

> The university, which I entered in 1873, first confronted me with a few palpable disappointments. Above all I was struck by the notion that I should feel inferior and not as a member of the *Volk* because I was a Jew. The former idea I rejected with a will. I have never comprehended why I should feel ashamed of my descent or, as one was beginning to say, my race. The membership in the folk community that was denied me I forwent without much regret. I thought that for an eager fellow worker it must be possible to find a small place within the frame of humanity even without such enrollment. But one consequence of these first impressions at the university that turned out to be important later on was that I became familiar so early with the lot of standing in the opposition and being banished by the "compact majority." Thus a certain independence of judgment was prepared.

The "compact majority" is a concept found in Ibsen's *An Enemy of the People—Volksfeind* in German.

Adler did not feel the same way. He was not at all openly cynical about his baptism, as Heine had been. Adler "became a Christian of the Protestant persuasion, feeling a spiritual danger from the isolation inherent in Orthodox Jewish faith" (p. 4). Other Jews gave up orthodox Judaism without converting to the Protestant persuasion, but even if Adler's rationalization is implausi-

[2] Ellenberger, p. 595.

ble he made it plain that he was afraid of the spiritual danger of isolation, and he was willing to take heroic—most Jews would have said unheroic—measures to meet it.

A page later we learn that

he felt himself put in the shade [we shall have to recall this image] by a model eldest brother . . . who always seemed to Alfred to be soaring far beyond him in a sphere to which he—for all his efforts—could never attain. Even at the end of his life he had not got wholly over this feeling.

Bottome tactfully fails to mention the brother's name, or perhaps Adler did not tell her that his name was Sigmund.[3]

Adler's father was very aggressive:

When he saw people with their legs crossed in a tram, he would push one foot down with his walking stick, saying politely, with a charming smile: "I do not like to clean my trousers on your shoes as I pass!" (p. 8)

The story is less interesting than the face Adler put on it when he related it to his biographer. It does not seem to have struck him or her that the use of the cane was neither polite nor charming. It should be added that Adler felt very close to his father, while his relationship to his mother was not good.

Is it legitimate to use Adler's biography in this way? A page later, Bottome says: "The following are Alfred's earliest recollections told in his own words: they were written for the guidance of his future biographer . . ." (p. 9). And in his own account he says:

Those who are familiar with my life work, Individual Psychology, will clearly see the accord existing between

[3] Ellenberger mentions the name without noting its significance. Eissler (1971) called attention to it (p. 371). His critique of Ellenberger in Appendix D is very powerful.

the facts of my childhood and the views I expressed in my studies of Organ Inferiority . . . . The similarity between my experiences and the basic views of I.P. is not without interest, when one considers the time I devoted in later years to:

Inferiority Feeling; as the motivating power of the striving for achievement. . . . (p. 10f.)

Above all we should know that as a child he had rickets and "suffered from spasm of the glottis." Here I am quoting from *Alfred Adler: The Man and His Work* by Hertha Orgler, who was for many years his close friend and coworker and whom he himself called the "standard-bearer of Individual Psychology."

When he cried or screamed he was in danger of suffocation. These attacks frightened him so badly that at the age of three he decided that he would not cry and scream again, and very soon after he got out of these attacks. . . . When he was three years old his younger brother died in a bed next to him . . . A year later he himself got pneumonia and was seriously ill. It was this illness which aroused in him the desire to become a physician. . . . Nothing could change this decision. Some time later . . . he already showed his remarkable faculty for drawing conclusions. (p. 16)

Before we take leave of Hertha Orgler, it should also be noted that, according to her, Adler's

personality emanated a quieting magic, and one felt his inner warmth and interest so strongly that there was immediate contact between him and the patient. He was even able to quiet raving maniacs and to cure them.

In addition to all his work, Adler always had time for social gatherings. . . . He was especially careful in helping his mother to cross the street. (p. 20)

Of course, not everybody saw him quite this way. Dr. Alphonse Maeder, a Swiss analyst and associate of

Jung, wrote Ellenberger about how he met Adler in March 1910 in Nuremberg:

> After I had read my report, Adler came to me and holding each button of my waistcoat, one after the other, started to explain his ideas to me. He wanted to win me for his theories. . . . There was something unpleasant in his manners . . . . (p. 591)

There is independent evidence that Maeder did not care for Viennese Jews, as we shall see when considering Jung's break with Freud. But Ernest Jones, who was far from being anti-Semitic, also failed to sense Adler's "quieting magic":

> My own impression of Adler was that of a morose and cantankerous person, whose behavior oscillated between contentiousness and sulkiness. He was evidently very ambitious and constantly quarreling with the others over points of priority in his ideas. When I met him many years later, however, I observed a certain benignity of which there had been little sign in his earlier years. Freud apparently had thought rather highly of him in the earlier years; he was certainly the most forceful member of the little group. Freud thought well of his book on defective organs and also considered he had made some good observations in the study of character formation.[4]

Study of Organ Inferiority appeared in Vienna in 1907 and in English translation in New York ten years later. It was a short book of less than one hundred pages. The idea that weak spots in the human system are more likely to suffer complications during a general infection was not new, but Adler suggested that diseases for which we find no cause may be caused by organ inferiority. Sometimes it takes a microscope to discover such inferi-

---

[4] Jones, II, p. 130f. See also his *Free Associations* (1959), p. 217f. Here Jones says that "in his successful period" Adler seemed "milder and mellowed, though more self-complacent."

ority, at other times there may be functional defects. Probably the most interesting point in the book was the suggestion that such inferiority may become a source of strength through "compensation." Even that idea was not altogether new. Ralph Waldo Emerson had devoted one of his best essays to "Compensation." Adler's point is much the same and also somewhat inspirational: Some people who either had eye disorders or came from families in which there were eye disorders became painters!

Although this was the only relatively major work Adler published before his break with Freud in 1911, it was not his first book. In 1898 he had published a monograph of 31 pages, *Health Book for the Tailor Trade*. It is very scarce and virtually unknown, but Ellenberger summarizes it neatly (p. 599f.). It manifests the social concern that remained one of Adler's central characteristics.

Adler was not much of a writer. In fact, most of his books were not actually written by him. His *Problems of Neurosis*, for example, was "edited by Philip Mairet"; and near the end of the Introduction we are told:

> The present volume is taken from lectures Adler had given in English. In 1928 Mairet was handed a sheaf of notes and reports of these lectures with the view of editing them into a book. Mairet was well qualified to do this. He was a journalist interested in philosophy and psychology . . .[5]

In his Introduction in the 1969 edition of Adler's *The Science of Living*, Ansbacher says (p. xiv):

> While his complete bibliography is very extensive, most of his books are based on lecture notes often edited by someone else. Furthermore, these notes are from series of

[5] Heinz L. Ansbacher, probably the most devoted and prolific of all of Adler's editors, on p. xxiii of the Torchbook Edition (1964).

lectures addressed to different audiences and cover essentially the same ground, so that there is considerable overlapping between the books.

The Nervous Character, which appeared in German in 1912, immediately after the break with Freud, is an exception. It was written by Adler himself, was his first book-length study, and was quite possibly his *magnum opus.* Yet it, too, shows that he was not much of a writer. Bottome has an explanation or two that may well go back to Adler himself:

> . . .writing bored him, and he often deliberately fogged his meaning (for no one could be clearer when he wished to be), in order not to be pinned down to a slogan or to limit the future growth of his subject. (p. 58)

One wonders whether Bottome could have felt free to attribute these ideas to her hero if he had not said something like this to her. But if he did, it would seem to bear out her suggestion that "Adler did not know himself as well as he knew others" (p. 41).

I have argued throughout this trilogy that fogging one's meaning and refusing to be pinned down do *not* contribute to the growth of the subject but help to account for the wretched state of the humanities in general and the philosophy of mind in particular. Moreover, Adler seems to have loved slogans, and Bottome herself tells us how in 1913 "he and his group made their final definition of the twelve chief tenets of Individual Psychology" (p. 103); and it takes her exactly two pages to state all of them. But before considering his ideas in 1913 we must return to *The Nervous Character,* which was published a year earlier.

> Adler's friend, Professor Z., says of it: "It is probably the most creative work of psychiatry in existence; but, until it is rewritten, perhaps in the form of a novel, very few people will understand it." . . .

When Adler wrote *The Nervous Character* he was laboring under two great disabilities. He was too poor to give himself the needed time to get his thoughts clear and in the right sequence (his servant, Sophie, describes how he often wrote far into the night); and he was himself living from day to day this Laocoön struggle with his own wife. (p. 98f.)

Apparently not all the "fogging" was deliberate; poor Adler wrote his *magnum opus* before having got his thoughts clear. Except for Bottome's odd metaphor, there is no evidence that Mrs. Adler was a snake, but it seems that Adler wanted the world to know that his ideas about "masculine protest" and the desire to "be on top" were nourished by his own struggles. He thought that "the accord existing between the facts of my childhood [and we may now add his married life as well] and the views I expressed" would be seen as supporting his views. Most readers may feel, on the contrary, that the connection is only too transparent and rather embarrassing because Adler assumed too readily that everybody was like himself. When we are told on top of that that "Alder did not know himself" very well—and this judgment seems to be supported by Adler's biography again and again—our confidence is diminished further. It seems at least possible that Adler was satisfied with surface explanations, if only because he did not have the needed time for deeper insights.

Specifically, he felt that his views about women were very emancipated, and he married a very intellectual woman of Russian birth. But his marriage turned into a prolonged struggle about who was "on top." He attributed his problems to everybody. Freud might have asked instead whether his inability to get along with his wife might be related to his prior relationship to his mother.

If Adler's capacity for rationalization exceeded his clarity, he nevertheless had unique gifts, according to

Bottome. Above all, "his memory was flawless" (p. 59) and "infallible" (p. 3); or so he thought. That, of course, would be a great boon for a psychologist and psychotherapist and relevant also to Adler's recollections of his break with Freud. Yet Bottome relates that "the Oedipus Complex was—as Adler was fond of relating—Jung's contribution, and received by Freud at first with marked distaste" (p. 64). Bottome even goes on to quote her master's exact words. Yet the Oedipus complex is found in Freud's letter to Fliess, October 15, 1897, and in *The Interpretation of Dreams* (1900), long before Freud even knew of Jung's existence. Nor did Jung ever claim to have discovered it.

Now one might think of saying in defense of Adler that Freud had not actually used the word "complex" and that others had said before Adler that this term went back to Jung or at least the Swiss. There are only two things wrong with this excuse. In the first place, it is not true. To be sure, Freud himself said very generously when he lectured at Clark University in 1909 that it was useful "to call a group of ideas that are invested with emotion and belong together a '*complex*,' following the example of the *Zurich* school (Bleuler, Jung, and others)."[6] But as a matter of fact, both Freud and Josef Breuer had used this term in 1895 and Jung only in 1904.[7] And to credit Jung with the discovery of the *Oedipus* complex shows an amazing lack of understanding of Jung as well as Freud.

The second thing that is wrong with this defense of Adler is more revealing because it explains Alder's mistake. Adler, though widely credited with the discovery of the inferiority complex, had initially resisted this

[6] *Werke*, VIII, p. 30.
[7] Freud, *Werke*, I, p. 122; Breuer later in the same work, *Studien-über Hysterie* (1977 ed.), p. 186. The whole problem is discussed at length in *The Standard Edition*, IX, p. 100f.

coinage—some say "because of its definitely Freudian ring"—but eventually "had to bow to the power of this word," in 1925.[8]

The mechanism at work in this mis-memory has been described by Freud and, as Freud himself acknowledged, also much earlier by Nietzsche. Memory is self-serving and often bows to pride or self-esteem.[9]

The same mechanism was obviously at work in another slip of Adler's memory for which we are indebted to another biographer, Manes Sperber. Adler had an elaborately detailed recollection of his self-healing when he was only six years old. On his way to school he had to pass a cemetery that filled him with anxiety. He got rid of his anxiety by forcing himself to climb over the wall a few times. Yet eventually he found out that, in fact, there had never been any cemetery on his way to school, and "that his heroic deed had in fact been mere fantasy." Eissler's comment is worth quoting:

> Suddenly, I understood the psychological root of many parts of his theory—for example, the assertion that mental and nervous diseases are "arrangements," as well as the frequent use of the word "tricks" in reference to symptoms and the general distrust of the patient's own words that is characteristic of Adler's approach. Indeed, the role that Vaihinger's philosophy of *as if* and of "fiction" plays in his sytem becomes psychologically far more understandable from Adler's own childhood recollection than it does from the observation of neurotic patients.[10]

---

[8] *The Individual Psychology of Alfred Adler: A Systematic Presentation in Selections from his Writings,* edited and annotated by H. L. and R. R. Ansbacher (1956, 1964), p. 256. See also the *Minutes* of February 1, 1911, in which Adler opposes "the adoption of the concept of the complex."

[9] See the beginning of Section 14 in the second volume of this trilogy.

[10] Eissler (1971), p. 373f., and Sperber (1970), p. 33f. (p. 14f. of the English version from which I quote).

Whether Adler's conceit that he was a great *Menschenkenner*, a wonderful judge of men, was really justified it may be impossible to decide at this distance. Again the contrast with Freud is interesting, for Freud and his most devoted followers, including Jones and Sachs, agreed that Freud was not much of a *Menschenkenner*. They seem to have had in mind what they saw as his long misjudgment of Adler and Jung. We shall come to that in due time, but perhaps Adler and Jung really were his most interesting associates; and after them Otto Rank and Sandor Ferenczi. Perhaps his judgment really was not that bad. Sachs and Jones, always loyal, had no comparable originality, but after Freud's death Ernest Jones wrote one of the finest biographies of all time. When one compares it with the work of Bottome, whom Adler wished to "write the story of his life in conjunction with himself," or Hertha Orgler, whom he called the "standard-bearer of Individual Psychology," one wonders about Adler's judgment of people. But it is, of course, entirely possible that they produced precisely what he wanted. Plainly, he did not consider Bottome's ignorance of philosophy, literature, and the whole intellectual climate from which Adler came a serious impediment.

Her only reference to Adler's relationship to Nietzsche is as incredible as the following:

> Adler's special contribution—Individual Psychology—was a "social training" and at the same time a literary movement. Men of all schools and parties were drawn to it for different reasons. The Socialists were attracted by a science that they could connect with Marxist theories. Adler's phrase: "Out of organic weakness of constitution springs the truth!" they took as direct support for Karl Marx's "The Truth is an economic factor." Hofmannsthal, Wassermann, Schnitzler, Auerheimer [sic], [Raoul Auernheimer], and Peter Altenberg, the poet, one of Adler's most intimate friends [I don't know if he was that,

but he was known not as a poet but as the author of short prose sketches]—the leaders of Viennese intellectual thought at this period—all joined the psychoanalytic circle [is that a Freudian slip? did they really prefer psychoanalysis to individual psychology?] and made their different contributions toward its theories.

If this could be taken seriously, it would be nice to know something about these contributions, but it is on a level with the immediately preceding claim that "Freud, Adler, and Stekel developed in the Caféhaus" (p. 62f.) and the statement about Adler and Nietzsche: "It was Nietzsche's solemn goal that he defended: 'Liberty is the freedom to do right' " (p. 200).

One cannot escape the dilemma: Either Adler was a very poor judge of people and at the very least his judgment was easily clouded by flattery, or he cared far more about some other things than he did about the truth. Of course, both of these alternatives could be true.

In fact, we cannot begin to understand Adler as long as we assume that his primary concern was with the truth, like Freud's or Nietzsche's. The epigraph of Manes Sperber's previously cited book on Adler reads: "There is no absolute truth, but what comes closest to it is the human community. ALFRED ADLER." This may be one of those cases where Adler "deliberately fogged his meaning," or where he lacked "the needed time to get his thoughts clear," but there is abundant evidence suggesting that he cared much more for "the human community" than he did for truth. I should like to distinguish three dimensions of this claim.

First, there is his baptism. Adler was evidently motivated by a desire for "human community." Sperber's immense admiration for Adler kept him from ever bringing up this subject in his many conversations with Adler. He himself was "a confirmed atheist," and

[l]ike every Jew of my persuasion, I had no objection to a genuine conversion—that is, a conversion prompted by belief; but I was inclined to detest those who became Christians out of opportunism. (p. 30f.)

He hesitates to call Adler an opportunist but was always "convinced that Adler was far and away the most radical atheist I have ever met."

Second, Adler had a strong messianic streak. Sperber feels that even Bottome, in her biography, does not fully succeed in giving the reader any adequate "sense of Adler's ceaseless activity" and adds that it simply cannot be done.

Adler always behaved as though it were up to him, and him alone, to spread his theories, which he saw as tidings that human beings needed more than their daily bread. He was surrounded by many faithful disciples and eager followers, but he wanted to bear the whole burden alone. (p. 224)

Ellenberger, too, relates that Adler "proclaimed that the most pressing need of mankind was the reform and spreading of education under the viewpoints of individual psychology" (p. 589). And: "With an almost messianic attitude, Adler expected his movement to conquer and transform the world through education, teaching, and psychotherapy" (p. 596).

Finally, Adler evidently had greater talents as an educator and psychotherapist than he did as a writer or thinker—or truthseeker. We do not really do Adler any service by fudging this distinction, which Ellenberger, for example, does not seem to grasp clearly enough when he says:

This kind of pragmatic psychology . . . does not pretend to go into matters very deeply, but to provide principles and methods that enable one to acquire a practical knowledge of oneself and of others. (p. 608)

Eissler comments on this passage that Adler should have informed Freud of all this "from the start."

> I can hardly think of anything that is less 'practical' . . . than psychoanalysis. If Ellenberger is right, then Adler really did not have any legitimate place as a member of the [Vienna Psychoanalytic] Society of which he was President [at Freud's suggestion]. After all, if someone's goal is to write a cookbook, he will remain forever an outsider in the company of chemists. (p. 368)

But it seems obvious that Alder was far from understanding all this "from the start," and that it never did become entirely clear to him. Talk of "practical knowledge" only compounds the confusion. If Adler did not know himself, Bottome, or Orgler very well, than we should not credit him with "practical knowledge" of himself and others. But we should leave open the question whether profound knowledge of oneself and others has enormous "practical" value and is a prerequisite for a good educator or psychotherapist.

Freud was far more interested in truth than in therapy, and he was far too disillusioned to entertain messianic hopes. In 1895 he concluded *Studies of Hysteria* by relating that he had often told his patients that their afflictions were probably related to their personal situations, which it was beyond his power to change.

> I do not doubt that it would be easier for fate than for me to clear away your affliction; but you will discover that much is gained if we succeed in transforming your hysterical misery into ordinary misfortune. Against the latter you will be able to put up a much better fight once your psychic life has got well again.

To return to Adler, Bottome compares him to "a revivalist preacher" and says, "those who knew Adler best . . . were well aware that when he said: 'What the world needs is this or that,' he would be prepared to give it to them" (p. 113). Nevertheless, the break between Adler and Freud has been adduced often to prove that *Freud's* attitude was not really scientific!

To determine whether it was or not, we must now consider the break. In a way, what requires explanation is that Freud and Adler could have been as close as they were for ten years and not that eventually they parted ways. Still, it is of some interest how precisely it came to the break.

37 ▶▶▶ It is a common mistake to suppose that when two outstanding individuals part ways it must be on account of some specific intellectual disagreement. When Adler and Jung decided to go their own ways, their reasons were not mainly intellectual, any more than Nietzsche's break with Wagner was due mainly to his dislike of *Parsifal*. In all these cases we must ask how compatible, or rather incompatible, the protagonists really were, and how it came about that they managed to travel on the same path for a few years. To understand their characters is to see that the break was inevitable.

Bottome says that Adler was impressed "when the famous book on 'Dream Analysis' was published" and "exclaimed with great earnestness" to a Viennese professor: "This man has something to say to us!" She claims further that the *Neue Freie Presse* published an article ridiculing the book, and that Adler then published "a strongly written defense" in the same newspaper (p. 56). Jones reported that "it has proved impossible, even after a thorough search" to find either the review or a reply by Adler in the *Neue Fremie Presse* (II, p. 8). Anyway, in the fall of 1902 Freud invited Adler, Wilhelm Stekel, whom he had analyzed, Max Kahane, and Rudolf Reitler, whom Jones calls "the first person to practice psychoanalysis after Freud," to "meet for discussion of his work at his residence." The suggestion may have come from Stekel. These five men then began to meet for discussion every Wednesday evening in Freud's waiting room, and they spoke of their "Psychological Wednesday Society." Jones, on whom I have relied here, also tells us that at the beginning of 1908 the society had twenty-two members, but that usually no more than eight or ten attended each meeting. The minutes of the meetings, generally recorded by Otto Rank, have been published in four volumes, first in English, and more recently also in the original German; they cover the period from October 10, 1906, to November 19, 1918, and are of interest because they summarize not only the remarks of the main speaker of the evening but also those of every participant in the discussions, including, of course, Adler as well as Freud.

Until 1908 all who attended had to participate in the discussions. In 1908 the Vienna Psychoanalytic Society was formed, and the meetings became a function of that society. In 1910 the International Psychoanalytical Association was founded, and Freud insisted that Jung should be its president. He was keen on its being truly international and not merely or even mainly a group of Viennese Jews. Adler and Stekel resented the appointment and felt slighted. Freud then retired from the presidency of the Vienna Society and asked Adler to replace him; and seeing that he had made Jung editor of the *Jahrbuch für Psychoanalytische und Psychopathologische Forschungen*, he agreed that a new monthly journal should be founded, the *Zentralblatt für Psychoanalyse*, to be edited jointly by Adler and Stekel. Five months later, however, Adler withdrew.

All of this leaves open the question what Freud and Adler had in common. Ellenberger says that Adler's favorite authors included Homer, Shakespeare, Goethe, Schiller, Heine, Nestroy, and Dostoevsky; also that he loved Vischer's novel, *Auch Einer*. If so, the two men shared at least some tastes. But on the same page (593) he also refers to Adler's "great talent for music" and interest in concerts—Freud was quite unmusical—and says: "Later, in his lonely years in New York, his only pastime was the frequenting of movie theaters." Clearly, the differences far outweighed any similarities.

The plain fact is that they never had much in common and never were close friends, but they did meet every Wednesday evening with a few others and discussed psychological problems that were of interest to them and that were quite different from the problems discussed by the establishment in those days. Among those who participated in these discussions, Adler was the most interesting and original, if we do not count Freud.

They were all outsiders who found some comfort in not being totally alone and isolated. They were able to talk with each other and usually had some common ground even when they disagreed. Nor was Adler blind at that time to Freud's merits. Freud's letter to Ferenczi, who practiced psychoanalysis in Budapest and was close to Freud's heart, makes clear what he felt on April 3, 1910:

> . . . I shall give up the leadership of the Vienna group . . . I will transfer the leadership to Adler, not because I like to do so or feel satisfied, but because after all he is the only personality there and because possibly in that position he will feel an obligation to defend our common ground. I have already told him of this and will inform the others next Wednesday. . . . I prefer to go before I need, but voluntarily. The leaders will all be of the same age and rank; they can then develop freely and come to terms with one another.
> Scientifically I shall certainly cooperate until my last breath, but I . . . can enjoy my *otium cum dignitate*. . . .
> The personal relationships among the Zurich people are much more satisfactory than they are in Vienna, where

one often has to ask what has become of the ennobling influence of psychoanalysis on its followers.[11]

Ludwig Binswanger's recollection of his first visit with Freud in Vienna is also relevant. He recalls attending a session with Freud's "adherents in his house—not more than six or seven." The minutes record that when he and Jung visited the meeting on March 6, 1907, Freud, Adler, Stekel, Rank, and eight other regular members were present. When the meeting was over, Freud said to Binswanger: "Well, have you seen these gangsters now?" *So, haben Sie jetzt diese Bande gesehen?* (p. 13). Earlier during the same visit, Binswanger had been distressed how Breuer had dismissed Freud with a "pitying-superior mien" and a gesture that "did not permit the least doubt that he was convinced that Freud had gone so far astray scientifically that one could no longer take him seriously and it was better not to speak of him." Until then Binswanger had not realized how radical the rejection of Freud and his ideas was, and then Freud's remark showed him "how lonely Freud still felt" and, of course, also "how sharp his judgments could be."

38 ▶▶▶ The simplest version of the break is to be found in Bottome. Adler had profited from his association with Freud.

> Owing to the fact that Freud had no time to handle all his patients, Adler in particular, who was acknowledged as the ablest physician of the group, took over more and more of Freud's cases. . . .
> Such opportunities as these, to a young man with his way to make in the world, were not to be lightly set aside; nor can the only bond between Adler and Freud have been an interested one. (p. 64)

[11] Jones, II, p. 71. The Latin phrase means "leisure with dignity."

Yet there was a fly in the ointment. Freud, to be sure, did not want the break, we are told a page later.

> . . . Freud begged Adler to reconsider their parting. "Why should I always do my work under your shadow?" Adler demanded. Those who reproach Adler, as if this were the petulant cry of an ambitious student, should remember that Adler was now in his late thirties [actually, he had turned forty in February and may well have felt: If not now, when?], a man of approved genius whose book, already published, *Organ Inferiority and Its Psychical Compensation,* ranked with Freud's "Dream Analysis."

Bottome never fails to be amusing, and we cannot lay at Adler's door such phrases as "approved genius" or "already published," or the fact that she italicized the title of Adler's book while placing Freud's, in an eccentric and inexact translation, in quotation marks. But seeing that *The Interpretation of Dreams* had appeared in English in 1913, and the third edition had appeared in 1932, it seems likely that Bottome had never seen it and that the ranking goes back to Adler.

Certainly, the immediately following sentences go back to Adler and give us his version of the break:

> Adler frequently explained in after-life that these words: "Why should I always do my work under your shadow?" were greatly misinterpreted by the psychoanalysts.
> What Adler really meant, and feared, was to be made responsible for the Freudian theories in which he more and more disbelieved [similar considerations, however, had not kept him from becoming a Protestant and never led him to leave the church], while his own work was either misinterpreted by Freud and his followers or pushed to one side. With every year that Adler worked with Freud his doubts grew stronger, until he came to believe that the whole process of psychoanalysis was inimical to the welfare of mankind [stirrings of his messianic mission]. This was the "shadow" under which

he would not work because he dared not to be made responsible for what he feared might be the results of Freud's thoughts upon mankind. Who shall say that he was mistaken while we are watching today the effects of a freed "libido" upon the civilized world?

It was Freud who pleaded for Adler's continuing with him, but it was Adler who had to make the greater sacrifice in order to leave him.

The sacrifice is not explained but may refer back to the loss of the patients Freud had sent him. One gathers that in his later years Adler came to see Freud as a threat to humanity, and others have reported that he said worse things about Freud. But what is scarcely credible is that anyone who had been associated with Freud for several years and who considered himself a greater psychologist than Freud should have really tried to explain "under your shadow" in this fashion. Nevertheless, this explanation, which Adler offered "frequently," according to Bottome, is also to be found in his own works, in a footnote in the fourth German edition of *The Nervous Character* (1928, p. 24). Here he protests against misinterpretations of

> my mild rejection, 'it was no pleasure to stand in his shadow'—that is, to be made an accomplice to all the absurdities of Freudianism, because I was a co-worker in the psychology of the neuroses.

If he ever gave a similar explanation of his admission that he "felt himself put in the shade by a model eldest brother" whose name was Sigmund and "who always seemed to Alfred to be soaring far beyond him in a sphere to which he—for all his efforts—could never attain," Bottome does not record it, although she herself adds: "Even at the end of his life he had not got wholly over this feeling" (p. 5).

In 1912 the first edition of *The Nervous Character*

appeared in German, full of attempts to explain not only neurosis but much of human conduct in terms of "feelings of inferiority," "masculine protest," the contrast of being "above" and "below" or "over" and "under" (*"Oben-Unten"*), "enhancement of one's personality by devaluing others," and "wanting to be the first." One of the oddities of the book that seems to have escaped even those who mention how poorly it is written and how unclear the thoughts are is the extraordinary number of words, page after page, that are emphasized in print, often for no apparent reason. They give the visual impression of someone constantly raising his voice and trying to overpower the reader.

When Adler left Freud he founded a group of his own that he called "Society for Free Psychoanalytic Research," a name that also appeared immediately, in 1912, on the title pages of a new series of monographs. This was unquestionably an attempt to take psychoanalysis away from its founder and to put Freud down. It did not endear Adler to Freud or, for that matter, to others, and Adler soon dropped this odious name and eventually called his approach or movement "Individual Psychology."

Those who find it amusing that Freud should have excommunicated Adler should take into account not only Adler's insistence that he left although Freud asked him to stay but also Adler's dogged insistence that he had never at any time been a disciple or follower of Freud's. When Abraham Maslow implied in a conversation with Adler in a New York restaurant, "a year or two" before Adler's death, that he *had* been, Adler "became very angry, flushed and talked loudly enough that other people's attention was attracted. He said that this was a lie and a swindle for which he blamed Freud entirely," and he called Freud a swindler and a schemer.[12] Around the same time, also a year or two before he died, Adler, in a conversation with Emmanuel Miller, a psychiatrist, "referred to Freud's psychoanalysis as that 'filth,' 'fecal matter.'"[13]

It would seem that Adler's attitude was not entirely scientific. Indeed, it was indistinguishable from the attitude of the medical establishment toward Freud at the time when Adler broke with him. Nor were these the words of embittered old age. Adler died in 1937, aged sixty-seven, and some of his admirers have actually suggested that if only he had lived longer he might well have become as successful as Freud, who died in his eighties. In any case, he had expressed himself in a similarly resentful way from the start, even before Freud stated his version of the schism in print in 1914.[14]

On July 5, 1914, Lou Andreas-Salomé wrote Freud that opposition to his ideas had to be understood in terms of "resistance" and enclosed a letter Adler had written her on August 16, 1913, which is printed under that date in her 1912–1913 diary (1958).[15] The letter shows how personal his attacks were even then.

> Do not think that a critical attitude makes me lose my composure. . . .
> My attitude toward the Freud school has, unfortunately, never had to take into account its scientific arguments. I always see only, and [so do] all my friends, busy snatching and pilfering [*Haschen und Mausen*] and all the scholar's shabby machinations [*Gelehrtenlumpereien*]
> . . .
> For me all this is proof that the Freud school does not believe at all in its own theses, rather wants only to save its investments. . . .

[12] Maslow, "Was Adler a Disciple of Freud?" in *Journal of Individual Psychology* (1962). The editor, H. L. Ansbacher, appended an article with the same title to this one-page "Note" and also concluded that the answer was no.
[13] Roazen (1975), p. 210.
[14] *Werke*, X, pp. 91ff. *The History of the Psychoanalytic Movement* was printed in March 1914.
[15] Her letter was prompted by her reading of Freud's *History*.

A word about Freud's "discovering" and "digging."
Every one of my patients makes similar discoveries. This
is not meant to be a devaluation. It merely points to the
"tricks." Freud has accepted his trick as real. This is what
is decisive. And now he is compelled to resort to further
tricks to cover his deficit. One question: Do you think
that people like us, if we had journals at our disposal,
would practice, and practice with such élan, the trick of
maintaining dead silence, of identification, and others?
My views may be false! But must they also be stolen on
that account?

Adler evidently felt enraged by Freud's dignified
silence; he was being ignored and felt put down. And he
had a great fear that others might steal his ideas. This is
understandable enough in people who are unable to
write, but was surely quite irrational in Adler's case,
considering that he did publish his own ideas, even if he
did not write particularly well.

Bottome relates how Adler, apparently after the First
World War, "felt that medical men . . . wanted to run
away with Adler's ideas," and she relates how on one
occasion when two doctors "came into the room to join a
discussion circle" he exclaimed: "Here enter the Plagia-
rists!" (p. 117).

According to the *Minutes of the Vienna Psychoanalytic Society*, Adler was not the only member of that
group who was concerned about plagiarism. The fre-
quency with which some of these men claimed priority
regarding ideas and worried about having their ideas
stolen is distressing, though perhaps understandable in
meetings that were designed to allow the participants to
try out bold ideas before committing them to print. On
February 5, 1908, Adler presented three motions to
reorganize the meetings, and Paul Federn added a
fourth: "The abolition of 'intellectual communism.' No
idea may be used without the authorization of its author.
Otherwise one would feel inhibited in free discussion."

Eduard Hitschmann added a fifth: "Personal invectives and attacks should immediately be suppressed by the chairman who should be given the authority to do this." One recalls Freud's comment to Binswanger about "these gangsters" as well as his letter to Ferenczi. But he kept silent for a long time during the discussion, as he usually did. Finally he spoke to oppose the fifth motion:

> *ad* 5. He is opposed. He finds it painful to reprimand anyone. If the situation is such that the gentlemen cannot stand each other and no one expresses his true scientific opinions, etc., then he has no choice but to give up the meetings. He had hoped—and is still hoping—that a deeper psychological understanding would overcome the difficulties in personal relations. He would make use of the authority offered to him only when people were disturbing the speaker by their conversation.
>
> He hoped for a certain degree of seriousness and candor and thanked the two sponsors of the motions for their frank approach to these painful topics. . . .
>
> However, the discussion concerning "intellectual communism" should be continued now . . .
>
> His own position on this question was precisely what it had always been. In his opinion, nothing essential should be changed here. . . . Besides, each person might say himself how he wanted his ideas to be treated. He personally waived all rights to any of his own remarks.[16]

Freud's attitude had always been clear. Honesty was all-important to him; psychoanalysis was an attempt to give honesty a new dimension; and Freud was exceptionally scrupulous in his efforts to give credit to his predecessors. The entire first chapter of his dream book, 65 pages in the original edition and 99 in the last edition in the *Werke,* was given over to discussion of the literature; and throughout his works one finds references to

[16] Cf. Freud's letter to Weiss, July 7, 1935.

the most unlikely forerunners, including a great many whom he had never read when he first published his ideas. He was also generous to a fault in adding mischievements discussed by others to later editions of *The Psychopathology of Everyday Life,* giving them credit. As noted earlier, he made "the Zurich school" a present of the term "complex" which, in fact, he himself had used earlier in the apposite sense. And in the Bibliography at the end of the first edition of *The Interpretation of Dreams* he listed 78 titles, not including anything by himself, and in a postscript called attention to a book published in 1898 which had come to his attention only as he was reading proofs but which announced a forthcoming book that was to deal with dreams.

By way of contrast, it is interesting to note that Adler's *The Nervous Character* has a bibliography entitled "Writings of the Author Quoted Above." Although he had published only one short book, less than a hundred pages long, which is cited constantly, he managed to list thirteen items.

Rather oddly, Paul Roazen, in *Freud and His Followers* (1975), kept claiming that Freud was perennially concerned about plagiarism but managed to ignore the fact that Adler was. He also kept referring to Nietzsche's anticipations of Freud but never once mentioned Nietzsche in connection with Adler, which is doubly odd seeing that Roazen's central chapter on Adler is called "The Will to Power."

Freud was sorry to have missed out on the discovery of the anesthetic properties of cocaine. This would have earned him a place in the history of "hard" science. But after his self-analysis and, more importantly, after the publication of *The Interpretation of Dreams,* he was no longer greatly concerned about priorities, especially in psychoanalysis, where his place was secure; and he was never paranoiac about plagiarism. He had accomplished something that was, as he saw it, more than commensurate with his limited abilities, and he was, in Hölderlin's words, "satisfied though my lyre will not accompany me down there." He had found peace.

Adler's paranoiac streak was not confined to fear that his ideas might be or actually had been stolen. "After Berlin had granted him the freedom of its city"—an honor Freud, whose ideas were offensive, was not offered—"he was made an honorary citizen of Vienna." But the mayor called him, according to Bottome (p. 102), "a pupil of Freud's. Adler flushed deeply at the mayor's ignorant blunder" and made a sarcastic reply. "The mayor, who was an ignorant fellow, remained quite unconscious of his blunder." But Adler was convinced that "an enemy out of the group he had left told the mayor beforehand that if he really wanted to please Adler, he should tell him that this honor was given him as a recognition of his merit as a pupil of Freud's."

This "cruel sting to his pride" is introduced by Bottome with the statement:

> Throughout his whole career, Adler received blow after blow from man or fate; he was far too sensitive a human being not to have smarted under each in turn. But, smart as he might, no blow that ever struck him could daunt him.

And more in the same vein. Others might say: The name of this game is "victim."

Ellenberger manages to be briefer than Bottome:

> The rejection of his application for Privat Dozent was a lifelong wound, as later was the Columbia University incident, and the blunder of the Mayor of Vienna (p. 593).

The University of Vienna would not appoint him a lecturer (*Privatdozent*) on the basis of *The Nervous Character*. This was one of the three great blows, though Bottome says:

Later, when the University of Berlin had given Adler an honorary degree [again, Freud's ideas were too offensive] and America had established a Chair of Medical Psychology for him in the Long Island College of Medicine [by special act of Congress? to console him for the failure of Columbia University to give him the position he coveted?] would have been glad of the slightest excuse to reconsider its former verdict; but when Adler was indirectly approached . . . he would not hear of it. (p. 101)

It does not matter greatly how much of this is true; the picture of Adler's character that emerges from various sources seems consistent. Incidentally: "In 1924 he was appointed a professor at the Pedagogical Institute of the City of Vienna, and his courses were attended by many teachers."[17] But while Freud was slowly dying of cancer and underwent thirty-three operations over a period of sixteen years without complaining, Adler felt that *he* was suffering blow after blow.

39 ▶▶▶ Since the issue has generated so much heat, it may be well to deal explicitly with the question of whether Adler ever was a pupil or disciple of Freud's. This can be done very briefly because Ansbacher's "Was Adler a Disciple of Freud?" in *Journal of Individual Psychology* in 1962 is scrupulously fair and detailed. Adler evidently gave different and conflicting accounts of how he came to the defense of Freud before Freud invited him and three others to join him once a week for discussion; and all of these accounts seem to be false. We cannot go back that far. But in an article in 1908 Adler said that he "could confirm Freud's view of the dream in all points." And!

[17] Ellenberger, p. 589.

The debt to Freud is acknowledged in most forceful words by Erwin Wexberg, who after the First World War was possibly Adler's most able coworker, and editor of a handbook on Individual Psychology. In his book on Individual Psychology, the most important textbook at the time, Wexberg even described Adler as "one of the oldest pupils and associates of Freud" . . . (p. 132)

That was as late as 1928 and makes one wonder whether the mayor of Vienna was really such "an ignorant fellow."

What Ansbacher did not know in 1962, and what makes Adler's reaction to the mayor's "ignorant blunder" even more irrational is how Adler had worded his resignation from the Psychoanalytic Society. When Freud wrote Jung about this, on June 15, 1911, he quoted Adler's letter: "Since I have no desire to carry on such a personal fight with my former teacher, I herewith tender my resignation."

In a way it is amazing that Adler should have forgotten so completely how he had thought of himself as Freud's pupil. But then one recalls Nietzsche's formulation of the theory of repression in *Beyond Good and Evil* (Section 68):

"I have done that," says my memory. "I could not have done that," says my pride and remains inexorable. Finally, my memory yields.

While experimental psychologists have had trouble confirming this theory, Adler did his best to illustrate it.

His overreaction to the "ignorant blunder" shows how strong his desire "to be the first" was, but it also shows that he had never learned from Nietzsche that resentment is a poison. The letter of resignation, of course, does not stand alone. On January 4, 1911, he addressed the Vienna Psychoanalytic Society, having announced as his topic "Controversial Problems in Psychoanalysis." He wished to spell out some of his new ideas. The *Minutes* say:

> The speaker stresses first that the ground for the examination of all these problems . . . was prepared by Freud's work, which was what made it possible even to discuss them.

At the end of the discussion of his paper he said that he "never wanted to dispute the fact that the germ of his views is to be found in Freud's teachings . . ."

At that time he was president of the Vienna Psychoanalytic Society, though it must have greatly hurt his ego that the members had not taken enthusiastically to Freud's suggestion and had urged Freud to stay on as leader of the group (April 6, 1910). In the discussion on January 4, 1911, Freud remained silent. But after Adler's second paper on his new ideas, which dealt with the crucial role of "masculine protest" in neurosis, Freud spelled out in detail how Adler's ideas seemed to him to differ radically from psychoanalysis. When the discussion was continued on February 8, Freud held his peace, but in the final discussion of the paper on "masculine protest," February 22, Freud completed his criticism. In his response Adler said that "his writings had been perceived by Freud and some colleagues as constituting a provocation; but they would not have been possible if Freud had not been his teacher."

In view of the fact that Freud and many others felt that he had departed from psychoanalysis, with its emphasis on the unconscious, and stressed "ego psychology" exclusively, Adler came to feel in the course of that meeting, as they apparently did, that his position as president of the society was untenable.

> At the following committee meeting, Adler resigns his position as chairman of the society because of the incompatibility of his scientific attitude with his position in the society . . .

On March 1, with Adler still attending, Freud was elected chairman by acclamation. But as late as May 24, 1911,

> DR. ADLER, having learned that at the preceding meeting [which he had missed] remarks were made that took up the point about his views once again, refers to the statement issued by the plenary session, which declares that the scientific viewpoint he represents is not in any way in contradiction to the findings of other authors, especially those of Freud. In referring to this resolution of the plenary session, he declares himself to be fully satisfied with that understanding.

He still participated at length in the discussion that evening, the last before the summer break, but at the next meeting, which was a special plenary session held on October 11, 1911, Freud announced that "since the last meeting of the society, the following members have resigned: Dr. Adler" and four others.

Other business followed, including Stekel's announcement of a trial paper "to be given by Ph.D. candidate Theodor Reik in November." Reik later wrote many books and made a name for himself.

Meanwhile Adler had founded a "Society for Free Psychoanalytic Research." The name clearly implied, as did that of the "Free University" founded in West Berlin in the 1950s, that the old institution was unfree. But some members of Adler's group still attended Freud's meeting. Freud asked them to decide within a week which group they wished to belong to. He and the board felt that one could not belong to both groups. C. Furtmüller argued against this view, but eventually a resolution was passed, by eleven votes to five, and six members resigned from Freud's group.

It is arguable that Adler, hardly less than his followers, would have liked to stay with Freud, and that it was Freud who precipitated the break. But it is as plain

Schriften des Vereins für freie psychoanalytische Forschung.
No. 1.

Psychoanalyse

und

Ethik

Eine vorläufige Untersuchung

Von

Dr. Carl Furtmüller

München 1912
Verlag von Ernst Reinhardt

Title page of Furtmüller's *Psychoanalysis and Ethics*, 1912.

as can be that any such view of the matter was totally incompatible with Adler's pride. Intent on being "the first," he also wished to be considered the one who had initiated the break. Of course, in such a complex interplay of personalities it is impossible to draw a sharp line.

Clearly, Adler was not satisfied to be nothing more than a follower. He did want to initiate something new. The remark about standing in Freud's shadow is significant, and a lot of other evidence shows this, too. But he would have settled for being Freud's successor. When Jung was appointed president of the International Psychoanalytic Association, this was a severe blow to Adler. When he was made president of the Vienna Society, he would have liked to be president not only in name. He would have liked to revolutionize the subject. But Freud and his more devoted followers found fault with Adler's ideas. Some ideas did not seem to them to be new but seemed only to amount to no more than new names for ideas long developed by Freud; many more seemed—though Freud put the matter more politely and took pains to be respectful toward Adler as a person—shallow and confused.

Under these circumstances Adler could not very well remain president of the society. He could have continued as a member, had he been willing to make plain where he agreed and where he disagreed. I shall have to return to this point later. But this was clearly unacceptable to him. He wanted to "be first." And since he could not be first in Freud's group he founded his own.

In sum, any notion that Adler was excommunicated by Freud is as absurd as the charge that he was an apostate. Ernst Federn's contributions to the discussion "Was Adler a Disciple of Freud?" comes as a shock:

According to a personal communication by Dr. Ludwig Jekels to me about the split between Adler and Freud, a last effort was made towards reconciliation, and Paul Federn, Eduard Hitschmann, and Jekels met Adler in a coffee house. My father cut the negotiations quite short by opening the talks with saying: "Adler, admit you are a Judas." Since my father did not deny the story it may well be correct.

Ernst Federn felt that this showed how the other members of the society did consider Adler a disciple even if Adler did not share this view. I feel that this story helps to explain Freud's exasperation with "these gangsters." It is doubly remarkable that Adler stuck with them as long as he did. It remains to be shown why Freud did.

Perhaps I should say expressly that, of course, I do not hold it against Adler that he left the society, or that he developed views very different from Freud's. For all my obvious admiration for Freud, I realize how difficult it must have been for men who were not born followers to develop fully and freely in his shadow or, if you prefer, in the immediate vicinity of so much brilliance joined with such consuming honesty. "Against great superiority of another human being nothing avails but love." (*Gegen grosse Vorzüge eines anderen gibt es kein Mittel als die Liebe.*) It may be easier to love a man like Freud from a distance or after his death than it was living in the same city, trying to develop different ideas in the same field, and testing them in weekly meetings with him and his disciples. In any case, it would be absurd to fault Adler for not having loved Freud.

Still, a glaring lack of self-knowledge coupled with frequent self-serving rationalization, and self-pity fused with blinding resentment raise questions about a man's conceit that he is the greatest living psychologist. The more one learns about Adler as a man, the better one understands why he is not known better.

Ironically, if one could believe Adler's insistence that he left Freud because he became convinced "that the whole process of psychoanalysis was inimical to the welfare of mankind," it would become difficult to solve our second riddle: Why do so many people see Freud as an intolerant dogmatist? As we have seen, Adler's version of the break is utterly misleading, but it remains to be shown whether a fuller study of the dispute might justify the verdict that concludes Heinrich Heine's long poem "Disputation":

> *Who is right, I do not know,*
> *But I am inclined to think*
> *That the rabbi and the monk,*
> *Yes, that both opponents stink.*[18]

40 ▶▶▶ The widely held view that Freud was an intolerant dogmatist owes a great deal to one author who has written three popular books on Freud that have been widely read and reviewed and even translated into other languages. Some of my most esteemed friends felt sure that they knew a number of things about Freud that actually were false, because they had read one of Paul Roazen's books; hence it seems necessary here to deal with him briefly before we proceed to a number of further problems.

Roazen's extreme bias against Freud has already

---

[18] This is one of the very rare cases where a translation of a great poet is better than the original. This is not because the translation is especially brilliant, which it is not, but because Heine, to set up the splendid last line, wrote a dreadful second line. English versions of Freud, including the quotations in the present volume, are, I think, never as good as the original German.

> Welcher Recht hat, weiss ich nicht—
> Doch es will mich schier bedünken,
> Dass der Rabbi und der Mönch,
> Dass sie alle Beide stinken.

been illustrated in connection with plagiarism.[19] I shall ignore his first book on Freud (1968) and be brief about the second (1969), which deals with Freud and Tausk and prompted Eissler to publish a volume of more than four hundred pages (1971) just to show how irresponsibly Roazen had defamed Freud. Although Eissler's book appeared in paperback, it was more than twice as long as the study it attacked as well as much more scholarly, and it never reached the same audience. My scholarly friends who were taken in by Roazen were not even aware of Eissler's *Talent and Genius: The Fictitious Case of Tausk contra Freud.*

It would be impossible to summarize Eissler's critique briefly or to unravel the complexities of the Tausk affair. But I should like to make three simple points of my own. First, Victor Tausk attended two Wednesday evening meetings in October 1909 before he was proposed as a member of the society on October 27. Even when still a guest, however, he intervened in the discussion to set Adler straight about "the problem of knowledge." On November 3 he became a member, and on November 24 he presented his first paper, entitled "Theory of Knowledge and Psychoanalysis." His paper ranged over the whole history of philosophy, from the Greeks to Spinoza and Hume, Kant and Schopenhauer, and was immensely ambitious. But he said more than once that Plato was Aristotle's immediate successor. In the discussion three

[19] Above, between footnotes 16 and 17. In Roazen (1969) one whole chapter is entitled "Plagiarism." Here the author finds one incident "in which Freud forgot one of his sources . . . a paper by Weiss" (p. 88). A footnote to a footnote, in the back of the book, gives an interview with Weiss as evidence; but when Eissler asked Weiss which paper it was, Weiss denied ever having said anything of the kind (1971, p. 182).

It seems to me that Roazen's concern with plagiarism is as excessive as Adler's was. He says: "The whole issue of plagiarism bothers all who write" (1969, p. 78). In all my life I have known only one professor, a logician, who was bothered by it; he was afraid that others might steal his ideas, and that was partly because he could not write.

people spoke, Adler at considerable length, before Freud began his remarks by saying that he "would like in the first place to correct a historical error. Plato is not a successor of Aristotle; he was the older man, and a student of Socrates." His comments were kindly and encouraging and ended with some constructive suggestions.

Here is what Roazen says about this incident (Eissler did not comment on this episode):

> Freud has sensed Tausk's latent rivalry for years. In the very first paper that Tausk presented to the Vienna Society, he referred to Plato and Aristotle, mistakenly making the latter into the former's master. Freud picked it up immediately: "Plato is not a successor of Aristotle; he was the older man, and a student of Socrates." The nucleus of rebellion lay there all along: Tausk began his relationship with Freud in competition and rivalry. (p. 111)

One gets the impression that Tausk was guilty of a mere slip of the tongue, and that Freud pounced on him immediately. In fact, one of the most striking points about Tausk, which one would never gather from Roazen's account, was the enormous gap between his ambitions and his ability.

Weiss recalls how Tausk, who was his friend,

> imitated Freud's haircut exactly. In a series of introductory lectures I heard him repeat almost literally the lectures Freud had given at the psychiatric clinic. I gained the impression that Tausk wanted to replace Freud and wished to be himself the founder of psychoanalysis . . . . (p. 24)

Lou Andreas-Salomé knew Tausk even better and had an affair with him for a while. Two entries in her

---

Adler found it difficult to write. Roazen is prolific, but his concern is plainly due to the fact that his books depend so heavily on what others have told him.

diary show the kind of deep psychological understanding of both Tausk and Freud that Roazen lacks entirely.[20] Most of the members of Freud's circle, including not only the Viennese but also Jung and most of the others, had never known a very great man until they met Freud. She had had an intense encounter with Nietzsche in 1882 and a long love affair with Rainer Maria Rilke; and then she had had more casual affairs with a large number of famous writers—perhaps to some extent surrogates for Nietzsche, who, her claims to the contrary notwithstanding, had not proposed marriage to her. It is remarkable that after she met Freud she considered him to be in a class by himself. In the journal entry entitled "Victor Tausk" she said:

> . . . Only now does Tausk's relationship to Freud appear to me in its full tragic dimension: for I understand that he will *always* get involved in the same problems and the same attempts at solutions on which Freud happens to be working—that this is no accident but the "making oneself a *son*" that is just as violent as the "hating the father for it." As if by telepathy, he will always occupy himself with what occupies Freud; he will never take the single step to one side that would give him space. This *seemed* to be due to the circumstances, but ultimately it is due to him.

The whole entry is full of deep sympathy and ends: "Brother animal, you." Roazen made *Brother Animal* the title of his book, but did not share these insights. He identified with Tausk, without fully understanding how much Tausk loved Freud.

Roazen feels that Freud insulted Tausk by refusing to analyze him and by letting Helene Deutsch analyze him. But enough has been said already to show why

---

[20] February 12/13, 1913 (p. 97f.) and "Victor Tausk," around September 1, 1913 (pp. 186–89, especially p. 188) = pp. 97f. and 165–68, especially 166, in the English version.

Freud could not analyze Tausk. For good measure one might add that Tausk was constantly worried that his ideas might appear in Freud's work before he could work them out, and that Freud as a matter of policy refused to analyze the members of the society with whom he met for discussion one evening a week.

Roazen tries hard to show that Freud was partly responsible for Tausk's eventual suicide. Yet he prints Tausk's "suicide note," that is, a letter to Freud dated July 3, 1919. There is agreement that he had deep psychological problems; but the suicide was clearly overdetermined, and it would serve no purpose here to try to unravel the various motives. He asked Freud to help his beloved fiancée and continued:

> I thank you for all the good which you have done me. It was much and has given meaning to the last ten years of my life. Your work is genuine and great; I shall take leave of this life knowing that I was one of those who witnessed the triumph of one of the greatest ideas of mankind.
>
> I have no melancholy, my suicide is the healthiest, most decent deed of my unsuccessful life. I have no accusations against anyone, my heart is without resentment, I am only dying somewhat earlier than I would have died naturally.
>
> I greet the Psychoanalytic Association, I wish it well with all my heart. . . .
>
> Please, also look after my sons from time to time. (p. 127f.)

When Freud informed Lou Andreas-Salomé of Tausk's suicide, he modestly failed to quote this note at length, but he was totally free of the usual kind of hypocrisy in the face of death and expressed his feelings with total honesty. Roazen finds Freud's letter "shocking" but fails to note that the recipient, who had loved Tausk, took no offense at all and responded in the same way; indeed she confessed that she felt very much as he did.[21]

In Roazen's eyes, Freud cannot do right.

> Marius [Tausk's son] cannot remember now how it was that his father's letter to Freud was returned. He visited the Freud apartment again, and he thinks Anna Freud gave him back the precious note, along with some other correspondence of his father's. It might seem odd of Freud to give Marius his father's letters. What was the boy to do with them? Freud was not helping Marius in any way. But he was finishing getting rid of Victor Tausk. Yet Marius did not perceive any of this as inappropriate. Paradoxically, he treasured the suicide note for almost fifty years as a sign of his father's good relations with Freud. (p. 127)

It would seem, on Roazen's own evidence, that what Freud did was not at all inappropriate. But, as in the case of plagiarism, Roazen is simply unable to recognize negative evidence.

Nineteen years later, in 1938, Marius was well-to-do and paid back the money his father's colleagues had given him to help him get through medical school. Freud had helped Tausk financially,

> so Marius wrote Freud to ask how much was owed him. . . . Though suffering from cancer of the jaw since 1923, . . . this secluded invalid of eighty-two remained as formidable [?] as ever; retaining all his sense of dignity and punctiliousness [??], Freud wrote back to say that he could not remember how much he had lent Marius's father, it could not have been much anyway, and it did not matter any more.

These incidents help to round out our picture of

[21] The two letters of August 1 and 25 are expurgated, with the places where material has been omitted clearly indicated, in the German edition of the correspondence (1966) but included without omissions in the English version (1972).

Freud's character. They also show how Roazen works with a preconceived notion of Freud's character and is impervious to evidence that shows him to be wrong.

41 ►►► *Freud and His Followers* (1975) is based in part on interviews with over seventy people who knew Freud personally as well as another forty who did not. But where we have the documents Roazen used, such as Freud's and Jung's correspondence, his account can be shown to be untenable, and that his bias has led him to ignore salient facts. And the *Minutes of the Vienna Psychoanalytic Society* show that his account of what happened there is quite fanciful. This point is worth stressing because so many people nowadays do not appreciate the difference between scholarship and repeating gossip.

Some of the other ways in which the book is unscholarly are also not peculiar to it but quite popular. Roazen gives no evidence of having read or at least checked the original German sources that he constantly quotes from inadequate translations. When he quotes letters, he does not furnish the dates, which are naturally the same in all editions and would also be more informative, but only the page numbers of the English versions. In Jung's collected works the paragraphs are numbered identically in the German and English versions to facilitate scholarly references, but Roazen again gives only the page numbers of the English translations. The number of notes in the back of the book gives a superficial impression of scholarship, but when the source is not what somebody or other told the author, it is often difficult if not impossible to determine the source, as there is no bibliography.

Simply to refute all of the falsehoods and misrepresentations in a single section of the book would lead us much too far afield. I shall confine myself largely to a single page (184). In view of what has just been said, it is ironic that Roazen should say of Freud: "He had what may now seem a rather primitive conception of the methodology of science." Then, to establish that Freud was a dogmatist, or to link him with dogmatism, we are told:

> One of Freud's followers at the time expressed his own [whose?] conception of science: "The natural scientist is a dogmatist; he lays down a principle and declares: that is the way it is."

Those who check the note in the back are referred to the *Minutes,* and the rare person who goes on to check the *Minutes* finds that the speaker was—Fritz Wittels, "the uninvited biographer" whom Freud considered "a pupil of Stekel's."[22] But one only needs to read in the *Minutes* how Wittels himself introduced this statement (November 18, 1908).

> He [Wittels] wishes only to specify the general difference between Freud's *Theory of Sexuality* and what he himself has said. . . . He has adopted a different—in a sense a higher—position.

And then Roazen's quotation follows! He saddles Freud with a view that Wittels opposed to Freud's position.

What is clear is that Roazen is in no position to pass judgments on sound method. He sees Freud as a dogmatist, and when he cannot quote Freud to show this, the quotes "one of Freud's followers" in a way that is bound to take in almost all of his readers. In this case one can at least check the assertion if one tries hard enough; when the references are to interviews one cannot. And an author who deals in this fashion with printed materials, and who does not recognize negative evidence when he

[22] Letter to Pfister, February 26, 1924.

himself quotes it, is hardly a reliable interpreter of large masses of oral material from which he selects what he chooses.

I am not suggesting that any of this involves deliberate deception, any more than I believe that the people he interviewed were deliberately inaccurate. But old people—by the time Roazen's preface was written forty-three of the people he had interviewed had died—are very apt to be wrong much of the time when they recall what happened over fifty years before. In Roazen's text one finds all kinds of confident assertions that are backed up in the notes simply by references to interviews. And his description of the Wednesday evening sessions that led up to the Freud/Adler break is based on recollections rather than the minutes that were published in 1974. It is an out and out travesty:

> The dispute between Freud and Adler hardly seems to have been a considered discussion of scientific differences. Freud was airing charges against Adler in full public view. . . . Freud outrightly denounced Adler. It was a trial and the charge was heresy. . . .
> The penalty was excommunication . . .

Every single sentence is a falsehood. The minutes show that Freud did discuss scientific differences, and did it very perceptively, distinguishing clearly between the *ideas*, which he criticized, and the *person*, whom he treated with respect. While Roazen had evidently not seen the third volume of the *Minutes*, which is relevant here, he knew the first two and hence had no excuse whatever for suggesting that these discussions were held "in full public view." On February 1 there were seventeen people, not counting Adler and Freud; on the twenty-second, eighteen. That "Freud outrightly denounced Adler" is also untrue and reflects the author's exceedingly unscientific, subjective, and rhetorical approach, which is designed to prejudice the reader against

Freud. The metaphors of trial, heresy, and excommunication, while not original with Roazen, are quite inappropriate and point in the same direction. Only a page later, he himself mentions that Adler kept attending the meetings for several months after these sessions, but once again Roazen simply fails to recognize negative evidence even when he himself presents it.

Roazen's treatment of Freud's insistence that members of his society must make a choice between Adler's meetings and his own and could not attend both raises a crucial question. He quotes Sachs as saying in his book that "most" of the six members who withdrew at that point "did not share Adler's views; their decision was influenced by their belief that the whole proceeding violated the 'freedom of science.' "[23] Perhaps Sachs was right that four people felt this, although according to the *Minutes*, not one of them said so. Even Furtmüller, who argued against Freud on this occasion and who was Adler's close associate,[24] said nothing of the sort. But Roazen leaves the reader to think that a majority felt that the "freedom of science" had been violated; and his readers are somehow given the impression that even "Sachs, loyal to Freud throughout," had to admit this.

Actually, Sachs introduces this issue only in order to deliver himself of a short discourse (more than three pages) on "freedom of science," what it means, and what it does not mean. He expounds "Freud's view—and incidentally my own too." But Roazen, having implanted in the reader's mind the notion that "freedom of science" was violated, has no time for any of that and simply ignores these issues.

Instead of recapitulating what Sachs said, I want to

---

[23] Sachs, p. 53. Roazen's page reference is wrong; see his pp. 185 and 570.
[24] The first monograph published by the *Verein für freie psychoanalytische Forschung* was Furtmüller's *Psychoanalyse und Ethik* (1912).

explain what I consider the crucial point. At the Wednesday evening meetings opinions were *not* aired "in full public view." Those who attended could try out some of their boldest ideas, which were often still quite far from being ready for publication, and then others would criticize these ideas very freely and often very sharply. Freud generally spoke quite late in the discussion, lest he inhibit it.

At the meeting of January 12, 1910, Fritz Wittels had analyzed Karl Kraus, the editor of *Die Fackel*, and called his talk "The *Fackel* Neurosis." He knew Kraus, having once worked for him, and they had had their difficulties. Freud said in the discussion: "Analysis is, indeed, supposed to make one tolerant, and such a vivisection could justly be reproached as being inhumane." As was his manner, he coupled such reproaches with great appreciation of the speaker as a person. But the essential point here is that he added: "He will surely guard against making his affects accessible to a wider circle, who would not have scientific esteem for them." Nevertheless, word of this meeting reached Kraus and led him to change his attitude toward psychoanalysis, which had been friendly until then. In fact, the enthusiastic review in *Die Fackel* of Freud's three essays on sexuality, in which "the anal character" was first introduced, along with other rather daring ideas, has already been mentioned.[25] From now on, however, Kraus could not resist punning on "psycho-anal," and his resentment of Freud knew no bounds. The connection between the Wittels paper and Kraus's change of mind is no mere matter of speculation but proved by a Kraus letter:

> This rabble now also has a journal at its disposal for its debates, and a symptom hunter whom I once fired, lays down the law [*führt dort das grosse Wort*], a rogue who

[25] Near the end of Section 25.

once reduced my detestation of the *Neue Freie Presse* to my "father complex"—in public.[26]

It was essential for Freud to keep these meetings small and to restrict them to members and an occasional guest while excluding troublemakers and declared opponents. People could not be expected to speak their minds freely without inhibition if they had to fear that members of the rival Society for *Free* Psychoanalysis might report on them to Karl Kraus, who would then try to pillory them in *Die Fackel.*

Before we consider Freud's own account of the matter, one final word about Roazen: He sometimes gives the appearance of being eminently unbiased and impartial—by striking a balance between truth and untruth. Here is an example that far transcends him; many people are confused on this point. Roazen writes:

> Ellenberger has written about Freud that even in the 1890s
>
> > There is no evidence that Freud was really isolated, and still less that he was ill-treated by his colleagues during those years . . .
>
> Freud may have been inadequately appreciated in Vienna, especially in his early years, but by the end of World War I he was world-famous.[27]

"*Even* in the 1890s" is an odd way of referring to the period before *The Interpretation of Dreams* appeared;

[26] Karl Kraus, *Briefe an Sidonie Nadherny von Borutin* 1913–36 (1974), p. 569: January 6, 1923. For the reason stated in the text above, said Kraus, he could not dedicate *Traumstück* to Sidonie. He had lampooned "Die Psychoanalen" in this playlet, which is a pastiche of parts of Goethe's *Faust*—"The Psychoanal Ones" say among other things: "In our hands all becomes filth"—and now Kraus did not dare link his name with a woman's. Freud had cited two of Kraus's witticisms in 1905 and 1908 (*Werke*, VI, p. 26—see also p. 83—and VII, p. 163), but ignored Kraus's attacks. *Traumstück* is included in Kraus, *Dramen* (1967).

[27] Roazen, p. 195; Ellenberger, p. 448.

that is, before Freud confronted the public as the founder of psychoanalysis. The opposition to him naturally came after that. Even before World War I, in 1913, the Austrian Department of Internal Revenue wrote him that "everyone knows that his reputation extends far beyond the frontier of Austria." Freud replied that he could not agree "that his reputation extends far beyond the frontier of Austria. It begins at the frontier."[28]

It has become fashionable in recent years to claim, as Roazen does, that Freud exaggerated "the extent and intensity of opposition to him and his work" (p. 195). Yet Freud worked in an environment in which people laughed when his name was mentioned,[29] and it is striking how free his books are of resentment, and even in his letters one finds no self-pity. Of course, he was thoroughly alienated in Vienna, not to speak of the rest of Austria; and beyond the frontier Adler and Jung received honorary degrees while he received none. To this day there is far more interest in Freud in the United States than in Austria. But resistance to Freud—which I distinguish from informed criticism of his ideas—continues abroad, too. How else is one to explain the fact that more than thirty or even forty years after his death books like Roazen's are widely applauded and translated?

[28] Jones, II, p. 390.
[29] Graf (1942), p. 469: "In those days when one mentioned Freud's name in a Viennese gathering, everyone would begin to laugh, as if someone had told a joke. Freud was the queer fellow who . . . imagined himself an interpreter of dreams. More than that, he saw sex in everything. It was considered bad taste to bring up Freud's name in the presence of ladies. They would blush when his name was mentioned. Those who were less sensitive spoke of Freud with a laugh, as if they were telling a dirty story. Freud was fully aware of this opposition . . . It was the manifestation of the same force which drove so many psychological stimuli into the unconscious; consequently, it now arose against any attempt at their uncovering. With conviction and certainty, Freud pursued his own way. He worked from morning till night . . ."

42 ▶▶▶ I confess that I first encountered Adler and Jung in the pages of Freud's *History of the Psychoanalytic Movement.* I was probably seventeen at the time and certainly not more than eighteen, and I realize that first impressions, especially those received in one's youth, often have great staying power. Nevertheless, I have generally found in the fields in which I did research that what I read as an undergraduate turned out to be untenable. It was only to be expected, therefore, that upon rereading Freud's account after I had done so much further reading it would strike me as embarrassing. Far from it, I now find it more masterly than I could realize before. The third and last section of the book[30] begins with an epigraph from Goethe:

Mach es kurz!
Am Jüngsten Tag ist's nur ein Furz.

Make it short!
On the last day it's but a fart.

In my effort to lay to rest all sorts of misconceptions and slanders, I have disregarded this wise admonition and shall not compound my felony now by summarizing Freud's version of what happened, too. But I cannot resist quoting a little of it:

Adler's striving for a place in the sun, however, also had one consequence that psychoanalysis is bound to appreciate. When, after the emergence of our irreconcilable scientific opposition, I got Adler to resign from the editorship of the *Zentralblatt,* he also left the Society and founded a new society that initially showed its good taste by adopting the name "Society for *Free* Psychoanalysis." But people outside, who are strangers to psychoanalysis, are evidently as ill equipped to appreciate the differences

[30] *Werke,* X, p. 84ff.

between the views of two psychoanalysts as we Europeans are to recognize the nuances that distinguish two Chinese faces. "Free" psychoanalysis remained in the shadow of the "official," "orthodox" version and was discussed merely as an appendage to it. Then Adler took the step that merits gratitude: he fully dissolved the ties to psychoanalysis and presented his doctrine separately as "Individual Psychology." There is so much space on God's earth and it is certainly justified that everybody who is able to do it should romp around unchecked; but it is not desirable that people should go on living under the same roof when they no longer understand each other and cannot get along any more. (p. 95f.)

To be sure, that was not all Freud had to say about Adler; he also commented on Adler's theories:

Adler's doctrine is characterized less by what it asserts than by what it denies; it thus consists of three elements of very unequal value: good contributions to ego psychology, superfluous but admissible translations of analytic facts into a new jargon, and distortions of these facts insofar as they do not fit in with the ego presuppositions.

Since psychoanalysis had concentrated on the unconscious, it had not paid much attention to the ego.

It was more interested in showing that all strivings of the ego had libidinous components mixed in. Adler's doctrine stresses the other side of the coin, the egoistic admixture in libidinous drives. Now this would be a palpable gain if Adler did not use this point to deny the libidinous impulse in favor of the ego drive component. In this way his theory does the same thing that all patients and our conscious thinking quite in general do: Rationalization, as [Ernest] Jones has called it, is used to cover up the unconscious motive. Alder is so consistent in this respect that he praises the intention to show women who is master, to be on *top*, even as the strongest motive of the sex act. I do not know whether he has championed these enormities in his writings, too. (p. 96f.)

This last point means, of course, that since Adler did not send Freud *The Nervous Character*, Freud did not buy it and felt relieved, as he wrote Jung (December 9, 1912) that he was under no obligation to read it. It may be recalled that even the worshipful Bottome found it no pleasure to read. And Freud had no reason to doubt that he was quite familiar with Adler's ideas. That is not to deny that Freud had the wit of Goethe's Mephistopheles, Heine, and Nietzsche.

He went on to say that psychoanalysis had long taken into account "the gain from illness" as well as the fact that if this gain is withdrawn, perhaps owing to changed circumstances, the symptom may be healed.

> These facts, which are not difficult to ascertain nor hard to grasp, receive the main emphasis in Adler's doctrine, while it is overlooked entirely that countless times the ego merely makes a virtue of necessity when it puts up with the most unwelcome symptom that has been forced upon it, comforting itself with the profit that attends it . . . The ego then plays the ridiculous role of the clown in the circus whose gestures are intended to persuade the audience that all the changes on the stage are brought about by his orders. But only the youngest members of the audience are taken in by him. (p. 97)

One might suppose that Adler championed Nietzsche's will to power against Freud's libido theory, yet this passage shows how in important ways Freud was closer to Nietzsche. Nietzsche's relevant ideas have been discussed in the second volume of this trilogy (especially in Sections 14 and 15), and Freud's image brings to mind Nietzsche's

> Your self laughs at your ego and at its bold leaps. "What are these leaps and flights of thought to me?" it says to itself. "A detour to my end. I am the leading strings of the ego and the prompter of its concepts."

Thus spoke Zarathustra in the chapter "On the Despisers of the Body." The point at issue here is of considerable importance for an understanding of Adler and his break with Freud; and we shall return to it in the context of a more detailed examination of their relationship to Nietzsche.

Two more points made by Freud in his account need to be mentioned here. Freud aims to show how little either organ inferiority or the feeling of inferiority—"one does not know which of these two" Adler means—can really explain. After all,

> an utterly overwhelming majority of people who are ugly, misshapen, crippled, or wretched do not react to their defects by developing a neurosis. (p. 100)

Nor does it help to say, as Adler did, that as children all of us are bound to feel inferior to adults; or—as Adler, also said, though Freud did not bother to mention this—that little boys are mortified when they realize how small their sex organs are compared to their fathers', or that little girls are bound to feel inferior when they discover that they have no penis at all. On the contrary, if all human beings have this experience it certainly comes nowhere near explaining why some few of them become neurotic.

Freud's final point may well have annoyed Adler more than all the rest: "The image of life that emerges from Adler's system is founded entirely on the aggressive drive; it leaves no room for love" (p. 102). Adlerians familiar with the messianic tinge of the later Adler and his constant emphasis on "community feeling" may well be baffled by this sally, but what Adler projected before the First World War was above all aggression, masculine protest, the desire to be on top, and—in person—resentment. Perhaps the later emphasis on community feeling was a case of overcompensation and in some measure a reaction to Freud's criticism. Of course, Adler had been a socialist in his youth, even a Marxist; but then Marxism is certainly compatible with resentment and aggression. While there is no doubt about Adler's later emphasis on love, there is ample room for doubt about his consistency. The Adlerians see their master as more loving than Freud and as optimistic, while Freud was, as they see it, pessimistic; but it is far from clear on what this love and optimism can be based if Adler's basic doctrines, developed before the First World War, were right.

The point that Adler had left no room for love was not a malicious rhetorical point but something Freud had felt for years. After reporting to Jung, on March 3, 1911, that he had resumed the chairmanship of the Vienna society, he went on:

> I now consider myself the executor of the revenge of the offended goddess Libido and shall also see to it more carefully than in the past that heresy should not take up too much space in the *Zentralblatt*. Behind Adler's seeming sharpness a large amount of confusion has become apparent. That a psychoanalyst could be so fooled by the ego, I should not have expected. After all, the ego plays the role of the clown in the circus . . .

Clearly, Adler's renunciation of depth psychology and what Freud perceived as his transparent rationalizations were at least as important to Freud as Adler's disaparagement of sexual factors in favor of masculine protest and aggressiveness. Indeed, in Adler's case these two "heresies" were two sides of the same coin. But before we consider Adler's ideas more carefully, along with his as well as Freud's attitude toward Nietzsche, something needs to be said about the whole concept of a psychoanalytic "movement" and Freud's mention of "heresy."

43 ▶▶▶ In his autobiography Ernest Jones suggested that the Viennese should never have spoken of a psychoanalytic "movement" because that term sounds religious rather than scientific. It led to talk, he says, of Freud as "the Pope" who expelled heretics from his "church."[31]

There are, as I see it, two questions that can be separated at least to some extent. The first has already been considered at length. Was Freud's attitude scientific, open-minded, and critical, or was he dogmatic and intolerant? Jones himself has furnished abundant evidence to show that Freud's attitude was scientific rather than dogmatic. The picture he gives on the pages immediately following the above suggestion and, above all, in his three-volume biography of Freud is supported by Binswanger's memoir and by Freud's correspondence with Jung, Abraham, Pfister, Lou Andreas-Salomé, and Arnold Zweig. A coherent image of Freud emerges from these ten volumes, and it does not contradict what we find in his works: He was strikingly open-minded, and his mentality was not "religious" rather than scientific.

In the very same letter to Jung in which he spoke of "heresy" he also said:

> I see at least with partial satisfaction that *The Interpretation of Dreams* is about to be overcome and must give place to something better, after it had seemed unimpeachable to me for a decade. So we have advanced substantially and beautifully.

What, then, are we to make of Freud's talk of heresy? I shall move from the particular to the general and comment on Freud's view of Adler before considering broader questions.

The imagery of the Pope and the heretics seems to

[31] Jones (1959), p. 205; cf. p. 212.

have been introduced by Jung during his first visit with Freud in Vienna, in March 1907. Freud wrote Jung on April 21, 1907, that what he knew of the work of Paul Sollier

> is hopeless chatter and a crude misinterpretation of nature. You will find that I am again raging like a Pope against heretics.

Three years later Freud wrote Jung, on March 6, 1910:

> Of the lectures I would like to ask you not to place the heretical ones, like Adler's (and perhaps also Marcinowski), in the first row; they would spoil the mood.

On November 11, Freud wrote Jung:

> My mood is not good because of the annoyances with Adler and Stekel, who are hard to get along with. Stekel you know; he has a maniac period and leads all my nobler impulses to despair; I am almost tired of defending him against all the world. . . . . Adler, a very decent and highminded [geistig hochstehender] human being is unfortunately paranoiac and pushes his scarcely intelligible theories so hard in the *Zentralblatt* that they must confuse all readers. Fights all the time about his priority, gives new names to everything, complains that he disappears in my shadow, and pushes me into the disagreeable role of the aging despot who won't let the younger generation come up. I would be glad to be rid of both of them since they also treat me badly personally. But it won't be possible. I would gladly let them have the *Zentralblatt*, and could expand the *Jahrbuch* to take care of the mounting pressure of material. But they won't want a break and yet cannot change. And at the same time there is their ridiculous Viennese local pride and their jealousy of you and Zurich. They are really people in whom psychoanalysis has not changed anything. The others in Vienna are well behaved but not exactly very able.

These complaints may comfort you in your local difficulties.

The *Zentralblatt* does seem to meet with a lot of interest and evidently was necessary.

Freud's letters are exceptionally straightforward and free of all deviousness. They show clearly how he felt and what the issues were. It therefore seems best to round out the picture with a few quotations from his letters to Jung. The next is dated December 3:

> Things are really getting bad with Adler . . . he reminds me of Fliess, one octave lower. In the second issue of the *Zentralblatt* . . . you will find a piece by him about your so-called little Anna. Read it carefully; otherwise it is hard to discover what he is driving at. His presentation suffers from paranoid vagueness. But this time one sees clearly how he wants to force a beautiful psychological diversity into the narrow bed of a single aggressive "masculine" ego current, as if a child thought only of being "on top" and playing the man while rejecting what is feminine. To bring this off, he must misinterpret a few things entirely, like planing off the genitals . . . Of course, between my conviction that the baby has been swaddled badly and that this is harmful and the danger that I may be considered an intolerant old man [*Greis* suggests a very old man, though Freud was then only fifty-four] who will not allow the younger generation to come up, I am in a very embarrassing situation with him.

Clearly, one very important motive of Freud's desire to be rid of Adler was that he could do without these constant frictions. As Lou Andreas-Salomé noted in her journal in February 1913, in connection with Tausk, ebullient and aggressive rivals in his immediate vicinity disturbed Freud in his own work and kept forcing him to come to terms with ideas prematurely, before he was fully prepared to deal with them. His creativity had its own rhythm, one might add; and she actually added:

That Freud considers this a disturbance and longs profoundly for that calm of quiet research which he enjoyed until 1905—until he founded the "school"—is certain; and who would wish that it were granted to him for ever and ever!

Yet she called her journal *In der Schule bei Freud*, "Going to Freud's School." And she was glad and profited from the fact that he did not withdraw into creative solitude.

On March 14, 1911, Freud wrote Jung that he was

waiting for an opportunity to drop both of them [Adler and Stekel], but they know it and hence their behavior is very cautious and conciliatory . . . In my heart I am done with both of them. Nothing will ever come of any of the Viennese; only little [Otto] Rank [who was then twenty-six], who is as bright as he is neat, has a future.

As one reads Freud's letters—not only the pieces quoted here—, one understands easily how eager Freud was in the end to terminate a very trying situation. Many professors consider it an excessive burden to teach twelve hours a week, although they never do anywhere near as much writing as Freud did. He saw four or five patients in a row from 8 or 9 a.m. till 1 p.m., day after day, and then several more in the afternoon until he had a late supper, and two nights a week he lectured at the university, while Wednesday evenings were reserved for the Psychoanalytic Society. He had no secretarial help, wrote all of his many letters by hand, and wrote a large number of seminal books and essays. The constant friction among the members of the Psychoanalytic Society must have been unbearable. Why, then, did he found a society? Why did he not go his way alone instead of becoming the head of a "movement"? Why did he found journals and then worry about "heretical" articles confusing the public?

Weimar Congress of the International Psychoanalytic Society, September 1911.
Far left, standing: Rank and Binswanger. Seated, second from left: Bleuler.
Far right, standing below two other men: Pfister.

Seated: _____, Lou Andreas-Salomé, Beatrice Hinkle,
Emma Jung. Above Lou: Ferenczi, Freud, _____, Jung,
Abraham.
Far left: Brill and Maeder (with small moustache) and
Hitschmann above him. Above Freud, right: Paul Federn
(with dark beard).

Seated, second from left: Toni Wolff. Standing, far right:
Jones and Stekel.
Above Jones: Marcinowski.
Above Wolff, right: Putnam.

44 ▶▶▶ Karl Jaspers, in his *General Psychopathology*, argued against Freud: "He does not disavow these pupils and is therefore partly responsible for them"[32] Max Weber's opinion of psychoanalysis was similarly influenced by his belief that "many of those who followed in the wake of Freud were too ready to justify what appeared to him as moral shabbiness."[33]

Freud knew that people judged psychoanalysis by his followers no less than by him. Hence Adler's doctrines and Stekel's lack of scientific scruples were sources of embarrassment for him. He had analyzed Stekel, who became one of his first supporters, and he repeatedly said in print that Stekel had made important contributions to psychoanalysis. Stekel had originality but relied on his intuitions and was not squeamish about inventing evidence.[34] If Freud stood by him, he was held responsible for him; if he disowned him, he was considered unwilling to tolerate originality.

One might not expect the same critic to make both points on facing pages, but as sober a man as Karl Jaspers did, being full of resentment against Freud. Nor is this passage in his *General Psychopathology* the only place in his works where his perennial campaign against Freud became comical.

In 1950, five years after the collapse of National Socialism, Jaspers published, in Germany, *Reason and Anti-Reason in Our Time* and pointed to Marxism and psychoanalysis as the two great examples of anti-reason in our time. In his repetitive insistence that Kierkegaard and Nietzsche were far greater psychologists than Freud, Jaspers conveniently ignored the fact that Kierkegaard was certainly a militant opponent of reason.

[32] 7th ed. (1959), p. 646. This pasasge goes back to 1913.
[33] Gerth and Mills (1946), p. 20.
[34] See Freud's letter to Stekel, January 13, 1924, in *Briefe*, and Jones, II, pp. 134–37; also Jones (1959), pp. 219–21.

In the passage in his *General Psychopathology* to which I have referred, Jaspers complained three times in less than one page that, unlike Kierkegaard and Nietzsche, "Freud himself remains opaque personally"—*undurchsichtig*, untransparent—as if Kierkegaard with all his pseudonyms and Nietzsche with his masks had been transparent! To this day scholars argue whether views put forward by Kierkegaard were really his own or only held by one or another pseudonym; and Kierkegaard was hardly free from self-deceptions. It would be no reason for complaints if Freud had actually been opaque as a human being. The demand that we ought to be transparent suggests shallowness. But there is a sense in which we can know Freud better than almost any other great personality—because he knew himself so well, was so honest, and wrote such incomparable letters. By comparison, Nietzsche's letters are so many masks and full of histrionics, while Jaspers' personality has never yet elicited the slightest interest.

Jaspers' *General Psychopathology* had so little impact that even Heidegger exerted much more influence on psychotherapy. Jaspers' criticisms of Freud are so irrational that they need to be explained psychologically, in terms of resentment and resistance. This is not an immunization strategy, for I am not trying to explain away reasonable criticism; I am trying to account for the fact that an otherwise generally reasonable man behaved so utterly irrationally in this case.

Jaspers' contradictory critique of Freud illuminates Freud's dilemma. If he did not disavow his pupils, he was held responsible for them; and if he did, he was charged with an intolerant, unscientific attitude.

Of course, Freud's differences with Adler and Jung were by no means solely scientific. Freud could remain friends with Binswanger and Pfister, who were clear and honest about their agreements and disagreements with him and Binswanger and Freud felt deep affection for each other. The problem with Adler was not only that Freud had to make clear what was and what was not psychoanalysis, what he was and what he was not responsible for; he also had to part company sooner or later with a man who resented him so much as an older brother that he made life a burden for both of them.

Two personality factors seem to me to have contributed greatly to the resistance to Freud. The first has already been analyzed in Section 17, and its relevance clearly stated at the end of that section. Freud did not consider himself a superior person; he felt that his uncompromising honesty was a matter of course; and it was only the other side of the coin when he felt that most people were rabble. His total straightforwardness about that is bound to strike many people as intolerant.

It was noted earlier, in Section 38, that after Lou Andreas-Salomé read Freud's account of the Adler schism she sent him a letter Adler had written her on August 16, 1913, in which Adler spoke of "snatching and pilfering" and claimed that Freud and his school did not believe their own theses but wanted only to save their investments. In his reply to her Freud said:

> The letter shows his specific venomousness, is very characteristic of him; I do not think it refutes the picture I have given of him. Let us speak plainly (then it will be easier to go on): he is a disgusting person.

And three days later, July 10, 1914, he mentioned the incident to Karl Abraham, without any self-pity, without wallowing in the unsavory details, but with his own occasional abrasiveness:

> Lou Salomé has sent me an exchange of letters with Adler that shows her insight and clarity in a splendid light, but also Adler's venomousness and meanness; and with such rabble, etc.!

Far from being able to identify with Freud, many people feel threatened by him. And that brings into play the second factor. He is a quintessential father figure. Apparently many, if not most, very critical readers see themselves as rebels against authority; and in the case of Freud they tend to identify with those who rebelled against him. This is understandable enough, but they overlook the fact that Freud was much more of a rebel and a revolutionary than Adler or, for that matter, Jung. Freud himself thought that both men felt that he had been too revolutionary, too abrasive, too offensive, and that both had wished to tone down the offense. The fact that much later both reaped honors that were denied to him suggests that he was right. And yet even those who see themselves as critics and as rebels do feel threatened by old Freud, who wrote to Arnold Zweig when Adler had died suddenly in May 1937:

> I don't understand your sympathy for Adler. For a Jew boy out of a Viennese suburb a death in Aberdeen is an unheard-of career in itself and a proof of how far he had got on. The world really rewarded him richly for his services in having contradicted psychoanalysis.

Jones has been criticized for publishing this remark, while Ernst Freud has been criticized for omitting it in the Freud/Zweig correspondence. It is one thing to applaud Nietzsche when he says in *Ecce Homo* (I, Section 5) that

> the rudest word, the rudest letter are still more benign, more decent than silence. Those who remain silent are almost always lacking in delicacy and courtesy of the heart. Silence is an objection; swallowing things leads of necessity to a bad character—it even upsets the stomach.[35]

[35] III, p. 208. The letter was dated June 17, 1936.

It is quite another matter to come face to face with such a complete lack of sorrow and hypocrisy in the face of death. Freud's corrosive honesty is experienced by many people as threatening: There is no hiding place. And they cannot identify with him because he always seems superior. In the official English translations he comes out much sterner than he does in the original German, which is often earthy, humorous, ironical. But the irony establishes a different kind of superiority; it shows us a man who usually sees the situations in which he finds himself quite clearly and, while having deep and sometimes painful feelings, is amused by it all. He keeps looking down upon himself and his predicaments; and people feel that he is looking down on them, too.

Of course, not all readers react the same way. Some are born followers or at least need a father figure. Others, including many writers and artists, have appreciated Freud immensely. Feeling about him as I do, I naturally feel that it is the depreciation of his personality that needs an explanation. But to be quite honest about that, I do not think that this is merely my subjective feeling. Most attacks on Freud—as distinguished once again from reasoned criticism of his theories—have been irrational and contradictory.

45 ▶▶▶ Did Freud need a "movement"? Could he have dispensed with his society and journals? Could his theory have gained the measure of acceptance that it did achieve if Freud had chosen to remain a loner, more or less like Nietzsche or like Kant? I doubt it.

Kant's case is not comparable, for he brought glad tidings. Nietzsche's psychology, on the other hand, met with so much resistance that eighty years after his death it is still scarcely known. Freud did need journals and collaborators.

The point of having journals was to present psycho-analysis to those who might be interested in it—and not to confuse people about what it was. Why Freud needed collaborators and journals was stated clearly, if inadvertently, by Max Webber in 1907 in a long report in which he advised against the publication of a paper by one of Freud's followers in a nonpsychoanalytical journal:

> What is needed is the creation of an *exact casuistry* of a bulk and a certainty that today, despite all claims to the contrary, does not exist, but will perhaps exist in two or three decades. One only needs to note how much Freud has revised in a single decade and how frighteningly small, in spite of everything, his material is even now, which is wholly understandable and *no reproach whatever*.[36]

Freud needed the help of others who would test his theories in a large number of cases; and where could they publish their findings and theories if nonpsychoanalytical journals turned them down? Many scientists have large numbers of graduate students and sometimes also a professional staff to assist them. Freud had none of that and initially developed his ideas on the basis of his self-analysis and a small practice. Had he continued that way, he would have been open to the criticism that his data were too limited by far to warrant any generalizations. For scientific reasons he needed collaborators but had no money to pay them.

In good times, more patients came to Freud than he could handle. He was thus in a position to distribute them among the members of his circle. But this involved questions of conscience for him when some of the members developed theories that he considered quite mistaken and harmful, and when he felt that their theories reflected their own unresolved psychological problems.

[36] Marianne Weber (1926), p. 379f.

He could not pay people to test his ideas, nor could he expect all of them to proceed in total isolation. He needed journals in which psychoanalytical articles could be published promptly, and meetings and conferences where the members could count on a free and uninhibited oral exchange of ideas.

That many of his collaborators, including some of the most "orthodox," were no great lights, nobody knew better than Freud. He clearly thought that Jung, Adler, and even Stekel were more interesting than the less independent members of his movement. When Paul Häberlin remarked how strange some of them were, Freud replied, according to Binswanger (p. 20): "I have always thought that the first to seize upon my doctrine would be swine and speculators." And when Häberlin asked why Adler and Jung had left him, Freud is said to have answered: "They wanted to become Pope for once, too."

46 ▶▶▶ It would be wonderfully ironic if at this point I could accomplish a dramatic reversal and show how, for all my admiration for Freud as a human being, Adler was really much closer to the truth. This would come as a surprise but would be understandable, considering my work on Nietzsche. After all, it is a commonplace, though not necessarily correct, that Adler revived Nietzsche's will to power.

Adler certainly saw himself as competing with Freud and wished with all his heart to "be above" and leave Freud "below." He hoped to beat Freud at his own game, first by taking away psychoanalysis from Freud and heading a new movement of *free* psychoanalysis, implying that he was at least morally superior. Then, when the world failed to see this, he called his movement "individual psychology," which brings to mind a wholly unintended contrast with group psychology.

When it came to book titles and coinages, he obviously was not in the same league with Freud; but that is surely a small matter. "Psychoanalysis" was a brilliant coinage, and all Jung came up with later was "analytical psychology."

Incidentally, though it seems to be assumed generally that "individual psychology" was Adler's coinage, it was not. The word had been used before, for example, by Sandor Ferenczi in 1908, in an article "Analytical Interpretation and Treatment of Psychosexual Impotence in Men."[37] And the long bibliography in the first volume of *Imago* (1912) was divided into "I. *Individualpsychologie*" (with ten subdivisions, including sexual psychology, dream psychology, occult phenomena, child psychology, characterology, biography, and aesthetics) and "II. *Völkerpsychologie*" (with five subdivisions, including mythology, psychology of religion, psychology of language, social psychology, and criminal psychology).

As a writer, Adler was not in the same league with Freud either. Again one may feel like saying that very few people are, and that this, too, is no serious objection to Adler. But the inadequacy of Adler as a writer was due to his inadequacy as a thinker. He was unable to develop a thought or an argument. Probably the most respected guide to his thought is *The Individual Psychology of Alfred Adler*, edited and annotated by H. L. and R. R. Ansbacher. It is subtitled *A Systematic Presentation in Selections from His Writings*. The interspersed comments, which take up much of the book, are scrupulous and informative. But what is utterly amazing is how

[37] In *Psychiatrisch-Neurologische Wochenschrift*, X (1908), reprinted in his *Bausteine zur Psychoanalyse*, Vol. II (1927), p. 209. When Ferenczi died in 1933, the Vienna Psychoanalytical Society held a memorial session in his honor, June 14, and Paul Federn said in his address that, as far as he knew, Ferenczi had been the first analyst to use the term *Individualpsychologie* (Federn, 1933, p. 308).

rarely two or three consecutive paragraphs of Adler's prose are consecutive in his books. The editors rarely found two whole pages of Adler usable. If this should sound confusing, it is; but an example may show what is meant. The book contains two and a half pages on "The Individual Child in School," which are clearly meant to be read consecutively. But the first, fourth, fifth, sixth, ninth, tenth, fourteenth, and fifteenth of these unnumbered paragraphs are taken from pages 52, 84, 81 and 73, 53, 126, 174–75, 56, and 54 of one of Adler's books; the second and the sixteenth paragraphs come from pages 6 and 30 of another volume; the third and eighth paragraphs from pages 184 and 227 of another book; while the seventh, eleventh, twelfth, and thirteenth are taken from three more different books. To treat a serious thinker that way would be unconscionable, but the editors have unquestionably performed a great service for Adler.

Let there be no misunderstanding: what they have assembled is not a collection of gems or of particularly vivid formulations. They have simply tried to follow some themes to the extent of giving the reader some notion of what Adler had to say on various subjects.

In 1929 Adler published *The Science of Living* in the United States. In 1969 it appeared in paperback, "Edited and with an Introduction by Heinz L. Ansbacher." The editor explained that most of Adler's books "are based on lecture notes often edited by someone else. Furthermore, these notes are from series of lectures addressed to different audiences and cover essentially the same ground, so that there is considerable overlapping between the books. The present volume is no exception . . . it would appear that it is based on lectures delivered to an American audience. But no editor is mentioned . . ." For the new edition the editor's wife made four kinds of changes:". . . 2. Occasionally sequences within a chapter were changed to achieve better organization. 3.

Some chapter headings have been altered to reflect the contents of the chapter more precisely." "Some" here means eight out of twelve.

It was a strange self-misunderstanding on Adler's part to suppose that he could beat Freud at his own game. His talents were altogether different, and we do him no favor if we keep on juxtaposing him with Freud, as almost everybody has done.

Adler's insistence on competing with Freud was neurotic: Instead of perceiving the realities of the situation, he remained stuck in his childhood and reenacted an altogether inappropriate sibling rivalry. Bottome considers Adler's discovery of the importance of "the family constellation" one of his ten "chief contributions to thought" (that is the title of her Chapter XVI). In the chapter on "The Family Constellation" in *Problems of Neurosis* we read:

> When we find so much resemblance between all first children, all second and all youngest children, we may well ask what part is left for heredity to play. . . .
> In later development, the second child is rarely able to endure the strict leadership of others or to accept the idea of "eternal laws." He will be much more inclined to believe, rightly or wrongly, that there is no power in the world which cannot be overthrown. Beware of his revolutionary subtleties! I have known quite a few cases in which the second child has availed himself of the strangest means to undermine the power of ruling persons . . .

Adler, of course, was a second child. But this does bring to mind astrology, albeit not—*pace* Popper—because it cannot be proved wrong. On the contrary, it invites statistical study.

Adler's bent of mind throughout the chapter on "The Family Constellation" appears to be completely unscientific. He constantly trails off into anecdotes and irrelevancies without even appearing to notice how he fails to support his sweeping generalizations. At the bottom of the page from which I have just quoted (p. 106) we read: "The youngest child is also a distinct type, exhibiting certain characteristics of style which we never fail to find." Never!

Actually, I read the description of "the second child" before I read that of the first, knowing that Adler was a second child. Then I wondered whether Robespierre had been a second child, but the books in my study were not clear on that point, and I felt it really did not matter that much. Imagine my surprise when I read about the first-born, just four pages earlier:

> . . . the eldest child is readier than others to recognize power and likes to support it. This is shown in the lives of scientists, politicians, and artists [at this point, I thought, popular astrology books would at least give you a dozen or more examples; but Adler does not bother], as well as in those of simpler people [his usual manner is to tell at some length about one patient]. Even if the person is a revolutionary we find a conservative tendency, as in the case of Robespierre.

That is the end of the discussion of the eldest, and after that one tends to lose interest in the whole theory.

The Ansbachers, understandably, piece together Adler's views about the eldest child from three other books—seven snippets—and ignore Robespierre. But in their long Introduction they suggest that it helps to see Freud as a representative of objective psychology and as tough-minded, and Adler as a representative of what they call subjective psychology and as tender-minded. The second contrast comes, of course, from William James, and it is from him that they derive the terms that they juxtapose in parallel columns, to describe Freud and Adler. Perhaps a few of these antitheses may help us here, especially the final one:

[Freud]	[Adler]
Empiricist	Rationalist
(going by fact)	(going by principles)
Pessimistic	Optimistic
Pluralistic . . .	Monistic . . .
Irreligious	Religious
Hardheaded	Feeling
Sceptical	Dogmatical

Here it is admitted that Adler was dogmatic, but in 1978 H. L. Ansbacher had second thoughts about that in his preface to an Adler anthology he called *Cooperation Between the Sexes*. To read Adler "in accordance with Adler's own overruling principles" means:

> (a) Sweeping generalizations are to be understood as statements of probability only. (b) Dogmatic or blunt statements must be taken as maxims, working hypotheses, or therapeutic devices. (c) Apparent reifications must be read and revalued as statements of processes.

In other words, Adler did not really mean what he said. Bottome had explained decades earlier why he was unable to say what he really wished to say. Her remarkable explanation is worth quoting once more in the present context:

> When Adler wrote *The Nervous Character* he was laboring under two great disabilities. He was too poor to give himself the needed time to get his thoughts clear and in the right sequence . . . and he was himself living from day to day this Laocoon struggle with his own wife. (p. 99)

One thinks of other writers and artists who triumphed over greater disabilities, but Bottome went right on to compare Adler with Beethoven. Adler's wisdom, she said in the very same paragraph,

> is the wisdom that has entered every beat of a man's heart. Like Beethoven, Adler might well have said: "My passions are the grapes that I tread out for mankind."

It would be less kind but possibly more hardheaded to say that his theories are so many rationalizations of his own predicaments.

It may be objected that this is what every great psychologist does, and that it is unfair to single out Adler. But I have shown, I think, that this is not what Freud and Nietzsche did. Whether he is interpreting his dreams or his mischievements, Freud does not make excuses for himself or offer rationalizations; rather, he exposes his shortcomings to the extent that the argument may require it, with a scientific detachment that is often quite astonishing. And he was generally very careful about generalizations—skeptical, in one word, not dogmatical.

We actually found that in his account of art as a substitute gratification he failed to take sufficient note of his own case and hence, if I am right, went wrong. Above all, his emphasis on sex was not due to his being oversexed. On the contrary, his own libido could be channeled largely into work and weakened early.[38] Adler's theories of inferiority feeling, and overcompensation, the aggressive drive and masculine protest, as well as the family constellation and the craving to be on top, not below, and to be the first were all derived from his firsthand experience and were so many ways of saying: Do not blame me! Others are no better! I have had some patients who are like that, too.

---

[38] See, for example, Freud's letters to Fliess, October 31, 1897, and to Jung, February 2, 1910, and Emma Jung's letter to him, November 6, 1912; also *Werke*, VII, p. 157.

We still have to ask whether some of these theories did not, after all, contribute a great deal to the discovery of the mind.

Looking back in 1931, Adler himself wrote:

> In 1908 I hit upon the idea that every individual really exists in a state of permanent aggression, and I was imprudent enough to call this attitude the "aggression drive." But I soon realized that I was not dealing with a drive, but with a partly conscious, partly irrational [an odd contrast] attitude toward the tasks which life imposes; and I gradually arrived at an understanding of the social element in personality . . .

The Ansbachers, who included this passage in their book, went on:

> In this connection, Bottome quotes Adler as saying to his friends with a grim smile, "I enriched psychoanalysis by the aggressive drive. I gladly make them a present of it."[39]

Under these circumstances one can hardly speak of Adler's theory of the aggressive drive as one of his contributions to the discovery of the mind. When he himself was "in a state of permanent aggression," he "hit upon the idea that every individual really exists" in such a state. But when he had founded a society of his own and calmed down, he "gradually arrived at an understanding of the social element in personality." Of course, that is not to say that there is, or is not, an aggressive drive in mankind. But when Freud introduced such a drive into psychoanalysis after the experience of the First World War and explained its relation to the death instinct, at a time when he had incipient cancer though he did not know it, did he really take it from Adler? Why from Adler rather than Nietzsche?

[39] Ansbacher (1956, 1964), p. 38; Bottome, p. 64.

The claim that Freud, after initially rejecting Adler's theory, eventually adopted it, is false. Adler was rejecting Freud's libido theories as well as his whole enterprise of depth psychology and claimed that he could explain everything in terms of masculine protest, aggression, and the desire to be "on top." Freud never embraced these views. What is revealing is that so many people have repeated this false claim, while we never seem to hear in this connection that Adler himself soon found that the tenets he had urged against Freud were in fact untenable.

It may be recalled that Adler's final paper at the Vienna Psychoanalytic Society was devoted to masculine protest, that it was discussed for a long time, and that Freud criticized Adler's views. Not long after, Adler abandoned his earlier notions about masculine protest. As the Ansbachers put it:

> When the striving for superiority and overcoming replaced the masculine protest, the term became limited to the more restricted meaning of the preceding paragraph. It referred to manifestations in women protesting against their feminine role. In girls "fighting and scuffling, climbing and chasing, exaggerated achievements in sports . . . point to dissatisfaction with the feminine role and to the 'masculine protest.'"[40]

In other words, this coinage was now reserved for uppity women who were not satisfied with their assigned sex roles.

In a later book, in 1978, Heinz Ansbacher said expressly:

> Adler did not always announce changes in his theory and terminology. Sometimes he even expressed himself as if his earlier views had never existed. The following extreme example of this tendency refers to the masculine

[40] P. 49, quoting from a book of 1930.

protest. Accusing his critics of quite misunderstanding him and doing him injustice, he writes . . . In all fairness, Adler could have faulted his critics only for not having kept up with his development . . . . (p. 283)

Yet Adler's strategy worked, and many people still accuse Freud of having been dogmatic or intolerant because he did not accept ideas that Adler urged against him, without noting that Adler himself abandoned these ideas soon after because they simply were untenable. We saw at the end of Chapter I how much the same thing happened in connection with Otto Rank's The Trauma of Birth.

47 ▶▶▶ As far as ideas go, undoubtedly Adler's most important contribution was concerned with inferiority. He rejected the notion of complexes and cannot properly be said to have discovered or coined "the inferiority complex"; nor did he develop any clear, consistent theory about it. Yet he more than anyone else called attention to the fact that many people are burdened with terrible inferiority feelings, and this was liberating in itself. The *Minko* or *Miko* (for *Minderwertigkeits-Komplex*) became a very widely used term in the German-speaking world, and people felt better for having a word for what ailed them. Above all, it helped to know that they were not alone.

Neither the concept nor the term of inferiority feeling is to be found in Adler's early *Study of Organ Inferiority* (1907). At that time, as the Ansbachers put it, he "was not concerned with anything so subjective as feelings" (p. 24). This feeling first appeared in Adler's work in 1910, in an article in which he did not yet attribute it to *all* children.

These objective phenomena frequently give rise to a subjective feeling of inferiority . . . Weakness, clumsi-

Adler's Break with Freud ▶ 251

ness, awkwardness, sickness . . . are all able to give a deep foundation for the feeling of inferiority in relation to stronger persons and to fixate it for life. This is especially true of the feeling toward the father. . . .

This is hardly much of a discovery, and the next paragraph does not help at all:

. . . Thus a wide area of originally childish value judgments is given. Accordingly, any form of uninhibited aggression, activity, potency, power, and the traits of being brave, free, rich, aggressive, or sadistic can be considered as masculine. All inhibitions and deficiencies, as well as cowardliness, obedience, poverty, and similar traits, can be considered as feminine. (p. 46f.)

Adler did not speak of an "inferiority complex" until 1925. According to the Ansbachers (p. 256), "the first use of the term attributed to Adler is found in an interview in *The New York Times* in the fall of 1925." Until at least 1930 he used the term merely "as a synonym for the feeling of inferiority in general, the normal as well as the abnormal." Later he used the term for "the abnormally increased inferiority feeling," but "the first usage left its mark." And then he also introduced a third usage in 1935, referring "to the means by which an individual 'explains to himself and others that he is not strong enough to solve a given problem in a socially useful way." The Ansbachers distinguish the second and the third meaning by speaking "for the sake of clarity" of the "inferiority [feeling] complex" and the "inferiority [symptom] complex." Even so they devote to the inferiority complex only a page and a half of quotations from Adler and two pages of editorial comments in a book that comprises more than five hundred pages. This would seem to show that even the most sympathetic expositors of Adler who are thoroughly at home in the whole range of his writings are unable to find anything approximating a theory of the inferiority complex.

Can we move beyond Adler and formulate an illuminating theory? During the *est* training many people speak about their problems, and it turns out that almost everybody has the same complaints: I am not good enough, and my relationships do not work. Of course, most of the people who take the training are not satisfied with their lives, and those who speak want help. Still, once I noticed how many people said they felt inadequate, I was led to wonder whether *everybody* does.

Freud, as we saw, felt that he was not a great man, and when people compared him with Goethe, he made gentle fun of them. Goethe, in turn, felt that it was foolish to rank him with Shakespeare, whom he considered a being of a higher order. Neither Freud nor Goethe was lacking in pride, nor was Shakespeare, as we know from his sonnets, but the sonnets also show that he knew feelings of inferiority at first hand. Vincent van Gogh had much more intense feelings of inadequacy. When one stops to think about it, it becomes obvious indeed that anybody who does not feel inferior to other people in some respects must be a victim of megalomania; also that as children all of us felt inferior—and were inferior—to adults. What does all this help to explain? Not much.

In fact, the whole concept of inferiority feelings, not to speak of the two kinds of inferiority complex, is really very misleading. It obscures a vital distinction. As children we *are* inferior to adults in height, weight, strength, knowledge, and ever so many other ways. As adults we continue to be inferior to millions of other adults in a multitude of ways. To realize this is the beginning of wisdom. But we must distinguish between inferiority in this sense and inadequacy. Freud felt inferior to many people in a number of ways—they had talents that he lacked and could do things he could not do, or could do things more quickly than he could do them—but he did

Adler's Break with Freud ▶ 253

not feel inadequate. He made the most of the gifts he had. The same applies to Goethe and Shakespeare.

> When, in disgrace with Fortune and men's eyes
> I all alone beweep my outcast state,
> And trouble deaf heaven with my bootless cries
> And look upon myself and curse my fate,
> Wishing me like to one more rich in hope,
> Featur'd like him, like him with friends possess'd,
> Desiring this man's art, and that man's scope,
> With what I most enjoy contented least;
> Yet in these thoughts myself almost despising,
> Haply I think on thee, and then my state,
> Like to the lark at break of day arising
> From sullen earth, sings hymns at heaven's gate;
> For thy sweet love remember'd such wealth brings
> That then I scorn to change my state with kings.

In sonnet 29 Shakespeare finds the kind of comfort that lovers have always sought; but what sustained him more often, and perhaps even when he wrote this sonnet, was using the talents he did have. The fact that his talents were quite extraordinary sharpens the point I wish to make. No matter how great a man's gifts may be, he is still bound to be inferior in a multitude of ways, and the inference from inferiority to inadequacy is invalid.

While *est* does not go in for analyses of this sort, it delivers the same message. Instead of telling people that they are not really inferior it tells them in so many words: Of course you are; so what? You are "perfect" nevertheless.

I had long thought that there was one case, oddly not mentioned by Adler, that could be illuminated by his theory and might even have inspired it. From 1888 until 1918, Wilhelm II was the German Kaiser; he had a malformed, stunted right arm from birth; and he was an immensely aggressive person who felt compelled to prove constantly what a man he was. Surely, he did bring to mind terms like masculine protest and overcompensation. Moreover, there are other men who were born with the same defect and who have also become unusually aggressive. In these cases Adler seemed to have a point, but Freud, unlike Adler, discussed the last Kaiser and offered a different explanation.

The Kaiser was still living at that time, albeit in retirement, and Freud therefore did not mention him by name, nor did he say specifically that the "very well-known" biographer who had based "the whole development of the character of his hero on the feeling of inferiority that had to be aroused by this physical defect" was Emil Ludwig. But Freud pointed out that Emil Ludwig had overlooked one crucial detail. Usually, mothers will try to compensate sick or otherwise disadvantaged children with redoubled love. But the Kaiser's proud mother withdrew her love from the child because of his defect; and after he came to power he "proved unequivocally by his actions that he had never forgiven her." Freud tried to explain this case in terms of "the significance of mother love for the child's psychic life."[41]

What splendid irony! Freud, the alleged "crypto-biologist," materialist, or reductionist, rejects the Adlerian attempt to explain behavior in terms of organ inferiority and insists on the crucial role of mother love.

Was Popper right when he suggested that all human behavior can be explained equally well by Adler's and by Freud's theories? I do not think so. One could examine similar cases, placing in one column those whose aggressiveness is counterproductive and keeps hurting them, and in the other those whose overcompensation is overwhelmingly constructive; and then one might ask whether Freud was right that it was the mother's attitude that made the difference. One could then go further and ask whether people with an inordinate need for constant attention and recognition

[41] *Werke*, XV, p. 72.

(*Geltungsbedürfnis*) felt insufficiently appreciated by their mothers, and whether Freud was right that nothing favored success more than having been the undisputed favorite of one's mother. Freud felt that he had been that; Adler thought, rather oddly, that Freud's theories must be wrong because he, Alfred Adler, had loved his father much more than his mother. In fact, as Bottome tells us (p. 7), "she and Alfred failed to understand each other." Again:

> Alfred had always been much less attached to his mother than to his father. She was colder in her nature, and it is probable that she preferred her first-born to Alfred. (p. 9)

Adler never ceased to compete with this first-born brother, Sigmund, and wished desperately to "be first."

Here one might venture a risky conjecture about the critic who has suggested again and again that "every conceivable case could be interpreted in the light of Adler's theory, or equally of Freud's," and who went on to say rather oddly that "according to Freud the first man suffered from repression (say, of some component of his Oedipus complex)" (Section 19 above). Actually, the Oedipus complex has only two components, one of which is the little boy's desire for his mother's undivided love. Why, then, did Popper choose this odd circumlocution? Why did he rank Adler with Freud? And why did he repeat the same ill-informed charges against Freud so often? Here is the conjecture for which there is actually a good deal of evidence. He may have felt so distressed by his looks and small stature that the concepts of the inferiority complex and overcompensation (or an inordinate desire for recognition and appreciation) struck him as having some *prima facie* appeal; and he often spoke of his father and rarely of his mother, who he may have felt did not appreciate him sufficiently. If she had loved him more, then, according to Freud, Popper would not have continued to feel all his life long, as Adler did, too, that all the recognition he got was sadly insufficient.

48 ▶▶▶ If it is a mistake to juxtapose Adler with Freud, following Adler's example, and if their talents were in fact quite different and he was neither much of a writer nor a profound thinker, what was he? The first of a new breed of gurus.

While Freud had practically considered it a point of honor to refrain from giving people religious satisfaction, Adler tried more and more to be inspirational. He moralized freely, had a strong messianic streak, and published such books as *The Science of Living* (1929) and *What Life Should Mean to You* (1931). While Freud was always much more interested in theory than in therapy, Adler's *The Nervous Character* consisted of a "Theoretical Part" that had three chapters with no subheads and a "Practical Part" that had ten chapters with almost forty lines of subheads. His admirers tell stories of how wonderful Adler was with children, with criminals, and with others whom he helped.

One of these stories seems splendid to me and shows Adler, the guru, at his best. Adler said that during the war he had had two patients who had their right arms amputated at the shoulder on the same day. According to Bottome (p. 150),

> Two years later both visited him in Vienna, by chance in the same week. One of them said to him: "Dr. Adler, I am helpless without my right arm. I cannot work; marriage is out of the question for me; I am a log of wood—not a man!" The second said: "Dr. Adler, I find I can get on beautifully without that right arm. I have a better job than before I lost it. I am married and have a fine boy! I sometimes ask myself why nature provides us with two arms when one suffices!"

When Freud developed a talking cure he made room, quite unwittingly, for a new kind of healer. Adler was the first to walk through the door Freud had opened, Jung, though in many ways very different, the second. Wilhelm Reich and Erich Fromm, each very different in turn, were among those who followed. Fritz Perls, who saw Freud in 1936 and felt rebuffed, became the bridge to another generation of gurus who had no direct ties to Freud or his pupils. As time went on, these gurus became more and more eclectic. If one sees Perls, who liked to be known as "Fritz," as the beginning of this secondary development, one might see Werner Erhard, who likes to be known as "Werner," as its culmination.

Having said in the discussion of Freud's therapy that it invites comparison with the great ocean liners, I welcome the search for more efficient and economical ways of helping people. We shall return to that question, if only briefly, in the final chapter.

The point here is that Adler comes out badly when we follow his lead and compare him with Freud. He needs to be seen as a link to those who walked the path he was the first to choose. Moreover, many of them did adopt or adapt his ideas without giving him credit. So did Jean-Paul Sartre. Many of these people felt, like Adler, that there was no need for depth psychology. And some also shared Adler's messianic streak and had visions of saving humanity.

49 ▶▶▶ Although Adler was somewhat paranoiac about people "stealing" his ideas, once he was dead a lot of people did just that. But since he could not really foresee that, his preoccupation with plagiarism must have had other sources. Perhaps his own relation to Nietzsche was the most important of these.

To be sure, Adler mentioned Nietzsche repeatedly in *The Nervous Character*, but without ever coming to

winn versprechenden Unternehmungen zurückschreckt, wie meist auch vor Verbrechen und unmoralischen Handlungen, so deshalb, weil er für sein Persönlichkeitsgefühl fürchtet. Aus demselben Grunde scheut er oft vor der Lüge zurück, kann aber, um sicher zu gehen, und sich vor Abwegen zu hüten, in sich das Bedenken nähren, dass er grosser Laster und Verbrechen fähig wäre. — Dass diese starre Verfolgung der Fiktion eine soziale Schädigung bedeutet, liegt auf der Hand.

Der Egoismus nervöser Menschen, ihr Neid, ihr Geiz, oft ihnen unbewusst, ihre Tendenz, Menschen und 'Dinge zu entwerten, stammen aus ihrem Gefühl der Unsicherheit, und sind bestimmt, sie zu sichern, zu lenken, anzuspornen. — Da sie in Phantasien eingesponnen sind und in der Zukunft leben, ist auch ihre Zerstreutheit nicht verwunderlich. — Der Stimmungswechsel ist abhängig vom Spiel ihrer Phantasie, die bald peinliche Erinnerungen berührt, bald sich aufschwingt zur Erwartung des Triumphes, analog dem Schwanken und Zweifeln des Neurotikers. In gleicher Weise erscheinen spezielle Charakterzüge, die alle der menschlichen Psyche nicht fremd sind, durch den hypnotisierenden Endzweck gerichtet und tendenziös verstärkt. — Sexuelle Frühreife und Verliebtheit sind Ausdrucksformen für die gesteigerte Tendenz, erobern zu wollen, Masturbation, Impotenz und perverse Regungen liegen auf der Richtungslinie der Furcht vor dem Partner, der Furcht vor Entscheidung, wobei der Sadismus einen Versuch darstellt, den „wilden Mann" zu spielen, um ein Minderwertigkeitsgefühl zu übertäuben.

Wir haben als leitende Kraft und Endzweck der aus konstitutioneller Minderwertigkeit erwachsenen Neurose die Erhöhung des Persönlichkeitsgefühls betrachtet, die sich immer mit besonderer Macht durchzusetzen sucht. Dabei ist uns nicht entgangen, dass dies bloss die Ausdrucksform eines Strebens und Begehrens ist, deren Anfänge tief in der menschlichen Natur begründet sind. Die Ausdrucksform selbst und die Vertiefung dieses Leitgedankens, den man auch als Wille zur Macht (Nietzsche) bezeichnen könnte, belehrt uns, dass sich eine besondere Kraft kompensatorisch im Spiel befindet, die der inneren Unsicherheit ein Ende machen will. Durch die starre Formulierung, die meist an die Oberfläche des Bewusstseins dringt, sucht der Neurotiker den festen Punkt zu gewinnen, um die Welt aus den Angeln zu heben. Es macht keinen grossen Unterschied aus, ob viel oder wenig von dieser treibenden Kraft der Neurotiker bewusst ist. Den Mechanismus kennt er nie, und ebensowenig vermag er es allein, sein analogisches Verhalten und Apperzipieren aufzuklären und zu zerbrechen. Dies gelingt nur einem analytischen Verfahren, welches uns durch die Mittel der Abstraktion, Reduktion und Simplifikation die kindliche Analogie erraten und verstehen lässt. Dabei stellt sich nun regelmässig heraus, dass der Neurotiker stets nach der Analogie eines Gegensatzes apperzipiert, ja dass er zumeist nur gegensätzliche Beziehungen kennt und gelten lässt. Diese primitive Orientierung in der Welt, den antithetischen Aufstellungen Aristoteles', sowie den pythagoräischen Gegensatztafeln entsprechend, stammt gleichfalls aus dem Gefühle der Unsicherheit und stellt einen simplen Kunstgriff der Logik vor. Was ich als polare, hermaphroditische Gegensätze, Lombroso als bipolare, Bleuler als Ambivalenz beschrieben haben, führt auf diese nach dem

Page from Adler's *On the Nervous Character, 1912.* Note the many emphasized phrases and the reference to "will to power" (Nietzsche).

grips with the problem of whether his own central conception was not derived from him. At the outset Adler paid his respects to Pierre Janet and Josef Breuer, then took issue with "*Siegmund* [*sic*] *Freud*," first of all for his "*conception of libido as driving force*," and opposed to it his own conception of

> the enhancement of the feeling of personality, whose simplest formula is to be recognized in the exaggerated "*masculine protest.*" This formula, "I want to be a whole male" is the guiding fiction in every neurosis . . . Around this guiding thought libido, sex drive, and inclination toward perversion also group themselves, *wherever they may have come from. Nietzsche's* "will to power" and "will to illusion" embrace many things in our view, which in turn has some points of contact with the views of [Charles] *Féré* and older authors . . .

Then we are told that Freud was wrong about "the *sexual etiology* of the neuroses and that it is

> Strange that *Freud*, a refined expert on the symbolic in life, was unable to . . . recognize the sexual as mere jargon, as *a way of speaking.*

Eventually (p. 18) it turns out that Adler's main idea "could also be designated as *will to power (Nietzsche).*" Of the many subsequent references to the will to power it will suffice here to cite one more from the "Theoretical Part": On page 38 Adler speaks of "the unconditional *primacy of the will to power.*" In the "Practical Part" all sorts of things are explained in terms of the will to power, which is sometimes introduced expressly under that name while many more times it is invoked implicitly.

Despite his intense concern about his own priority and originality, Adler never faced up to the question of his own relationship to Nietzsche. He more or less gave the impression that he was only borrowing a convenient name or phrase from Nietzsche, as he did when he spoke of the neurotic patient's reenactment of childhood patterns as "the 'recurrence of the same' *(Nietzsche)*" (p. 15). He never considered the problem of whether he was not championing Nietzsche's will to power against Freud's libido theories. Many people always felt that this was what he did, and this also helps to account for the lack of interest in Adler. He never seemed all that original.

His followers, on the other hand, gathered from him "that the drive for power in Adler's sense has nothing in common with Nietzsche's will-to-power," to cite Manes Sperber's extreme formulation (p. 82). Adler's originality, which mattered so much to Adler himself, became a dogma for them. They did not even bother to look into this question to find out for themselves whether the view so succinctly formulated by Sperber was right.[42]

Of course, it would be a mistake to claim that Adler was really very close to Nietzsche. Adler was less close to Nietzsche than Freud was. Briefly, Adler was *Nietzsche without depth.* Recalling Jaspers's odd complaint that Freud was not transparent as a human being, one might say that Adler *was* and that this indicates a certain shallowness. Nietzsche was very complex, and Freud thought that it was probably impossible to understand him fully at this distance;[43] but he also "several times said of Nietzsche that he had a more penetrating knowledge of himself than any other man who ever lived or was ever likely to live."[44] As a human being, Adler was

[42] After the Ansbachers had discovered my *Nietzsche* (1950), a session at the Ninth Annual Meeting of the Association of Humanistic Psychology in Washington, D.C., in September 1971 was called "The Will-to-Power Re-examined," and then they printed the three papers, including my "Nietzsche's Concept of the Will to Power" and Heinz L. Ansbacher's "Adler's 'Striving for Power' in Relation to Nietzsche," in their *Journal of Individual Psychology,* May 1972. Clearly, Adler himself had not invited such reflections.

[43] Letters to Arnold Zweig, May 12, 1934, and July 15, 1934.

[44] Jones, II, p. 344. See Section 12 of the second volume of this trilogy.

the opposite of Nietzsche. He did not know himself at all well but seems easy to understand a few decades after his death. His constant rationalizations—of his baptism, of standing in Freud's shadow, of his own aggressiveness, to recall three examples—are indeed transparent.

Nietzsche was the first great depth psychologist and taught us to listen with the third ear. He called our attention to the importance of rationalizations and said: "Consciousness is a surface." Adler felt that there was no need for any depth psychology. His will to power theory differs from Nietzsche's by not reaching down below the surface. Since Freud had chosen a Latin epigraph for *The Interpretation of Dreams*, Adler naturally had to place a Latin epigraph over *The Nervous Character*. Freud's called attention to the underworld, Adler's to the importance of opinions.[45]

That brings us to the third way in which Adler was the opposite of Nietzsche. He had a great regard for public opinion and did not wish to give offense. His baptism and his completely unconvincing explanation of it speak volumes.[46] So do his remarks near the end of his life when he called Freud's psychoanalysis "filth" and "fecal matter."[47] Nietzsche had said:

> If a psychologist today has *good taste* (others might say, integrity) it consists in resistance to the shamefully *moralized* way of speaking which has gradually made all modern judgments of men and things slimy.[48]

One of Adler's followers should have the final word on the contrast. I can do no better than quote Bottome

---

[45] "Everything hangs on opinion. Not only ambition, profligacy, and avarice defer to it; our suffering conforms to it. One is as wretched as one thinks one is." Seneca, *Epist.*, 78.13.

[46] See Section 36 above.

[47] See Section 38 above.

[48] *Genealogy* III, Section 19, discussed in Section 17 of the second volume of this trilogy.

once more, for the last time. She quotes him as saying that

> "what the world chiefly wants today is *Gemeinschaftsge-fühl* [a sense of community]."
> What a platitude in the middle of a war! . . .
> But those who knew Adler best listened carefully, for they were well aware that when he said: "What the world needs is this or that," he would be prepared to give it to them.
> The difference between a platitude and a truth is, after all, only that between an uncontrovertible fact *stated*, and a deeply experienced fact *felt*. . . .
> But the Nietzscheans could not bear it. Whatever else they had joined Adler for—these Will-to-Power men could not put up with this menial goal. (p. 112f.)

This is a rich passage indeed. One of its implications would seem to be that Adler's truths were deeply felt platitudes. Nobody could say that of Nietzsche or Freud. Nor were Nietzsche and Freud as intent as Adler on giving the world what it wanted or telling it what it wanted to hear. And instead of preaching community feeling they communicated a sense of integrity that involved standing alone against the compact majority, "being the bad conscience of their time."[49] It was their ethos to swim against the stream. Adler, we recall, converted to Protestantism because he was afraid of the "spiritual danger" of isolation.

Nevertheless, Adler's many explanations of behavior in terms of the will to power provide a good deal of material that lends support to Nietzsche's theory. The way he put his points often does not commend itself; much of his talk about masculine and feminine is embarrassing; and he tended to make a virtue of being simplistic. Still, he provided cases from his practice as a psychotherapist that support Nietzsche's theories.

[49] Nietzsche, *Beyond*, Section 212.

50 ▶▶▶ Now we can no longer avoid the question of Freud's relationship to Nietzsche. Actually, there are two problems. First, if it is a mistake to see Adler and Freud as two significant alternatives because Adler really was not in the same league as Freud, then we must juxtapose Freud and Nietzsche. Second, Freud's attitude toward Nietzsche and the question of what he owed to Nietzsche are also of some interest. I shall take up the second point first.

In the autobiographical sketch of 1925 Freud said that he had not been influenced by Schopenhauer and continued:

> I have read *Schopenhauer* very late in life. *Nietzsche,* the other philosopher whose intimations and insights often coincide in the most amazing way with the laborious results of psychoanalysis, I have long avoided for precisely this reason; for I was concerned less about priority than about the preservation of my open-mindedness.[50]

Is this credible? Coming from Freud, yes. He must have meant that when people told him that Nietzsche had said many similar things, he preferred to work out his own themes in his own way, at his own speed, and did not wish to be influenced by Nietzsche's formulations one way or the other—either to accept them or to make changes to show his own independence.

Passages similar to this one include two published only in the 1960s but uttered orally in 1908. Both are found in the *Minutes.* In the discussion of the third part of Nietzsche's *Genealogy of Morals* on April 1, 1908,

> PROF. FREUD stressed above all his peculiar relationship to philosophy; its abstract nature is so uncongenial to him that he finally renounced the study of philosophy. Nietzsche, too, he does not know; an occasional attempt to read him was smothered by an excess of interest. In

[50] *Werke,* XIV, p. 86.

spite of the similarities which many people have pointed out, he can give the assurance that Nietzsche's ideas have had no influence at all on his own works.—To show how complicated and sometimes strange the origin of new ideas is he used this occasion to relate the genealogy of his conception of the sexual etiology of neurosis—something he remembered only when he was trying to justify himself after this idea had been rejected. Three important physicians had expressed this idea in his presence: Breuer, Charcot, and Chrobak.[51]

On October 28 of the same year the Wednesday evening meeting began with a very poor talk on Nietzsche's *Ecce Homo* by a minor figure, Adolf Häutler. Most of the discussion concerned Nietzsche as a case rather than Nietzsche's ideas. That observation applies also to Adler's and Freud's remarks. But Freud made three points that are worth quoting here. The book cannot be discounted as a product of insanity. "What shows that this work by Nietzsche must be considered fully valid and is to be taken seriously is the preservation of mastery in the form of the work." Then Freud said: "The degree of introspection achieved by Nietzsche had never been achieved by anyone, nor is it likely ever to be achieved again." Finally, only four sentences later,

> Professor Freud still wished to remark that he was never able to study Nietzsche: partly on account of the similarity between his intuitive insights and our laborious investigations, partly because of the wealth of ideas in his writings that, whenever he tried to read him, kept him from reading more than half a page.

At first glance, this seems hard to believe. It may even seem to contradict the preceding remark about the

[51] Freud mentioned this also in his *History of the Psychoanalytic Movement* (*Werke*, X, pp. 50ff.) and in his autobiographical sketch (*Werke*, XIV, p. 48).

degree of Nietzsche's introspection and Jones's report that "Freud several times said of Nietzsche that he had a more penetrating knowledge of himself than any other man who ever lived or was ever likely to live."[52] How could Freud have known that, if he never read much Nietzsche? That question is not unanswerable. The compliment must have been based on his reading of *Ecce Homo* in the fall of 1908, coupled with his reading a few months earlier of Nietzsche's *Genealogy of Morals* and particularly of the penetrating discussion of "ascetic ideals" in the third part; for Nietzsche himself had lived an ascetic life. Still, the compliment is utterly extraordinary because one would think that the whole point of psychoanalysis was to make possible more penetrating self-knowledge than had been available before. In effect, Freud was running down his own accomplishments as well as his own self-knowledge. How can we explain that? Here we cannot get beyond conjecture, and that will be more "educated" and probable if it takes into account additional evidence. To that end we must turn to the last decade of Freud's life and consider his correspondence with Arnold Zweig, who was an outstanding novelist as well as an essayist.

Zweig wrote Freud (December 2, 1930) that he was thinking of writing an essay "about your relationship to Nietzsche." He outlined some of his ideas about this topic—the central notion was that Freud had executed in detail "what Nietzsche saw intuitively as a task"—and having done this at some length, suggested that Freud should write a little book on the will to power of politicians. Freud replied that he could not write such a book:

> I know too little about the human striving for power, since after all I have lived the life of a theoretician. . . .
> Your essays I will get here. The one about the relation-

[52] II, p. 344. See Section 12 of the second volume of this trilogy.

ship of Nietzsche's influence to mine you should really write; after all, I don't have to read it. Write it some time when I am no longer around and you feel haunted by memories of me.

On April 28, 1934, after he had left Berlin-Grunewald for Haifa, Zweig wrote Freud another long letter about Nietzsche. This time he thought of writing a novel about Nietzsche's breakdown in Torino. He asked for Freud's and perhaps also Lou Andreas-Salomé's help and promised to dedicate the book to Freud. In his reply Freud tried to talk him out of his plan because it seemed impossible on the basis of available information to understand Nietzsche's psyche well enough, and he did not like the idea of a portrait that might not be faithful to the real Nietzsche. Then he added:

> Whether these are my real arguments against your plan I do not know. Perhaps the relationship to him into which you are moving me also plays a role. In my youth he signified for me a nobility I could not attain; a friend of mine, Dr. Paneth, had got to know him in the Engadin and had written me a great deal about him. Later my attitude toward him was roughly like that in your *Bilanz.*

Zweig's attitude in *Bilanz* had been mainly hostile. Paneth had met Nietzsche in Nice, where he saw a good deal of him between December 26, 1883, and March 26, 1884—not in the Engadin, in Switzerland, where Nietzsche spent several summers. Presumably, Paneth's portrait of Nietzsche in his letters to Freud was not far different from that which we find in his letters to his future wife, and I have included pertinent quotations in a chapter on Freud in another book.[53] The qualities Paneth stressed were "not a trace of false pathos or the prophet's pose," a "completely inoffensive and natural manner,"

[53] *From Shakespeare to Existentialism*, p. 324.

and total dedication to his work in spite of severe health problems. "Through his physical pains he had got rid of his pessimism—from defiance, in order not to let himself be bullied by pain." "He is a thoroughly honest human being."

> He is completely convinced of his mission and of his decisive importance. In this faith he is strong and superior to all misfortune, physical suffering, and poverty. Such a contempt for all external instruments of success, such freedom from all that smacks of cliques or advertising, is impressive.

One might have thought that Freud, after reading letters that presumably drew much the same picture, and feeling about Nietzsche as he did then, would have gone on to read some of Nietzsche's books—in the 1880s. The idea that he did this and then lied about it twenty-five years later can be ruled out on the basis of our knowledge of Freud. I have never found him to be dishonest about anything. That he read more than only a half a page here and there and then forgot about it is conceivable, the more so because he developed a less friendly attitude toward Nietzsche when Nietzsche became fashionable in the 1890s and his sister's caricature of him was widely accepted. If this should have been what actually happened, it would explain why Freud praised Nietzsche's self-knowledge so extravagantly (to make it up to him) and why he simultaneously ran down his own self-knowledge as well as the value of his discoveries (to punish himself for his forgetfulness and for having failed to give sufficient credit to Nietzsche earlier).

This hypothesis involves accusing Freud of having conveniently forgotten something, which really is not at all likely when one considers all the circumstances. After all, the question of Nietzsche's influence on him came up again and again. Yet his extraordinary praise of Nietzsche's self-knowledge at his own expense clearly seems to involve the two factors just cited: punishing himself and making an extravagant effort to compensate Nietzsche for something. For what?

The member of Freud's circle who knew most about Schopenhauer and Nietzsche was Otto Rank. He called some parallels to Freud's attention. In an unpublished letter of January 21, 1931, to George Wilbur, who later became editor of *American Imago*,[54] he wrote:

> Your discovery of Nietzsche's influence is quite correct, particularly in earlier days, because lately I have emancipated myself from him too [and not only from Freud]. But in stressing his influence on my development don't [*sic*] overlook the tremendous influence he had on Freud inasmuch as he has influenced all European thinking (Freud read Nietzsche only in his later years but was spiritually under his influence from the beginning—just as he was under Schopenhauer's, although he denied both).[55]

Rank was in a position to know that Freud read Nietzsche only late, and his testimony to that effect is valuable. That Nietzsche's thought helped to shape the intellectual climate in the 1890s and in the first decade of the twentieth century—in other words, during the period when Freud developed psychoanalysis—is also a fact. But the further claim that Freud "was spiritually under his influence from the beginning" is vague and plainly meant to put down Freud. A letter Rank wrote to his biographer, Jessie Taft, on February 8, 1933, is as clear on that score as could be: While reading D. H. Lawrence,

---

[54] He succeeded Hanns Sachs in 1947 and subsequently served as honorary editor from 1963 until 1976.
[55] Reading Rank's many letters to Wilbur at an autograph dealer's, I was struck by the immense difference between Rank's letters and Freud's. Rank's are quite undistinguished, and I found none of the others half as interesting as this one.

> I felt that he was the greatest psychological philosopher
> since Nietzsche because more human (but certainly
> greater than Freud and all the rest of "fiction writers"?).[56]

More human than who? That is left as unclear as the
reason for the question mark. But what is clear is the
resentment toward Freud and the attempt to put him
down, which throws more light on Rank's feelings in the
1930s than on Freud. (See Section 34 above.) Here it
only needs to be added that Rank's parting present to
Freud—in 1926, for Freud's seventieth birthday—was an
elegantly bound edition of Nietzsche's works that he had
sent immediately after his own departure from Vienna.
Roazen was surely right when he noted, without referring to the two letters I have cited:

> It was as if Rank's gift were saying, "you accuse me of
> taking from you, when look what you have taken from
> Nietzsche."[57]

Only Freud had not made any such accusation.

In view of what we have learned about Freud's
mind from his works, his letters, the *Minutes,* and those
who knew him well, it seems plain that he felt he owed
Nietzsche something and also that he somehow felt
a little guilty (I can see no other explanation for his
punishing himself the way he did). There seem to have
been two reasons, neither of which might have been
sufficient by itself. He had never given Nietzsche
sufficient credit for his creation of depth psychology and
had slighted him in a way by not reading him and by not
indicating all the points on which Nietzsche actually had
priority. Freud had been scrupulous about other, minor
figures, while in a way treating Nietzsche less well. Add
to that his immense admiration for Nietzsche in the

[56] Taft, *Otto Rank* (1958), p. 175.
[57] Roazen (1975), p. 412.

1880s, when he had associated Nietzsche with "a nobility I could not attain"—and no further explanation is needed.

Still, Freud had long owned a set of Nietzsche, which made Rank's opulent gesture only that much more poignant. Oddly, Freud's letter to Fliess of February 1, 1900, was among those omitted by the editors when they published *The Origins of Psychoanalysis,* and it remained for Max Schur to include it in *Freud: Living and Dying* (1972). The fact that it was written a couple of months after the appearance of *The Interpretation of Dreams* bears out Freud's later claims. But I cannot forgo quoting two sentences that precede the crucial reference to Nietzsche. They are very striking and support my picture of Freud as anything but the scion of nineteenth-century scientific materialism.

> For I am actually not at all a man of science, not an observer, not an experimenter, not a thinker. My temperament is essentially that of a conquistador, I am nothing but an adventurer if you want to translate it, with the curiosity, the boldness, and the tenacity of that type. . . .
>
> I finally treated myself to Nietzsche [*Ich habe mir jetzt den Nietzsche beigelegt*], in whom I hope to find words for a great deal that remains mute in me, but have not opened him yet. Too inert so far.[58]

Surely, the two paragraphs are not altogether unrelated. Of course, Freud was a man of science and a thinker. But far from feeling at home with the nineteenth-century

[58] The German text is given on p. 547, and the translation is mine. Schur's English version appears on p. 201f., along with an interesting footnote in which Schur links this passage with another letter to Fliess (April 14, 1898) in which Freud had said of a guide who boasted that "he had already been in thirty-six holes," meaning caves: "I recognized his conquistador exploits as an erotic equivalent." The guide himself said "a minute later . . . 'It's like with a virgin; the farther the better!'" Schur suggests that Freud thought of his own exploits as also involving sublimation.

scientists with whom so many who have written about him have linked him, he felt more of a kinship with Nietzsche. Nevertheless, the letter suggests that before 1900 he really had not read much Nietzsche, and that even then he felt some resistance to exposing himself to Nietzsche.

This resistance was still in evidence in 1908, when Freud and his circle considered Nietzsche at two meetings more as a case than as a psychologist, with the exception of that one sweeping compliment. Freud refused to read Nietzsche the way Nietzsche would have wanted to be read—or the way Freud would have wanted to be read. Another reason for making it up to him and running himself down.

We still have to ask whether Freud's revision of his theories after the First World War had something to do with the fact that in 1908, if not before, he had read *Genealogy of Morals* and *Ecce Homo,* and then possibly more of Nietzsche after that. One cannot prove this, and the revision was in any case overdetermined and clearly not due mainly to things Freud had read. Still, there is a compelling reason for believing that after 1912 he was reminded of Nietzsche more often than before. That year Lou Andreas-Salomé approached Freud and quickly became his friend, which she remained until her death in 1937. She had been very close to Nietzsche in 1882 and had later published a book on him (1894; 3rd edition, 1924), and she provided an unexpected link with Nietzsche.

One might suppose further that Freud must have heard a great deal about Nietzsche from her, but there is good reason to believe that she refused to talk about Nietzsche with Freud. Having tried to talk Zweig out of writing a book about Nietzsche, Freud wrote him on May 22, 1934, that advising against it did not strike him as a sufficient service to a friend; he had complied with Zweig's request.

I have therefore asked Frau Lou whether her cooperation might be available. I enclose her reply, which you might return to me.

Frau Lou's words could hardly have been more emphatic:

That is for me an *altogether unthinkable* collaboration, even if it were ever so slight, ever so remote! That is something I cannot touch; full of horror, I ward it off. Please tell the man with the strongest expressions and for ever.—Moreover, how right you are to advise him urgently against the Nietzsche plan.[59]

Her overreaction must seem puzzling unless one knows how she had thoroughly misrepresented her relationship with Nietzsche before she met Freud. Above all, she had claimed falsely that he had proposed marriage to her.[60] She admired Freud immensely, and he liked and respected her; but if she had ever agreed to speak with him about Nietzsche she would have faced the dilemma of either confessing her perfidy or lying to him.

Still, there is one theory in the later Freud that was surely derived directly, albeit unconsciously, from Nietzsche. The account of the origin of conscience in Chapter VII of *Civilization and Its Discontents* (1930)— "Aggression is introjected, internalized"[61]—is anticipated in Nietzsche's *Genealogy of Morals*, in Section 16 of the second essay. That essay is entitled " 'Guilt,' 'Bad Conscience,' and the Like," and Nietzsche argues:

All instincts that do not discharge themselves outwardly *turn inward*—this is what I call the *internalization* of man.

[59] In a footnote to Freud's letter to Zweig; also in Freud's correspondence with her, May 16 and 20, 1934.
[60] See Binion's *Frau Lou* (1968) and Kaufmann's *Nietzsche*, pp. 48–64 of the 3rd or 4th edition.
[61] *Werke*, XIV, p. 482.

The passage, that ends "*that* is the origin of the bad conscience" has been quoted and discussed in Section 25 of the second volume of his trilogy, along with its influence on Freud.

51 ▶▶▶ Now we must finally face the problem of what to make of the difference between Freud's depth psychology and Nietzsche's. They may be similar in ever so many ways, yet Nietzsche tried to explain human behavior in terms of the will to power while Freud tried to explain as much as possible in terms of sex. Or did he? Is this not a caricature of Freud? He himself insisted that he had always been a dualist. Before the First World War he had contrasted the pleasure principle and the reality principle.[62] After the war he had revised his theories:

> After long hesitation and vacillation we have resolved to postulate only two basic drives, the *Eros* and the *destruction drive*. (The opposition of the drives for self-preservation and preservation of the species as well as that of self-love and object love still falls within the Eros.) The goal of the former is to produce ever larger units and to preserve them, thus cohesion; the goal of the other one, on the contrary, to dissolve what hangs together and thus to destroy things. Regarding the destruction drive we can think that its final goal seems to be to transform the living into an inorganic state. We therefore also call it *death drive*. If we suppose that the living arrived later than the lifeless and developed out of that, then the death drive obeys the previously mentioned formulation that a drive desires the return to a former state.[63]

[62] *Werke*, VIII, p. 232 explains the reality principle succinctly.
[63] *Werke*, XVII, p. 71.

Now one might have thought that Freud would have considered the question of how his dualisms fare when they are compared with Nietzsche's psychological monism. But he never did. In fact, he did not think of Nietzsche as, so to say, in Adler's camp, denying the importance of sex or even the desire for pleasure. Here the German terms are crucial. *Beyond the Pleasure Principle* is in German *Jenseits des Lustprinzips.* When George Sylvester Viereck had a long conversation with Freud in 1926, with the express intention of including his account of it in a forthcoming book— *Glimpses of the Great* (1930)[63a]—he said to Freud toward the end: "Psycho-analysis has given new intensities to literature." Freud replied:

> It also has received much from literature and philosophy. Nietzsche was one of the first psycho-analysts. It is amazing to what extent his intuition foreshadows our discoveries. No one has recognized more profoundly the dual motives of human conduct, and the insistence of the pleasure principle upon unending sway. His Zarathustra says:
>
>> Woe
>> Crieth: Go!
>> But Pleasure craves eternity
>> Craves quenchless, deep eternity.

Viereck's translation of the end of Nietzsche's poem (in the penultimate chapter of *Zarathustra*) is neither quite literal nor very beautiful. In my translation of *Zarathustra* I rendered *Lust* as joy:

> *Woe implores: Go!*
> *But all joy wants eternity–*
> *Wants deep, wants deep eternity.*

[63a] Freud referred to this interview as pleasant. (*Werke*, XIV, p. 393).

At this point we must recall a passage from Freud's *History* that has already been cited in Section 42 above. Psychoanalysis, said Freud in 1914, was

> interested in showing that all strivings of the ego had libidinous components mixed in. [Nietzsche might well have agreed and occasionally said the same thing, though he did not do anywhere near as much as Freud did to show this.] Adler's doctrine stresses the other side of the coin, the egoistic admixture in libidinous drives. Now this would be a palpable gain if Adler did not use this point to deny the libidinous impulse . . . (p. 96)

in a way that favored constant rationalizations. Adler eventually went so far as to call Freud's preoccupation with libido "filth" and "fecal matter," and there was ample reason all along to suppose that his repudiation of Freud's concern with sexual etiologies was of a piece with his conversion to Protestantism and motivated in part by a desire for community feeling and his horror of the dangers of isolation from the compact majority.

Nietzsche was the opposite of Adler in all of these ways, and Freud considered Nietzsche a precursor and not an antagonist. Moreover, Freud tried not only in 1914 but even more so after the war to absorb Nietzsche's central insights into psychoanalysis. One could actually characterize Freud's later version of psychoanalysis as an attempt at a synthesis of Nietzsche and early Freud.

That is not to say that Freud thought in the end that he now had created an all-embracing system. On the contrary, one of the many points on which he sided, in effect, with Nietzsche against Adler was that he opposed inclusive systems. With Nietzsche's opposition to systems I have dealt at length in this chapter on "Nietzsche's Method" in my *Nietzsche*. Freud's even less systematic denigration of systems was introduced in a lighthearted way in Section 6, where we noted how he liked to quote Heine's derision of the German philosophy professor:

> with his bathrobe rags and long nightcaps
> he mends the world and plugs all the gaps.[64]

When discussing Adler in his *History* Freud said of psychoanalysis:

> It has never claimed to furnish a complete theory of the whole of human psychic life but merely demanded that its results should be used to amend and correct what knowledge we have acquired elsewhere. The theory of Alfred Adler goes far beyond this aim . . . (p. 93f.)

Similar passages recur throughout Freud's writings down to the book on which he was still working when he died, his *Outline of Psychoanalysis*. Here he distinguished three "psychic qualities": conscious, preconscious, and unconscious, and then commented:

> Presented in this general and simplified form, the doctrine of the three qualities of what is psychic seems to be a source of unfathomable confusion rather than a contribution to enlightenment. But it should not be forgotten that it is not properly speaking a theory but merely a first report [*Rechenschaftsbericht*] about the facts of our observations, that it sticks as closely as possible to these facts and does not try to explain them. The complications it uncovers may make understandable the peculiar difficulties with which our investigations have to wrestle.[65]

It would be idle to expect any definitive answer to the question how Nietzsche might have reconciled Freud's findings with his own psychology, which was obviously even more tentative. He was only twelve years

---

[64] See also the quotation from the *Minutes* in Section 12 above.
[65] *Werke*, XVII, p. 83.

older than Freud; and had he lived as long as Freud did, he would have died in 1927 and could have read almost all of Freud's major works. I certainly could not imagine him rejecting Freud's libido theories either as filth and fecal matter or, dogmatically, because they did not coincide with his own attempts to get as far as he could with the will to power. After all, he said that "it was Christianity . . . that first made something unclean of sexuality: it threw *filth* on the origin, on the presupposition of our life." Nor does this formulation in the penultimate section of *Twilight of the Idols* stand alone; this was one of his central themes. And in Section 75 of *Beyond Good and Evil* he suggested, without ever elaborating this point very much: "The degree and kind of a man's or woman's sexuality reach up into the ultimate pinnacle of their spirit." It would have been entirely in his spirit to try to integrate Freud's ideas with his own—as Freud tries to integrate Nietzsche's with *his* own.

Where does that leave us? Far from the notion that every conceivable case can be interpreted quite easily in Adler's fashion or in Freud's.[66] In fact, Freud never claimed that he could explain every bit of human behavior, and to explain some cases proved to be so hard that it took years, and not every case by any means was solved by him to his own satisfaction. Leaving aside Adler now and turning to Nietzsche instead, it would be ludicrous to claim that by invoking the will to power we can adequately explain every bit of human behavior and solve even the most recalcitrant cases, curing every neurotic.

We need to recall Freud's concept of overinterpretation,[67] which is very close to Nietzsche's spirit and invites comparison with Nietzsche's comments on interpretation and perspectivism: "Every neurotic symptom and even a dream is capable of overinterpretation and

[66] See Section 19 above.
[67] See Section 20 above.

actually demands nothing less for its full understanding." We also recall Freud's remark, quoted a few pages back, right after the lines from *Zarathustra*, that "all strivings of the ego had libidinous components mixed in" and that it is "a palpable gain" to be shown "the egoistic admixture in libidinous drives."

In sum, no single explanation can really explain human behavior; it can at most illuminate human behavior and allow us to see something we had not seen. Rarely is what we are shown so striking and relevant that we may feel we need to know no more. This, it seems to us, was just what we were looking for; it answers our question; we are satisfied. But then somebody may call our attention to a point that we had overlooked, and suddenly a dimension has been added to our understanding.

All of this happens so regularly that there is simply no end of examples. An accident may be considered a paradigm. Why did it happen? The road was icy at that point. And the driver of the small car was in a great hurry because he was late for a crucial appointment, because the person who had promised to pick him up had not come. And his reflexes were slower than usual because he had had hardly any sleep that night because his mother had died the day before. And just before the accident his attention was distracted for one crucial second by a very pretty girl on the side of the road who reminded him of a girl he had once known. Yet he might have regained control of his car if only a truck had not come toward him just as he skidded into the left lane. The truck driver might have managed not to hit him, but . . . If we add that the truck driver had just gone through a red light and was, moreover, going much faster than the legal speed limit, the policeman who witnessed the accident, as well as the court later on, might discount as irrelevant everything said before the three dots and be quite content to explain the accident simply in terms of the truck driver's two violations. *He* caused the accident. But that does not rule out the possibility that the other driver had a strong death wish because his mother had died, or that he punished himself for looking at an attractive girl the way he did so soon after his mother's death, or that the person who had let him down was partly to blame.

In this case more than one person is involved, but the picture is not essentially different when there is only one. Why am I writing this book? Why are you reading it? Why did I choose this example? Why do I admire Freud so much? Why do I not admire Adler more than I do? Why does *Oedipus Tyrannus* move so many people so deeply?

To take up the final question, Freud ventured an explanation in his *Interpretation of Dreams*, just before the footnote in which he introduced "overinterpretation." I have argued at length in another book that Sophocles's tragedy contains five central themes: man's radical insecurity, human blindness, the curse of honesty (supreme honesty, however admirable, usually does not make the honest person happy, nor those who are very close to him or her), the inevitability of tragedy in some situations, and finally the highly problematic nature of justice. It would be pointless in the present context to recapitulate the whole demonstration which in any case was not designed mainly to explain the effect of the play. What is essential here is merely that the effect is overdetermined. My five themes do not rule out Freud's suggestion any more than his suggestion rules out my five themes, and it would be fatuous to say that there cannot be five themes, that there must be one sole explanation for the deep effect of the tragedy.

Simplistic minds are confused by more than one explanation. They like to be told that every tragedy is due to the hero's "tragic flaw": Hamlet allegedly can't make up his mind, Othello is jealous and Macbeth ambitious, and Oedipus has a temper. To ask whether human behavior is to be explained by the will to power or by libido is on that level. Some so-called explanations are illuminating, most are not. Nietzsche and Freud, like nobody else, developed ideas that illuminate a great deal, if not all, of human behavior and contributed more than anybody before or since to human self-understanding or, if you prefer, to the discovery of the mind.

Some people suppose that there must be one true explanation that differs from all others by appealing to facts from which one could have predicted what is to be explained. Two things are needed, according to this model: the facts and covering laws. To explain something that had remained unexplained so far, one has to discover either a fact or a law.

All the things that had to happen to make an accident inevitable defy the imagination, and precisely the same is true of historical events and individual experiences generally. If even one of the great-great-grandmothers of one of the protagonists had succumbed to measles or diphtheria in her childhood, or if even one had refused the advances of her husband the night in which the child who eventually became an ancestor of one of the protagonists was conceived, then that protagonist would not have existed and the event would not have occurred as it did.

Suppose we were told not to go that far back. We might be asked to describe only what was the case five minutes before the event in question. In that case the explanation would consist in a full and accurate description and a listing of the applicable laws. But this model still raises enormous difficulties.

One simply cannot describe fully everything that was the case. Every description involves interpretations, and all understanding and explaining depend on selection. Those who try to tell us everything exhaust our patience and confuse us without explaining anything.

Suppose the truck in our example had been loaded with books. Need we really have a full description of every page of every book? And what would be a full description? Would it proceed in terms of chemical elements? Molecules? Temperature? Arrangement of the type? The meaning of each word? The plots, numbers of characters, or kinds of argument?

An explanation provides an answer to a question, and as long as no question is specified or understood, no explanation can be given. The question of why a particular event happened is elliptical. We need to know what is already known and what in particular is not understood as yet. In other words: What precisely is the problem? Once we are told that, we may be able to point to a fact that is relevant but had been overlooked, or we may be able to point out a frequent, though not necessarily universal, correlation. We may be able to say: There are many cases in which the conjunction of such and such events has precisely this kind of a consequence.

Now we may be pressed further: If somebody knew all the relevant facts along with all possible interpretations and all "natural laws," would such an agent be able to predict our future actions and experiences in detail? I doubt it, I hope not, but I cannot predict for certain that this is impossible. Those who claim to know that this is possible or that it will happen are dogmatists. I am a skeptic and resigned to my insignificant place in the universe. And for us human beings all explanations involve interpretation and selection. Under these circumstances, an explanation can always be supplemented and is never final. A work of art can be finished; science and philosophy are open-ended.

52 ▶▶▶ Before we leave Vienna for Zurich to have a look at Jung, we should consider for just a moment the popular notion that Freud's long residence in Vienna either explains or at least greatly illuminates psychoanalysis. Many people have said something like that for decades, and in the 1970s not only this conceit became quite fashionable, but it came to be supposed that cities might quite generally throw some light on the great men who lived there for a while. We shall confine ourselves to Freud and Vienna.

Those who try to explain Freud or psychoanalysis in terms of Vienna never seem to mention Adler, who was actually born in a suburb of Vienna while Freud was born in Freiberg in Moravia. Was Freud, who hated Vienna, more Viennese than Adler, who loved it?

Vienna, we are told, was full of new ideas in Freud's time. But when Jones once said precisely that, adding that it must be interesting to live there, Freud replied: "I have lived here for fifty years and have never come across a new idea here."[68] That must have been about 1910. On the same page Jones quotes a letter of March 11, 1900—"I hate Vienna almost personally, and in contrast to the giant Antaeus I gather fresh strength as soon as I remove my foot . . ."—and a letter of September 22, 1898—"It is a misery to live here; this is no atmosphere in which to maintain the hope of achieving anything difficult." He also said it disgusted him, and he found it "physically repulsive." And as early as 1886 he wrote from Berlin, where he spent several weeks on his way home from Paris: "I believe I should have died on the journey if I had had to travel direct from Paris to Vienna."

This overwhelming hatred was plainly not merely an understandable reaction to the poor reception of his ideas, which Graf described unforgettably (footnote 29 above); it long antedated the development of psychoanalysis. Jones refers to the "illiberal and anti-Semitic atmosphere, combined with the memory of his poverty-

[68] Jones, I, p. 293. See also Sachs, Chapter II.

stricken years that followed the wrenching away from his beloved Freiberg." No doubt, that had a lot to do with it, but what matters here is that Vienna really did not influence Freud except insofar as he reacted against it.

The remark about the lack of new ideas must strike many readers as extraordinary. Schorske's *Fin-de-siècle Vienna* contains an article on Freud, originally published in 1973, as well as pieces that deal with Gustav Klimt and Oskar Kokoschka, Arnold Schoenberg and Hugo von Hofmannsthal. Not one of them is ever mentioned in Freud's works or in Jones's three-volume biography, except that Jones at one point rejects Bottome's curious claim that Hofmannsthal and various other luminaries "joined the psychoanalytic circle."[69] Freud was not interested in their work and had no ear for music.

Despite his immense interest in literature and art, Freud lived in another world that was much more German than Austrian. Viereck reports that Freud said to him in 1926:

> My culture, my attainments are German. I considered myself a German intellectually, until I noticed the growth of anti-Semitic prejudice in Germany and in German Austria. Since that time, I consider myself no longer a German. I prefer to call myself a Jew. (p. 30)

This report is entirely consistent with what we have found. Goethe and Nietzsche defined the tradition in which Freud placed himself; he loved Lessing, who influenced his style; and two German Jews, Heine and Börne, who had hated each other, meant a great deal to him, too, especially Heine. Beyond that, his horizon was European: Leonardo and Michelangelo, Shakespeare and Dostoevsky, and Ibsen. Thomas Mann, Stefan Zweig, and Arnold Zweig admired him and wrote about

---

[69] Jones, II, p. 8. The Bottome passage is cited in Section 36 above, after footnote 10.

him, and he carried on an interesting correspondence with Arnold Zweig. Among his Viennese contemporaries he did like Arthur Schnitzler. But had he lived in Berlin instead of Vienna, there is no reason to believe that his work would have been greatly different.[70]

Of course, some knowledge of the environment in which a thinker lived can add a dimension to our understanding of his work. But in Freud's case this dimension has been vastly overestimated, and those who have dealt with fin-de-siècle Vienna have not dealt with *Freud's* Vienna but have concentrated on people in whom he took no interest, without telling us that he ignored them. Even so, one could say some illuminating things about, say, Freud and Gustav Klimt, showing how different they were. Klimt's art teeters on the edge of prurience and often crosses over. Few painters who are taken seriously have ever painted so much that is so bad. But even his best work is distinguished by a style that is diametrically opposed to Freud's. It is sumptuously ornamental, luxuriant, rich, and it depends heavily on the appeal of nudity; even his portraits are utterly lacking in psychological subtlety. His is an art of surfaces, lacking in depth.[71]

[70] Peter Gay (1978) comes to the same conclusion. I also agree with him when he says of some recent writers that he rejects "their construction of 'Vienna' " and "*that* Vienna is an invention of cultural historians in search of quick explanations" (p. 33f.).

[71] Schorske's attempt in *Fin-de-siècle Vienna* (1980) to find depth in Klimt is wholly unconvincing: "His figure of Philosophy suggests the dark rhapsodic language of Zarathustra's 'Drunken Song of Midnight,' " he says and then quotes the song, but entirely misses its meaning. He introduces "Desire" where Nietzsche had "Joy" or "Pleasure" (see above between footnotes 63 and 64). The difference is crucial for the climax and conclusion of *Zarathustra* as well as Nietzsche's doctrine of the eternal recurrence of the same events; but either way it makes no sense at all to claim that "Nietzsche's explication of his Midnight Song in the glowing finale of *Thus Spake Zarathustra* reads as though written to elucidate Klimt's painting." Nietzsche's world, tone, and style were as remote from Klimt's as were Freud's.

Moreover, it seems to me that if one wanted to distill the spirit of Vienna during the two decades preceding the First World War, sound method would require some contrast with other cities during that period. How did Viennese painting at that time differ from the works of Ernst Ludwig Kirchner and Emil Nolde, Karl Schmidt-Rottluff and Erich Heckel, Wassily Kandinsky and Franz Marc, Edvard Munch and Paul Klee? How could a book in which all of these artists are simply ignored along with Dante Gabriel Rossetti and Edward Burne-Jones possibly tell us what was distinctive in fin-de-siècle Vienna? And how could one have reason to believe that Freud was somehow typically Viennese if one simply ignores the question of whether he had more in common with his contemporaries in Vienna than with people elsewhere? These questions of method far transcend one or two books on Vienna. They are meant to suggest that Freud needs to be understood in an altogether different context.

PART ▶

Discovering Jung's Mind ▶▶▶

53 ▶▶▶ For all its critical analysis psychology has not yet managed to root out its psychopaths. . . . In the critical psychology of the future there will be a chapter on "The Psychopathology of Psychology.". . . There is no thinking *qua* thinking; at times it is a pisspot of all unconscious devils. . . Often *what* is thought is less important than *who* thinks it. But this is assiduously overlooked. *Neurosis* contradicts every psychologist, for he is at odds with himself. In such cases psychology is nothing but the systematized fight against one's own insecurity.

Except for one small change, this outburst appears in a letter Jung wrote February 28, 1943, to a student. The one change I have made is to substitute "psychology" and "psychologist" where Jung wrote "philosophy" and "philosopher." If Jung had been right about philosophy, his statement should not lose its truth when this change is made, for psychology is no more privileged than philosophy. His point of departure in this letter was Heidegger, and in the Heidegger chapter of this trilogy (in Section 42) this passage was quoted as Jung wrote it, and there it can also be seen how, toward the end of the letter, Jung specifically included Kierkegaard, Hegel, and Nietzsche in his attack.

I do not accept this reductionist attitude, which finds clear expression in the words "nothing but." Jung's remarks about Hegel, Kierkegaard, and Nietzsche are absurd, and his comment on Heidegger's "inflated language" can hardly be taken seriously: "Only listen to one seminar on psychiatry and then you will know where this language can also be heard." This wildly emotional overreaction suggests that in Heidegger he sensed his own shadow (a conception we shall consider later), but without understanding this himself. Whether his final strictures are applicable to Jung himself remains to be seen.

I shall concentrate on the discovery of Jung's mind and try to illuminate his break with Freud, which was the most crucial event of his adult life. He never got over it and kept dealing with it in various ways until he died. While it is impossible to cover all of his psychology here, I shall deal with some of his major concepts in this chapter and then consider a single book in depth in the next.

It may be well to note some asymmetries between the collected works of Freud and Jung before we begin. In German, Freud's collected works comprise seventeen volumes and a large index volume.[1] The writings are offered in chronological order, and six volumes contain a single work. Asked for a good overview of the whole of psychoanalysis, one would point, without hesitation, to the introductory lectures of 1916/17 and the seven lectures Freud added to this sequence in 1933; and anyone who did not wish to give the subject that much time could be referred easily to several briefer summaries by Freud himself. Asked what Freud's major works were, one would point, again without any hesitation, to *The Interpretation of Dreams, The Psychopathology of Ev-*

[1] For no very good reason, Volumes II and III form a single volume.

eryday Life, and *Beyond the Pleasure Principle,* to which one might perhaps add *Three Contributions to the Theory of Sex,* the book on jokes, *Totem and Taboo, The Ego and the Id,* and possibly *Civilization and Its Discontents.*

Jung's collected works comprise eighteen volumes, supplemented by *General Bibliography* and *General Index.*[2] The writings are not arranged chronologically, and fifteen of the eighteen volumes contain miscellaneous pieces, usually written during entirely different periods of Jung's life; for example, from 1904 to 1937, or from 1907 to 1958. Of the remaining three volumes, number 5 offers a single work, *Symbols of Transformation,* but in the 1952 revision of the text originally published in two volumes in 1911 and 1912. I cannot help feeling that Jung and his editors neither had a clear conception of his development nor wished others to see how he had developed. Their approach was more systematic than historical or developmental.

The editors of Freud's works followed the precedent of editions of Goethe and Nietzsche that were arranged chronologically. Jung's editors, in keeping with his own wishes, departed from this example and tried for a more systematic arrangement that, owing to his very unsystematic turn of mind, did not work out at all well; and when the same material was eventually made available in paperback, another effort was made to present essays with similar themes in one volume, resulting in an entirely different grouping. A typical paperback volume draws on more than one hardcover volume.

Moreover, Jung never wrote the kind of introduction or survey that Freud wrote. There is no one work by him that integrates his many publications into a single whole. Although he wrote copiously, his bent was really strik-

[2] Volume 9 is actually two volumes, (9.I and 9.II), each with separate pagination. The totals I give for both Freud and Jung follow the editors' numbering and disregard these oddities.

ingly unsystematic. Nor could one point to a few of his books and say, without fear of contradiction, that they are his masterpieces on which his reputation rests, for better or for worse.

Finally, Jung's German style is such that he is bound to gain in English translation, like Kant, while Freud, like Goethe, cannot but lose a great deal in translation. In English, the immense difference between Freud's style and Jung's is flattened out. Nor have Jung's translators been content to make his prose clearer and leaner; they have made other improvements as well. In an article that Jung published in Germany in 1934, for example, he said:

> The Aryan unconscious has a higher potential than the Jewish; that is the advantage and disadvantage of a youthfulness that is not yet totally alienated from the barbarous.

In *The Collected Works* the word "Aryan" is placed in quotation marks throughout this paragraph,[3] suggesting subtly that Jung did not really mean it, and "not yet totally alienated" (which sounds more like a compliment) is turned into "not yet fully weaned." Of course, most of the slight inaccuracies in the English versions are not particularly tendentious, though sometimes it is hard to decide whether admiration has not had its share in them. While it may seem to be nitpicking to give examples, it would be worse to make an unsubstantiated charge of this sort; and many readers may well wonder why I have made my own translations in this case, too, when Princeton University Press has produced *The Collected Works* as well as Jung's letters so handsomely. Here, then, is one more example. In one of his last letters to Freud (18 December 1912) Jung said: "I recognize my

[3] 10, 353f. = Volume 10, paragraph 353f. These figures apply to the American as well as the Swiss edition. Where the American edition differs, I identify it as "A."

insecurity vis-à-vis you, but have the tendency to keep this situation honest and absolutely decent." In the published English translation this becomes: "I admit the ambivalence of my feelings towards you, but am inclined to take an honest and absolutely straightforward view of the situation." *Anständig* is "decent" and not "straightforward," and there is no reference to any view in the original; but these are trifles, while Jung's recognition of his insecurity is highly significant. The word he uses, *Unsicherheit*, is the same we encountered in the letter to the student at the beginning of this chapter. There, incidentally, the same translator (R. F. C. Hull) has "uncertainty." Anyone who relies on the published translations of Jung is bound to miss all sorts of niceties.

54 ▶▶▶ Jung's contrast of the introverted and extraverted character may well be his most familiar and most widely cited contribution to the discovery of the mind. It is presented in *Psychological Types* (1921), one of the three works that take up one entire volume (6) of *The Collected Works*. The book has eleven chapters, and the first nine deal with the historical background of Jung's typology. Chapter I deals with classical and medieval thought, II with Friedrich Schiller, III with Nietzsche's contrast of the Apollonian and Dionysian in *The Birth of Tragedy;* each of the following four chapters deals at length with a relatively minor writer, VIII with William James, and IX with Wilhelm Ostwald.

No doubt, I am more interested in intellectual history than most scholars, not to speak of readers who have no special interest in scholarship; but what is one to make of these hundreds upon hundreds of pages? If I point out that the discussion of Nietzsche's contrast of two types displays a crass misunderstanding and that the latter contrast of Richard Wagner as "an advocate of love" and Nietzsche as "an advocate of power"[4] is downright embarrassing, I am sure to be told by Jung's admirers that his claim to fame obviously does not rest on his competence as an intellectual historian. But what is at stake here is actually much more interesting than meets the eye.

To appreciate that we must note first of all that the break between Wagner and Nietzsche was by no means merely a biographical incident that can be ignored by those who are interested in Nietzsche's work rather than his life. Nietzsche wrote three books on Wagner, and the last two were designed to explain the break. In fact, *Nietzsche contra Wagner* was his last book, and he put into it some of the most profound and best-written passages from his earlier works. Anyone who wants to gain some understanding of Nietzsche could hardly do better than devote a half hour to reading this little book.[5]

Of course, Wagner's *Tristan und Isolde* is a celebration of love, but Nietzsche admired and praised it to the end. What Nietzsche did not admire was Wagner's nationalism, his hatred of the French, and his virulent anti-Semitism. Moreover, Nietzsche's attempt to understand Wagner psychologically was one of the major sources of his theory of the will to power. Nor did Nietzsche criticize Christianity as the religion of love; he tried to show how it was born of resentment.

Not only Jung's juxtaposition of Nietzsche and Wagner but his whole typology represents an attempt to come to terms—with Freud. In 1917 Jung had published an essay[6] that later became the first of the *Two Essays on Analytical Psychology* (Volume 7 of *The Collected*

---

[4] 7, 453 = A7, 408.
[5] In *The Portable Nietzsche* the complete text comprises pp. 661–83.
[6] *Die Psychologie der unbewussten Prozesse.* It was actually an extensive revision of an article Jung had published in 1912 before his break with Freud. In Vol. 7 the 1912 piece appears in an appendix. The 1917 essay is called "On the Psychology of the Unconscious."

Works), and there Chapter II was called "The Eros Theory" and dealt with Freud, while Chapter III was called "The Other Point of View: The Will to Power" and dealt with Adler-Nietzsche, who were treated as if they had offered the same theory and did not need to be distinguished.

It would be hard to say whom Jung misrepresented more: Nietzsche or Freud. Yet Jung's misunderstanding of Nietzsche is much less interesting than his crass failure to understand Freud. After all, a great many intelligent people got Nietzsche wrong, including some who kept writing about him, as Jung did; but Jung had been close to Freud for almost seven years, and one might have thought that few people would have been in a better position to know him well.

One could easily quote page upon page to show what I mean, but if one wants to single out a very few consecutive lines, these may do:

> There is not only the drive to *preserve the species* but also the drive of *self-preservation.*
> *Nietzsche* evidently speaks of this latter drive, namely of the *will to power.* Whatever else is instinctual is for him always part of the retinue of the power will: from the point of view of Freud's sexual psychology, a glaring error, a misunderstanding of biology, the blunder of a decadent neurotic. For every adherent of the sexual psychology will find it easy to demonstrate that every-thing high-pitched and heroic in *Nietzsche's* world view and view of life is nothing but [*nichts anderes sei als*] a consequence of the repression of and the failure to recognize the drive that *this* psychology considers funda-mental. (38f.)

Nietzsche, of course, was far from identifying the will to power with the instinct of self-preservation; he contrasted them. And Freud, unlike Jung, was far from lumping together Adler and Nietzsche; he never ran down Nietzsche's ideas as "the blunder of a decadent neurotic"; nor did he ever try to prove what was, according to Jung, such a very simple matter for him to demonstrate. This sort of crude reductionism was espoused by Jung himself in the letter cited at the beginning of this chapter—"Nietzsche drips with violated sexuality"—but never by Freud. In fact, we have seen how Freud struck the diametrically opposite note in a letter to Arnold Zweig in 1934, telling Zweig that it was impossible to fathom Nietzsche, who had signified to him "a nobility I could not attain." Sections 50 and 51 above show abundantly how little relation Jung's Freud in that 1917 essay bears to the real Freud.

On the back of the paperback edition of *Two Essays* the publisher says, plausibly enough: "This volume has become known as perhaps the best introduction to Jung's work," and that it presents "the essential core of his system." The two essays "sum up his attempt to integrate the psychological schools of Freud and Adler into a comprehensive framework." This seems fair enough to me. After giving us his reading of Freud in Chapter II and of Nietzsche-Adler in Chapter III, he presented his own typology in Chapter IV. Here, as in *Psychological Types*, the two basic types, extravert and introvert, are offered to account for the differences between Freud on the one hand and Adler and Nietzsche on the other. Jung claimed to "rise above the opposition and to create a theory that would do justice . . . to both equally" (65).

Under these circumstances it is no small matter if Jung actually failed to do justice to both and if he badly misunderstood the three psychologists whom he thought he knew best: Freud, Adler, and Nietzsche. I believe I have shown in the preceding chapters how far he was from understanding them. But it may help if we also consider the two sentences that follow upon our last quotation:

To this end a critique of the two theories introduced here is indispensable. Both theories are apt to reduce a high-pitched ideal, a heroic attitude, nobility of feeling,[7] or a conviction in a painful manner to a banal reality . . .

And Section 67 begins:

The two theories of neurosis . . . are destructive and reductive.[8] They say to everything, "You are nothing but . . ."

Jung is plainly fighting straw men whom he has endowed with his own projections. The attitude to nobility that he ascribes to his self-chosen opponents was as far from their actual outlook as the "nothing but" which we have encountered only in a letter written by Jung himself, many years later.

On the face of it, it is extremely odd both that Jung should have ascribed reductionism to Freud so persistently (we shall encounter more examples later on) and that he himself should have exploded the way he did in his letter to the student. I conjecture that he projected upon Freud some things he found in himself and did not like. So far, of course, the evidence is insufficient to substantiate this surmise, but we shall encounter other instances that give strong support to it.

55 ▶▶▶ In *Psychological Types* the two central types, extravert and introvert, are introduced near the end of the first chapter, in the section on Abelard, in the context of an extended juxtaposition of

[7] "Nobility of feeling" is Hull's rendering of *ein Pathos*, which defies literal translation.
[8] "Destructive and reductive" is again Hull's very elegant translation of *auflösend und reduktiv*.

Freud and Adler. This is one of the places where the translator, Hull, has genuinely improved Jung's involuted prose style, which in the original has "former" and "latter" and altogether lacks the vigor of the English version, which is nevertheless entirely accurate:

> Freud's view is essentially extraverted, Adler's introverted. The extraverted theory holds good for the extraverted type, the introverted theory for the introverted type. (86 = A91).

> Freud's as well as Adler's point of view is one-sided and is characteristic only of one type. (86 = A92).

In Chapter IV of the first of the *Two Essays* we find the same notion. It was the schism of Freud and Adler that led Jung to postulate his two types to account for the differences between Freud's and Adler's theories.

At first glance, this seems as reasonable as can be. It may seem as if Jung had learned from Hegel that if two outlooks conflict the chances are that both are one-sided; also that each outlook needs to be considered together with the person who holds it. What is nevertheless wrong with Jung's solution is that his portraits of Freud and Adler are unrecognizable. To show this, I turn to Chapter X of *Psychological Types*, where the two basic types are described at length.

The extravert "admires the new tenor because all the world admires him," while the introvert "does not admire him, not because he dislikes him but because he is of the opinion that what all people admire does not have to be admirable for that reason" (628 = A563). This is very clear and would pose no problem for us if Jung had only said that Adler was the extravert and Freud the introvert. But Jung, of course, has claimed precisely the opposite in order to account for their differences.

Surely, it was Freud who defied public opinion and felt that being a Jew and considered inferior by many people at the university taught him "a certain independence of judgment" and accustomed him to "standing in the opposition" to the "compact majority," while Adler converted to Christianity although he did not believe in it, "feeling a spiritual danger in the isolation" that he associated with being a Jew (Section 36 above). It was Adler who was concerned with what all the world wanted and who stressed community feeling, while Freud's self-image was that of a loner.

The example of the tenor is merely clearer and crisper than much of the rest of Jung's exposition, but otherwise it is entirely representative of the contrast he drew,

> The former [the extravert] orients himself on the basis of the external facts that are given; the latter [the introvert] reserves for himself a view that is interposed between himself and the objectively given. Now, when orientation by the object and the objectively given predominates in such a way that the most frequent and most important decisions and actions are conditioned not by subjective views but by objective conditions, then one speaks of an extraverted attitude. When this is habitual, one speaks of an extraverted type. When a person thinks, feels, and acts or, in one word, lives in a way that corresponds *directly* to the objective circumstances and their demands, in a good as well as a bad sense, he is extraverted (628 = A 563).

Jung's notion that Freud's theory "holds good for the extraverted type, the introverted theory [Adler's] for the introverted type" is as ill conceived as his notion that Freud was an extravert and Adler an introvert. He thought that because libido or Eros involves an outside object, the person who can be helped by Freudian therapy is extraverted. He failed to notice the elementary fact that the Freudian patient does *not* behave "in a way that corresponds directly to the objective circumstances" any more than Freud himself did. The patient's conception of father and mother does not depend on "the external facts that are given" or on the way they look to all the world; the parents are seen in a highly subjective way. Similarly, Jung's notion that, because the will to power comes from inside, Adler's psychology holds good for introverts overlooks the fact that those who seek power in business or politics are often much closer to the type Jung describes as extraverted.

So far, then, it would seem that Jung's typology as well as his understanding of the two psychologists with whom his own name has been linked most often was strangely muddled. The typology was designed to explain something that it utterly failed to explain.

Now, this is the second case in which we have found that Jung totally misrepresented Freud. Does this case support my earlier conjecture that Jung projected upon Freud some things he found in himself and did not like? I think it does. The portrait of the extraverted type has strong conformist features. It is not an accurate portrait of Jung by any means, but he did have these tendencies and evidently was not aware of them. Instead he attributed them to Freud.

56 ▶▶▶ The last point is of sufficient importance to warrant a closer look. It is highly unlikely that a man should develop a typology of this sort without giving some thought to his own case. Did Jung consider himself an introvert or an extravert? The answer is clear: he always considered himself an introvert. Even when he was interviewed for BBC television in July 1955 and asked outright, "Which are you?" he responded: "Oh well. [Laughs.] Everybody would call me an introvert."

Here Jung defers to the opinion of all the world or, as he says, "everybody"—that he is an introvert. But is that really what everybody would say? The interview appears with over fifty more or less similar pieces in C. G.

Jung Speaking: Interviews and Encounters, edited by William McGuire and R. F. C. Hull (1977). The very existence of this book or, if you prefer, the fact that Jung loved to give interviews to journalists, suggests that he was something of an extravert. Nobody could have put together a comparable book by or about Freud.

Freud's life was quite withdrawn; it involved hardly any public appearances, and he preferred to share his ideas with the world by writing in peace and quiet. Journalists were anathema to him. An interview with William Leon Smyser represented a rare exception. Freud's letter consenting to it is worth quoting. It was written from his home, December 7, 1928:

> I have made it a rule for myself not to receive any . . . journalists from America. Also I do not know, if you plan to devote to me a chapter in your book, what profit you hope to derive from a personal encounter with me. I am no poet, no artist, and if you take an interest in my writings then you have fully satisfied, I think, your conscientiousness as an author.
> So I should really ask you to forgo your intended visit with me. But since you have already met my wife and my son, it seems too unfriendly to me to stick to my habits in your case, too. I am prepared to talk with you next Sunday (the 9th), at my home around 3:30 p.m. Let me know by telephone . . . whether I am to expect you, and promise me not to present any difficult philosophical questions.[9]

This incident is also interesting because Smyser subsequently published a rather long piece in the *New York Herald Tribune Magazine* in 1929 in which he said: "Like Goethe, Freud would have liked to become a sort of scientist-poet." It seems unlikely that an American journalist would have made that up out of whole cloth,

[9] In the author's collection.

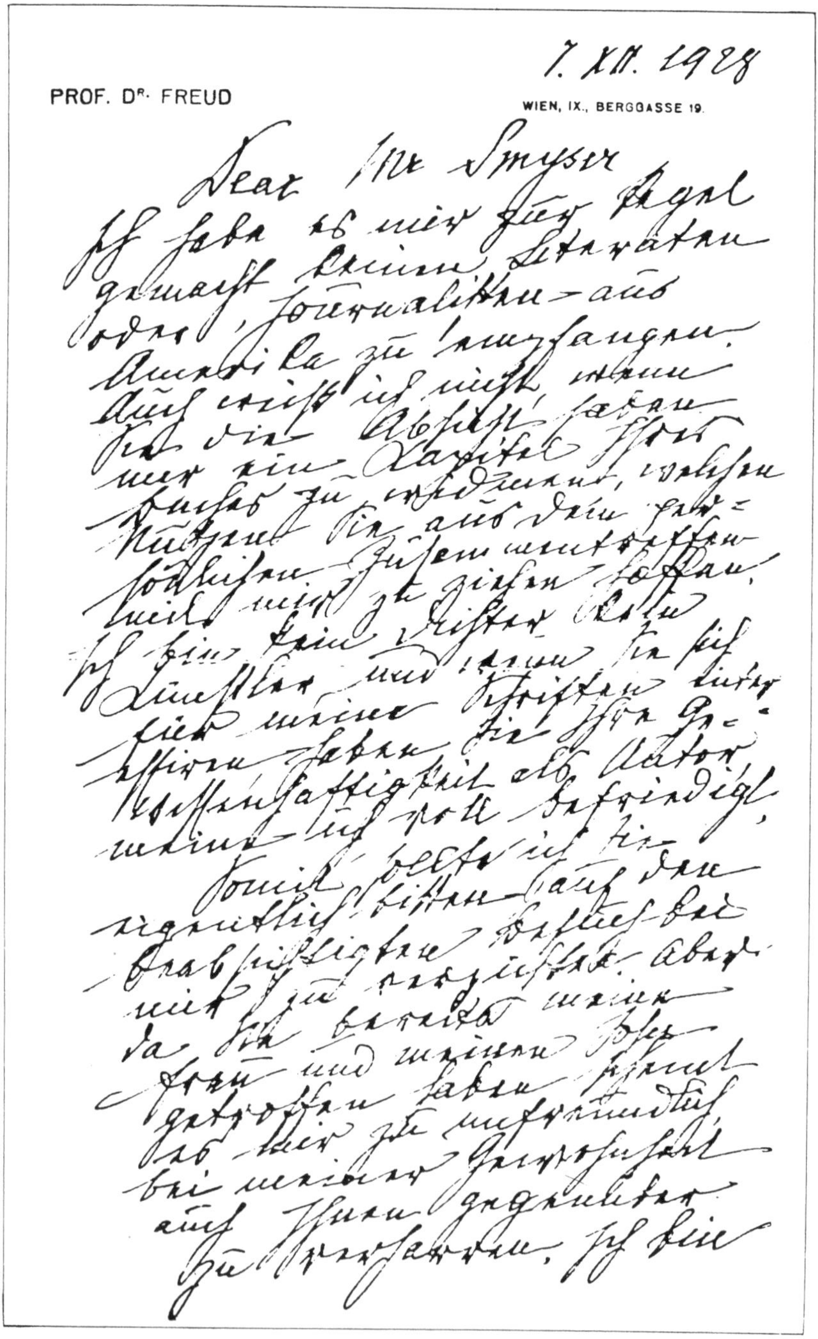

Freud's letter to an American journalist. Not published before.

and the quotation goes well with the picture of Freud and his poetic science presented in the present volume.

To return to the main point, in important ways Freud seems much more introverted than Jung. The single most obvious point is surely Jung's boisterous laughter which has been described by many people who have written about him. Albert Oeri, who had known Jung from childhood, mentioned in the reminiscences he wrote on the occasion of Jung's sixtieth birthday in 1935: "Carl burst into whoops of wild Indian laughter, an art he retained all his life."[10] Charles Baudouin, founder of the Institut de Psychagogie at the University of Geneva, noted in 1945 how when Jung gave "himself up to one of his hearty laughs over some story" his face turned red.[11] Lou Andreas-Salomé, writing in her diary about the Munich Psychoanalytical Congress in September 1913, which she attended with Rilke, compared Jung and Freud:

> Who is more dogmatic and in love with power is clear from even a single glance at both of them. Two years ago, Jung's booming laughter gave expression to a sort of robust cheerfulness and exuberant vitality, but now his seriousness speaks of pure aggression, ambition, and intellectual brutality. (p. 190)

Oddly, Jung seems to have felt, too, that his will to power far exceeded Freud's, but he took this for evidence that he was introverted. Nietzsche, of course, would have said that the will to power sought different expression in Freud and Jung. Freud's will to power reached its goal mainly through writing, and being as good at writing as he was he did not need journalists and newspapers, nor did he have any desire to attract attention by loud laughter. Perhaps a passage from *The Dawn*

[10] *Jung Speaking*, p. 4.
[11] *Ibid.*, p. 147.

(Section 348) is also relevant, although it was written before Nietzsche introduced the concept of the will to power:

> *The feeling of power.*—One should distinguish well: Those who still want to gain the consciousness of power reach out for all means and do not spurn any nourishment for it. But those who have it have become very choosy and noble in their tastes . . .

The Jung we meet in *C. G. Jung Speaking* is pretentious, self-important, and unhumorous, quite lacking in the ironical self-disparagement that was so characteristic of Freud, who took great pride in his work but felt nevertheless that he himself was not important and that, as he put it in his letter to "the uninvited biographer" (see Section 10 above), "the public has no claim to my person." What is striking again and again is how Jung saw himself as an expert on almost anything he was asked about by some journalist and how susceptible he was to flattery. This—in the perspective of Nietzsche's psychology—is surely the will to power of the weak or, to revert to Jung's letter to the student, a perennial fight against his own insecurity.

He is particularly embarrassing when "Diagnosing the Dictators" in 1938 and 1939 (pp. 115–40). One of the best-known American foreign correspondents of the time, H. R. Knickerbocker, asked him:

> What would happen if you were to lock Hitler, Mussolini, and Stalin in a room together and give them one loaf of bread and one pitcher of water to last them a week? Who would get all the food and water, or would they divide it?

Without any appreciation of the humor of the question or any sense of his own lack of sufficient knowledge of these three men, Jung immediately launched into a magisterial disquisition and answered all of Knickerbocker's follow-up questions in the same omniscient manner. Of course, he was anything but omniscient, and the contents of his remarks are no less embarrassing than their tone. I do not want to get into the question of Jung's attitude toward Hitler at this point but feel that at least a few very short examples should be given to show what I mean:

> The outstanding characteristic of his [Hitler's] physiognomy is its dreamy look. (p. 117)

> The Jews got their inferiority complex from geographical and political factors. (p. 122)

> If he [Hitler] is not their true Messiah, he is like one of the Old Testament prophets: his mission is to unite his people and lead them to the Promised Land. (p. 123)

> Every German man would like to dress like an Englishman. (p. 125)

> . . . the goose step . . . really is a most impressive step. (p. 127)

> . . . the only way to save Democracy in the West [said Jung in October 1938]—and by the West I mean America too—is not to try to stop Hitler. (p. 132)

Such brief examples are inadequate. Much of that volume is of that order, and any reader should ask himself whether what Jung says of Hitler in his second diagnosis of the dictators does not also apply to himself:

> It is certain that Hitler does not understand himself; if he did he would not be lacking in a sense of humor and would not take himself so seriously. (p. 138f.)

The fact that I find the Jung of C. G. Jung Speaking rather unattractive may well tell as much about me as about him. But the reason for introducing this book here is that it offers a portrait of Jung as an extravert. Naturally, that was not all there was to him, and the introvert we encounter in Memories, Dreams, Reflections, the posthumously published autobiographical work on which Aniela Jaffé collaborated with him, is much more remarkable. But where does that leave Jung's famous contrast of introvert and extravert?

In the first of the *Two Essays* Jung himself remarked:

> Above I have emphasized what I see as two main opposite types and have called them the *introverted* and *extraverted* types. William James already noted the existence of these two types among thinkers. He distinguished them as "tender-minded" and "tough-minded." (80)

In a sense, then, this typology is not new and is perhaps more useful when applied playfully than it is when one tries to make a theory of it. Jung himself certainly was a mixed type in whom both tendencies were highly developed, and that was only one of the ways in which he was deeply at odds with himself. Freud, though almost a pure introvert according to Jung's, I think, very inadequate characterization of the two types, also had some extraverted tendencies; for without those one would withdraw into oneself and not confront the world with publications. Adler, though much more an extravert than Freud, was no pure type either.

In *Psychological Types*, as already noted, a whole chapter is devoted to William James's typology, and there Jung also cites the characteristics of the two types that James listed in parallel columns. They have already been quoted above in Section 46, where it was noted that two Adlerians felt that it was helpful to see Freud as tough-minded, empiricist, pessimistic, pluralistic, irreligious, and skeptical, and Adler as tender-minded, rationalistic, optimistic, monistic, religious, and dogmatic. Had Jung accepted this scheme, and fully accepted the identification of the introverted with the tender-minded, he might have ended up with the concession that Freud was skeptical and empiricist while he himself was dogmatic and rationalistic. That contrast is actually more suggestive than Jung's typology. Freud really was much more skeptical than Jung, and Jung was much more of a dogmatist than Freud, and Jung's doctrine of archetypes stood in a rationalist tradition that goes back to Kant, Leibniz, and Plato.

Jung, however, did not fully accept James's typology, and he frequently insisted that Freud was dogmatic and that he himself was above all an empiricist. "I'm not a philosopher, I'm an empiricist," he said in English, in a letter to Swami Devatmananda, February 9, 1937, and went on to speak about the

> doctrine of karma. This is a doctrine which one can believe or disbelieve. Being not a philosopher but an empiricist, I'm missing the objective evidence.

Although there have been many empiricist philosophers, Jung liked to insist that he was not a philosopher but an empiricist and developed this contrast further in a letter to Zwi Werblowky, June 17, 1952. It also appears in his works (9.I, 149): "I am an empiricist, not a philosopher." In a radio interview in 1955 he explained his break with Freud as due to Freud's "scientific materialism," which "was the sort of philosophy I couldn't subscribe to. . . . Mine was merely the empirical point of view."[12]

Before we consider Jung's break with Freud, it must be noted that Jung's typology is more elaborate than indicated so far. Since he is immensely prolix and his own descriptions are, as we have seen, of dubious service to his cause, let me quote Anthony Storr's admirably succinct summary:

> Jung considered that, just as either extraversion or introversion tended to be the predominant attitude of any given individual, so either thinking, feeling, sensation, or

[12] *Jung Speaking*, p. 261.

intuition tended to be the predominant function. He further postulated that thinking was opposed to feeling, and sensation to intuition. This meant that the person who was chiefly adapted to the world through thinking would be likely to function poorly in matters of feeling.[13]

Storr goes on to say on the next page: "I think it is fair to say that this further classification of types is one of Jung's least satisfactory contributions." And he concludes his chapter on the typology: ". . . the quaternity of the four functions has been discarded by all except the most dedicated Jungians, and is, I suspect, little used even by them."

Seeing how much space Jung himself devotes to this "quaternity," it is, of course, tempting to go into more detail here, but in the end that would serve little purpose. Henry Murray was much more sympathetic toward Jung than Storr:

> Considered *in toto* Jung's description of type differences are more insightful, richer in anecdote and reference and more suggestive theoretically than anything that is to be found in the literature of personology. It is, therefore, particularly unfortunate that he did not systematically set down in one place a condensed list of what he considered to be the crucial indices of extraversion and introversion, respectively. This would have clarified his position . . .

Jung's typology has had little influence in America, he went on to say, because "amid the abundant illuminations in Jung's book one runs a foul of many vague metaphors, confusions and contradictions."[14]

This verdict is on the kind side and in any case does not raise any question about "the literature of personology" as a whole. Typologies have an instant appeal because they allow people to play games with them.

[13] *C. G. Jung* (1973).
[14] Murray, *Explorations in Personality* (1938), p. 233.

Isaiah Berlin once wrote a little book called *The Hedgehog and the Fox*, proposing a very simple but suggestive dichotomy; W. H. Auden made gentle fun of it in *The New Yorker*, dividing people into Alices and Mabels; and later Nancy Mitford juxtaposed "U" and "not U." Jung went out of his way to establish that his typology was serious, inflating it into a huge tome in which he included a vast, if not really very scholarly, historical survey; but in the end its "cash value," to use another term from William James, is small. For every one of his observations that is insightful there are many others that are appalling.

Jung's classification of the four men who are also considered at length in the present trilogy speaks for itself. Of how much use could his eight types be when Kant and Nietzsche turn out to be the same type and in fact the two most striking examples of "the introverted thinking type," introduced as such in the first paragraph under this heading? A typology that has no place for the immense differences between these two types surely leaves much to be desired.

Or consider once more Jung's conception of Freud as an extravert and Adler as an introvert, which, as he himself insisted repeatedly, was the inspiration of the whole typology. Here is Murray's characterization of these types, which is more orderly and systematic than anything we find in Jung:

> The extravert's course of action is determined by his desire for social approval; being no better than his day, he is gratified by any sort of praise or public acclaim. The introvert, on the other hand, is more apt to do something solely because it pleases him; he rejects easily won applause and is only satisfied when he comes up to his own exacting standard. . . . The extravert is vain, the introvert proud. The extravert keeps his eyes on what others are doing and he conforms to and is moulded by the groups of which he is a member . . . The extravert

takes the prevailing moral order for granted, he may or may not succeed in living up to it but he rarely doubts that what the "best people" say is "Right"; the introvert, on the other hand, is more apt to reject accepted dogmas and come to his own conclusions; he may not be actively defiant but he is often radical in his sentiments . . . dislikes suggestions, wants to follow his own routine without interruption . . . preferring to "go it alone," to make his own decisions and be solely responsible for his achievements. (p. 235f.)

What is one to think of a psychologist who presents this dichotomy, even if the various points are scattered over many pages, and tells us that it was originally prompted by an attempt to understand the schism between Freud and Adler—when his contribution to such an understanding is that Freud was an extravert and Adler an introvert? If Jung had not said all this again and again, one would assume it was a slip of the pen because, according to these criteria, Freud would seem to be the quintessential introvert and Adler incomparably more extraverted.

Much later, Jung himself tried to some extent to clarify his classification of Freud. In a letter of August 26, 1941, written in English, he reminded his correspondent, "Now I knew both Freud and Adler personally." I shall quote only some of his other observations:

As you know, Freud himself was neurotic his life long. . . . Freud as well as Adler underwent a change in their personal type. . . . In his personal psychology . . . [Freud] underwent a tremendous change in his life. Originally he was a feeling type and he began later on to develop his thinking, which was never quite good in his case.

Most of us, I suppose, would settle gladly for being able to think half as well as Freud did, and even Jung admits that "Freud was the far greater mind than Adler."

The letter of February 18, 1957, written when Jung was in his eighties, is similar but, if anything, blurs the picture even more. Again Jung insists that Freud changed fundamentally, although it seems to me that neither his works nor his letters, not to speak of Jones's three-volume biography, bear this out.

> On the basis of an accurate knowledge of his character, I consider him to have been originally an introverted feeling type with inferior thinking. When I got to know him in 1907 this original type was already neurotically blurred. . . . Freud, then as later, presented the picture of an extraverted thinker and empiricist.

To whom? Obviously to Jung, but that only goes to show how far Jung was from perceiving the Freud we know from his letters to Jung and to many others, from his works, from Lou Andreas-Salomé's diaries, and from the records left by ever so many other highly intelligent people who knew him at least as well as Jung ever did.

57 ▶▶▶ Freud's and Jung's friendship and break can be described briefly. One may be pardoned for sometimes feeling that the friendship is harder to explain than the break, and that the break was somehow inevitable while the friendship was not. The same applies to Freud and Adler and also to Wagner and Nietzsche. Yet the friendship really is not that difficult to understand.

It is not in the least surprising that Jung should have been immensely impressed by Freud's *Interpretation of Dreams*. He made use of Freud's ideas in his own work, stated his admiration for Freud in print, and went to Vienna in 1907 to meet Freud. As he put it in his autobiographical *Memories, Dreams, Reflections:*

Freud in 1906. The photograph he sent to Jung.

We met at 1 p.m. and talked virtually without interruption for thirteen hours. Freud was the first really great man I encountered. No other human being I knew then was in the same class. There was nothing trivial in his attitudes. I found him extraordinarily intelligent, keen, and remarkable in every way.

Freud was fifty at that time and the author of four books that insured his immortality, while Jung was thirty-one and had just published his first book. When Freud offered him his friendship and made it clear that he esteemed him more than any of the members of the Vienna Psychoanalytic Society, and before long asked him to become president of the International Psychoanalytical Association, it is no wonder that Jung was delighted. Even if he had not felt particularly insecure, it would have been stunning to be asked by Sigmund Freud to become his successor.

Nor is it hard to see why Freud should have felt about Jung as he did. He realized that psychoanalysis looked as if it were merely a local Viennese phenomenon, and to make matters worse all its major practitioners were Jews. Moreover, he was unimpressed by most of his followers. Adler had a little more originality than the others, but Freud never felt much enthusiasm for Adler. Jung struck him as much more remarkable. Being a Swiss and the son of a Protestant pastor, he conferred on psychoanalysis the international standing that Freud felt it deserved and needed.

One could say that Freud had had three traumatic experiences of resistance. First, he encountered it as a Jewish student at the University of Vienna. That helped him to develop a certain independence of judgment. Then, Josef Breuer, who had a woman patient who had virtually invented her own talking cure, pulled back in alarm when her transference confronted him with her sexual needs for which he was quite unprepared; and eventually Breuer turned against him. Finally and most importantly, when Freud presented his findings to the world, he met with a great deal of scorn and ridicule.

The importance of these three experiences can hardly be overestimated, and Freud's friendship and break with Jung cannot be understood apart from it. Above all it is essential to realize how lonely both of these men felt when they found each other.

Those who feel persuaded that the resistance to psychoanalysis during its early years has been greatly exaggerated should bear in mind that when Freud met Jung the six hundred copies that had been printed of *The Interpretation of Dreams* had not been sold yet: "It took eight years to sell them,"[15] and the second edition did not appear until 1909. Graf's description of how people laughed when Freud's name was mentioned has already been cited (in footnote 29 in Chapter II). In his autobiography Jones remarked: "Since the libido theory played a central part in the psychoanalytical doctrine, the whole range of sexual bawdiness was opened up" (p. 225). And in the second volume of his Freud biography he tells of a prominent professor at the 1910 Congress of German Neurologists and Psychiatrists in Hamburg who, when Freud's theories were mentioned, banged his fist on the table and shouted: "That is not a topic for discussion at a scientific meeting; it is a matter for the police" (p. 109). In Volume I Jones tells of a Viennese professor who concluded a lecture on hysteria before an audience of four hundred students:

> You see that these sick people have the inclination to unburden their minds. A colleague in this town has used this circumstance to construct a theory about this simple fact so that he can fill his pockets adequately. (p. 361)

[15] Jones, I, p. 360

Wilhelm Stern, a psychologist of considerable reputation, said in a scholarly journal in 1901: "Uncritical minds would be delighted to join in this play with ideas and would end up in complete mysticism and chaotic arbitrariness."[16] This final quotation throws a great deal of light both on Freud's initial attitude toward Jung and on his later apprehensions.

Caring passionately about psychoanalysis, Freud could scarcely be indifferent to Jung's embrace of his cause. Jung had obtained his medical degree in Switzerland in 1902, worked at a major center for psychiatric studies, and—this seemed terribly important then—was neither Viennese nor Jewish. He was uncommonly erudite, full of ideas, and looked very impressive and respectable. He seemed to Freud to be ordained to save psychoanalysis from seeming to be no more than the creed of a few Jews in Vienna. Here was the beginning of a new era for psychoanalysis, the more so because Jung clearly was more interesting and promising than any of Freud's earlier disciples.

I do not mean to imply that either man was opportunistic. There was a genuine community of interest. Moreover, Jung, having in effect lost his father, was emotionally ready to find a new father, while Freud, every inch a father, welcomed the new son with open arms. There were deep emotional bonds between them, and in this respect their relationship was quite different from that between Freud and Adler.

Given our hindsight, it seems obvious that their close association could not last. Unlike Jones and Sachs and some of Freud's other disciples, Jung was not a born follower but a man who needed to develop his own ideas in his own way, at his own speed, exploring the unknown and making his own mistakes before he found his own way.

[16] *Zeitschrift für Psychologie und Physiologie der Sinnesorgane,* XXVI (1901), p. 133. Cited by Jones, I, p. 361.

Why, then, could the two men not have remained personal friends, like Freud and Binswanger? They came too close to each other too quickly. In their different ways both men had been exceedingly lonely and sought more in their friendship than was realistic. Having met in 1907, they visited the United States together in 1909 to appear at Clark University with Brill, Jones, and Ferenczi as representatives of psychoanalysis, and Freud made Jung president of the International Psychoanalytical Association in 1910. How, then, could Jung depart in important ways from psychoanalysis and try out new ideas without either taking psychoanalysis away from Freud, suggesting to the public that Freud's ideas were dated and were only, as it were, the *Old* Testament, or breaking with Freud, resigning his post, and creating his own new psychology?

Some readers may well feel that this question is not really unanswerable and that with sufficient good will, tact, and wisdom the two men might well have found a way. But Jung was very short on tact and wisdom in 1912 and felt, as many a son does, no less hostility than love toward his adopted father. And the more patient and fatherly Freud became, the more annoyed and rebellious Jung became, feeling that he did not want and need a father any more. He clearly did not understand himself very well at that time—nor later, for that matter—and was deeply at odds with himself. His letters show a man dissatisfied and angry with himself, with a great deal of anger to spare.

Should not Freud have had wisdom enough for both? After all, he was fifty-six by then and had published more important contributions to the discovery of the mind than any man before him. He, too, was at odds with himself in a way he did not fully understand. With the publication of his three essays on sex and his book on jokes he had completed the first phase of his psychoanalytic work in 1905; and when he embraced Jung and talked to him about becoming his successor, Freud felt old and thought his work was done. Nor did he publish another major work until *Totem and Taboo* appeared in two installments in 1912 and 1913, almost simultaneously with Jung's first ambitious work, which appeared in two installments in 1911 and 1912. As it happened, Freud was to publish many more important works for a long time after that and was actually extremely creative even in the last decade of his life, before he died at eighty-three.

In a way, his fault was, to anticipate one of Jung's fascinating dreams about Freud, that he refused to die. But given his own love of Shakespeare, he might have realized that he made Lear's mistake of turning over his crown too early, long before he was really ready to retire. By doing that he created an almost impossible situation, first with Adler, whom he made president of the Vienna Psychoanalytic Society, and then also with Jung as president of the International Association.

To put it plainly, he was wrong in thinking that his work was done when in fact it was not done, and that he was ready to retire when he actually was nowhere near ready to retire. He mistook seven lean years—not a severe drought but still quite a change from the preceding seven years of plenty—for the end.

Nietzsche said in an early fragment: "The errors of great men are venerable because they are more fruitful than the truths of little men."[17] Some of Freud's errors were fruitful in a number of ways, and perhaps this one was, too. The frictions he generated, though initially hurtful to him, helped to generate some of the pearls he produced later.

He may have felt that he had earned a rest, but we may be fortunate that he did not get it. The competition of Adler and Jung was not pleasant by any standard.

[17] *Werke*, I, p. 393.

Neither man behaved very chivalrously. But even as Nietzsche felt that perhaps he owed more to his sickness than to his health,[18] Freud, too, may have gained a good deal from these disagreeable challenges. They reawakened his fighting spirit, led him to return from his premature retirement, and spurred him on to do some of his best work.

58 ▶▶▶ To understand why the close association of the two men could not last is one thing; to see how it came to an end is another, and to untangle that story seems to be more difficult. The concrete realities involving two complex human beings are bound to be more complicated than such a general construction as I have offered here. Nor is it surprising that Freud's account of what happened is somewhat different from Jung's. What is perhaps surprising and what makes the whole issue much more significant than it would be otherwise is that Jung tried to cope with the break for the rest of his life, offering many different explanations of it. The break with Freud became for Jung the most important event of his adult life, and by exploring how he dealt with it over a period of fifty years, from 1911 until his death in 1961, we can discover a great deal about his mind and work. We shall see how it was not only his typology that represented an attempt to cope with Freud and be done with him. Had this typology been successful, and if Jung could really have persuaded himself that he had now assigned his proper place to Freud, there would have been no need to return to Freud again and again as he did down to his *Answer to Job* and his autobiographical reflections.

[18] Preface to *The Gay Science* and Epilogue of *Nietzsche contra Wagner*.

Of course, the fact that Freud could deal with the break once, very briefly, in 1914 and then be done with it, while Jung had such a hard time of it does not prove that Freud's account is right while Jung's many attempts to explain it can be dismissed. Obviously, the break was less important for the older man who played the role of the father and had more than one son than it was for the younger man. It may help to recall the break between Nietzsche and Richard Wagner, in 1878. Fully ten years later, Nietzsche published *The Case of Wagner,* and still after that he composed *Nietzsche contra Wagner.* Had Wagner at all seen fit to describe the break, one page might well have sufficed him; but it does not follow that this page would have been more accurate or revealing than Nietzsche's two short books.

Still, Freud's concise account of the matter in his *History* is as insightful as it is brief, and it seems sensible to begin with it before we venture into greater complexities. As usual, no summary can hope to improve on Freud's own presentation, and his whole *History,* about seventy pages in length, is eminently worth reading. Here I can only hope to single out what seem to be the most important points about Jung's break with Freud.

In 1912 *Jung* boasted in a letter from America that his modifications of psychoanalysis had overcome the resistance of many people who until then had not wanted any part of it. I replied that this was nothing to boast of; the more he would sacrifice of the laboriously attained truths of psychoanalysis, the more he would see the resistance decrease. The modification of which the Swiss were so proud was again [as in Adler's case] none other than the theoretical downplaying [*Zurückdrängung* brings to mind *Verdrängung,* repression] of the sexual factor. I confess that right from the beginning I understood this "progress" as an adaptation to the demands of fashion that went too far. (p. 102)

Freud also refers to Jung's insistence on "the right of youth to throw off the fetters into which tyrannical old age that has become rigid in its views would like to cast it."

> *Jung's* argument *ad captandam benevolentiam* [to gain favor with the audience] rests on the all too optimistic premise that the progress of humanity, of culture, of knowledge has always proceeded in an unbroken line. As if there had never been epigones, reactions, and restorations after every revolution. . . . The approximation to the point of view of the crowd, the surrender of an innovation that is felt to be unwelcome, make it improbable from the start that *Jung's* correction of psychoanalysis could lay claim to being a liberating feat of youth. In the end it is not the age of the doer that is decisive but the character of the deed.
>
> Of the two movements discussed here *Adler's* is undoubtedly the more significant; radically wrong, it is nevertheless distinguished by consistency and coherence. *Jung's* modification, on the other hand, has loosened the connection of phenomena with instinctual life; it is, moreover, as its critics (Abraham, Ferenczi, Jones) have stressed, so unclear, opaque, and confused that it is not easy to take a position about it. Wherever one touches it, one must be prepared to hear that one has misunderstood it, and one does not know how one is to arrive at a correct understanding. It presents itself in a peculiarly vacillating way, now as "a very slight variation that is not worth all the clamor raised about it" (*Jung*), now as a new gospel that marks the beginning of a new era of psychoanalysis, indeed, a new world view for all others. (pp. 103ff.)

The main point is clear enough, but one is bound to wonder whether it is fair. To decide about that we must consider *The Freud/Jung Letters* and, beyond that, Jung's attitude toward public opinion. For the present it must suffice to note that Jung wrote Jones on February 25,

1909: "Both with the students and with patients I get on further by not making the theme of sexuality prominent." And Jones also reports that in September 1909, on the occasion of the visit to Clark University, Jung said,

> he found it unnecessary to go into details of unsavory topics with his patients; it was disagreeable when one met them at dinner socially later on. It was enough to hint at such matters and the patients would understand without plain language being used.

It seems reasonable to assume that Jones told Freud. What makes the issue complex is that on the one hand there is other evidence as well, as we shall see, for Freud's interpretation of the downplaying of sex, while on the other hand one may well feel that Jung was right that Freud had made too much of sex. We shall have to return to both issues, and eventually it will be seen that Freud's reference to Jung's argument *ad captandam benevolentiam* was almost prescient.

In connection with the last paragraph quoted from Freud one must remember that it was published in 1914. Freud had felt for a long time that Jung was much more remarkable and promising than Adler, but here he was dealing not with two human beings but with two new movements, and the only book one could point to as perhaps expressing Jung's new point of view was *Wandlungen und Symbole der Libido*, which was anything but the manifesto of a new movement. But it is interesting in connection with what Freud said in his *History* that the word *Libido* was dropped from the title when the book was translated into English.[19]

[19] Literally, "Transformations [or simply: Changes] and Symbols of Libido." An "Authorized Translation" by Beatrice M. Hinkle appeared in 1916 under the title *Psychology of the Unconscious: A Study of the Transformations and Symbolisms of the Libido. A Contribution to the History of the Evolution of Thought.* In 1952 Jung published a very extensive revision of this work. Only the

Initially the book had appeared in two installments in the *Jahrbuch für psychopathologische und psychoanalytische Forschungen*, which Freud had asked Jung to edit. Freud's reaction to the first part, which appeared in August 1911, was totally friendly and positive though not detailed. On August 20, when he had only cut and turned the pages, he said he felt proud that his own essay should appear "at the beginning of such important things," praised Jung, and indicated that he himself had begun to work "in a field where you will be surprised to find me." He also said that he was "burning to read your work *Wandlungen und Symbole der Libido*." Jung's reply began: "Your letter has made me extremely happy. I am after all very receptive for recognition granted by the father." He was on tenterhooks regarding Freud's hint about his own work. In his next letter Freud explained that his work

dealt with the same theme as yours, the origin of religion. Lest I distract you, I did not mean to talk about it. But since I see from my first reading of your essay in the *Jahrbuch* (I must read it a second time; for the present Ferenczi has taken the volume away from me) that you know my result, there is no need to be mysterious, which is a great relief. So you already know, too, that the Oedipus complex contains the root of religious feelings. Bravo!

On November 6, Emma Jung, Carl's wife, wrote Freud that in a previous letter she had mentioned his libido book

because I knew how tensely Carl was waiting for your opinion; he had already often said earlier on that you would certainly not agree with it, and hence he awaited

_____

revised version has been included in *The Collected Works* (Vol. 5) under the title: *Symbols of Transformation: An Analysis of the Prelude to a Case of Schizophrenia.*

your discussion rather apprehensively. Of course, this is still a residue of his father complex (or mother), which probably is getting resolved precisely in this work; for Carl really ought not to worry about any other opinion when he considers something right. Perhaps it is all to the good that you did not react right away lest you confirm him in this father-son relationship.

In his long letter of November 12, which deals with a number of questions, Freud commented once more on Jung's essay:

My reading on the psychology of religion progresses only slowly. One of the most beautiful works that I have read now (again) is that of a well-known author on *Wantlungen und Symbole der Libido.* Many things are expressed so well that one's memory will retain these definitive formulations. Sometimes I have the impression that Christianity provides too narrow a horizon. . . . But this is the best work that the promising author has published so far, though not the best he is still going to achieve. In the section on two kinds of thinking I regret his great erudition. I should have preferred it if he had said everything in his own words. Every thinker speaks his own dialect, and the many translations are exhausting.

The rest of this letter is no less interesting, but the last sentence quoted here suggests strongly that it may be better not to translate still more, not even Freud's friendly reactions to the second and last installment, November 12 and 29. What is crucial for our purposes is that he showed he had read it with interest and that he said nothing hurtful, although Jung had sent him some rather unfriendly letters by that time.

Now it is remarkable that Joseph Wheelwright has recounted in *Psychological Perspectives* (2, pp. 171ff.) that Jung himself claimed that he sent the book to Freud and that

It came back by return mail, pages uncut, obviously unread. Scrawled across the fly leaf, Freud had written: "Widerstand gegen den Vater" (Resistance to the father) and was signed S. Freud. I asked Jung how he felt, and he said that he turned to his wife, Emma, and said: "I feel as though I had been thrown out of my father's house."

In a letter to *The Journal of Analytical Psychology*,[20] in whose pages this story had been given further currency, William McGuire confirmed that he himself had heard Wheelwright tell this story at a symposium on Freud and Jung. But he also pointed out that the copy of the bound book with Jung's inscription was not only kept by Freud and not returned to Jung, but that the old Freud even took it along to London, where it is still to be found in his library. And Jung's inscription reads: "Laid at the feet of the teacher and master by his disobedient but grateful pupil."

When Jung said in later years, as he often did, that he had been sure that this book would cost him Freud's friendship, he was exaggerating a little, but he certainly had been apprehensive about it. When he went on to say that he had been right and that it did cost him Freud's friendship, his memory played him a trick; and his memory played him quite a few tricks regarding Freud. When Jung broke with Freud he had not written a book that represented an altogether new direction, and when Freud wrote his *History* in 1914 Jung, unlike Adler, had not yet staked out any clear position.

Above all, it is simply false, however often it has been claimed, that Freud excommunicated Jung for heresy. Jung decided to strike out on his own, like Adler. Once Adler had pointed the way, Jung, aged thirty-seven, came to feel: If not now, when?

[20] London, January 1976 (Vol. 21.1, p. 94f.).

59 ▶▶▶ The publication of *The Freud/Jung Letters,* admirably edited by William McGuire, who has supplied invaluable footnotes, makes it possible to trace the friendship and break between the two men in detail. Of course, Freud was right when he said that it is easier for the reader to deal with a single author and become accustomed to his voice, while constant translations of quotations are exhausting. In this case one might simply refer those interested in the details to the published correspondence. But in German it comprises over seven hundred pages, in English more than six hundred, and previous accounts of what happened seem to me to be quite misleading. To establish a new reading of the break one has to deal with the evidence in some detail.

In September 1911 Freud visited Jung in Zurich, stayed three days at his house, and then traveled to Weimar with Carl and Emma Jung to attend the Third International Psychoanalytical Congress. On October 12 Freud informed Jung that Adler and company had left the Psychoanalytic Society. On October 30 Emma Jung wrote Freud an extraordinarily lovely and sensitive letter, expressing some apprehension about the Freud/Jung relationship.

> I do not know whether I deceive myself when I think that in some way you do not quite agree with the *Wandlungen der Libido.* You did not discuss it all, and yet I think that it would do both of you so much good if you would once discuss it thoroughly. Or is it something else? Please tell me what it is, dear Professor, for I cannot bear to see you so resigned . . .

Is it something about his children? "My husband, of course, knows nothing of this letter . . ."

It seems reasonable to assume that she felt that Jung was disappointed that Freud had not said more about the first installment of his book. And it is, of course, interesting that she felt she could confide in Freud. We do not have Freud's replies to her letters.

Near the end of his letter of November 2, Freud says: "A morose senex really ought to be slain without remorse." Apparently he felt old and somewhat discouraged.

Emma Jung's letter of November 6 may well be the most moving letter in the whole volume. I have already quoted from it a few pages back. She went on to recall a conversation in which Freud had spoken of his family. "You said: the marriage has long been amortized; now nothing is left but—to die." And finally:

> You can imagine how delighted and honored I feel by the confidence you show in Carl; but it almost seems to me at times as if you were giving too much; don't you see in him rather more than is necessary as the successor and fulfiller?
> Why are you thinking now of handing things over instead of enjoying your well deserved fame and success? . . .

Freud's gracious comments on Jung's essays in his letter of November 12 have already been quoted. The next passage that adds something significant to our story is a paragraph in Freud's letter of November 30:

> What you mean when you speak of extending the libido concept to make it applicable to schizophrenia would interest me very much. I am afraid that there is a misunderstanding between us at this point, as happened once before when you said in an essay that libido was for me identical with every kind of desire, while I hold the simpleminded premise that there are two drives and that only the energy of the sexual drive could be called libido.

In his reply of December 11 Jung confessed that it was a

remark in one of Freud's analyses[20] that had "triggered a booming echo in me."

On December 17 Freud complained, as he sometimes did, that his work on *Totem and Taboo* was not progressing well.

> I see from the difficulties of this work that I am not at all cut out to be an inductive researcher; my bent is wholly intuitive, and I have imposed an extraordinary discipline on myself when I set out to establish psychoanalysis, which can be discovered purely empirically.

It seems to me that the letters show clearly that the break was not due to scientific differences, although Jung kept feeling apprehensive that Freud might become intolerant.

On March 3, 1912, Jung wrote that he had some "opinions that are not yours, although even this is not certain—for it is impossible to discuss everything in letters." He assumed that Freud would not hold this against him, and he was always prepared to change his opinions, bowing to one who knew better. "I would not have sided with you if a little heresy did not run in my blood." And then he quoted (with a few sentences omitted) from the final section of Part One of Nietzsche's *Zarathustra:*

> One repays a teacher badly if one always remains nothing but a pupil. And why do you not want to pluck at my wreath?
>
> You revere me, but what if your reverence tumbles one day? Beware lest a statue slay you.
>
> You had not yet sought yourselves, and you found me. Thus do all believers.
>
> Now I bid you lose me and find yourselves; and only when you have all denied me will I return to you.

Jung himself added immediately after this quotation: "Such things you have taught me through psycho-

[20] *Werke,* VIII, p. 311.

analysis." Nor did Freud take exception to what Nietzsche said.

> What you go on to say about necessary intellectual autonomy and reinforce with the quotation from Nietzsche I applaud without reservation. But if a third person could read this passage, he would ask me when[21] I had made such attempts at intellectual oppression; and I would have to say: I don't know. I think never. Adler, to be sure, made similar complaints, but I am convinced that he allowed his neurosis to speak. But if you feel that you want to have more personal freedom from me, what better can I do than renounce my urgency and lodge my unoccupied libido elsewhere while waiting until you have discovered that you can tolerate more intimacy? You will find me ready again. In transition to this reserved position I scolded very softly. You would consider me dishonest if I had not reacted at all.
>
> Why, I repeat, this "pensive mood"? Do you believe of me that I am looking for someone else who could be to me at the same time a friend, helper, and heir, or that I expect to find such another soon? If you do not believe that, then we are at one again, and you'd better apply your thoughts to the work on libido.

This was on March 5. On April 21 Freud mentions again how he looks forward to the second part of the work on libido. He assumes that the "Declaration of Independence" must have referred to that, and he will show that he knows how "to listen and accept or wait until something becomes clearer to me." The discussion of libido continues off and on without any significant change in tone on either side.

A new tone is struck when Jung felt deeply offended by what he took to be a personal slight. Freud had visited Ludwig Binswanger in Kreuzlingen, Switzerland, in

[21] Freud wrote: why—as noted in the German and English editions, in a footnote. I take it that he was also thinking: why would I have done such a thing?

IMAGO

ZEITSCHRIFT FÜR ANWENDUNG DER PSYCHO=
ANALYSE AUF DIE GEISTESWISSENSCHAFTEN
HERAUSGEGEBEN VON PROFESSOR S. FREUD

SCHRIFTLEITUNG:
I. 3.   OTTO RANK / DR. HANNS SACHS   1912

Über einige Übereinstimmungen im Seelenleben der Wilden und der Neurotiker.

Von SIGM. FREUD.

II.

Das Tabu und die Ambivalenz der Gefühls= regungen.

Tabu ist ein polynesisches Wort, dessen Übersetzung uns Schwierigkeiten bereitet, weil wir den damit bezeichneten Be= griff nicht mehr besitzen. Den alten Römern war er noch ge= läufig; ihr s a c e r war dasselbe wie das Tabu der Polynesier. Auch das ἄγος der Griechen, das K o d a u s ch der Hebräer muß das nämliche bedeutet haben, was die Polynesier durch ihr Tabu, viele Völker in Amerika, Afrika (Madagaskar), Nord= und Zentral= Asien durch analoge Bezeichnungen ausdrücken.

Uns geht die Bedeutung des Tabu nach zwei entgegenge= setzten Richtungen auseinander. Es heißt uns einerseits: heilig, ge= weiht, andererseits: unheimlich, gefährlich, verboten, unrein. Der Gegensatz von Tabu heißt im Polynesischen noa = gewöhnlich, allgemein zugänglich. Somit haftet am Tabu etwas wie der Begriff einer Reserve, das Tabu äußert sich auch wesentlich in Verboten und Einschränkungen. Unsere Zusammensetzung »heilige Scheu« würde sich oft mit dem Sinn des Tabu decken.

Die Tabubeschränkungen sind etwas anderes als die religiösen oder die moralischen Verbote. Sie werden nicht auf das Gebot eines Gottes zurückgeführt, sondern verbieten sich eigentlich von selbst; von den Moralverboten scheidet sie das Fehlen der Ein= reihung in ein System, welches ganz allgemein Enthaltungen für notwendig erklärt und diese Notwendigkeit auch begründet. Die Tabuverbote entbehren jeder Begründung; sie sind unbekannter Herkunft; für uns unverständlich, erscheinen sie jenen selbstverständ=

The second installment of *Totem and Taboo* in *Imago*, 1912.

May 1912, without also visiting Jung in Zurich and, Jung claimed, without even informing him in time for him to have met Freud somewhere. It may seem tedious to go into such a relatively petty question, but this "Kreuzlingen gesture" became a cause célèbre, and neither the break between the two men nor Jung's mind can be understood very well apart from it.

In brief, then, Binswanger had been operated on for a malignancy, and while he told Freud about it he asked him not to tell anybody about the cancer.[22] Freud's letter to Binswanger, April 14, 1912, is very beautiful, but he could not get away to visit his friend until May and then notified Binswanger and Jung of his visit with the same mail. Jung, however, kept believing that he had not been notified in time and said at the end of his letter of June 8:

> That you did not feel like seeing me on the occasion of your Kreuzlingen visit I must explain in terms of the situation about my theory whose development by me you find so disagreeable. I hope that later on it will be possible to reach an understanding about the disputed points. I must proceed alone, it seems, for a long stretch of the way, with the Swiss stubbornness that you know.

The somewhat tortuous prose here mirrors a state of mind that does not come across in the official English translation, which is a little crisper and more elegant.

In his reply of June 13 Freud explained the situation fully and patiently, and wrote about other matters as well, at some length. Jung did not answer until July 18! I quote this letter in full:

> About your last letter I did not know what to say until now. Now I can only say: I understand the Kreuzlingen gesture. Whether your policy is the right one will be revealed by the success or failure of my next works. The

[22] See Binswanger (1956), pp. 52ff.; also Jones, II, p. 144f., and Schur (1972), pp. 262ff.

distance I have always kept will preserve me from any imitation of Adler's disloyalty.

On August 2, Jung wrote again, saying among other things:

Adler's book I shall also subject to a critical scrutiny, not without also emphasizing what is indecent in it.

My American lectures are finished now and will contain several proposals for changing certain theoretical formulations. This step was hard. But I shall not overcome my father following Adler's recipe, as you seem to suppose. That would not be like me.

He never did write a piece on Adler along the lines suggested here, but we shall see about that. Before we consider Jung's report about his American experience and the eventual resolution of the Kreuzlingen matter, we must turn away from *The Freud/Jung Letters* for a moment to see how Jung's letters, just quoted here, affected Freud.

On July 22 he shared Jung's letter of the eighteenth with Binswanger, and on July 29 he explained that he did not suffer from Jung's behavior; he had learned from past experiences and had withdrawn his libido from Jung some months ago. On September 22, finally, he said in a longish letter: "Toward Jung I shall be happy to take any step that may lead to an external reconciliation; internally, however, nothing is likely to change in me anymore." As for Jung's work on libido, Part II, which Freud had received about ten days before,

this is certainly discussable and would not provide any occasion at all for a personal conflict, any more than his earlier errors (I consider the new view also erroneous). That can be taken care of at leisure.[23]

[23] Binswanger, pp. 59–61.

The final phrase, *in aller Ruhe,* implies that this did not upset Freud in the least. Jung's behavior, on the other hand, would have hurt him deeply if he had not managed to withdraw his libido from him. I am purposely using the word Freud himself used because it is important to note that Freud did not associate libido with sex in the *narrow* sense, and it did not remain for Jung to liberate it, as it were.

What we have discovered here is worth emphasizing. One way of doing that is to note that the day before he wrote Binswanger the last letter cited here, Freud wrote similarly to Jones, who paraphrases the letter he got: "Freud expressed the opinion that there was no great danger of separation, but that former personal feelings could not be restored."[24]

What Freud failed to see was how badly Jung wanted a separation, without having the courage and insight to realize this himself. In retrospect it is clear, at least to me—but I aim to show this—that Jung wanted Freud to reject him. To leave Freud would have burdened him with terrible guilt feelings. If only Freud would take the initiative, then Jung could be on his own without feeling that he had betrayed his master.

All of this may sound very psychoanalytical, but as a matter of fact neither Freud nor Jung nor their disciples seem ever to have understood this. It now remains to be shown that these suggestions are not fanciful but supported by very strong evidence. But before we go any further we should recall the *Zarathustra* quotation. What Jung quotes to Freud is a teacher saying to his pupils that they must leave him and deny him!

While working on his libido book, Jung expected Freud to disown him once he read it. Emma Jung saw his anxiety but failed to recognize Jung's wish that this should happen. Eventually, when Freud did not behave

[24] Jones, II, p. 145.

as Jung expected him to behave, Jung's wishful fantasy blotted out reality for him and he convinced himself that Freud had actually returned the book to him unread with an inscription that meant that Freud had thrown him out. If only that had really happened, he need not have felt guilty.

Meanwhile, he fantasized that Freud had rejected him when he went to Kreuzlingen to see Binswanger. When Freud explained the matter to him, he "did not know what to say," maintained an insulting silence for almost a month and a half, and then wrote a letter that was designed to put an end to their friendship while stoutly maintaining that it was Freud who had ended it.

Why did Freud fail to see this? Why has all this not been seen long ago? Freud was too inclined to believe in a reality behind the mask, and so was Jung, who came to feel that what was wrong with Freud's psychoanalysis was that it did not go down deep enough into the past. What I am saying is that what is real is up front, right there before us, for all to see. But those who have never learned from Nietzsche and Freud how to see are almost bound to miss it.

60 ▶▶▶ On November 11, 1912, Jung wrote Freud:

Just back from America, I hasten to tell you about myself. I could have done this from America, to be sure, but I was so busy there that I neither felt like writing nor had time to write.

. . . Of course, I also made room for my ideas, which in places deviate from previous views; I mean especially in regard to libido theory. I have found that my version of psychoanalysis won very many friends who had previously been baffled by the problem of the sexuality of neurosis. . . . I feel no need to run away from you if you care to appreciate our endeavors objectively. I regret it exceedingly if you believe that only resistance to you has decided me to make certain changes. Your Kreuzlingen gesture has offended me and still does. I prefer direct confrontation. What is at stake for me is not moods but insisting on what I consider true. No personal consideration for you can keep me from that.

On the other hand, this letter should show you that I do not by any means feel the need to cut off my personal relationship to you. I do not identify you with an axiom. I have always endeavored to see to it that you are treated entirely justly, and shall always do this, regardless of how our personal relations should develop. . . .

The letter continues in this curious, provocative tone, actually suggests to Freud that expediency (*Opportunität*) alone would indicate that Freud should be nice to him, and then returns to the subject of his great successes in the United States.

This is obviously the letter to which Freud referred in his *History*. There he mistakenly said that it was "a letter from America," having forgotten that in fact Jung had not written him from August 2 until November 11. He evidently recalled this letter as the single most crucial one in connection with the break but found it too painful and unnecessary to reread it once more.

One may well feel that the point that Jung "won very many friends who had previously been" put off by the emphasis on sex was the last thing he should have stressed in a letter to Freud. It was insensitive to use this as an argument—unless this point really was important to Jung. Freud naturally assumed that it was. But the whole letter was insensitive and calculated to offend. Ostensibly, Jung asks that their personal relationship should continue, but sentence upon sentence seems designed to make that quite impossible.

Freud, who for almost five years had begun every letter, *Lieber Freund* (Dear friend), replied promptly:

Lieber Herr Doktor,

I greet you upon your return home from America, no longer as tenderly as in Nürnberg the last time—you have weaned me successfully from that—but still with enough sympathy, interest, and satisfaction in your personal success. . . . That you have reduced much resistance with your modifications, you really should not put down on your credit side, for you know that the further you choose to depart from the innovations of psychoanalysis, the more assured are you of applause and the less is the resistance.

Of my objectivity and the continuation of our relationship you may be certain; I have the same view of the right to personal variations . . .

The way you stick to the "Kreuzlingen gesture" I find incomprehensible and insulting, but there are things that cannot be taken care of in writing.

A reprint of your lectures I look forward to with great anticipation, for from your big work on libido [meanwhile Emma Jung had sent Freud Part II], of which I liked some parts extremely well—the whole, not—I have been unable to gain the desired enlightenment about your innovations. . . .

Later the same month, Freud and Jung met in Munich at a conference about association business, took a long walk together, and finally cleared up the misunderstanding about the "Kreuzlingen gesture." Freud had written Binswanger and Jung the same day, May 23, about his forthcoming brief visit. According to Jones,

Jung suddenly remembered that he had been away for two days on that week-end. Freud naturally asked him why he had not looked at the postmark or asked his wife when the letter had arrived before leveling his reproaches; his resentment must evidently come from another source and had snatched at a thin excuse to

Freud in 1912.

justify it. . . . Jung accepted all the criticisms and promised to reform.[25]

This was a triumph for Freud, and he was elated at lunch. There was an animated discussion that involved death wishes and the way the heretical, monotheistic pharaoh Akhenaton had erased his father's name from his monuments; and Freud complained that the analysts in Zurich had begun to ignore his work and name in their recent publications. Suddenly Freud fainted, as he had done in Bremen, on the way to the United States, after persuading the anti-alcoholic Jung to have some wine. Jones wrote Ferenczi that "his attacks could be traced to the effect on him of his young brother's death when he was a year and seven months old" and he, in effect, triumphed over his young rival.[26] On December 8 he wrote Jones:

> . . . six and four years ago I suffered from very similar though not such intense symptoms in the *same* room . . . There is some piece of unruly homosexual feeling at the root of the matter.[27]

On January 1, 1913, finally, he shared a more detailed analysis with Binswanger in which he said: "Feelings I held back, this time against Jung as formerly against a predecessor, obviously play the main part" (p. 64). There is a whole book entitled *Why Freud Fainted,* but most of

[25] Actually, according to a note in *The Freud/Jung Letters,* the letter of May 23 should have arrived on the twenty-fourth, but Jung wrote Freud on the twenty-fifth (the Saturday of the weekend when he is said to have been away for two days), from home, asking why he had not heard from Freud for so long. A number of possible explanations come to mind: Jung could have written on the twenty-fourth and possibly misdated his card, and Freud's letter might have arrived on the twenty-fifth; or Jung could have been away from home when he sent the card.
[26] Jones, II, p. 146.
[27] Jones, I, p. 317.

it does not really deal with this question.[28] For our purposes, the aftermath is much more important.

There is, first, Freud's letter to James J. Putnam about what had happened in Munich. On November 28, Freud wrote that his talk with Jung had cleared the air.

> Theoretical differences need not cloud it. On the libido question I shall scarcely be able to accept his modifications since all of my experiences speak against this conception.[29]

Jung's first letter after the meeting could not have been more pleasant and filial, but it was the last such letter Jung ever wrote. It began:

> I am very happy about our Munich meeting, for on this occasion I have really understood you for the first time. I became conscious of how different from you I am. This insight will suffice to change my whole attitude essentially. Now you may really rest assured that in our personal relationship I shall not abandon you. Please forgive my errors, which I will not excuse or extenuate. I hope that I shall succeed in making this insight that I have gained at last the guiding line of my actions. I find it very painful that I did not attain this insight earlier. I could have spared you so many disappointments.
>
> I still worried a great deal how you may have got back to Vienna, whether you did not wear yourself out again by traveling at night. Please let me know how you are, even if it is only a few words on a card.

Beware of people who say: "I shall not abandon you." They are thinking of abandoning you. Jung protested too much that he would not imitate "Adler's disloyalty" and that "I shall not overcome my father following Adler's recipe . . . That would not be like me."

[28] Samuel Rosenberg (1978).

[29] *The Freud/Jung Letters*, note before Jung's letter of November 26.

Freud replied on the twenty-ninth:

> . . . it was not easy for me to moderate my demands on you; but . . . on my part our relationship from now on will always retain the afterglow of our former intimacy. I think we really have to invest some new capital of good will for each other, for it is easy to foresee that we shall engage in objective controversies, and after all one always gets irritated a little when the other person insists on having his own opinion.
>
> Now I gladly answer your questions. My Munich condition was no more consequential than the similar attack in the Essighaus in Bremen; it faded in the evening and allowed me to sleep splendidly that night. According to my private diagnosis it was once again a qualified migraine . . . , not without psychic content that I unfortunately lack the time right now to track down. The dining room of the Park Hotel, incidentally, is disastrous for me. Six years ago I first experienced such a state there, and four years ago another. In short, a little piece of neurosis that one really ought to attend to. . . .

Most of the rest of this letter concerned business matters, and there was nothing that could have provoked Jung. Yet the last words quoted here enraged him: *Also ein Stückchen Neurose, um das man sich doch kümmern sollte.* The implication was surely that Freud planned to analyze it, and his previously cited letters show that he did.

Jung's reaction was astonishing. At the top of his reply of December 3 he wrote: "This letter is an impudent attempt to accustom you to my style. Watch out!" Then he thundered about Freud's reference to a *"Stück Neurose"* (the published English version has "bit of neurosis" both times and misses Jung's slight misquotation with its escalation). It must be taken seriously; he himself had suffered on account of it. Eventually:

> As for this piece of neurosis, I may perhaps call your attention to the fact that you begin *The Interpretation of*

Dreams with the minor chord of the confession of your own neurosis—the dream of Irma's injection—identification with the neurotic who needs treatment, which is very revealing.

Our analysis came to an end [on the voyage to the U.S.] with your remark, "You could not surrender yourself analytically *without losing your authority.*" This sentence engraved itself in my memory as a symbol of all that was to come. But I did not kiss the rod [literally: crawl to the cross].

I am writing you now as I would write to *a friend;* that is *our* style. I therefore hope that you won't feel offended by my Helvetic loutishness. . . .

What I demand of the psychoanalysts is not the infantile libido of admiration and recognition but merely understanding of the connections of ideas I have produced. The psychoanalyst uses his psychoanalysis wretchedly as a bed of sloth,[30] the way our opponents use their belief in authority. Whatever could make them think is [alleged to be] conditioned by some complex. This protective function of psychoanalysis remained to be discovered. . . .

At first glance, this letter seems hard to understand. What had Freud done to enrage Jung like that? It is indeed illegitimate to use psychological analysis as an excuse for not coping with rational arguments, but this reaction to Freud's letter was scarcely rational. Is it saying too much that Freud in a faint had looked like Freud dead, and that Jung could have put up with him a little longer if only Freud had had the good grace to die soon? The affront was that Freud had said that his condition was not serious. If it were not for the first of Jung's dreams about Freud around this time—and we shall consider Jung's dreams about Freud together, soon—this might be a rather daring surmise. But it is noteworthy that Jung actually said in the second sen-

[30] The official translation "just as supinely dependent" misses the point, as well as the allusion to Goethe's *Faust*, line 1692.

tence of his letter: "This 'piece' must be taken very seriously in my opinion, for what is at stake, as experience teaches, is *usque ad instar voluntariae mortis.*'" It was as good as a voluntary death.

Freud replied promptly on the fifth:

Lieber Herr Doktor,

Do not worry again that I might bear you a grudge for your "new style." I think that in internal relations among analysts, no less than in analysis itself, every form of honesty is permitted. The abuses of psychoanalysis to which you point, in polemics and to fend off what is new, have made me pensive for some time. I do not know whether they can be prevented entirely, and for the present I can only recommend against it the little household remedy that every one of us should concern himself more intensely with his own neurosis than with his neighbor's.

Forgive me when I reverse the proportions of your letter and give more space to practical matters . . .

Toward the end of his letter Freud, far from denying his neurosis, said: "On one point I venture an emphatic contradiction: My neurosis did not harm you, as you suggest." Freud may well have felt that the opposite was the case: A combination of a residue of homosexual leanings and excessive fatherliness had led him to be, if anything, too generous.

Jung's reply began:

Since you have tolerated my "new style" pretty badly, I shall tune down my lyre again a few notes, just for the present. . . .

I want to inform you, furthermore, that I am plotting to review Adler's book. I have succeeded in descending into its abysses, and I found delectable things that deserve to be hoisted higher. For the man is actually somewhat insane. . . . The style is entirely "praecox" [schizophrenic]. The consequences are significant: insofar as a man does not make a masculine protest against women (woman = below = inferior), he is below = inferior = feminine. Ergo, almost all men are women. One would not have thought that. . . . The man is witty, by God.

When Jung wrote this, he had already written in his foreword to *The Theory of Psychoanalysis*[31] (the New York lectures that appeared in print in 1913):

It was only after I wrote these lectures in the spring of 1912 that I became acquainted during the summer of the same year with Adler's book *On the Nervous Character.* I acknowledge that Adler and I have reached similar results on various points; but I must here forgo a more detailed discussion.
Zurich, fall of 1912   C. G. JUNG

He never published a hostile review of Adler's book. "He gave not unfavourable treatment to the book and to Adler's theories generally in his paper at the Munich Congress, Sept. 1913."[32] And we have already seen how later on Jung treated Adler's theory as on a par with Freud's, both being equally one-sided, one holding good for introverts, the other for extraverts. That verdict actually implied that Adler's theories hold good for Jung; and he certainly treated Freud to a spectacular display of "masculine protest."

It is noteworthy how consistently Jung ran down Adler in his letters to Freud, and how he kept protesting that he would not follow Adler's example and abandon Freud. It is not clear what is schizophrenic about Adler's bad prose. One feels like asking: Who is it that is somewhat schizophrenic?

The point can scarcely be missed that Jung keeps identifying with Adler while telling himself and Freud

[31] 4, before paragraph 203. An editorial note to Jung's letter calls attention to this fact.
[32] Quoted from the same editorial note.

that Adler is bad. When Jung reassures Freud repeatedly that he will not act like Adler, he is plainly reassuring himself—fighting his own insecurity. But now he had painted himself into a corner from which there was scarcely any possibility of escape. Soon, his foreword would appear acknowledging his agreement with Adler on various points. He was now totally at odds with himself, not only in his soul but in writing, on the record.

Freud replied December 9 that he was pleased that Jung intended

> to criticize Adler's book. Apart from the contents, this step should also help to clarify things politically by putting an end to the expectations, frankly expressed here, that you will after all "swing over" to him. . . .
> I greet you cordially and follow you gladly through all the variations of the lyre that you handle with such virtuosity.

In Jung's brief reply only one short paragraph is relevant here. From a forthcoming critique by Adler's associate Furtmüller, Jung has "been able to see that the Viennese prophets are not right about the 'swinging over' to Adler." This, of course, is a stunning *non sequitur*. How could one of Adler's associates prove anything about Jung's intentions? What Furtmüller wrote could be relevant only if the Adlerians had forestalled Jung's intentions by attacking him. The next sentence compounded the confusion: "Even Adler's accomplices refuse to recognize me as one of yours." Jung plainly meant "as one of theirs" (*als einen der ihrigen*) but wrote *Ihrigen*.

Freud promptly replied to answer a question about business and continued:

> Taking everything objective personally is not only a (regressive) human peculiarity but also quite especially a Viennese failing. . . . Are you "objective" enough now to appreciate without anger the following miswriting?

And then Freud quoted Jung's last sentence, underlining *yours*, and signed, without further comment: "Nevertheless wholly yours, Freud."

The second sentence of Jung's reply has already been quoted at the end of Section 53: "I recognize my insecurity vis-à-vis you . . ." Having said that, Jung became more and more enraged:

> But I want to call to your attention that your technique of treating your pupils like your patients is a *mistake.* Thus you produce slavish sons or impertinent rascals (Adler-Stekel and all those impertinent gangsters who make Vienna unsafe [*die ganze freche Bande, die sich in Wien breitmacht*]. I am objective enough to see through your trick [an Adlerian term]. You demonstrate all the symptomatic actions all around you; thus you reduce your whole environment to the level of sons and daughters who blush as they admit the existence of faulty tendencies. Meanwhile you always stay on top [another Adlerian term] very neatly as the father. . . . "Who is it that really has the *neurosis?*"
>
> You see, my dear professor, as long as you labor with stuff like that, I could not care less about my symptomatic actions, for they don't mean a thing compared to the very considerable beam in the eye of my brother Freud.—For I am not at all neurotic—touch wood!

Jung went on to tell Freud, in case he had not got the point yet, that *he* was neurotic; also that perhaps he *hated* neurotics.

> Adler and Stekel . . . have become childishly impertinent. I will stick to you in public while preserving my views, but will begin secretly in my letters to tell you for once what I really think about you. I consider this way the most decent.
>
> You will scold about this peculiar act of friendship, but perhaps it will do you good just the same.

It certainly was a peculiar letter. His anger blinded him to the fact that his mischievement had let the cat out of the bag: that he had already sided with Adler in a foreword that was about to be published, while he was telling Freud how he would dissect Adler in public—which he never did. Had Freud not called this slip to his attention, could the "friendship"—or what was left of it—have lasted?

Jung's wild accusations of Adler are once again full of projections. What right has the writer of that letter to call Adler "childishly impertinent"? Most striking, however, is Jung's insistence that he himself is not at all neurotic while Freud is. Freud had made a point of admitting that he had found some neurosis in himself that required attention. Yet Jung later turned things upside down in this matter, too, claiming that *he* had discovered what Freud had failed to see, namely that we all are somewhat neurotic, and that neuroses and complexes are not all bad but can become creative. This had been Freud's view all along. Thus he had written to Ferenczi, on November 17, 1911 (Jones, II, p. 452): "One should not try to eradicate one's complexes, but come to terms with them; they are the legitimate guiding forces of one's behavior in the world."

Once more Freud wrote a totally unruffled, patient, and friendly reply, dated December 22; but he did not mail it. It was found among his papers and is printed both in *The Freud/Jung Letters* and in Freud's *Letters*, with a suitable note. On reflection, he seems to have decided that enough was enough and that he really would be better off without this peculiar friendship. After discussing some business matters, the letter of January 3 that he mailed continued:

> In your last letter there is only one point that I can answer at some length. Your premise that I treat my pupils like patients is demonstrably incorrect. . . . In

fact, since Stekel finished his treatment with me about ten years ago he has not heard another word from me relating to his analysis; and in the case of Adler, who never was my patient, I have used analysis just as little. . . . Here you have made things just as easy for yourself concerning the basis for your construction as you did in the case of the famous "Kreuzlingen gesture."

For the rest, your letter is unanswerable. It creates a situation that would create difficulties in oral communication and is totally beyond resolution in writing. It is understood among us analysts that nobody needs to be ashamed of his piece of neurosis. But anyone who, while behaving abnormally, shouts incessantly that he is normal arouses the suspicion that he lacks insight into his illness. So I suggest to you that we terminate our private relationship altogether. I lose nothing that way, for my affective bond to you has long been no more than the thin thread of the aftereffects of earlier disappointments; and you can only gain from this since you recently confessed in Munich that a more intimate relationship to a man had an inhibiting effect on your scientific freedom. Take you full freedom then and spare me the alleged "acts of friendship." We are agreed that a human being should subordinate his personal feelings to the general interests in his field.

Their scientific collaboration was to continue, Freud concluded. His letter crossed in the mail a letter from Jung written the same day. Jung's tone was once again so truculent that Freud must have felt relieved that he no longer needed to respond. Here is part of Jung's letter:

> As you know, in the understanding of psychoanalytical truths one gets just as far as one gets inside oneself. If one has neurotic symptoms [as Freud, unlike Jung did, according to Jung], one will also lack understanding somewhere. Where, events have already shown. When I am frank with you in this unvarnished manner, it is for your own good even if it hurts.
> I think, my honorable intention is entirely clear . . .

Indeed, he was an honorable man and extraordinarily self-righteous. When he received Freud's last personal letter—after that Freud wrote once more, on January 27, entirely about business matters—Jung replied January 6, 1913:

> I will defer to your wish to give up our personal relationship, for I do not force my friendship upon anyone. For the rest, you will know best yourself what this moment means for you. "The rest is silence."

It wasn't really. Not only did Jung still send Freud quite a few business letters, but he kept writing about Freud, talking about the break, and giving interviews about it in later years.

He had finally managed to get Freud to terminate the personal relationship, although despite all provocations, Freud refused to play the part that Jung had assigned to him: Freud did not excommunicate him. On the contrary, Freud felt that theoretical differences could be discussed.

In fact, Jung remained president of the International Psychoanalytical Association and was even reelected at the Munich Congress in September 1913. Those who felt that he should not be reelected, like the Viennese, Karl Abraham, and Jones, abstained. Lou Andreas-Salomé, who attended the Congress with Rilke, noted her impressions in her diary:

> At the Congress the Zurich contingent sat at one table facing the Freud table. One can say in one word what characterizes their behavior toward Freud: not that Jung deviates from him but that he does it as if these deviations were required to save Freud and his cause. When Freud resists *that*, the matter is twisted as if he were incapable of scientific tolerance, were dogmatic, etc. Who is more dogmatic and in love with power is clear from even a single glance at the two of them. (p. 190)

In a letter to Pfister, December 27, 1919, Freud referred to an article that had been submitted to him and that he thought of publishing after deleting a comparison of Jung's style with his own as well as "mention of a private remark by Jung that he did not spurn me but . . . merely corrected me and made me 'housebroken' ['*zimmerrein*']."

Freud wrote his *History* late in 1913. It has already been discussed briefly in connection with Adler, in Section 42. Still, three brief quotations from it may round out the present picture:

> I merely wish to show that—and in what points—these doctrines deny the principles of analysis and therefore should not be discussed under this name. (p. 93)

> I am happy to admit, of course, that everybody has the right to think and write as he pleases, but he does not have the right to pass it off as something that it is not. (p. 106)

> I can only conclude with the wish that fate may grant a comfortable ascent to all who have become uneasy during their stay in the underworld of psychoanalysis. The others should be permitted to bring their labors in the depths to a conclusion, unmolested. (p. 113)

Finally, in 1914, Jung resigned from the presidency of the Association and the editorship of the *Jahrbuch*, then also from the Association, and also from the University of Zurich, which had never granted him the title of professor. According to his own testimony in *Memories, Dreams, Reflections*, Jung found it "impossible for three years" after he finished the libido book "merely to read a scholarly book." He was deeply disturbed and went through a very profound psychological crisis. In fact, he was not at all sure that he might not become mad.

Meanwhile, the Zurich contingent resigned with Jung. We must not think of this secession merely in terms of two men; two groups were involved, the Viennese and the Swiss. They had never been on good terms, but Freud and Jung had managed to keep these two factions together. In the article on Jung, the *Encyclopaedia Britannica* (1974) says that "he resigned from the society and was the cofounder (with A. Maeder) of a new school in Zurich." It does not mention that at that time Maeder wrote Ferenczi, the leading Hungarian analyst, that "the scientific differences between the Viennese and the Swiss resulted from the former being Jews and the latter 'Aryans.'" Jones continues (II, p. 149):

> Freud advised Ferenczi to answer on the following lines. "Certainly there are great differences . . . But there should not be such a thing as Aryan or Jewish science. Results in science must be identical, though the presentation of them may vary. . . ."

On January 1, 1913, Freud wrote James Putnam:

> Scientific differences are unavoidable in the development of a science, and even errors have much that proves helpful, as I have been able to find out in my own case. But that such deviations and innovations of a theoretical nature had to appear with so much injury of reasonable personal feelings, that does not do much credit to human nature.
>
> That I consider Jung's new ideas "regressive" errors is a matter of course and does not prove anything to others. On that score everybody has to consult his own experiences and his impression of the arguments he has heard. My impression is that of a *déjà vu.* I have experienced all of this in the resistance of the nonanalysts, and now it is repeated in the resistance of the half-analysts.

Two Swiss analysts remained Freud's lifelong friends: Ludwig Binswanger, who tried later to blend Freud and Heidegger and thus became a founder of existential analysis, and Oskar Pfister, who practiced analysis but was a Protestant minister. They disagreed with Freud about many things, but that never clouded their friendship in any way. Freud did not mind disagreement as long as those who did not accept his theories were frank about it and did not confuse the public about what was and what was not psychoanalysis.

To return to Jung, his letters to Freud created a record that disproves much of what he later said about the break. Freud kept Jung's letters, even as Jung kept Freud's. But Jung and his collaborator did not consult these letters when putting together *Memories, Dreams, Reflections.* Jung may have found it too painful to go back to the record; and he evidently preferred to make it easy for himself in his constructions—to quote Freud—as he "did in the case of the famous 'Kreuzlingen gesture.'" It certainly was much easier not to be confused by the facts.

While Jung kept insisting in the letters that he would have liked to remain Freud's friend, he insisted in later years that their friendship was really finished on one or another occasion, as early as 1909. Since he quoted Nietzsche to Freud, one might quote Nietzsche to Jung:

> The strength of a spirit should be measured according to how much of the "truth" one could still barely endure— or to put it more clearly, to what degree one would *require* it to be thinned down, shrouded, sweetened, blunted, falsified.[33]

Freud was close to Nietzsche in this respect; Jung does not fare well when measured by this standard. It remains to be seen whether this weakness—and I think it is a weakness—makes itself felt in Jung's analytical psychology.

[33] See footnote 90 in Section 21 above.

61 ▶▶▶ It is no objection to a book by a philosopher, psychologist, or critic, if we find that the book deals to some extent with the author's own personal problems. Nietzsche's Zarathustra actually began his discourse "On Reading and Writing" by saying: "Of all that is written I love only what someone has written with his blood." But it makes a crucial difference whether the author realizes that he is dealing to a considerable extent with himself, as Freud did in *The Interpretation of Dreams,* for example, and as Nietzsche did, too, or whether he fails to see this, as Adler apparently did when he assumed that what was true of *him* was true of all men and women. In this respect, too, Jung belongs with Adler, not with Freud.

Something needs to be said here about Jung's libido book to which in later years he repeatedly ascribed Freud's break with him. It first appeared as "Contributions to the History of the Development of Thought" (to cite the subtitle of the original German version), but the title and subtitle of the final revised version were much more modest: *Symbols of Transformation: An Analysis of the Prelude to a Case of Schizophrenia.* His first book, published in 1907, had also dealt with schizophrenia; and since the publication of *Memories, Dreams, Reflections* it is obvious that when he worked on his libido book he himself was on the verge of a schizophrenic breakdown.

In a 1952 interview with Mircea Eliade (included in C. G. Jung *Speaking*) Jung said that when the First World War broke out,

> nobody was happier than I. Now I was sure that no schizophrenia was threatening me. I understood that my dreams and my visions came to me from the subsoil of collective unconscious. What remained for me to do now was to deepen and validate this discovery. And this is what I have been trying to do for forty years. (p. 233f.)

This is the conclusion of an interview that involved two very remarkable men. It may well be more significant than a great deal that has been written about Jung. Obviously, he had not understood in 1911 and 1912, during the period covered by the letters I have quoted, what he understood in 1952.

His interest in schizophrenia was prompted by his own condition, and he felt that if his visions and dreams came from the collective unconscious then he was not schizophrenic. This inference, of course, leaves much to be desired, but it is crucial for an understanding of Jung to know that he himself conceived of his attempts to establish that there is a collective unconscious and, we might add, that there are archetypes, as a form of self-justification. If only he could validate these claims, then he was not mad after all.

This sounds strange when it is stated so unemotionally, and it is essential to understand that Jung's attitude was anything but cold and objective. He was a Swiss depth psychologist, claimed to have some notion of the disasters of a world war, and was not swept up in the hysterical jingoism that made so many shortsighted people rejoice when the First World War broke out. He must have been frightened out of his wits that he was about to go mad if he could say that nobody was happier than he when the war broke out.

All this leaves open the question of whether there actually is a collective unconscious and whether there are archetypes. Jung's admirers generally seem to assume that if one does not share these beliefs it must be because one considers them to be irreconcilable with a scientific world view. I do not. While Jung's conceptions are rooted in Kant and Plato, the notion that all human minds are constituted the same way and share certain ideas or symbols that as a matter of fact are found among people everywhere and in all ages is not at all disturbing to a scientific mind. There could be a physical basis for that. In fact, the whole idea is much less strange than the ability of various migratory birds or butterflies to find their diverse ways.

The two serious objections to Jung's ideas on this subject are, to my mind, that there seems to be insufficient evidence to warrant them (much of the alleged evidence can be accounted for by diffusion of ideas from one place to others), and that most of the talk about archetypes explains nothing. Jung's theory allows for great exhibitions of erudition which, however, needs to be distinguished sharply from scholarship. Erudition is extensive knowledge acquired chiefly from books. Scholarship involves intellectual self-discipline, which consists in the scrupulous consideration of objections and alternatives.

Most of the literature on archetypes and the collective unconscious is distinguished by utterly tedious, pointless erudition coupled with a stunning lack of any even elementary concern with objections and alternatives. Erich Neumann's *Ursprungsgeschichte des Bewusstseins*, with a preface by Jung—translated as *The Origins and History of Consciousness*, although the title plainly means "The History of the Origins of Consciousness"—provides a perfect illustration.

It is not unfair, I think, to introduce Neumann here before returning to Jung's libido book. Neumann, says Jung in his preface, has been able to "give a coherent account of the whole field whose full extent the pioneer [Jung] can survey only at the end of his life's work." Moreover, Jung had told Neumann that the only point in Volume I of the manuscript to which he took exception was that Neumann had referred to the "castration complex." He returned to this point in a second letter, discussing the question at some length both times, and in the second letter he also insisted that "sacrifice" is a symbol.[34] It seems clear that while Freud tried to im-

[34] Letters of July 1 and 19, 1947.

press on his pupils how important it was to learn not to be dogmatic and to endure a piece of the truth, Jung simply failed to understand what constitutes dogmatism—namely, the refusal to consider objections and alternatives. Neumann's book is quintessentially dogmatic and operates with a notion of evidence not far different from the tracts of theologians who "prove" points by citing a few Biblical verses that are far from proving what they claim. He is delighted when he finds something "in Syria, Asia Minor, and even in Mesopotamia." Diffusion is never even considered as an alternative explanation. Even when the net is cast wider, "from Egypt to India, from Greece and Asia Minor to darkest Africa," the possibility of diffusion certainly needs to be discussed. All of these areas, including parts of India, were part of Alexander's empire; only "darkest Africa" was not, but the evidence from that part of the world belongs to modern times. But let us return now to Jung's libido book.

The first chapter contrasts "The [!] Two Kinds of Thinking": "*directed thinking* and *dreaming or fantasizing.*" Freud was very kind when he criticized this chapter only for the superabundance of quotations. Its main fault, which also disfigures much of Jung's other work, is surely irrelevant erudition.

The last four pages of that chapter are by far the most interesting and revealing, though neither Jung himself nor Freud seems to have noticed what they reveal. People, says Jung, may go back to archaic ideas. As an example he chooses a priest in a story by Anatole France. This man was terribly concerned with the fate of Judas and finally pleaded for a sign that Judas was saved. When he felt a heavenly touch on his shoulder, which he took for such a sign, he told his superior that he would now go out into the world to preach God's infinite mercy.

Now comes a typical Jungian digression: The story

of Judas is mythical and involves "the malicious betrayal of a hero." It brings to Jung's mind "Siegfried and Hagen, Balder and Loki." The traitor always comes from among the "closest associates" of the hero. He then thinks of Caesar and Brutus, who were historical characters; but Jung goes on to remark that the myths express "the psychological fact that envy does not allow humanity to sleep, and that all of us harbor, in a hidden recess of our heart, the wish that the hero should die." Jung is speaking about himself. Why does he generalize like this?

In effect, Jung answers this question in the next paragraph, after first offering a general rule about myth:

> *What is propagated is not just any account of old events, but only what expresses a universal thought of humanity that is rejuvenated again and again. . . .*
>
> But why does our pious Abbé torment himself with the old Judas legend? . . . he separated from the Catholic Church and became a *Swedenborgian.* Now we understand . . . *He was the Judas* who betrayed his Lord. Therefore he had to make sure first of all of the divine mercy . . .[35]

It was his own personality that "wished to win a way to freedom through the solution of the Judas problem." Jung goes on and on like this. He even asks: What might the priest "have said, had he been told confidentially that he was preparing himself for the Judas role? And what in ourselves do we consider immoral . . . ?" Eventually, Jung says plainly what he is doing: For this priest

> Judas became the *symbol* of his own unconscious tendency, and he needed this symbol in order to be able to reflect on his unconscious wish. The direct coming into consciousness of the Judas wish would have been too painful for him. *Thus there must be typical myths . . .*

[35] My translations are based on the 1912 edition. The significance of Jung's preoccupation with Judas and of several points discussed in the next section has been noted by Rosenberg (1978).

Warum aber quält sich unser frommer Abbé mit der alten Judas-
legende?

Er ging also in die Welt, um das Evangelium der Barmherzigkeit
zu predigen. Nach einiger Zeit trat er aus der katholischen Kirche
aus und wurde Swedenborgianer. Nun verstehen wir seine
Judasphantasie: er war der Judas, der seinen Herrn verriet; deshalb
mußte er sich vorerst der göttlichen Barmherzigkeit versichern, um
ruhig Judas sein zu können.

Dieser Fall wirft ein Licht auf den Mechanismus der Phantasien
überhaupt. Die bewußte Phantasie kann von mythischem oder
anderem Stoffe sein, sie ist als solche nicht ernst zu nehmen, denn sie
ist von indirekter Bedeutung. Nehmen wir sie doch als per se wichtig,
so wird die Sache unverständlich, und man muß an der Zweckmäßigkeit
des Geistes verzweifeln. Wir sahen aber im Falle des Abbé Oegger,
daß seine Zweifel und Hoffnungen sich nicht um die historische Person
des Judas drehen, sondern um seine eigene Person, die sich durch die
Lösung des Judasproblems den Weg in die Freiheit bahnen will.

Die bewußten Phantasien erzählen uns also an einem
mythischen oder sonstigen Stoffe von noch nicht oder nicht
mehr anerkannten Wunschtendenzen in der Seele. Wie
leicht verständlich, kann eine seelische Tendenz, der man die Aner-
kennung versagt und die man als nicht existierend behandelt, kaum
etwas enthalten, was zu unserem bewußten Charakter gut paßte. Es
handelt sich um Tendenzen, die man als unmoralisch und überhaupt
als unmöglich bezeichnet und gegen deren Bewußtmachung man den
stärksten Widerstand empfindet. Was hätte wohl Oegger gesagt, wenn
man ihm vertraulich mitgeteilt hätte, daß er sich selber für die Judas-
rolle präpariere? Was aber bezeichnen wir in uns als unmoralisch
und nicht existierend oder wünschen wenigstens, daß es nicht exi-
stiere? Es ist das, was in der Antike breit an der Oberfläche lag, nämlich
die Sexualität in ihren vielfachen Erscheinungsformen. Wir dürfen
uns darum nicht im geringsten wundern, sie an der Basis der meisten
unserer Phantasien zu finden, wenn schon die Phantasien ein anders-
artiges Aussehen haben. Weil Oegger die Verdammung des Judas
unverträglich mit der Güte Gottes fand, so dachte er über diesen Kon-
flikt nach: Das ist die bewußte Kausalreihe. Nebenher geht die
unbewußte Reihe: weil Oegger selber Judas werden wollte, ver-
sicherte er sich vorerst der Güte Gottes. Judas wurde für Oegger
zum Symbol seiner eigenen unbewußten Tendenz, und er brauchte

Page about Judas from Jung's libido book, 1912.

Why must there be? Even as the priest needed to reassure himself that Judas was saved before he felt free to become a Judas, Jung had to reassure himself that "all of us harbor . . . the wish that the hero should die" and that what he was about to do was merely the reeanactment of a primordial myth. Was it really?

Whatever we do, we can find parallels in myth and in history, as well as in literature. I fail to see that this in itself diminishes our responsibility or the difference between those who act heroically and those whom envy does not permit to sleep.

Indeed, the drama of the Freud/Jung break has what one might call, speaking loosely, archetypical features. I myself should not have compared Jung with Judas, Hagen, or Brutus, and it does make a difference after all that Jung did not kill Freud or help others to kill him. Insofar as Jung and Freud reenacted a timeless drama it was surely the drama of father and son. The more fatherly and patient and forgiving the older man may be, the more intolerable he becomes for the younger man who needs to go his own way. The son feels the need to strike out for himself and make his own mistakes, but is often nasty about it because he is deeply troubled and at odds with himself.

Jung kept blaming Freud all his life and was not above misremembering things in self-serving ways. About that one may well say: Who doesn't do that? Isn't it a common human failing? It is, but scholarship and science depend on systematic attempts to housebreak ourselves.

Psychoanalysis had been conceived in that kind of scientific spirit. It was meant to add a new dimension to honesty. Jung's new version of it, analytical psychology, was indeed regressive or, if you prefer, counterrevolutionary. It provided new forms of escape.

62 ▶▶▶ To show this, I now turn to consider three of Jung's dreams and two of his fantasies. The first two dreams are found in the Freud chapter of *Memories, Dreams, Reflections*. While working on his libido book, Jung "had significant dreams that already pointed toward the break with Freud." This way of putting the point brings out clearly the attempt to decline responsibility. "One of the most impressive" involved "an aging man in the uniform of an Imperial customs official" who paid no attention to Jung. Somebody told Jung that it was "the spirit of a customs official who had died years ago. 'He is one of those who could not die,' was what was said." Jung's first association with customs was censorship, and, to be brief, "I could not reject the analogy with Freud." Jung seems to have realized that part of him was impatient for Freud to die.

Now, this dream was immediately followed by a second dream; or as Jung put it, "after a hiatus there followed a second very remarkable part." In this dream Jung encountered "a knight in full armor." His face was covered by a helmet with eye slits, and over his chain armor he wore a white tunic with a red cross woven into it both in front and in the back." This dream, says Jung, made an enormous impression on him, but he could not understand it. He was upset and knew no way out.[36] "The knight and the customs official were diametrically opposite figures," for the knight "had vitality and was wholly real." After meditating about this dream on and off for years, Jung eventually figured out that it was significant that the knight belonged to the twelfth century, when alchemy first developed—and so forth. It never seems to have occurred to him that the red cross might signify a medical man, and that the knight might be a crusading doctor, namely Freud. Jung had been

[36] The short paragraph summarized in the last two sentences is missing in the American paperback edition.

upset that Freud had refused to share with him some intimate information that might have enabled him to interpret one of Freud's dreams. Now, in the dream he was completely covered from top to toe, and one could not even see his face.

It would be silly to claim that this was all there was to the dream. I have not even related all the details Jung mentioned, and there may have been more that he did not commit to print; nor do we know his associations when he woke up. What is significant in the present context is merely that the descent into the distant past serves to obscure what is up front. It functions as an escape.

The third dream is found in the next chapter (p. 183 = A, p. 179f.). Jung found himself in the company of a brown-skinned youth, a savage. He heard Siegfried's horn "and I knew that we had to slay him. We were armed with rifles . . ." And "we shot him, and he collapsed, dead." Now Jung felt "disgust and contrition about having destroyed something so great and beautiful." He fled. A voice told him that he must understand the dream, immediately. Finally, the voice said: "If you do not understand the dream you have to shoot yourself."

> I had a loaded revolver in my bedside table and was frightened. Then I reflected once more, and suddenly the meaning of the dream dawned upon me: "This is the problem that is being played out in the world!" Siegfried represents what the Germans wanted to realize, namely making one's own will prevail heroically. "Where there is a will there is a way!" I wanted the same thing. But now that was no longer possible. The dream showed that the attitude embodied in Siegfried, the hero, no longer suited me. Therefore he had to be killed. . . .

There is no need to go on quoting. Obviously, an interpreter at this remove cannot be sure about *the* meaning of the dream; but he can be sure that it is false that such a dream has only one meaning. The escape function in this case is underlined not only by "the meaning" but also by the impersonal "dawned upon me." Jung disclaims all responsibility, does not work his own way step by step, but relies on a sudden revelation: *plötzlich ging mir der Sinn des Traumes auf.* There are many mysteries we cannot fathom. Why would a doctor in Switzerland, on the night of December 18, 1913, have a loaded revolver in his bedside table? But what is not particularly mysterious is that Siegfried is surely not only a symbol of "what the Germans wanted to realize" but also Sig(mund) Freud. If anyone should have doubts about that, they may perhaps be laid to rest by recalling how Siegfried and Hagen were introduced in the first chapter of the libido book along with Jesus and Judas. The brown-skinned savage might be Adler, but it hardly matters. What is important is to see once again how the Jungian interpretation functions as an escape from the here and now.

Two fantasies remain to be considered. The first, introduced by Jung a page later, involves "an old man with a white beard and a beautiful young girl. . . . The old man declared he was Elijah . . . The girl . . . called herself Salome! . . . What a strange pair: Salome and Elijah!"

Typically, it took Jung years to figure out that the motif of "an old man accompanied by a young girl" is found in many myths. In *Memories, Dreams, Reflections* this realization serves as a point of departure for a quick display of erudition. Oedipus and Antigone are left out, and what is up front is ignored again. At the Munich Congress in September 1913, Lou Salomé sat with Freud. We know from the famous photograph taken two years earlier at the Weimar Congress how stunning she looked. Indeed, "a strange pair." But why was Freud represented by Elijah? "Like an Old Testament prophet he undertook the task to dethrone false gods," Jung himself said at the end of the Freud chapter. Moreover, Elijah was considered the herald of the messiah—in the New Testament, too—and Jung presumably sometimes thought of Freud as his forerunner. Finally, seeing that Jung boasted repeatedly that he knew philosophy in general and Nietzsche in particular as Freud did not, and how Jung had cited Nietzsche's counsel to break with the master for the sake of one's independence, it must have rankled him to see Freud's visible link with Nietzsche. Here was the woman Nietzsche had been so close to—so close to Freud.

> Soon after this fantasy another figure emerged from the unconscious. It had developed out of the figure of Elijah. I called it Philemon. Philemon was a pagan and brought up an Egyptian-Hellenistic mood with a Gnostic coloring
>
> . . .
>
> Psychologically, Philemon represented superior insight. He was a mysterious figure for me. At times he almost seemed physically real to me. I walked up and down with him in the garden, and he was for me what the Indians call a guru.

Again Jung writes about Philemon at some length but misses two of the most striking points. One is that he made a painting of Philemon, and it looks unmistakably like Freud. The other one is that the New Testament contains Paul's Epistle to Philemon, in which Paul asks Philemon to take back his thieving runaway slave and forgive him.

For good measure, Philemon is also a character in the final act of Goethe's *Faust*. In *Memories, Dreams, Reflections* Jung tells us near the beginning of the chapter "Student Years" how he split his own personality into a number one and number two, and how Faust was to his mind "a living equivalent of number two." Much later in the book, near the end of the "Tower" chapter, he tells us how when Faust "caused the murder of Phile-

154

Jung's painting of Philemon, from his Red Book.

mon and Baucis, I felt guilty, as if I myself had participated in the past in the murder of these two old people."
Thus Faust/Philemon correspond to Judas/Jesus, Hagen/
Siegfried, Brutus/Caesar, and Jung/Freud. "I considered
it my responsibility to atone for this guilt or prevent its
repetition." But instead of realizing that he felt guilty for
having treated Freud rather shabbily, and instead of
asking himself whether he might tell Freud how he felt
and try to clear the air, he escaped once again into
erudite reflections.

There was a story that his grandfather Jung had been
Goethe's illegitimate son. This story "seemed to explain" his "strange reactions to *Faust*." From there we
move on to "that concept which the Indian calls karma,"
to Jakob Burckhardt, Nietzsche, Wotan, "the catastrophe
of 1914," Mephistopheles as the "uncanny shadow" of
Faust, and eventually we are told:

> Later I consciously linked my work to what Faust had
> passed over: respect for eternal human rights, the recog-
> nition of what is old, and the continuity of culture and the
> history of the spirit.

These high-flown words, however, are less illuminating
than Aniela Jaffé's footnote: Originally, Jung inscribed
over the entrance gate to his house in Bollingen, in Latin,
"Philemon's Sanctuary—Faust's Atonement." Later,
"when the place was walled up, he placed these words
over the entrance to the second tower." It would seem
that he never got over his guilt feelings vis-à-vis Freud,
but instead of understanding this and taking appropriate
steps to make it up to Freud and get rid of his guilt
feelings, he used his erudition as blinders—and kept
slandering Freud.

63 ▶▶▶ When Jung referred to Mephistopheles as the "uncanny shadow" of Faust, he referred to one of his archetypes. Below the personal unconscious, in which we may find what we have forgotten and repressed, there is, according to Jung, the collective unconscious whose contents are "archetypes."

In *The Collected Works* these introductory reflections are found in volume 9.I.1–4 and followed eventually by a rather odd lot of papers and discussions of "the Anima Concept" (1936/1954), "the Mother Archetype" (1938/54), "Rebirth" (1940/50), "the Child Archetype" (1940), "the Kore" (1941), and "the Trickster Figure" (1954). In volume 9.II we encounter "The Ego," "The Shadow," "Anima and Animus," "The Self," "Christ, a Symbol of the Self," "The Sign of the Fishes," "The Prophecies of Nostradamus," four more discussions of the fish, and three other pieces. In the *General Index* to the works we find roughly three and a half columns of references to the shadow, which Jung mentioned constantly, but there seem to be only two places in which the shadow is mentioned in more than three consecutive paragraphs.

The arrangement of *The Collected Works* makes it impossible, as I have implied earlier, to see where a concept is introduced for the first time or to note how, if at all, Jung's view of it may have changed. (The chronological arrangement of Freud's works makes it easy to compare early and late uses of the same term, and Freud generally took care to explain his concepts.)

In the case of the shadow, the index volume at least refers us to a definition. In the first of the *Two Essays* Jung said:

> The personal unconscious contains lost memories, painful ideas that have been repressed (forgotten on purpose), so-called sub-threshold (subliminal) perceptions, that is, sense perceptions that were not strong enough to reach

Jung's painting "Encounter with the Shadow," from his Red Book.

consciousness, and finally contents that are not yet ripe for consciousness. It corresponds to the figure of the *shadow* that frequently appears in dreams. (7, 103)

"It" can only refer to the personal unconscious, which is here said to correspond, whatever that may mean, to the shadow. This does not seem to make sense because the personal unconscious surely does not appear frequently in dreams as a figure, although the contents just mentioned do, of course, appear in dreams. Moreover, it seems odd to call the personal unconscious an archetype that is found in the collective unconscious. But at this point we are offered the aforementioned definition, in a footnote:

> By *shadow* I mean the "negative" part of the personality, namely the sum of the hidden, disadvantageous qualities, inadequately developed functions, and contents of the personal unconscious.

This is rather a mixed bag, and it is far from obvious that we profit from having a single term for it that keeps appearing in passing throughout Jung's works. Such doubts are strengthened when we recall our point of departure: Jung considers Mephistopheles Faust's shadow. This may sound impressive, suggestive, and profound to people who do not know Goethe's *Faust* very well; but after rereading that footnote definition anyone who does know the play well is bound to feel that the definition does not quite fit. It is a truism that Goethe found both Faust and Mephistopheles in himself, even as he found both Götz and Weislingen, and Tasso as well as Antonio in himself, but the definition of the shadow does not really fit Mephistopheles, Weislingen, and Antonio, any more than it would be quite right to say that Faust is Mephistopheles's shadow, and so forth. And the claim that the shadow is an archetype does not help at all and only adds to the confusion.

The first time Jung discussed the shadow at any length was in 1946, in a BBC radio talk that was subsequently published in *The Listener*. It was called "The Fight with the Shadow," and Jung, whose own behavior during the Nazi period had come in for a great deal of criticism and will be discussed soon, lectured the Germans: "In Hitler every German should have seen his own shadow" (10, 455). This curious notion seemed to imply that the Germans share a racial unconscious. During the Nazi period Jung had also suggested that the Jewish unconscious differed from the Aryan. If so, we would have at least three kinds of unconscious: personal, racial, and collective; but Jung was not consistent about this, nor did he generally stress the notion that a whole people shares a shadow.

The only other place where Jung discussed "The Shadow" at any length is a section with this title that comprises three pages that "are taken from a lecture" Jung gave in 1948 (9.II.13ff.). Here we are told that the shadow is "the most accessible" of all the archetypes and "the easiest to experience . . . for its nature can in large measure be inferred from the contents of the personal unconscious"—except in cases where it is the positive qualities that happen to be repressed. It is said to require great moral effort to become conscious of one's shadow, for it involves recognition of "the dark aspects of the personality as present and real." This, however, is necessary for real self-knowledge and requires hard work over a long period of time.

These remarks as well as a few others that follow do not altogether resist an attempt at sympathetic understanding. One can see what Jung is driving at, but not only could it be said better and more clearly than he says it; what is more important here is that it could be said better without introducing any archetype.

Perhaps the vital point can be made best by choosing another literary example: *The Brothers Karamazov*.

There are four brothers, and the clue to the character of each is that whatever is embodied explicitly in one is implicitly present in the other three. Alyosha's devout soul contains Smerdyakov's wickedness, Mitya's passion, and Ivan's skepticism—nor would Ivan be so troubled if his philosophy had come more easily to him, and if Alyosha were not within him fighting his position. So, too, Nietzsche's sister was, as it were, the embodiment in the flesh of that part of his character which he tried, all his adult life long, to overcome. That he was really not entirely unlike her is true enough but misses the more significant point: because he was cursed with the same heritage that came to full flower in her, his philosophy was a triumph of integrity. "My *strongest* characteristic is self-overcoming. But I also need it most."[37]

When I wrote that more than thirty years ago, I was not aware of Jung's concept of the shadow, and I did not mean to imply—using this term now—that each of the brothers Karamazov had precisely three shadows and no more, or that Nietzsche had only one. In fact, according to Jung the shadow is always of the same sex as the person who has it, which is another one of his dogmatic *obiter dicta* for which no argument whatsoever is offered. Taking Nietzsche's case, it is worth asking whether the people whom he attacked with some emotion, notably Richard Wagner, did not seem to Nietzsche to have qualities that he had, too, and disliked. But it would be fatuous, I think, to say that Wagner was Nietzsche's shadow. Insofar as I myself feel some emotion about Kant, Heidegger, or Jung, it is worth asking myself whether they have qualities that I have, too, and dislike—notably qualities of which I was not aware in myself until I put this question to myself and took some trouble answering it. This pluralistic approach—looking at all the figures in reality and myth as well as such

[37] Kaufmann, *Nietzsche* (1950), p. 44f.; p. 74 of the 1974 edition.

classes of people as, say, pimps or rapists, whom one abhors—seems much more fruitful to me than all the discussions of archetypes.

The notion that each of us has just one shadow owes something to Jung's schizophrenic splitting of his own personality, and it can also be used easily to shut out a great deal that it would be more comfortable not to see. Of course, the very image of a shadow suggests—rightly, I think—that we have many shadows. Incidentally, Nietzsche had called one of his books *The Wanderer and His Shadow* (1880); it begins and ends with a dialogue between the two, and the shadow reappears in the last part of *Zarathustra,* in which a whole chapter bears the title "The Shadow."

Jung's rather loose talk of archetypes opened up a new game for scholars that one could play without really being very scholarly—that is, without self-discipline— and *that* is a gift for which many people are always grateful. One only needs to recall ordinary language philosophy, which allowed philosophy dons, professors, and students to play endlessly with such phrases as, "wouldn't it be rather queer if someone said," or "suppose some said." Jung made it possible for people to go archetype hunting, looking for shadows, fish, tricksters, wise old men, and above all the great mother. Erich Neumann had a marvelous time going on and on about "The Uroboros," and Jung himself loved to speak of the psychopomp. One frequently gets the impression that the authors of this sort of literature feel: the more arcane, the better. They seem to feel that not being understood by ordinary educated people is a warrant, or a condition, of being scientific.

What matters most, however, are not bad manners but rather that Jung gave a tremendous boost to something against which Kierkegaard and Nietzsche already had raised their voices. Nietzsche had pointed to the dangers of the hypertrophy of the historical sense, and

Kierkegaard, much earlier, had pointed out how scholarship can function as a diversion, a distraction, an escape from ourselves. I confess to a fascination with *some* scholarship, not all, but find the Jungian literature full of undigested and indigestible erudition that seems to have no other function than distraction from the central task of depth psychology: a better understanding of ourselves and our fellow men.

Today scholars tend to be rather polite, but perhaps Jung's occasional "Helvetic loutishness" should be balanced with a passage from a letter that Pfister, the Swiss pastor, wrote to Freud:

> I have finished for good with the Jungian manner. These hermeneutic acrobatics which pass off every kind of muck as a higher marmalade of the soul, and all perversions as holy oracles and mysteries, and try to smuggle a little Apollo or Christ into every upset soul, are no good. It is Hegelism transposed into psychology: everything that is must be reasonable. If only this theory were reasonable![38]

64 ▶▶▶ Although Jung claimed that the shadow was "the most accessible" of all the archetypes and "the easiest to experience," and that we must recognize our shadow if we would know ourselves, Jung plainly did not recognize his own weaknesses at all clearly. Seen in this perspective, *Memories, Dreams, Reflections* is a very curious document. On the first page of the Prologue Jung says:

> Thus I have undertaken today, in the eighty-third year of my life, to relate the myth of my life. I can . . . only "tell stories." Whether they are true is no problem. The question is only, is it *my* fairy tale, *my* truth?[39]

[38] July 19, 1922. The published English version is quite inadequate.
[39] *Märchen* means fairy tale, not, as the English version has it, fable.

This sounds beautiful and brings to mind the title of Goethe's autobiography, *Aus meinem Leben: Dichtung und Wahrheit*—Out of My Life: Poetry (or Fiction) and Truth; also Nietzsche's rather unusual autobiographical work, *Ecce Homo: How One Becomes What One Is*. Yet it is a strange conclusion for the life's work of a depth psychologist who saw himself as having gone far beyond Nietzsche and Freud. Will it really do to tell fairy tales about Freud, to whom a whole chapter is devoted, and to cover oneself with a disclaimer of that sort? And the work is curiously lacking in depth psychology and strangely pre-Freudian. P. J. Stern remarked in his *C. G. Jung* (1976) that

> Jung failed to mention Bleuler even once. This omission was quite a feat. Jung seemed to have completely erased from his memory the unselfish teacher to whom he owed a great deal intellectually and who had so generously smoothed his path. But, then, gratitude toward fatherly sponsors was never one of Jung's strong points. (p. 56)

What is rather more remarkable is that he did not mention Toni Wolff (1888–1953), whom he first encountered as a patient in 1909 and thought he cured of schizophrenia. He became her lover, and eventually she moved into his house, where Jung lived with her and Emma and his family. (Stern devoted a whole chapter to her and also discussed the theories about women that Jung developed to rationalize what he did.)

Of course, there were many good reasons for not telling the world about Toni Wolff.[40] I can do no better than quote once more Freud's words to his "uninvited biographer":

[40] "Jung's letters to his close friend and collaborator Miss Toni Wolff were returned to him after her death in 1953 and were destroyed by Jung, together with her letters to him." *Letters*, 1, p. xi.

I naturally would never have wished or asked for such a book. It seems to me that the public has no claim to my person and also cannot learn from it as long as my case—for ever so many reasons—cannot be made fully transparent. You think differently about this and have therefore been able to write this book.

We should be clear about what kind of a book Jung's *Memories, Dreams, Reflections* is. It may seem to be the fearless voyage of a depth psychologist into hitherto unfathomed abysses, the log of a man who has faced up to his own shadow and attained a degree of self-knowledge not possible until he discovered the collective unconscious and the archetypes. Actually, it is the story of a man who required the truth to be shrouded and falsified; a man who, like so many Victorian gentlemen, had a mistress but found sex an unsavory subject that it was better not to talk about; a man who was remarkably self-indulgent and self-righteous and who felt a great need at the end of his life to engage in a lengthy exercise in self-justification. In the process, he escaped again and again in various directions, as we have seen when considering some of his dreams and fantasies, while he systematically ignored what was up front.

I do not feel that the public has any claim to know about Jung's relationship to Toni Wolff and Emma Jung, and I have never written a biography. But any biography or autobiography of Jung that simply ignores all of this would have to be extremely subtle and perceptive to avoid a far-reaching falsification of his character. It would have to be doubly careful to look for possible projections, meaning instances in which Jung projected some of his own qualities and problems upon others. But Jung's book abounds in projections and excuses.

Instead of introducing altogether new material at this point, I shall confine myself to his treatment of Nietzsche and Freud. As a student, Jung studied Kant on

Sundays, he says, but hesitated to read Nietzsche "because I felt insufficiently prepared. Nietzsche was much discussed at that time but for the most part repudiated." Since it seems odd that he should have felt that he was adequately prepared to read Kant on his own but not Nietzsche, one may wonder whether the main reason for not reading him might have been that he was in such bad repute, the more so since Jung goes on to enlarge on that point before he finally says:

> These things, however, did not serve me as a pretext for postponing the reading of Nietzsche [an odd remark since the reader is not wondering about pretexts but about the real reasons]—on the contrary, they would have been the strongest inducement for me [why the subjunctive? were they not an inducement after all?]—but it was a secret dread that I might perhaps be similar to him, at least regarding the "secret" that isolated him in his environment. Perhaps, who knows, he had inner experiences, insights about which unfortunately he wished to talk and was understood by nobody? Evidently, he was an oddity, or at least was taken for one, for a *lusus naturae* [sport of nature], which I did not wish to be under any circumstances. I was afraid of the possible realization that I, like Nietzsche, was "Another One" [title of a novel by F. T. Vischer that Freud and Adler admired].

What Jung was afraid of was after all isolation from—or he says, in—his environment. And he goes on, where we have left off, making excuses for himself. After offering a Latin disclaimer that means, "if it is permitted to compare something small [himself] with something great [Nietzsche]," he proceeds:

> . . . he was a professor, had written books, and had thus scaled dreamlike heights; he, too, came from a theologian's house, to be sure, but in Germany, which was large and expansive and reached to the sea, while I was merely a Swiss and came from a modest pastor's house in little

village on the border [smaller than Röcken, where Nietzsche was born?]. He spoke polished High German, knew Latin and Greek, perhaps also French, Italian, and Spanish, while I was secure only in Waggis-Basel German. He, in the possession of all these splendors, could after all afford a certain oddness while I must not know in what way I might be similar to him. (p. 108f. = A, p. 101f.)

"So this was the poodle's core!" to quote *Faust* (line 1323). The long list of excuses that begins with "did not serve me as a pretext" comes down to the admission that he was afraid of being thought different. Or was he perhaps not afraid of what others might think of him but only of finding out that he really *was* different—or mad? No, Jung continues:

In spite of my fears, I was curious and decided to read him. It was the *Untimely Meditations* that first fell into my hands. I was carried away by boundless enthusiasm, and soon I also read *Thus Spoke Zarathustra*. That was, like Goethe's *Faust*, one of my most powerful experiences.

Jung was led to reflect on himself, he says. But the most striking point of what follows—as it were, the moral of the story—is that Nietzsche was naive and incautious enough to speak to others of the unmentionable. "I, however, realized very soon that one makes bad experiences that way."

Was Freud right about Jung in his *History*? Was Jung's attitude toward Freud's emphasis on sex colored by such considerations? No, one feels, that would be placing too much weight on insufficient evidence. But Jung, looking back in his eighties, goes on to say explicitly:

I reached the insight that one gets nowhere when one does not speak of things that are familiar to all. Those who are naïve in this respect do not understand what an insult it is to one's fellow men when one speaks to them of what is not familiar to them. Only writers, journalists, and poets are forgiven for such wickedness.

Two points may seem to speak against my construction. In the first place, Jung himself certainly wrote about unfamiliar things and actually had a predilection for arcane erudition. But that is not the point at issue here. What is significant is that he showed so much concern for the reactions of other people to one's work—and failed to realize this. He ascribed this concern to the extravert and called Freud an extravert, while he considered himself an introvert. Instead of recognizing his shadow, he projected the qualities he did not like in himself upon Freud.

Then there is, of course, a lot of sarcasm in the passages quoted here. But that does not really affect the point made here. Moreover, it is revealing that in Jung's works and letters we find neither the detached humor that is so notable in Freud nor the lucid and incisive wit of Lessing, Heine, and Nietzsche. There is almost always something in Jung's humor that brings to mind the German word *verbissen*. Dictionaries say it means sour-tempered, but *beissen* means to bite, and *sich verbeissen* is an expression used of a dog that locks its teeth on something and won't let go. *Sich etwas verbeissen* means to swallow something, especially one's anger, or even to choke on it. All of these associations are pertinent to Jung's dogged sarcasm. He quite lacked what Nietzsche called "light feet," and he never seems to be able to let go of himself and his heavy seriousness. Far from the wit that exposes something in a sudden flash, Jung's humor lacks speed and typically impedes communication. He cannot move on or say simply what he wants to say, and quite often what comes across is mostly his anger or—Nietzsche's word seems wholly appropriate—his *ressen-*

timent. We shall encounter many examples of it in his *Answer to Job.*

Nietzsche, for all his wit, was certainly not free of resentment, but he made no secret of that. His campaign against resentment was part of his self-overcoming. Jung does not seem to have realized how full he was of resentment, and how it distorted not only his prose but also, more importantly, his perceptions. It attached itself to all of his major rivals—Nietzsche, Freud, and Adler—and helps to account for his failure to see them as they were.

Having vented his resentment against Adler in his letters to Freud, he decided later to play off Adler against Freud as having championed a view of roughly equal merit. But since Adler hardly had sufficient stature, he conflated Adler and Nietzsche to the point of claiming not only that they offered the same doctrine, which, of course, they did not, but even that they were the same psychological type. Nietzsche and Adler! Can one really imagine Nietzsche converting to Protestantism to escape from the dangers of spiritual isolation?

We are always led back to the fact that Jung needed reality, external as well as internal, "to be thinned down, shrouded, sweetened, blunted, falsified." This is hardly the recipe for a great psychologist. Nor did Jung have the insight to quote the line from Baudelaire's poem to *The Flowers of Evil* that T. S. Eliot quoted in *The Waste Land:*

Hypocrite reader! My own image! Brother!

65 ▶▶▶ Jung's criticisms of Freud after their break revolved around four major themes. Three could be discussed largely on the basis of the Freud chapter in *Memories, Dreams, Reflections.* The fourth involves what Jung saw fit to print in Nazi Germany about Freud as a Jew.

Jung's first charge was that Freud was an exponent of an essentially reductive materialistic science. This incredible claim is still widely believed by many people who have no idea who originated it. In a letter of May 26, 1934, that is altogether remarkable the crucial point is formulated very memorably: "Freud previously accused me of anti-Semitism because I could not abide his soulless materialism."

In an article that appeared in 1932, Jung claimed that Freud constructed "a rigid system that might rightly be charged with absolutism"; he casually mentioned "his greater contemporary Nietzsche," as the Nazis did, just to put down Freud, without taking the trouble to discover or spell out Nietzsche's psychological insights; he said of Freud that "one of his favorite maxims is Voltaire's 'Écrasez l'infâme,'" although this motto, which is actually found in the penultimate line of Nietzsche's *Ecce Homo*, is nowhere to be found in Freud's work; and then he proceeded:

> With a certain satisfaction he invariably points out the flaw in the crystal; all complex psychic phenomena like art, philosophy, and religion fall under his suspicion and appear as "nothing but" repressions of the sexual instinct.[41]

It is tempting to say that all this is "nothing but" a web of lies and projections. It is on a level with the "Kreuzlingen gesture" and the claim that Freud returned the libido book to him, unread, with an inscription that Jung could quote although the whole story was

[41] 15, 44ff. Cf. *Memories*, p. 164 = A, p. 149. Hermann Hesse "had several analytical sessions" with Jung, around 1921, but came to feel that Jung had no "genuine relationship to art" and that analysts "lack the organ for it" (Jung, *Letters*, 1 (1973), p. 575).

made up. It was what Jung had expected to happen; and when it did not happen, he eventually thought it did. The falseness of this first charge has been demonstrated at length in the present book.

The second charge was that Freud was a dogmatist whose dedication to the truth left much to be desired. This is an odd charge to make in a book that more or less begins with the statement that the author can only " 'tell stories.' Whether they are true is no problem. The question is only, is it *my* fairy tale, *my* truth?" Nevertheless, this charge, too, has been accepted widely but has been refuted, I hope, in the present book.

The story about Freud and truth that has attracted most attention is found in *Memories, Dreams, Reflections*. In 1909, on the boat to the United States, Jung and Freud analyzed each other's dreams. Jung asked Freud to furnish "some details about his private life" that might enable Jung to say more about a particular dream. According to Jung, Freud said: "I cannot risk my authority." (The wording here is not quite the same as in Jung's letter of December 3, 1912, cited in Section 60.) Jung continued:

> At this moment he had lost it. This sentence engraved itself in my memory. In this sentence the end of our relationship was already decided for me. Freud placed personal authority above truth.

Jung's letters show clearly that the penultimate sentence is a falsehood. And the final sentence is slander. The preposterous implication is plainly that Freud did not consider truth as high a value as he should have, and that honesty was for him not the virtue it was for Jung. It was at most a particular piece of truth—the added something that Jung might have discovered about the dream—that Freud did not take to be of supreme value. But even that makes little sense, for though Jung had to stop at that point, nothing prevented Freud from continuing the analysis of that dream without Jung's help.

Whether Freud did or did not speak of his authority, we have no way of telling. One would think that the obvious word would have been discretion. There was something he did not wish to tell Jung, but it would have been insulting, even if it was reasonable, to express doubts about Jung's discretion. After Freud's death, if not before, Jung made remarks to several people about the neurosis for which he claimed to have treated Freud and, according to a professor at a theological seminary, also talked at length about people other than Freud who had been involved in this very dream.[42] But it is not really relevant whether Jung was discreet or not. Freud did not want to talk to him about some problems that involved others and then in some sense feel at his mercy. He was not untruthful. Why, then, did Jung suggest that he was? To exculpate himself. A mere two pages later Jung related how Freud asked him something in connection with a dream, and "I told him a lie" (p. 164 = A, p. 160).

[42] John M. Billinsky's interview appeared in the *Andover Newton Quarterly* in November 1969 and was subsequently given wide currency by *Time*. It was presented as a dialogue, with all of Jung's remarks in quotation marks, and introduced: "What follows is a copy of remarks recorded on May tenth, 1957." People who knew Jung extremely well were sure that he could not have said some of the things he was quoted as saying, and in conversation the author admitted eventually that his dialogue was written up from memory later in the day. Regarding the insinuation that Freud was "intimate" with his wife's sister, those who were perhaps closest to Jung insisted that, according to what Jung had said more than once about Freud's character, this was absolutely wrong. Even Roazen, whose attitude toward gossip differs sharply from mine, is "inclined to reject" this tale for reasons of his own (1975, p. 62). See also note 38 in Section 46 above, and the text above note 65 in Section 17. Perhaps Jung expressed himself ambiguously, and Billinsky made the most of that.

66 ▶▶▶ When I visited Jung in 1953, I said that Freud had often been portrayed as a dogmatist but that on reading him I had not found this to be true; he had struck me as remarkably open-minded. Jung replied: "I myself have heard him say: 'We need a dogma against the mud tide [*Schlammflut*] of occultism.'" What struck me most was that it did not seem to occur to Jung that this image might refer to the dangers Jung had brought to Freud's poetic science. Jung felt that the quotation proved that Freud was a dogmatist.

In *Memories, Dreams, Reflections* this saying is introduced to support the strange claim about Freud that "sexuality meant for him a *numinosum*." Rudolf Otto, in his book on the holy (*Das Heilige*, 1917; translated as *The Idea of the Holy*, 1923), introduced *numen* and *numinous* to designate the terrifying but at the same time fascinating divine presence that is encountered in many religious experiences, and Jung suggested that sexuality had for Freud a religious function. This seems wholly implausible. What was distinctive in Freud's attitude toward sexuality was precisely his sobriety, the lack of drama and emotion. In this respect there was clearly a great difference between Freud and Jung, which comes out clearly in the opening words of Jung's libido book:

> Anyone who can read Freud's *Interpretation of Dreams* without . . . moral indignation over the stark nudity [*Nudität*] of his dream interpretations . . . will surely be impressed deeply . . . .

Emotionally, the man who wrote that was obviously much less liberated and much more Victorian than Freud.

Now we shall see where an attempt to track down the remark about the mud tide leads us. We must begin with the passage in which this remark appears in *Memories, Dreams, Reflections*:

I still remember vividly how Freud said to me: "My dear Jung, promise me never to give up the sexual theory. That is what is most essential. You see, we must turn it into a dogma, an unshakable bulwark." This he said to me full of passion and in the same tone in which a father might say: "And promise me one thing, my dear son: Go to church every Sunday!" Somewhat surprised, I asked him: A bulwark—against what?" Whereupon he answered: "Against the black[43] mud tide—" here he hesitated for a moment to add: "of occultism." At first it was the "bulwark" and the "dogma" that startled me; for a dogma, that is, an indisputable confession, one posits only where one wants to suppress doubt once and for all. But that no longer has anything to do with scientific judgment, but only with a personal drive for power.

This was a blow that struck into the life marrow of our friendship. I knew that I would never be able to reconcile myself to this. What Freud seemed to mean by "occultism" was just about everything that philosophy and religion, including parapsycholoy, which was just coming up in those days, had to say about the soul.

On the evidence submitted in the present book up to this point, I dare say that what we have here are not memories but dreams and reflections. The words attributed to Freud do not ring true at all. They conflict outright with Freud's attitude toward dogmatism; and one naturally has to go on to ask when he is supposed to have adopted this attitude toward the occult; also, when this blow was struck into the life marrow of the friendship. Jung is specific on that point: the conversation took place in Vienna in 1910.

An editorial note in *The Freud/Jung Letters* (138J) says politely that "there is no other evidence that Jung visited Freud in Vienna after 1909." In fact, the negative evidence in the correspondence is overwhelming. There

[43] "Black" and "bulwark" were not mentioned in our conversation.

is no trace of such a meeting. But then Jung said a page earlier, "our first meeting took place in Vienna in February 1907," though it actually took place March 3, 1907 (note after 16J); and since the two men did meet in Vienna in 1909, it seems reasonable to suppose that "1910" was merely a slip and Jung meant 1909. This surmise is supported by the fact that the letters Jung and Freud exchanged in April 1909 show that during the 1909 Vienna visit they did indeed discuss occult phenomena. But these letters also show that Freud could not have said what Jung later claimed he said, and that no blow was "struck into the life marrow of our friendship." Jung's first letter after the 1909 meeting begins:

> Annoyances and patients and all the other chores of daily life have overwhelmed me again and have really got me down during the first two days. Now I am emerging again slowly and am beginning to bask in the sunshine of my memories of the days in Vienna.

In the course of the same letter Jung speaks without embarrassment of a case he is treating that involves "exquisite spook phenomena." The whole letter is worth rereading in this connection and totally incompatible with the story in the posthumous book. It ends: "Your grateful Jung."

Freud's reply of April 16 shows how undogmatic his attitude toward the occult was. But his reference to the "evening when I formally adopted you as my eldest son and anointed you my successor and crown prince" suggests strongly that this must indeed have been the occasion that Jung later misremembered. It is tempting to quote this letter at length because it illustrates Freud's open-mindedness, his skepticism, and his humor so well; but the letter is long, and two samples must suffice:

> My faith, or at least my readiness to have faith, faded away with the magic of your personal presence; from

some inner motives, it again seems quite improbable to me that anything of that sort should occur; the de-spirited furniture confronts me again . . . Yes, that is how boys are; what they really enjoy is after all only trips on which they do not have to take us along, where we with our short breath and tired legs cannot follow them.

The last paragraph of the letter reads:

Thus I shall be able to hear with interest further news about your researches into the spook complex as an enchanting delusion that one does not share.

Although it seems clear that the 1909 meeting in Vienna was what Jung had in mind, one still must ask whether Freud could not possibly have spoken the words Jung ascribed to him, although neither in 1910 nor in Vienna. But when Freud returned to the subject of the occult in the spring of 1911, his attitude was as undogmatic as ever. The right word for it was still skepticism, not dogmatism. On May 12 he wrote Jung:

I know that your inmost inclinations drive you to study occultism, and I do not doubt that you will return home richly laden. There is nothing to be done against that, and everybody does right when he follows the chain of his impulses. Your reputation, based on your *Dementia*, will hold up quite a while against the reproach of "mystic." Only do not stay in those tropical colonies; it is important to govern at home.[44]

And on June 15: "I promise to believe everything that can be made reasonable in some way. Not with pleasure; that you know." Jung was unable to appreciate that the willingness to accept what one would be more pleased not to believe is the very essence of a scientific attitude.

[44] See also the letters to Ferenczi, May 1, 1911 (254J, note), and October 6, 1909 (158F, note, which also contains other relevant references).

Freud's concern was clearly due to the worry that the preoccupation with spooks might compromise the scientific respectability of psychoanalysis for which he had worked so hard against great odds. But his attitude was totally different from that ascribed to him by Jung. It is admirable that Aniela Jaffé included three fine passages from Freud's letters in an appendix to *Memories, Dreams, Reflections*. That seems to me to illustrate a truly scientific spirit.

Incidentally, the account in *Memories, Dreams, Reflections* draws heavily on unpublished "Notes on the Seminar in Analytical Psychology Conducted by Dr. C. G. Jung, Zurich, March 23–July 6, 1925, Arranged by Members of the Class." And it is noteworthy that in these notes the dictum about the mud tide is not to be found. It is not clear whether Jung ever mentioned it before our 1953 conversation.

Once again we have found Jung projecting upon Freud a part of himself he did not like. It was Jung who felt that truth was not everything, that it was all right to tell fairy tales that one could immunize against criticism by calling them "*my* truth." It was Jung who was a dogmatist insofar as he never understood that a truly scientific attitude consists in the scrupulous consideration of objections and alternatives—indeed, the willingness to consider inconvenient facts. Instead of facing up to all this, he was content to lecture others about the shadow while he accused Freud of insufficient respect for truth and of dogmatism.

67 ▶▶▶ Jung's third charge against Freud is on a different level. He spoke at some length of "Freud's bitterness." What Jung says on that score is not really worth quoting at length. Once again, it is pure projection:

There is no worse bitterness than that of a human being who is his own worst enemy. According to his own saying, he felt threatened by a "black mud tide"—he who above all others had tried to plumb the black depths.

Reading *The Freud/Jung Letters*, one is struck again and again by Jung's bitterness, not by Freud's; and this bitterness Jung was not able to outgrow. It is nowhere more in evidence than in his *Answer to Job* (1952). Freud, on the other hand, was quite remarkably lacking in bitterness and at peace with himself.

To be sure, he was disillusioned; but disillusionment and bitterness are not at all the same thing. It is really astonishing how the books and papers Freud published are free of bitterness and resentment against the critics and detractors. Not only did he manage to ignore them instead of engaging in polemics, but like a great composer, he created a peaceful world in which he takes us for walks, pointing out new sights to us and answering our questions, always in good humor and never impatient or angry. Jung himself seems to have noticed this when he wrote Freud on March 7, 1909: "The high degree of security and serenity that distinguishes you does not characterize me on the whole." For the sake of consistency and pertinent associations with other passages we have considered, I have rendered *Sicherheit* as "security," but here "assurance" would be a little more idiomatic. Still, the assurance that is meant is grounded in security, and the man who had it did *not* "feel threatened" from inside.

Another witness is more astonishing: Martin Buber. He did not like psychoanalysis and at one point thought of writing a book against Freud. Lou Andreas-Salomé talked him out of that.[45] But late in life he told Jochanan

---

[45] Martin Buber, *Briefwechsel aus sieben Jahrzehnten*, ed. Grete Schaeder, Vol. I (1972), p. 94.

Bloch how he had gone to see Freud in 1903 or 1904 to talk about a friend, and how deeply Freud had impressed him.

> He had the "calm sea of the soul"—I think Schopenhauer called it that—a great tranquil resoluteness and superiority. I have never encountered anything like it elsewhere.[46]

This passage is so beautiful, I could scarcely believe that Buber should have spoken that way of Freud whom, I thought, he did not like. So I asked Bloch about it and checked it also with others who had been especially close to Buber, and there is no doubt he said it—and even less that he was right.

What Buber described so well is what we find in *The Freud/Jung Letters*; and although Jung claimed, as we have seen, that Freud's personality changed, this was probably another projection. I see no evidence at all that Freud changed in this respect between 1904—which ws before Jung ever saw him—and 1939 when he died.

Stefan Zweig, a very sensitive novelist who also wrote some insightful biographical sketches of, among others, Freud and Nietzsche, had known Freud in Vienna and visited him once more in London. His account of this visit in his last book,[47] published posthumously

---

[46] Jochanan Bloch (1977), p. 301: *"Ihm war die 'Meeresstille der Seele' eigen, . . . eine grosse ruhige Entschiedenheit und Überlegenheit. Mir ist es sonst nie so begegnet."*

Perhaps this is also the place to quote from the last page of Binswanger's reminiscences what Freud's widow wrote him when she thanked him for his letter of condolence: ". . . in the fifty-three years of our marriage no angry word ever passed between us . . ."

Freud seems to have found peace through his work and an exceptionally harmonious marriage. Jung seems to have created a situation in his home that reflected his own lack of peace—and he seems to have given Billinsky the impression that *Freud* had created such a situation in *his* home. See note 42 and the text for note 40 above.

[47] *Die Welt von Gestern* (1944, 1970), pp. 301ff.

after his suicide in Brazil, is deeply moving and corroborates the picture given of Freud in the present book. When Zweig went to see the old man in exile, dying of cancer after more than thirty operations, he was "secretly a little afraid to find him embittered . . . and found him freer and even happier than ever . . . 'Have I ever lived more beautifully?' "

68 ▶▶▶ Jung's fourth charge against Freud revolves around Freud's Jewishness and was developed at length in a German journal in 1934. There has been a good deal of discussion about Jung's assumption of the editorship of a journal published in Nazi Germany, and his defenders have insisted that this act does not prove that he was an anti-Semite. Of course, it does not, but the whole issue is a red herring, like the question of whether it was wicked of Heidegger to accept the rectorship of the University of Freiburg in 1933. In such matters it may be difficult to know what to do; one may believe that one can do some good by accepting such a post; and it seems obvious that a professor of philosophy or an analytical psychologist is not necessarily endowed with particularly good judgment in such matters. If Jung had accepted the post and then used it to publish a critique of what was being done in Germany, nobody in his right mind would ever have accused him of anti-Semitism merely for having become editor of the *Zentralblatt*. The issue in his case, as in Heidegger's, is what he actually published.

Nor am I interested in the question of whether what he did publish should or should not be called anti-Semitic. The label does not matter; what he published does matter and rounds out the picture of his attitude toward Freud. Anyone who wants to discover Jung's mind could hardly ignore this material. I shall concentrate on "The State of Psychotherapy Today" (1934).

Freud is introduced thus:

Freud bases himself, with fanatical one-sidedness, on sexuality, covetousness, on the pleasure principle . . . It almost seems as if in this doctrine the covetousness of human nature had been elevated to the status of being the fundamental principle of psychology.[48]

Much of the article consists of a denunciation of Freud and, to a lesser extent, also of Adler—in a journal in which they could not reply. Halfway through the article, Jung pointed out that their faults were due to their being Jews. They see our weak spots: "The Jews have this peculiarity in common with women; being physically weaker [than whom?], they have to aim at the chinks in the armor of their adversary . . ." (10, 353). This image brings to mind Jung's dream in which Freud wore armor and Jung looked for an opening. And now, after all these years, Jung has found the chink in Freud's armor and attacks him fearlessly in a German journal, in 1934, as a Jew.

The Aryan unconscious, on the other hand, contains explosive forces and creative seeds of a future yet to be fulfilled . . . The still youthful Germanic peoples are entirely capable of creating new cultural forms, and this future still lies in the darkness of the unconscious of every individual as seeds bursting with energy and capable of a tremendous flame [nothing less than a holocaust, in fact]. The Jew, being something of a nomad, has never yet created a cultural form of his own and probably never will, since all his instincts and talents presuppose for their development a more or less civilized host nation. [In other words, the Jew is—as the Nazis insisted—a parasite.]

[48] 10, 340. Hull translates the same word first as "concupiscence" and then as "desire and greed." Freud, incidentally, always treated at least one patient free of charge and lived much more modestly than Jung did.

   . . . The Aryan unconscious has a higher potential than
the Jewish . . . In my view it has been a grave mistake of
medical psychology to date that it simply applied Jewish
categories, which are not even obligatory for all Jews, to
Christian Teutons or Slavs.

This would seem to involve a major revision of Jung's
typology. Freud's psychology no longer holds good for
extraverts but only for Jewish extraverts, Adler's for
Jewish introverts—and Jung's types, for whom? It
also seems to involve a major revision of the notion of
the collective unconscious. But let us see how Jung
continued.

   Thus, it declared the most precious secret of the Germanic human being, the creative ground of his soul,
which abounds in intimations, to be a childishly banal
morass, while my warning voice was suspected for decades of anti-Semitism. This insinuation issued from
Freud. He did not know the Germanic soul any more
than did his Germanic parrots. Has the tremendous
phenomenon of National Socialism, which a whole world
contemplates with amazement, taught them better?
Where was the unheard of tension and momentum when
there was no National Socialism as yet? It lay concealed
in the Germanic soul, in that profound ground which is
anything but the garbage pail of children's unfulfillable
wishes and unresolved family resentments. A movement
that takes hold of a whole people has also become mature
in every individual [and cannot possibly be immature, it
seems]. Therefore I say that the Germanic unconscious
contains tensions and possibilities that medical psychology must take into account in its evaluation of the
unconscious. Its business is not with neuroses but with
human beings; and precisely this is the beautiful privi-
lege of medical psychology . . . . (353f.)

   After the Second World War, in 1946, Jung collected
some of his recent essays and added an Afterword, or

Epilogue, in which he piled up quotations to prove that he had understood very well what happened in Germany in the thirties—even before it happened. Having done this at length (458–71), he admitted that "the figure of the Führer at first struck me as merely ambivalent" (472).[49] This is an odd way of saying—or not saying—that Jung's attitude toward Hitler was ambivalent in 1934. But this point, which alone seems crucial, is buried in thirty pages of boasts about Jung's prescience.

In 1946, moreover, he proclaimed over the BBC, as we have seen (in Section 63): "In Hitler every German should have seen his own shadow." *Every* German? But not Jung? Not even in 1946?

In the 1934 essay we find some statements that many of Jung's admirers applaud, however embarrassed they may be by the passages quoted so far; for example:

> A neurosis is by no means a merely negative thing, it is also something positive. Only a soulless rationalism reinforced by a narrow materialistic outlook [that is, the view Jung kept attributing to Freud] could possibly have overlooked this fact. (355)

> *Not how one gets rid of a neurosis is what the sick person has to learn, but how one endures it.* (360)

In *The Freud/Jung Letters* Freud had admitted that he was neurotic while Jung insisted that *he* was not. All along, Freud taught, as we have seen, what Jung here passes off as his own doctrine, which Freud, as a Jew, could not grasp. But on this point Jung recalled the truth in *Memories, Dreams, Reflections*, though naturally without any self-criticism: Freud

> had taught me that all the world was a little neurotic and that one must therefore be tolerant. But I was by no

[49] Actually, Jung had been on the enthusiastic side in his interview on Radio Berlin, June 26, 1933, in *C. G. Jung Speaking*, especially p. 64f. See also p. 92f. (1936).

means of a mind to be satisfied with that but wanted to know how one could avoid a neurosis (170f. = A, p. 167).

But even then Jung had to insist in the very next sentence that, of course, he was right and Freud wrong:

> I had seen that neither Freud nor his pupils could understand what it meant for the theory and practice of psychoanalysis when not even the master could get over his own neurosis.

Now the tables are turned again, and Freud was wrong in 1909 when he espoused the view that Jung urged against him in 1934, emphasizing it in print. Jung seems to have been one of those people who care much less about what might be true than they do about being right and about always having been right.

Not surprisingly, Jung was criticized in print, in a leading Swiss newspaper, as soon as his 1934 article had appeared. He defended himself in "A Rejoinder to Dr. Bally," which appeared in *Neue Zürcher Zeitung* (1934) and is also included in *The Collected Works* (10, 1016ff.). Of course, he stuck by his guns, but in the end at least took note of the fact that, even if he was right about everything, one might "object, why raise the Jewish problem today of all days and in Germany of all places? Pardon me, I raised it long ago . . ."

While his admirers, like Heidegger's, keep suggesting that he was guilty merely of a temporary error, Jung insisted in 1934 that his essay represented his considered views. In his defense, if that is the right word, he quoted two passages in the next issue of the paper, one written in 1927, the other as early as 1918. Indeed, he had said as early as 1927 that "it is an inexcusable error to accept the conclusions of a Jewish psychology as generally valid." And in 1918 he had already contrasted "Jew" and "Aryan." But he quite failed to see that even if he had said things of that sort on two previous occasions, the last of them seven years before, he had chosen an odd time and place to enlarge on this theme at such length.

He was surely right that his essay of 1934 did not merely represent a momentary slip. It had strong roots in his mind, and he was also right when he suggested in the final paragraph of his "Rejoinder" that the theme could be traced back all the way to his break with Freud in 1913. His closest associate, Alphonse Maeder, had said even then, as noted earlier, that "the scientific differences between the Viennese and Swiss resulted from the former being Jews and the latter 'Aryans.' "

The last thing I should wish to claim is that Jung was consistent. What makes the whole issue doubly sensitive is the fact that many of his most eminent disciples, associates, and editors were and are Jews, for example, Erich Neumann, Gerhard Adler (among other things the editor of Jung's letters), and Aniela Jaffé (the co-editor who also collaborated with Jung on *Memories, Dreams, Reflections*). The list could easily be lengthened.

Aniela Jaffé's short book on Jung (1968, English 1971) contains a chapter on "C. G. Jung and National Socialism" that points out that Freud also juxtaposed Jews and Christians (1971, p. 87f.). She overlooks the fact that Freud went on to say, as we have seen: "But there should not be such a thing as Aryan or Jewish science. Results in science must be identical . . ."[50] Her chapter ends with Gershom Scholem's letter to her, saying that after the war Jung had said to Rabbi Leo Baeck: "Well, I slipped up." This remark hardly shows much sensitivity. Nor did Jung see that his high hopes regarding Hitler made a mockery of his boasts that he understood the Aryan, and specifically the Germanic soul, as Freud did not. On the evidence, Freud understood it and Jung did not.

[50] See Section 60, as well as Binswanger, p. 60.

One can see why most Jungians would rather ignore this whole issue. However one looks at it, it is painful. Jung said in his "Rejoinder":

> The Jewish problem is a complex, a festering wound, and no responsible doctor could bring himself to apply methods of medical hush-hush in this matter. (1024)

Never mind "the Jewish problem." Jung's writings on it and, more generally, Jung's attacks on Freud are a wound that we cannot hush up if we want to understand Jung.

The letter Jung wrote to Wolfgang Kranefeldt, a German psychotherapist, on February 9, 1934, also belongs to this complex. Jung suggested that Aryan psychotherapists might call the attention of the German government to the fact that Freud's and Adler's points of view, which were still propagated publicly, were specifically Jewish and demonstrably *zersetzend*. The Nazis constantly associated this last epithet with the Jews. It has no precise equivalent in English, but "disintegrative" comes close. Jung went on to say that, while nothing further could be done if the spread of these Jewish gospels pleased the German government, it was possible after all that the government might not be pleased.[51]

It is noteworthy that "the tremendous phenomenon of National Socialism" led Jung, living in safety in Switzerland, to panegyrics about "the Germanic soul." It was not just a German phenomenon to him; it came out of his own soul, too. He identified with it. And he felt that what was bad for the Jews was good for his own analytical psychology. Until then he had to share the stage with two rivals of whom one was very clearly superior to him. Now he could denounce and defame Freud to his heart's

---

[51] *Autographen & Urkunden aus den Jahren 1930 bis 1972:* Lagerkatalog Nr. 608 der Gesamtfolge, J. A. Stargardt, Antiquariat, Marburg. #29 described and quoted extensively from twenty-seven letters and cards Jung sent to Kranefeldt. The above account is based on the complete text of the letter.

content while stressing how different his psychology was from Freud's.

What Jung said to Baeck is much less interesting than what Baeck had written long before in his essay "Romantic Religion" (in *Judaism and Christianity*, translated by Walter Kaufmann, p. 275):

> A spirit is characterized not only by what it does but, no less, by what it permits, what it forgives, and what it beholds in silence. The Christian religion . . . has been able to maintain silence about so much that it is difficult to say what has been more pernicious in the course of time: the intolerance that committed the wrongs or the indifference that beheld them unperturbed.

Jung was not even content to be silent.[52]

69 ▶▶▶ Jung's psychology does not illuminate his own conduct as well as Adler's seems to. In *Memories, Dreams, Reflections*, Jung actually speaks of his inferiority feelings, and we have encountered his profound sense of insecurity at every turn. He overcompensated for his basic timidity and sense of inferiority by developing a boisterous laugh and an aggressive manner. And when the time seemed ripe, in 1934, his will to power declared itself openly. Still, there is something shallow to my mind in Adler's disquisitions on these matters, and I prefer to recall Nietzsche's aphorism from *The Dawn:*

[52] There is an interesting mischievement in *C. G. Jung Speaking*, p. 268. In 1955, when Jung turned eighty, he was asked whether he had congratulated Freud on *his* eightieth birthday. "The answer was no, and Jung explained it at some length. Some time around 1933, he had sent a patient to Freud in Vienna with a detailed medical report and a friendly letter. Freud did not respond. Since then they had never had any contact." A footnote says: "Actually 1923." Why did Jung say 1933? That was the year the Nazis came to power, and Jung presumably recalled, though he did not mean to say, that he had not been content merely to be silent.

> Those who still want to gain the consciousness of power reach out for all means and do not spurn any nourishment for it. But those who have it become very choosy and noble in their tastes . . .

Freud, though Jung kept reassuring himself that he was neurotic all his life long, was an exceptionally powerful character, distinguished by "a great tranquil resoluteness and superiority" (to recall Buber's sketch of him), and confronts us as the very image of nobility. Jung was, for all of his protestations of his health, a sick soul who gives no evidence of having fathomed its own sickness. William James took the sting out of the phrase "sick soul" when he contrasted it very sympathetically with the "healthy soul" in his *Varieties of Religious Experience*. But I am not alluding to Jung's battle with schizophrenia, which calls for sympathy and even admiration. The sickness he did not recognize as such was the resentment that kept gnawing at him all his life. Had he really had any grasp of Nietzsche, of whom he spoke constantly, emphasizing that he, unlike Freud, had read him, he would have known that *ressentiment* can poison a man's character; also how it can be fought. That he failed to see this is not a minor oversight, rather odd in a man who actually gave seminars of Nietzsche's *Zarathustra*, but a flaw that in 1934 assumed world historical dimensions. When *ressentiment* exploded in Germany and prepared for mass murder, Jung felt a profound kinship with what happened across the border and coined a phrase that included him, too: the Germanic soul.

If Adler's psychology and Nietzsche's help to illuminate Jung, what about Freud's? Having read Freud, one would predict that Jung must have felt insufficiently loved by his mother. And in the chapter on his childhood in *Memories, Dreams, Reflections* Jung, born in 1875, tells us how he was quite ill in 1878:

> My sickness must have been related to a temporary separation of my parents (1878). My mother was in a hospital in Basel for several months, and her ailment was presumably the consequence of her disappointment in her marriage. An aunt, twenty years older than my mother, looked after me. The long absence of my mother was very hard for me to cope with. Since that time I have always been suspicious as soon as the word "love" was mentioned. The feeling that I associated with the "feminine" was for a long time: natural unreliability. "Father" meant for me reliability and—*Ohnmacht.*

The last word has been translated as "powerlessness" in the official version, which is not wrong. But what it actually means more often is a fainting spell, and *ohnmächtig werden* is the German equivalent of "to faint." Surely, this helps to explain Jung's absurd overreaction to Freud's fainting spell: It triggered childhood, not to say childish, emotions.

> While my mother was away, our maid took care of me. . . . She had black hair . . . and was quite different from my mother. . . . The type of the maid later became an aspect of my anima.

The anima is one of Jung's archetypes. While the shadow is said to be always of the same sex as oneself, the anima—or in women the animus—is always of the opposite sex. The conception is as suggestive as, on closer examination, it turns out to be unclear. In any case, Jung concludes this paragraph by saying that this later became for him the quintessence of the feminine. One naturally wonders whether Toni Wolff resembled her in some ways. The picture of the Weimar Congress of 1910, in which she sits in the front row, as does Emma Jung, suggests that she did, but I have no way of being sure, nor any wish to pursue these matters. Still, we shall have occasion to see in the next chapter how Freud's psychology helps to explain some great oddities in Jung's work.

70 ▶▶▶ Jung, much more even than Adler, became a guru. Many of his patients did not have specific symptoms when they came to him but sought help in finding a meaning for their lives. And Jung himself stressed his eclecticism (16, 74f.)

> The clinical material at my disposal is of a peculiar composition: new cases are decidedly in the minority. Most of them already have some form of psychothera- peutic treatment behind them with partial or negative results. About a third of my cases are not suffering from any clinically definable neurosis, but from the senseless- ness and aimlessness of their lives. . . . Over two thirds of my patients are in the second half of life. (16, 83)

Among Jung's patients were wealthy American women, eager to do something for the cause. Eventually, the publication of his collected works, in English and German, was subsidized, and the volumes were produced very beautifully and underpriced, and then also made available in extremely attractive paper- backs. The Bollingen Series, established for this pur- pose, made room not only for Jung but also for a few other prestigious writers as well as a number of works dealing with Oriental religions, thus providing a very appealing setting for Jung.

By far the best-selling title of the series—and of all the books published by Princeton University Press, which eventually acquired the series—is the *I Ching*, translated into English from the German version done by Richard Wilhelm, with an introduction by Jung. Many readers of that book—or rather people who have con- sulted it (it is, after all, a book of ancient Chinese oracles and not a volume to be read straight through)—have gone on to read—or perhaps only to consult—some of Jung's writings. Others have been led to Jung by Heinrich Zimmer's beautifully illustrated books on India. The growth of interest in the religions of the East has been a boon for Jung.

Freud confronts us, as Jung himself noted in his final eulogy at the very end of the Freud chapter in *Memories,* as a man not altogether unlike an Old Testament prophet. He is, in one word, very demanding. He sets standards of honesty that we can hardly hope to satisfy. The most natural reaction to that is resentment.

Jung makes no demands on us. He provides diversions and escapes. Readers who are aware of Jung's rebellion against Freud are only too ready to believe that Freud was an intolerant, dogmatic old tyrant while Jung was a revolutionary. But Jung was an archetypal counter-revolutionary.

Freud's account of Jung in his *History* (cited in Section 58) was as perceptive as most of what Jung wrote on Freud is obtuse. Among the points one might add to it is that people prefer stories and fairy tales—soothing diversions—to austere challenges.[53]

What Jung actually had to say about Oriental religions should come as something of a surprise. In view of his comments about the Aryan unconscious, one might suppose that he had a special feeling for ancient India, while China and Tibet might have defied his understanding. If a Jew like Freud, who had lived all of his life among "Germanic" people and was one of the all-time masters of the German language, failed to fathom the Germanic soul, how could Jung, who knew little about China and Tibet except for a few German translations of old texts, have been in a position to illuminate this material? Was the "Aryan" bit after all no more than a device to put Freud in his place? The chink in Freud's armor was that he was a Jew whose psychology was—as

[53] This point, made by Baeck in his highly polemical contrast of Judaism and Christianity (see end of Section 68 above) is as relevant as can be to Freud and Jung. Even those who would not accept Baeck's portrait of Christianity might well concede this claim.

the Nazis said of Einstein's theories—Jewish science. That very convenient idea created a place for Jung.

Jung's major writings on the Oriental religions include his "Psychological Commentary on the Tibetan Book of the Great Liberation" (written in 1939 and first published in 1954), his "Psychological Commentary on the Bardo Thödol (the Tibetan Book of the Dead)" (1935), the "Preface to the I Ching" (written in 1948 for the English edition and published in 1950), and his "Preface to Suzuki: The Great Liberation" (1939). In the bulky eleventh volume of the German collected works these four pieces total exactly a hundred pages. The same volume contains three more short pieces on Eastern religions that comprise another forty pages, and Volume 10 contains another two essays, written in English and published in *Asia* 1939, right after Jung's return from a trip to India.

The first of these essays is "The Dreamlike World of India," the second "What India Can Teach Us." They are on the same level as most of the material in *C. G. Jung Speaking* and embarrassingly trivial. It is tempting to illustrate this charge by citing some of Jung's observations, which he presented, as was his manner as if he were a great expert, but no sample could allay the suspicion that the essays must also contain great profundities. I shall quote only the final paragraph of the second essay:

> If you want to learn the greatest lesson India can teach you, wrap yourself in the cloak of your moral superiority, go to . . . Konarak . . . covered with the most amazing collection of obscenities . . . and then analyze carefully and with the utmost honesty all your reactions, feelings, and thoughts. . . . You will have learned something about yourself, and about the white man in general . . . . (1013)

In this case the German translator tried to make Jung's choice of words less embarrassing by placing

Konarak. (Photograph by the author, 1971.)

quotation marks around the German equivalent of "obscenities," as the English translator did with "Aryan." It tells us a good deal about Jung's mind that he should have considered this "the greatest lesson India can teach you." It also bears out my earlier claim that, regarding sex, he was much less liberated than Freud.

Jung felt a very strong hostility to India, which is indeed about as different from Switzerland as a country can be, but Konarak, which is actually one of the most beautiful and impressive places in the whole world, could be used to put down the West and vent his bitterness. Other Western apostles of the East have used India in much the same way to revenge themselves upon their hated Christian upbringing, although they really detested India. Joseph Campbell, the editor of *The Portable Jung*, is an outstanding example.

The section on India in *Memories* begins: "The voyage to India (1938) did not issue from my own intention, but I owe it to an invitation . . ." He was immersed in alchemy at the time; he took along "the first volume of the *Theatrum Chemicum* of 1602" and studied that.

> I avoided encounters with all so-called "holy men." I passed them by because I had to make do with my own truth and was not permitted to accept anything else but what I could reach myself. It would have seemed to me like theft if I had wished to learn from holy men or to accept their truth for myself. Their wisdom belongs to them, and to me belongs only what issues from myself.[54]

I have been to India several times and feel that avoiding "holy men" requires no excuse, but Jung's rationalizations rest on a strange confusion. After all, one can talk with people without any intention of accepting their ideas or convictions. It is doubly odd that, feeling as he

[54] The last sentence is missing in the English version.

did, Jung should have felt called upon to tell the West upon his return what is "the greatest lesson India can teach you." It is triply odd that Jung should have said these things when one recalls that he wrote commentaries and prefaces for Tibetan and Far Eastern texts. Obviously, he disliked India and Indian wisdom. His letters leave no doubt about that, and one of them—duly printed in the *Letters*—really ought to be better known.

On October 19, 1960, less than a year before his death, he sent it to *Encounter,* for publication, and it was also used later as a postscript in the German edition of Arthur Koestler's *The Lotus and the Robot.* No major writer has published a more devastating attack on the wisdom of the East, and specifically on India and Japan, than this book. Admirers of Eastern wisdom generally dismiss it, whether they have read it or not, as hopelessly lacking in sympathy and understanding. Erik Erikson, in *Gandhi's Truth* (1969), refused to come to grips with Koestler's detailed critique of Gandhi and mentioned the book only in one short footnote that dealt quite inadequately with a single point (p. 460). Displaying a truly mordant wit, Koestler dealt scathingly with things that he felt should be ridiculed. I feel that his book should be read and that those who see more merit in Oriental wisdom ought to deal with his critique, as George Woodcock, for example, did to some extent in his short book on Gandhi. I also wish that it were better known that Jung said in print: "In essentials I agree with Koestler's critique."

Jung also said that he did find something in Zen, less in Yoga, but that he opposed attempts to gain experiences through exercises. Moreover, he felt that Westerners should stay closer to home—a point he also made in the India section of *Memories.*

The next section in that book is called "Ravenna and Rome." Most of it deals with mosaics he saw in Ravenna and describes at length, although afterwards it turned out that they had not been there. He came to feel that this experience defied explanation, the more so because his travel companion (Toni Wolff) had seen them, too. This incident, to which Jung devotes several pages, is significant in at least two ways. First, his capacity for vividly remembering in the form of external experiences what in fact were internal realities—or to hallucinate—may help us understand his stories about the book Freud returned to him unread and about Freud's remark about the mud tide. Second, his interest in matters that seem to defy scientific explanation also helps to account for his vogue in the last third of the twentieth century. Freud has been assimilated to a dogmatic rationalism or scientism—erroneously, and at least in part owing to Jung's incessant claims to this effect. Jung, on the other hand, is seen as a prestigious ally in the fight against the disenchantment of the world.

Rome receives barely more than half a page, for the simple reason that Jung, who lectured Westerners that they should stay closer to home, never went there.

> In 1917[55] I went by boat from Genoa to Naples. I stood at the railing as we sailed along the coast on the latitude of Rome. Back there was Rome! There was the still smoking and fiery hearth of ancient cultures, locked in the tangled roots of the Christian and occidental Middle Ages. There was antiquity still living in all its splendor and wickedness.
> I always wonder how people can travel to Rome as one does, for example, to Paris or to London. . . .
> When in 1949, already in old age, I wished to make up for what I had missed, I fainted as I bought the tickets. After that the plan of a trip to Rome was laid aside once and for all.

[55] 1917, in the midst of the war, is obviously a slip. The English version makes it 1912. Actually, it was 1913 (see *The Freud/Jung Letters*, 350J, note 1).

Freud's fainting has elicited considerable interest, presumably because the world likes to be reassured that such a great and inconvenient man had clay feet. Jung's fainting and Jung's rage at Freud for having called his (Freud's) fainting a little piece of neurosis that needed looking into have been ignored, although Jung kept bringing up Freud's neurosis, first in his letters to Freud and then on all sorts of occasions after the break.

The distance from Zurich to Rome is just over four hundred miles, and train service was excellent. But here was Jung writing about the I Ching and the Tibetan Book of the Dead without exploring his own backyard, or rather his own background. He knew very well what Rome had long meant not only to Catholics but also to non-Catholic German-speaking people. For Luther and Goethe trips to Rome had been turning points in their lives, and Jung also knew how much his first trip to Rome had meant to Freud. But Jung felt that the impression might be too much for him. He had written his dissertation on the occult; the occult also figured prominently in his recollections of Freud; and it seems to me that what he liked about the occult was precisely that it was occult. There were things he would rather not see, that he felt he was not up to seeing. He would rather write about Tibet or alchemy than cope with what lay right in front of him.

PART ▶ IV

Jung's Answer to Job ▶▶▶

71 ▶▶▶ *Answer to Job* (1952) is Jung's most intimate book, as we are told in an editorial note; it is also the most embittered. It was written when Jung was in his seventies, and one might have expected him to be a wise old man who had found peace. But the resentment that pervades the book is so great that it interferes not only with communication but also with the thought process. Jung seems to be so angry that he loses control, and one sometimes wonders whether he still knows what he is saying. Still, he heeds his own advice in this book, and instead of writing about Tibet or China he wrestles with the religion on which he had been raised. He writes about the Bible and the problem of human suffering. This problem—how God could have permitted the outrages of Auschwitz and other such atrocities—was troubling millions of people.

A rational analysis of this problem might have begun by pointing out that its traditional form depends on certain premises that characterize later Judaism and Christianity, but not the religion of the earlier parts of the Hebrew Bible, nor Hinduism, Buddhism, Confucianism,

Taoism, or Homer's outlook. In all of these religions the immense human suffering we find in the world is taken for granted and raises no particular difficulties of a philosophical nature. But when it is assumed that there is one, and only one, God who is both all-powerful and all-good and just, then the question arises why there is all the suffering there is. If he cannot help it, he is not all-powerful; if he can but does not choose to, he is not all-good.

If we assume, on the other hand, that God is evil from the human point of view, or merely that he is not all-good, or that he is all-good but not all-powerful, or that there are two or more gods of whom at least one is evil, or that there is no god, then the problem of suffering does not arise. The outrages remain, but the question how God could permit these things to happen does not arise. All "solutions" of this problem always come down to the denial, usually not overt, of one of the distinctive premises that the problem entails. Generally, it is God's omnipotence that is denied, in effect. The Book of Job is unusual insofar as it explicitly denies God's justice.

Jung does not analyze the problem in this manner. For that matter, the problem is not usually attacked in this straightforward way. But Jung does not at all define either his own problem or the problem of Job as it is presented to us in the Bible. He pours out his heart, writing first about the Book of Job, then about the New Testament, and finally about "the promulgation of the new dogma of the Assumption of the Virgin Mary." When he comes to that (11, 748ff.), he lashes out at Protestants with a great deal of bitterness for not appreciating this dogma. His heavy sarcasm is unmistakable throughout. What precisely he means to say is much harder to discern, and I am not sure that he himself could have answered that question.

One cannot give brief illustrations of opacity or the failure of an author to communicate his ideas. Brief quotations leave the reader wondering whether they have been chosen fairly and whether the context does not make things clear. Long quotations of opaque passages are tedious and still leave open the same questions. But the book is not only available in paperback but also included in its entirety in *The Portable Jung* because the editor, like many of Jung's admirers, considers it especially beautiful.

A few quotations may at least convey something of the flavor of the book. Section II begins:

> Since the Omniscient looks into all hearts and Yahweh's eyes "roam over the whole earth," it is really much better when the interlocutor of the eighty-ninth Psalm does not become conscious too quickly of his slight moral superiority over the unconscious God, or even conceals it from himself, for Yahweh does not love critical thoughts that might in any way detract from the supply of recognition that he demands. (575)

The tone is unusual but the idea can be made out. It is, in brief, that the God of the Old Testament is not all-good. Once that is assumed, the problem of suffering is taken care of. But Jung is less concerned to solve a problem than to vent his anger. Two paragraphs later we read:

> Since the chosen people used every opportunity to break away from him, and Yahweh felt it of vital importance to tie this indispensable object (which he made "godlike" for this very purpose) definitely to himself, he proposed to the patriarch Noah a contract . . .

Anyone who knows the Bible may wonder at this point whether he has read right, seeing that there were no Jews in Noah's time—and the Jews are specifically mentioned in Jung's text. No matter how often one reads this paragraph and the whole section either in the published English version, from which I have quoted for once, or in the original German, there is no way of getting around this anachronism; but the sarcasm is so heavy that most readers do not even notice such a detail. One is transposed into a world where rational considerations do not appear to have much relevance.

The next paragraph begins:

> Despite such precautionary measures [meaning the rainbow], the contract had gone to pieces with David, an event that left a literary deposit in the Holy Scriptures, to the chagrin of a few pious people who thought about what they read.

Jung seems to assume that Job really lived after David's time, and he treats the Biblical tale of Job as if it had really happened just the way it is reported, with God as a very human, all too human, and by no means all-good character in it.

There is an important sense in which Jung's approach is as unliterary as that of any fundamentalist. This may sound paradoxical because Jung makes such a point of being disrespectful. Yet his blasphemous tone shows how unliberated he was in these matters. He evidently felt that what he found and said was shocking. Yet his approach to the Book of Job depends entirely on not treating the book as the work of a human author who might have had some purpose in writing it. Jung was not at all concerned with either the psychology or the intentions of the human author; his concern was with God's psychology—assuming that God really did and said the things he is reported in the book to have said and done. But Jung further confused the issues by also attributing to God quite a few actions and thoughts that are not mentioned in the Bible. Some of these come from post-Biblical sources and show some measure of erudition, but Jung's use of such material was highly selective and permitted him to develop his image of God (as a psychologically interesting character) in accordance with his own needs.

Although the approach is in one sense that of a fundamentalist, it is in another sense that of a rationalist like Voltaire, who heaps scorn on God's outrageous conduct. To give at least one example:

> One has to give oneself an account of the fact that within a very short span of time dark needs are piled up: robbery, murder, premeditated bodily injury, and denial of due process. Aggravating considerations include the fact that Yahweh does not show at any time compunction, remorse, or sympathy but only lack of consideration and cruelty. A plea of unconsciousness cannot be considered valid inasmuch as he flagrantly violates at least three of the commandments that he himself decreed on Sinai. (581)

Omniscience and Wisdom are personified, following late traditions that became prominent in Gnosticism, and in some passages one gains the impression that, in addition to everything else, God had an affair with Sophia (Wisdom). When Jung speaks of "the pneumatic nature of Sophia" (613), one wonders how he could have failed to know T. S. Eliot's famous line about the woman who "gives promise of pneumatic bliss." It is a strange world into which Jung transposes us: "If Yahweh had consulted his Omniscience, then Job would not have been one up on him. But in that case so many other things would not have happened either" (583).

As usual, Jung did not consider even the most obvious objections or alternatives to his interpretation. Nahum Glatzer, one of the foremost Judaic scholars of our time, has assembled more than thirty such readings in *The Dimensions of Job: A Study and Selected Readings* (1969). He did not include Jung because he considered Jung's "interpretation of Job 'a purely subjective reaction' (as stated [by Jung himself] in the Preface to the book) but in no way an 'Answer to Job'" (p. 46). While this is not the place to reargue my own reading of Job,[1] it is essential to contrast it with Jung's on one crucial point.

As I see it, the author of the Book of Job attacks the conventional wisdom that he ascribes to Job's friends. They maintain throughout that God is good and just (his omnipotence is never questioned in the book) and that Job's suffering proves that he must be guilty and deserves his suffering. The author lets us know at the beginning that this view is wrong, and in the end he has God say expressly to Job's friends, twice: "You have not spoken of me what is right as my servant Job has." Thus the author agreed with his Job that God is not good and just. But resistance to views that conflict with one's own deep-rooted preconceptions is so great that most interpreters through the ages have failed to note this and have restated, more or less overtly, the spurious wisdom of Job's friends.

Jung, of course, rejected the conventional wisdom, but without seeing that this is what the biblical book does, too. He totally misrepresented God's rebuke to Job's friends:

> Let that be as it may, in any case Yahweh finally calmed down. The therapeutic measure of acceptance without resistance [which Jung ascribes to Job] has proved itself once again. All the same, Yahweh is still a little nervous regarding the friends of Job: They 'might in the end not speak of him what is right' [a footnote refers us to Job 42:7, which actually says: 'You have not spoken of me what is right.' The English version quietly corrects the misquotation]. The projection of the doubter thus extends also—rather comically, one really must say—to these solid and slightly Philistine gentlemen, as if God-knows-what depended on what they thought. But that human beings can think—and even about him—that is enragingly uncanny and is to be prevented in some way.

[1] Presented initially in *The Faith of a Heretic* (1961), Chapter VI, and reprinted and commended by Glatzer.

It is after all too similar to what his footloose, vagrant son [evidently, Satan] often springs on him so suddenly and that hits him so disagreeably in a weak spot. . . .(601)

Jung claimed that he was dealing with God as a psychological reality (751), but he evidently was not clear in his own mind about what that might mean. He obviously did not think that he was dealing only or even mainly with his own psychological problems. He thought he was talking about "an archetype of wholeness that is encountered in the unconscious and spontaneously manifests itself in dreams, etc." and that this archetype "possesses a certain central position that brings it close to the image of God" (757). Let us suspend judgment about whether there are archetypes and allow the possibility that there might be. The question still remains how we are to read passages like these.

Jung did not discuss the author of the Book of Job, nor the meaning of the book to generations of readers, first Jews and later also Gentiles. His approach is profoundly unhistorical and does not trace the development of the conception of God. He himself was not altogether clear about that and occasionally bowed in the direction of those who have made much of the evolution of the conception of God in the Bible. But if one is serious about that, one must first try to place the composition of the Book of Job in time and offer some hypothesis about its probable date. One might also say something about the figure of Satan and its development. But Jung had no time for history, and his talk of archetypes suggests more or less Kantian structures of the mind that can be discovered once and for all. Still, they might emerge into consciousness only gradually, and this seems to be one of the themes of *Answer to Job*. He failed to see, however, that this brings us back to the history of the conception of God in the Bible, a topic on which a great deal had been written during the hundred years preceding the publication of Jung's book. Oddly, he did not only ignore all of this literature but also managed to see himself as a pioneer who had the almost unheard-of courage to see that in some parts of the Bible God behaves in a way that is not all-good. Instead of tracing a development, which would require some attention to probable dates, he talked about *God's* psychological problems in an extremely sarcastic manner, taking as much pleasure in his blasphemies as a schoolboy. Often it is not clear what Jung was doing apart from gaining some emotional relief for himself.

In an editorial note of June 1972, in the English paperback edition, we find a quotation from a letter Jung wrote to Aniela Jaffé, July 18, 1951: "If there is anything like the spirit seizing one by the scruff of the neck, it is the way this book came into being." Perhaps one could say more modestly that something in Jung's unconscious no longer allowed itself to be denied and that he wrote the book as if under compulsion. In another letter, quoted in the same note, he said: "The motive for my book was an increasingly urgent feeling of responsibility which in the end I could no longer withstand." If one omits the rather high-sounding "of responsibility," the picture seems clear enough.

By way of taking leave of Jung's discussion of the Old Testament, let us consider one more passage:

> We naturally do not know why one found out only so late . . . that long before the marriage with Israel Yahweh had a relationship with Sophia. [Actually, most people, including Biblical scholars, still have not found out about that.] Nor do we know the reason why in the older traditions the knowledge of this first alliance got lost. [This is an odd way of saying that nothing of the sort is to be found in early traditions.] It was likewise only very late that one heard about the awkward relationship of Adam to Lilith. Whether Eve was just as uncomfortable a wife for Adam as the people . . . were for Yahweh,

eludes our knowledge. [With his unliterary, fundamentalist approach, Jung writes as if he were dealing with historical facts of which we have only partial knowledge.] In any case the family life of the primeval parents was not all fun: Their first two sons represent the type of the hostile pair of brothers; for in those days [when Cain and Abel were living?] it apparently was still the custom to translate mythological motifs into reality. (619)

That final clause boggles the mind. Was it really "the spirit" (one of Jung's archetypes) that had seized Jung, or was it not rather a long delayed adolescent rebellion against the Bible stories on which he had been raised, and particularly against God the Father? That it was the Father, the Jewish God of the Old Testament, that provoked this late explosion of Jung's anger becomes plain when Jung turns to consider the New Testament.

72 ▶▶▶ Jung's totally divergent approaches to the Old and the New Testament show how much he was still under the influence of his childhood upbringing and how little he had succeeded in emancipating himself from the religious instruction he had received as the son of a parson. Moreover, he would not have become so angry if he had been more emancipated.

Jung's reading of the New Testament in *Answer to Job* is essentially that of a liberal Protestant who lacks the courage for an attack on his own convictions and is content to repeat unexamined clichés. "A certain philanthropic and universalistic tendency makes itself felt" (637). We also hear of Christ's love of mankind (646) and of "the God of love and *summum bonum*" (651). The many passages in the Gospels about hell and eternal damnation are ignored, nor is there any place in Jung's account for Jesus's saying to his disciples:

And if anyone will not receive you or listen to your words, shake off the dust from your feet as you leave that house or town. Truly, I say to you, it shall be more tolerable on the day of judgment for the land of Sodom and Gomorrah [that is, for the greatest evildoers] than for that town [even if there should be people in it who have done good deeds?]. (Matthew 10:14-15)

It is arguable that there is a more "philanthropic and universalistic tendency" in the Book of Jonah; but liberal Protestantism had taught very dogmatically that the conception of God in the New Testament was more loving and represented a stupendous new development, and Jung gives no evidence of having thought seriously about this problem. In flat defiance of the fact that in the Old Testament there is no devil and that Satan plays scarcely any role at all—even in the Book of Job none whatsoever after chapter 2, verse 7—Jung claimed that Satan plays "a subordinate role in the Gospels that in no way recalls the former intimate relationship to Yahweh" (650). The intimacy here depends on projecting into the prologue to Job Goethe's Prologue to his *Faust*. Jung also ignored the fact that even in the Book of Job, not to speak of the rest of the Hebrew Bible, Satan is not the Lord of Hell, and that there is no eternal damnation, as there is in the New Testament.

The parochialism of Jung's upbringing is also in evidence when he calls "the Roman Catholic Church the direct heiress and developer of historical Christianity" (655) or says that "Christendom consists of two separate camps" (754), thus reading out of history the Eastern churches. Nor does the textual evidence in the New Testament keep Jung from saying of "Christ's redemptive work"—no translation could capture the theological flavor of *das Erlösungswerk Christi*—that "He reconciles God with man and liberates him from the calamity of God's wrath, which threatens him with eternal damnation" (658). Where do the texts say, in flat defiance of all the ancient and medieval dogmas of Catholicism and of Luther's as well as Calvin's teachings, that most of humanity will *not* be eternally damned?

Accepting liberal Protestant notions that became popular only in the nineteenth century, Jung kept suggesting that all men will be saved, and instead of arguing for his view, considering objections and alternatives, he said:

> The old view, which is based on Christ's own view of the matter [!], asserts that he came into the world to save man, who was threatened by God, and that he suffered and died. Furthermore, he believed that his own bodily resurrection would assure all God's children of the same future. (663)

If only God had seen to it that "Christ's own view" had found expression in the Gospels, which constantly ascribe very different views to him, humanity might have been saved much suffering.

Finally, Jung does find hell and damnation in the last book of the New Testament, the Revelation of Saint John the Divine. Nowhere, however, is his double standard in reading the Old Testament and the New more blatant than here. Far from reading this text in the unliterary, rather fundamentalist way in which he read Job, assuming that what we are told is the literal truth, Jung suddenly asks what made the author of the book say things like that; and he offered a psychological explanation. It depends on the rather eccentric assumption, which scholars do not accept and for which no evidence is given, that the author was also the author of the Epistles of John in the New Testament (698). He had wished to become perfect, according to Jung, but what we find in the Revelation—and if we do not find it there we certainly find it in Jung's book—is "less a metaphysical mystery than first of all the eruption of long pent-up negative feelings" (708).

The Revelation, says Jung,

> contradicts all notions of Christian humility, tolerance, love of the neighbor and the enemy, of a loving father in heaven . . . A veritable orgy of hatred, wrath, revenge, and a blind rage for destruction that simply cannot find enough fantastic images of horror, erupts . . . (708)

It is nice that Jung disowned all that, but noteworthy that, although this book is the conclusion of the New Testament, he called it, as any liberal Protestant would, un-Christian. He ignored the central insistence in the Gospel according to John that only those who take the sacraments and have faith in God's only begotten son can be saved. By Jung's standards, Luther and Calvin, Saint Augustine and the Jesus of the Gospels were all un-Christian. Christian is what Jung says is Christian, and Jewish is what he says is Jewish.

He reads selected texts from the Old Testament in an unliterary way, as if they did not reflect the intentions of a human author but told us how it actually happened, and he reads selected texts from the New Testament in a very different manner, trying to fathom the psychology of a writer whose book does not fit Jung's preconceptions. At one point he even invokes the possibility of "a perplexed transcriber" who might have got the text wrong (712). Such a double standard—one for you and one for me—is hardly sound method or a good way to illuminate "the unconscious"—except one's own. But to discover oneself in this way one would have to understand first of all what one is doing. And Jung was far indeed from that.

Section XIII ends:

> The passion that breaks through in this Revelation bears no trace of the feebleness or serenity of old age, for it is infinitely more than personal resentment; it is the spirit

of God itself that penetrates the weak mortal shroud . . . (717)

There is no evidence that the author of the Revelation was old, but the reference to old age brings to mind Jung's self-description that in his seventies he had reached old age. Both times he refers to *hohes Alter*. He seems to be defending himself in this passage. But is he not deceiving himself?

What has been said so far does not suffice to explain the full measure of Jung's anger or the strong emotion with which he wielded his double standard. Something is still wanting to make sense of it all. But the missing link is easily supplied. In *Answer to Job* the Jewish Father, in the Old Testament, can do no right, while the Christian Son, in the New Testament, can do no wrong. Jung is still fighting Freud.

73 ▶▶▶ Obviously, that is not all there is to it. Above all, the three parts of the book still do not fit together. That *Answer to Job* should deal with the Book of Job in the Old Testament requires no justification. That it should also deal at great length with the New Testament does require some explanation, and Jung provides this in the terms of traditional Christian theology. The Father has treated Job cruelly, but the Son has suffered as much as Job and is thus redeeming mankind. Jews and unbelievers are not likely to see how this answers Job, but it is at least understandable that a pastor's son should think that every question raised in the Old Testament receives its answer in the New Testament.

That still leaves the question of how the long third part of the book about the dogma of "the bodily assumption of the Virgin in heaven," which Jung proclaims as "the most important religious event since the Reformation" (752) is related to the first two parts. It seems to have very little to do with Job. It underlines the fact that *Answer to Job* has very little to do with Job.

Jung tried in this book to work out some deeply personal problems. He had, as he himself put it, "reached the age of seventy-six before daring to catechize myself" (738). It is really remarkable that a man who considered himself a great psychologist and who wrote voluminously about religion, priding himself on understanding religion far better than Freud did, should have waited that long.

His pent-up resentment did not abate in his discussion of the dogma that Pope Pius XII had proclaimed. The Protestant world was shocked at the time because the dogma seemed to contravene all ecumenical tendencies. It was widely considered incredibly reactionary and "medieval." Whatever the Pope's reasons were, he certainly was less sympathetic to feminism than, say, Freud;[2] nor was Jung's wrath at the Protestant reaction due to any sympathy for feminism. Yet this bitterness about the Protestant parsons is far clearer than his logic; what he communicates is more than anything else his violent personal feeling.

To understand that, one must first of all take note of what the new dogma claimed. It asserted that the Virgin Mary was *bodily* assumed into heaven. I am not persuaded of the universality of the Oedipus complex, but I note with amazement how Jung, at the age of seventy-six, gives free vent to his bitter hatred of the Father, extols the Son, and then, in a book that deals ostensibly with Job, suddenly pours out his resentment of the Protestant parsons who will not have it that the Mother was bodily united with her Son, if only in heaven.

[2] Christopher Lasch, "Freud and Women," in *New York Review of Books*, October 3, 1974, dealt very sensibly with a subject on which Freud has often been misrepresented.

I did not approach *Answer to Job* with the slightest wish to force a Freudian scheme upon it, least of all the Oedipus complex, of which I assumed Freud had probably made too much. Nor did it dawn upon me for a long time that Jung was still fighting Freud in this book. It still took me another nine months until, after I had worked my way through the book again, the pieces finally fell into place when I realized that I still had not accounted for the final part of *Answer to Job*.

At last the immense resentment that is so disturbing in this work of old age can be understood. Hatred of the Jewish father God of the Old Testament mingles with resentment of Freud and of Protestant parsons and draws upon Jung's infantile hatred of one Protestant pastor in particular, Jung's father, who according to Freud was resented for not allowing the mother to be bodily united with her son.

While this does not prove that everybody has an Oedipus complex, and Freud himself thought that most people manage to resolve theirs as they grow up, it would be difficult to find a clearer example of a man who never managed to resolve his Oedipus complex. This is really amazing when one recalls that Freud had designated Jung as his successor. Surely, Jung must have given some thought to his own Oedipus complex. We must recall the incident of the book that he thought, and told people, Freud had returned to him with the inscription "Resistance to the Father." He knew very well that Freud thought that Jung had Oedipal feelings, but he set out to prove Freud wrong, and though Freud did not return the book to him he imagined the slight so vividly that he even pictured the inscription. That, he felt, is what Freud thinks; but that involves an insufficient regard for my reasoning. Freud, he complained, always expected him to have dreams in which his death wishes for the father would find expression, but Freud was wrong. His dreams were very different. But when he related them late in life, he enabled us to see that he did dream about the slaying of Siegfried, and we have also analyzed his preoccupation with Judas and his fantasies about Philemon. All that time, however, Jung refused to come to grips with his own Oedipus complex, until it finally came out into the open in his *Answer to Job*.

My analysis of this book provides, it seems, a finishing touch on the portrait I have drawn of Jung and my account of his break with Freud. But in such matters no brush stroke is ever the last, and as long as one does not close one's mind to further evidence one keeps making discoveries. I must still relate one such discovery. But first I want to ask why *Answer to Job* seems "beautiful" to the editor of *The Portable Jung* and many others. It naturally appeals to people who share some of Jung's resentments, if only those of the Old Testament and of Protestantism, not to speak of the father.

74 ▶▶▶ *Answer to Job* suggests forcibly that a depth psychologist who does not understand himself and his own problems will write about himself and his own problems whatever he is writing about. But is that not what all of us are doing anyway unless we more or less emulate the mathematicians and escape from ourselves? The extent to which psychologists and philosophers, as well as poets and novelists, write about their own problems is widely underestimated, but the difference between those who realize what they are doing, as Goethe, Nietzsche, and Freud did, and those who do not, like Kant, Heidegger, and Jung, remains noteworthy. The trouble with those who do not understand what they are doing is that their unwillingness to face up to their problems distorts their perception of the things they write about.

Jung's own verdict was actually harsher and brings to mind the curse pronounced by Sophocles' King

Oedipus upon the slayer of Laius, when Oedipus did not realize that he himself was the man on whom he pronounced judgment. When writing a book on the Bible, one has to be selective, concentrating on some texts to the exclusion of others. The best one can do is to make a point of always looking for objections to one's reading and alternative interpretations. Jung failed to do this. He ignored inconvenient themes in the Gospels, no less than the whole Book of Jonah and most of the Old Testament. Yet Jung himself said:

> If one prefers not to read the eighty-ninth Psalm—if, in other words, one is a shirker—the matter will not end there. Whoever commits fraud once will do it again— particularly when it comes to self-knowledge. The latter, however, is demanded by the Christian ethic in the form of the examination of conscience. They were pious people who maintained that self-knowledge paves the way to knowledge of God. (661)

Jung was as self-righteous as Oedipus pronouncing his curse and could be quite as sanctimonious as the pastors he hated.

Incidentally, it is strange that he should have found the eighty-ninth Psalm so upsetting. A person not stuck in the problems of his childhood and adolescence, penning an answer to Job in the 1950s, would have been upset by Auschwitz, Nagasaki, and a multitude of recent horrors, all of which Jung passed over in silence.

75 ▶▶▶ While I was finishing the first complete draft of "Jung's Answer to Job," I was asked what I thought of the idea of publishing some lectures Jung had given in his early twenties to the Zofingia Society (of Students) at Basel University. I was sent

photocopies of the manuscripts[3] but did not look at them until the draft was finished. Then I was astonished to find how perfectly they rounded out the picture. Here was a find almost comparable to the discovery of Hegel's early "theological"—or rather anti-theological—writings. Suddenly one could see Jung's development in a new and clearer light.

In a lecture "On the Border Areas of Exact Science," probably delivered in 1896 or 1897, Jung attacked "the whole materialistic-skeptical conception of modern natural science." If only Jung had made clear in later life that what he could not stomach was Freud's skepticism rather than the dogmatism that he falsely ascribed to him!

Henri Ellenberger reports in *The Discovery of the Unconscious* (1970):

> This talk was so successful that the assembly [of students] unanimously decided to recommend Jung's talk for publication in the central journal of the association. It is not known why it was not accepted by the editorial committee in Berne. Gustav Steiner points out that the great success of this talk contradicts what Jung wrote in his autobiography, namely, that whenever he told his fellow students about spiritism, they reacted with derision . . . (p. 687f.)

In a lecture delivered in 1898, "Thoughts about the Essence and Values of Speculative Research," he reinterpreted Kant's conception of the thing-in-itself, attacked the hope that soon everything might be explainable in causal, scientific terms, and invoked Schopenhauer and Eduard von Hartmann, his "spiritual heir."

None of this would be worth mentioning if it were not the prelude for the fascinating lecture of January 1899, "Thoughts about the Conception of Christianity with Reference to the Doctrine of Albrecht Ritschl."

[3] Jung's lectures will be published, and the English version will be brought out by the Princeton University Press.

Here is what Jung wrote during the period when Freud wrote his *Interpretation of Dreams,* published in November 1899. (Where my translation is unidiomatic the German original is, too. I have tried to capture the flavor of Jung's prose.)

> The figure of Christ must necessarily be placed again in the conception he had of himself. . . . The transworldliness of his essence that he himself asserted must be received as such, *talis qualis,* in our modern consciousness. If we do not do that, then we are no longer Christians, for we are not entitled to bear any longer the name of him whose conception we do not share. [Jung did not doubt—any more than in *Answer to Job*—that he knew what Jesus thought!] But as long as we call ourselves by his name, we are morally constrained to accept his doctrine in all particulars. Even what seems impossible *must* be believed, or we abuse the name of Christian. It is a hard word, one will cry, a *sacrificium intellectus!* . . . If our Christianity is to have any contents at all any more, then we must again accept the metaphysical world of ideas of original Christianity. We thus drive a painful thorn into our flesh, but we must do it for the sake of our name as Christians.[4]

Then Jung referred again to Eduard von Hartmann, the author of *The Philosophy of the Unconscious.*[5] It was in this way that Jung was led to the unconscious, and it was against this background that he discovered *The Interpretation of Dreams and Freud.*

What at first does not seem to fit is Jung's account in his autobiography of his discovery of Nietzsche, which he places in the very period when he gave these lectures. But on reflection one sees that these lectures help to

[4] Ellenberger's two-and-a half line summary is very odd: ". . . a talk on the theology of Albrecht Ritschl, whom he criticized for his denial of a mystical element in religion."

[5] See Section 11 of the second volume of this trilogy.

explain why Jung said that he was "insufficiently prepared" for Nietzsche and postponed reading him, while
he had no such hesitation about reading Kant. Very
probably, it was reading Nietzsche that put an end to
Jung's Christianity—or drove it underground—and made
him ready to embrace Freud. Yet Freud appealed to him
not only, and not mainly, as the heir of Nietzsche, but
rather as the explorer of the unconscious and the enemy
of the science of the time. As one reads these early
manuscripts one is led to wonder how Freud and Jung
could have been friends for almost seven years.

It took Jung almost forty years after he left Freud
before he finally wrote *Answer to Job*. That book has a
foreword entitled *Lectori Benevolo*. Before his 1899
lecture he had placed a foreword entitled *Praefatio
auditori benevolo!* And that began: "One will be understandably surprised that a medical man . . . should leave
his craft to talk about theological matters." Not until 1952
did he finally publish his ideas about such matters. In the
end he returned to his beginnings—and still did not find
peace. Even then his bitterness bore testimony of his
deep division against himself. He postured as an icono-
clast, speaking blasphemously about God the Father, as
proud of his wit and daring as any adolescent, but at the
same time went back to the reverence for "Christ" that
had been so striking in the lectures he gave as a student.

76 ▶▶▶ In the end we shall also re-
turn to the beginning of these reflections on Jung, to his
attack on Heidegger and his plea that philosophy should
root out its psychopaths. Jung's first letter to Künzli,
whom he wrote soon after how philosophy was a system-
ized fight against one's own insecurity, is an even more
astonishing document. Arnold Künzli was a student who

had said in a review of one of Jung's books in a student newspaper that "much in Jung is still the romantic vision of a creative spirit, occasionally at the expense of scientific empiricism." Although Künzli apparently had not said anything worse than that, Jung felt so piqued that he sent Künzli a long handwritten letter, February 4, 1943:

> . . . Supposing that my attitude really does exhibit such easily recognizable faults, how do you square this with the fact that I unite at least seven honorary doctorates upon my unscientific and/or benighted head? I am, by your leave, an honorary member of the Academy of German Scientists and Physicians, a Fellow of the Royal Society, Doctor Scientiae of Oxford and Harvard University, and was one of the four guests of honor and representatives of Swiss science at the Tercentenary of the latter university. Do these august bodies really consist of nothing but simpletons incapable of judgment, and is the philosophical faculty of Zurich University [which had never given Jung a chair] the brain of the world?

This extraordinary outburst shows how, so late in life, Jung was still fighting his own insecurity, seeking reassurance in his honorary degrees.

About the Harvard degree: The committee at Harvard had wanted to give Freud an honorary degree but was assured by Erik Erikson that there was no chance at all that Freud would accept. It was 1936, the year he turned eighty. Had their offer been rejected, the next offer would have been made by a different committee, and the psychologists wanted very much to honor a psychologist. So they offered the degree to Jung.

Jung stayed with Stanley Cobb, Professor of Neurology, and put his shoes outside his bedroom door to have them shined. Cobb polished them, but when he introduced Jung to a large audience, he introduced him as "Dr. Freud."[6]

Perhaps one should not say that Jung, who never visited Rome, could be counted on to take a boat to India or America to receive a degree. Surely, most professors would gladly do the same. Yet Freud had not been wrong in feeling that to Jung public acceptance meant rather more than it should to a great psychologist. It is also interesting to compare Jung's letter to a student, boasting of his honorary degrees, with a lovely letter William James, a great psychologist of a different type, wrote to F. C. S. Schiller at Oxford:

> I hope you are not serious about an Oxford degree for your humble servant. If you are, pray drop the thought! I am out of the race for all such vanities. Write me a degree on parchment and then send it yourself—in any case it would be but your award!—and it will be cheaper and more veracious.[7]

Nietzsche and Freud thought that great spirits were skeptics, but one might suppose that a depth psychologist would not even have to be a great spirit to be somewhat skeptical about public honors. Jung, however, was an anti-skeptic. And it does not seem to have occurred to him that, a generation after Freud had revolutionized our thinking, some professors felt that it was time to bestow some recognition on this new direction in psychology, but that Freud's emphasis on sexuality and his views on religion made it much more diplomatic to honor Jung.

[6] Roazen (1975), p. 296, drawing on information from Henry Murray. Murray confirmed all of this in a letter to me.

In 1980 Harvard University bestowed an honorary degree on Freud's daughter Anna, who had won a name for herself with her own publications half a century earlier (she was born in 1895)—and the Austrian government gave a gold medal to Sigmund Freud's maid, Paula.

[7] Gay Wilson Allen (1967), p. 429f.

77 ▶▶▶ Künzli had kindled Jung's wrath by questioning how scientific he was. It was terribly important to Jung to be considered no less scientific that Freud, if not more so, but at the same time not opposed to religion. Like Kant, Jung wanted to reconcile science and religion. And in Jung's case as in Kant's that, as much as anything, accounts for his wide appeal.

At his funeral ceremony in the Protestant church in Küsnacht the pastor called him "a prophet who had stayed the overwhelming flow of rationalism and had given man the courage to have a soul again." The same theme has been sounded often since then. Jung has been proclaimed a religious figure, and R. C. Zaehner actually proclaimed him nothing less than "A New Buddha"![8]

The folder used to publicize the first Panarion Conference, held in Los Angeles in September 1975, read in part:

> We want to attract those who have the profoundly spiritual attitudes which in Jung's definition characterizes [sic] religion. . . . Theologians, historians, and other scholars who may not subscribe to Jung's concepts and terminology but whose original work is inspired by a genuine religious experience and attitude will feel themselves welcome.
>
> They, and the small group of men and women who are convening this conference share the belief that the future of man depends largely upon understanding all of the necessities of the psyche. One of these necessities is a relationship of the psyche to transcendental facts . . .

"Transcendental," like the whole project of reconciling science and religion, brings to mind Kant. He, of course, tried to distinguish sharply between "transcen-

[8] Zaehner, *The Concise Encyclopaedia of Living Faiths* (1959), Chapter 11.

dental" and "transcendent"; and what is meant here is what Kant called "transcendent," that is, what transcends all possible experience. Or is it? There is also talk of "genuine religious experience" and, in the next and final sentence, of the "transcendental needs" of the psyche. Presumably it is not really the needs that are transcendent, but the soul is taken to have a profound need for "facts" that transcend—what? All possible experience, to use a Kantian phrase? Hardly. Rather, reason.

Of course, this is a mere folder, replete with misprints, in which Jung is hailed as "the discover [*sic*] of the collective unconscious." Clearly, the details of such a publication are of no consequence; what matters is the sentiment nurtured by Jung.

In a lecture of May 1897, "Some Thoughts about Psychology," Jung had referred to "*Immanuel Kant*, the sage and prophet of Königsberg, who has been called [by whom?], with some justification [really?], the last philosopher."

Jung went back to Kant, but not the Kant who was one of the leading spirits of the enlightenment. What Jung quoted is a remark from Kant's lectures that seems to provide for a right to believe.

> Something can be accepted problematically when it is altogether clear that it is *possible*. We cannot prove it apodictically, but *nobody can refute it either* that such spirits should not exist.

It is a pity that Jung, for all his erudition, never discovered Mark Twain, whom both Nietzsche and Freud admired. The last quotation brings to mind some of Mark Twain's reflections on the Church of the Holy Sepulcher (in *The Innocents Abroad*):

> If even greater proofs than those I have mentioned are wanted, to satisfy the headstrong and the foolish that this is the genuine center of the earth, they are here. The

greatest of them lies in the fact that from under this very column was taken the *dust from which Adam was made.* This can surely be regarded in the light of a settler. It is not likely that the original first man would have been made from an inferior quality of earth when it was entirely convenient to get first quality from the world's center. This will strike any reflecting mind forcibly. That Adam was formed of dirt procured in this very spot is amply proven by the fact that in six thousand years no man has ever been able to prove that the dirt was *not* procured here whereof he was made.

At the beginning of the next chapter, in which Mark Twain describes the Via Dolorosa in Jerusalem, he mocks another religious argument in a way that also brings to mind the frequent accumulation of erudite "evidence" in the works of Jung and Erich Neumann. He relates how, when Saint Veronica wiped away the perspiration on Jesus' face,

> the print of the Saviour's face remained upon the handkerchief, a perfect portrait, and so remains unto this day. We knew this because we saw this handkerchief in a cathedral in Paris, in another in Spain, and in two others in Italy. In the Milan cathedral it costs five francs to see it, and at St. Peter's, at Rome, it is almost impossible to see it at any price. No tradition is so amply verified as this of St. Veronica and her handkerchief.

To return to the young Jung, he quotes from Kant's early book on Swedenborg (1763), which long antedates his critical philosophy: "I confess that I am very much inclined to affirm the existence of immaterial beings in the world and to include my soul in this class of beings."

Jung's fundamental concern, like Heidegger's, was religious, and though Heidegger dealt prominently with the pre-Socratics and with Nietzsche, and Jung with China and Tibet, it was some sort of Christian Gnosti-

Masks. (Photograph by the author, 1979.)

cism they sought to revive. Yet they did not come out into the open, presenting arguments that others might examine critically. Jung and Heidegger were at pains to hide even from themselves what they were doing.

The picture of Jung that has emerged from my work is not what I myself expected. Even when the final draft of this volume was finished, I still kept asking friends who thought better of Jung than I did where they found his major contributions to the discovery of the mind. I wanted to give a balanced account and, if possible, end on a positive note. But I have come to the conclusion that there are no great contributions. Jung obstructed the discovery of the mind but, in effect, contributed a fascinating case history.

Incidentally, the way the chapter on Adler turned out surprised me, too. I do not wish to imply that I began with great admiration for either Adler or Jung, but seeing that some people of whom I thought well and whom I liked admired them, I should have preferred not to hurt their feelings. On the other hand, what makes research exciting is, of course, that it is not a matter of backing up preconceived notions but a voyage of discovery.

Should we say in the end that Jung and Adler failed to look behind their own masks? No, what I have stressed throughout is that what is crucial is up front and that Jung's descent into the depths was an escape, not only for himself. Jung also provided new forms of escape for others.

PART ▶ V

Mind and Mask ▶▶▶

78 ▶▶▶ The claim that what is crucial is up front seems to contradict the central notion of Nietzsche's and Freud's depth psychology. I have hailed Nietzsche's idea that "consciousness is a surface" and his philosophy of masks as major contributions. Now I may seem to have reached a position that is irreconcilable with some of the major insights I have ascribed to Freud and Nietzsche. To be sure, in the final paragraph of my discussion of Nietzsche's philosophy of masks I said that "the image of the mask with its implicit dualism of appearance and reality is certainly questionable." And that section (29) ended:

> Perhaps—Nietzsche himself suggests in many late passages—there are only appearances and no ultimate reality behind them . . . and perhaps there is no self. Perhaps individuals have no essence or nature; and if they did, it might be said to be their task to overcome it. . . . It is part of Nietzsche's profundity that he raised these questions. We shall return to them in the final chapter of this trilogy: "Mind and Mask."

Now the moment of truth has come.

Actually, the solution of this problem has been up front all along. The second major contribution to the discovery of the mind with which I credited Goethe was that "man is his deeds." In the first chapter of this trilogy (Section 8) I explained how "Goethe implicitly called into question the existence of the mind" and how "we can dispense with the concept of mind as an entity." But instead of repeating what is to be found in the first two volumes, I shall now address myself directly to the apparent contradiction.

We are—at least in part—what we have done, written, and dreamed. But our consciousness shuts out *most* of this—and not only most of *this*. Our consciousness is highly selective and takes in very little of what is up front. It is rather like a telephoto lens and often altogether out of focus. Three generalizations about what we usually do *not* see may prove helpful.

First, we tend not to take in what does not interest us. After seeing a number of other people, I rarely recall what they wore because I am not particularly interested in clothes. But I usually notice what books people have on their shelves, which is something many other people do not take in. Further examples are so easy to come by that there is no need for further illustrations.

Second, we do not take in things for which we have no eyes and ears because we lack the needed background; for example, necessary information or experiences. An expert looking at a patient or a plant, a painting or a text will see a great deal that escapes the novice. Similarly, there is a great deal that children who see a performance of a play by Sophocles or Shakespeare are bound to miss, and as one grows and develops one is likely to make ever new discoveries when going to performances of the same tragedies.

Third, we tend not to take in what we would very much rather not see or hear. This is the insight Nietzsche formulated succinctly in *Beyond Good and Evil:* " 'I have done that,' says my memory. 'I could not have done that,' says my pride and remains inexorable. Finally, my memory yields." Freud, as we have seen, applauded and developed this suggestion.

The claim that what is crucial is up front or meets the eye does not commit us to agree with Adler or with Sartre when they say that we really see it very clearly and merely lie about it. I am far from withdrawing my critique of Sartre (in Section 28 above). It is extremely difficult to see clearly ever so much that lies right in front of us, notably including ourselves, our own parents, and quite generally people with whom we are deeply involved emotionally. The present volume abounds in examples that include Adler's and Jung's self-images, their images of Freud, Bottome's image of Adler, and Freud's initial image of Jung. But it may be helpful to give at least one extended illustration at this point.

In "The Development in Psychoanalytic Theory toward a Humanistic Orientation" one of Adler's most devoted followers, H. L. Ansbacher, has argued that we must distinguish *"The Phases of Freud"* (1886–1900, 1900–1923, and 1923–1939), and that this throws *"New Light on the Adler-Freud Relationship."* Freud I was "the Freud whom Adler joined," and the decision to join him was as reasonable of Adler as his decision to separate from Freud II. Freud III allegedly came close "to Adler's position that Freud only a few years earlier had derided as being nothing but ego psychology." To substantiate this account, H. L. Ansbacher furnishes a "table" in which "Passages from Freud's (1905) Case of Dora" appear in the left column, while "Similar Passages from Adler's Later Writings" appear in the right column, with "Key Phrases Italicized." The "surprising similarities" are said to show Adler's consistency: He did not change, Freud did.

Yet the table brings to mind a feature that has appeared now and then in *The New Yorker* under the heading "Department of Funny Coincidences." The point of that feature is that the "surprising similarities" between the left and right columns are due to the fact that one writer has taken something from the other, without acknowledgment. In the case at hand one might suppose that it met the eye that Adler was less original than he thought and that Freud had long seen the things of which Adler later made so much; only Freud had integrated them into a larger picture instead of claiming that this was all. This, of course, was what Freud himself said in his *History of the Psychoanalytic Movement* (1914), and earlier than that in his letters to Jung. Ansbacher proved Freud to have been right without seeing that this is what he did. It is doubly ironic that Adler was so concerned about people stealing *his* ideas without proper acknowledgment.

As long as I have mentioned the notion that there were three Freuds rather than one, it should be added that this strikes me as implausible, and that the dates are altogether untenable. This, too, meets the eye: all of the passages that are said to represent Freud I (that is, the period from 1886 to 1900) are taken from three consecutive pages of a paper of 1905.[1] Freud kept revising his theories, most notably in *Beyond the Pleasure Principle* (1920), but he never adopted the positions of Adler's *Nervous Character*.

And what might an Adlerian say when you point out such things to him? "I don't like the conclusions you draw from the similarities. They refer to a Freud whom almost nobody would recognize as such." But if that should be true, it would only go to show how little knowledge of Freud most people have.

The point of this example is, of course, that the case at hand is typical: It is extremely difficult and rare for people, even scholars, to see what threatens their world

[1] *Werke,* V, pp. 203–5.

view or calls into question the meaning of a large part of their lives. In such cases it is by no means proof of greater wisdom, intelligence, or virtue if another person, who has no reason to feel similarly threatened, sees what meets the eye. The classical story making that point is Hans Christian Andersen's fairy tale "The Emperor's New Clothes."

The swindlers told an emperor that they could weave very fine fabrics and make clothes for him that had the special quality of being quite invisible to all who were not fit for the offices they held, or who were impossibly dull. He commissioned new clothes but then began to worry that he himself might not be able to see them, and hence sent an old minister to see how the tailors were coming along. He did not see a thing but pretended to admire their work, and so did another official, and eventually also the emperor himself. When a great procession was held at which the emperor was expected to wear his new clothes, everybody admired and praised them until a little child exclaimed: "But he has nothing on!"

Surely, that fairy tale was meant to illuminate much that goes on in the academic world, and it does. Students and professors, but also many people outside the academy, pretend they see what in fact they do not see, because otherwise they might be considered incompetent or stupid; and eventually they persuade themselves that they do see all sorts of things. Conversely, they refuse to see that the emperor is naked or that famous people who are supposed to have all sorts of great merits really are quite devoid of them.

The tendency to see what we are supposed to see and what everybody else in our circle claims to see is very powerful. Children may occasionally get away with the admission that they do not see it, but one of the functions of schools, from the first grade, if not kindergarten, to the doctorate, is to make them see it. The person who steadfastly refuses may be dismissed as stupid and incompetent, or resented as a troublemaker. As long as one has to pretend, it saves one's self-respect as well as a great deal of psychic energy if make-believe turns into genuine belief.

In sum, what is crucial is typically up front and not hidden in unfathomable depths, but it does not follow that it is therefore easy to see. What is needed is often great courage and strength of character.

SIGHT

I

People see what they know is there
Though what they know is often false
And one does not know what one does not dare:
Our vision stops where our courage halts.

II

Sight is an arrow. You need more than aim;
For the crucial string you need guts.
Even the lame
Could walk through the open gate
Which the coward shuts
Complaining of fate.

79 ▶▶▶ Is a writer's work a mask behind which an all too human individual hides? Or is it the work that shows us the real person while the shy individual—for example, the soft-spoken and polite Nietzsche—is a mask? Was Jung's extraversion and booming laughter the mask of an introverted sick soul? Or was the introvert whom we encounter in the posthumous autobiography an artful mask?

The answer to all these questions is: No. The work is a sustained deed no less than a person's behavior, and both are real. I have not tried to unmask Goethe, Kant, or Hegel; Nietzsche, Heidegger, or Buber; Freud, Adler, or

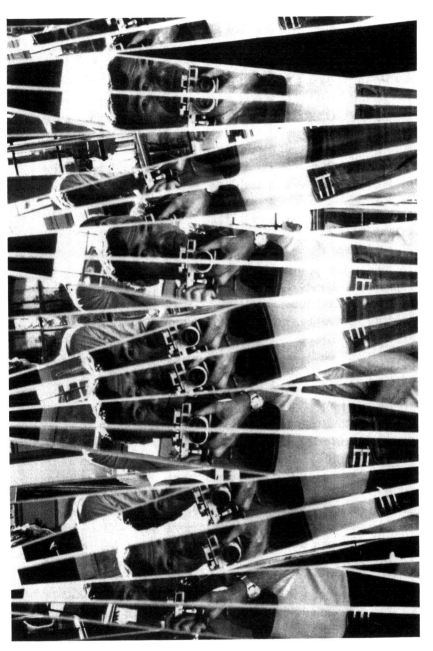

Faces. (Photograph by the author, 1979.)

Jung. Far from claiming that one or another thing is only a mask or mere appearance while something else shows us the reality, I have sought to discover the mind of each writer *in* his work and not behind it. Nor have I followed the example of those who find the real Heidegger in, say, *Being and Time* while dismissing his 1934 book or his later writings as irrelevant. In no case have I concentrated on a single work or period to the exclusion of the rest; it has always been my aim to show how the whole oeuvre hangs together and how the man and his work are of one piece.

It is a common error to take one mask for the whole person, and those who try to correct this mistake often suppose that the person is to be found behind the mask. In fact, most people have many masks; but as long as "mask" suggests that what is real can be found by ripping off the mask, it seems better to drop this misleading metaphor. People are more or less complex and multifaceted, and one could say that at least some of them have many faces. Given our eyes, we cannot see all of these faces at once, but anyone who sees only one or two, or who discounts one or more because they do not fit his image of the person, goes astray.

In 1607 a man named Conrad Andreae published an attack on Martin Luther that he called *Zweyhundert Luther*, meaning two hundred Luthers. It consisted of well over two hundred quatrains, each with a short title, such as "Humble Luther," "Thieving Luther," "Translating Luther"—arranged alphabetically, but with many of the epithets beginning with the same letters. Facing the first two verses appeared a full-page woodcut showing Luther with seven very different heads. In the West people have rarely been portrayed with many faces, while in Indian art this theme is common. The picture of Luther was part of an attack on him, and in English "double-faced" is opprobrious. But I am suggesting that we all have many faces.

This is a truism regarding so-called Renaissance men. It is fairly obvious in the cases of Leonardo and Michelangelo, Goethe and Nietzsche. But none of the nine major figures considered in this trilogy had only one face. In no case have I made a sustained effort to show all their faces, nor does it really make sense to say that any one has, say, ten faces, neither more nor less. The point is rather that we should go out of our way to find a few and see how they are of one piece and reveal a single mind.

While there is no mind as a separate entity, there is a person, not meaning the body, that we find in a person's deeds—and in the case of writers in their writings—and I call that mind.

80 ▶▶▶ "You are your body." "You are not your body." Such propositions are not the form of truth, as Hegel noted in the preface to his *Phenomenology*. Some philosophers have a genius, many more a talent—most philosophy professors a meager talent—for concealing urgent problems from themselves—and hiding—behind a web of words that they call concepts. They divert themselves and their students and readers by playing chess with words. Every move is a proposition or a series of propositions that is called an argument. (For philosophy as chess see the last section of Volume I.)

You are your body, and what your body does you do. Yet others can know you without ever having seen your body, and they can know a great deal about you without knowing how your body looks. We are our bodies, but not only our bodies but also our deeds; and a writer's deeds include his writings. We know Goethe, Kant, and Hegel; Nietzsche, Heidegger, and Buber; Freud as well as Jung and Adler through their writings, and we sometimes call what can be known of them in this way their minds.

Instead of saying that "man is his deeds" or that we are our bodies, it would be better to say: We are our lives and works. We are unfinished as long as we live and work and can add a few lines that could place the whole picture in a new perspective. We are not finished until we are dead. While we live we are like a speaker in midsentence who cannot be understood fully until he has had a chance to finish. What is still coming could change the apparent meaning—although most speakers are painfully predictable.

As long as we live we can say: We are not nothing but what we have done and failed to do; we are all that, but not only that. It is up to us to show how much of this was merely background, skins we shed, or failings over which we triumphed. Our lives and we ourselves are works in progress that we can reinterpret and remake while we have time and strength.

What might look pathetic if it were the end could actually make what follows look better, as when a student starts with poor work and after a year has improved enormously. Compare the painting such a student does after a year with a painting of more or less the same quality done by a master who has deteriorated. If "we are our deeds" meant that you could take a painting and say "that is the painter, no more, no less," it would be madness. The painting has to be seen in the context of what came before and after, as a rung on a ladder or a way station. Individuals are not one or another deed but all of their lives and works—and unfinished until their lives and works are done.

Those who consider themselves finished, whether they are proud of it or in despair, do not realize that they are still alive. For them self-discovery could mean the realization that they need not remain what they are and that they can actually remake their past, too, by giving it unexpected meanings. Of course, that is not done by setting to work on one's past in a deliberate effort to reinterpret it. It is done by coming to life and using what one has. Using it gives it new meanings incidentally, without our giving it any thought. One discovers oneself through living; but it is possible to live without discovering oneself. In fact, it is easy. To discover something one has to look or listen, and most people are afraid of doing that.

It is widely supposed that true knowledge of the mind depends on introspection and that other minds cannot be known as well as our own because knowledge of other minds must do with empathy, which cannot be quite as reliable as introspection. German philosophers, beginning with Wilhelm Dilthey and Heinrich Rickert, tried doggedly to distinguish the methods of the natural and the mental sciences (*Geisteswissenschaften*), assuming that this was so. (See Section 11 above.) These notions owe something to Kant's idea that the self is concealed behind appearances and, of course, to Descartes's dualism of matter and mind. Ultimately, they are rooted in Plato's metaphysics, with its distinction of appearance and reality and its roots in the Orphic doctrine that the body is the tomb or prison of the soul. Heidegger and Buber owe a great deal to this dualistic tradition. On the penultimate page of the First Part of *I and Thou* Buber actually said, in words that bring to mind Kant:

> The It-world hangs together in space and time.
> The You-world does not hang together in space
> and time.

He held that the You could not be approached with the methods of the natural sciences or of any science. It could not even be grasped in intuition. It could not be grasped at all. It had to be encountered, like God.

I do not deny that there is an element of truth in that, yet I have insisted throughout on the needfulness of an essentially scientific approach; and what I mean by that is the method of conjectures or hypotheses that are hardened or destroyed in the fire of objections and alternatives. If we are our lives, and the minds of people who write are to be found in their works, then the knowledge of mind does not depend on introspection. In fact, I have tried to show that in some ways it is more difficult to know one's own mind than to know the minds of some other people. Kant and Hegel, Heidegger, Jung and Adler did not know themselves at all well. They would have done better if they had relied less on their intuitive sense of themselves and had managed to look at their own writings and actions in a more detached way.

All this is not meant to imply that the proper study of mind can dispense with the imagination and must be, to use a highly misleading cliché, coldly scientific. The point is rather that science is not altogether different from poetry and art; great scientists have a great deal of imagination.

What is needed in natural science no less than in discovering the mind is enough imagination to bring up hypotheses, objections, and alternatives, as well as a highly developed critical faculty that persists in evaluating them. Such evaluations do not depend on a position that is held dogmatically and considered immune against criticism. One asks oneself: What objections and alternatives might an intelligent person present at this point? One willingly considers many views, not only one's own. That requires, to repeat it, imagination as well as critical acumen. Freud had both gifts, many orthodox Freudians have neither, and Jung had some imagination but a profoundly uncritical mind. He usually failed to consider even the most obvious objections and alternatives.

A cartoon once showed a patient lying on a couch, who says: "I am Napoleon." The analyst sitting behind him replies: "I am Freud." Even Jung and Adler bring to mind that cartoon, not to speak of less well-known psychotherapists.

Freud's superiority is due in some measure to the

fact that he learned a great deal from Goethe and that he was not corrupted by Kant. Goethe had opposed the dualistic tradition that in his own time found expression in Kant's philosophy. He did not see science as altogether different from art, or nature as altogether different from mind, nor did he believe in a noumenal self or in essences that might hide behind phenomena. In effect, he rejected the metaphor of the mask, and instead of looking for timeless structures he insisted on the crucial importance of development.

When he was about seventy, Goethe wrote a poem that is more remarkable for its contents than for its form, which is not very poetic:

"To nature's core"—
You Philistine!—
"created minds can't penetrate."
Me and my kin
you should not irritate
with words that we abhor.
Where we are, we assume,
we're at the core.
"Happy are those to whom
she merely shows her skin."
For sixty years I've heard this tedious lay
and cursed one or another dunce
discreetly. To myself I say:
She offers all quite willingly.
Nature has neither core
nor skin,
for she is all at once.
You'd better test yourself to see
if you are core or skin.[2]

The discovery of the mind has been obstructed by the false idea that it is a hidden core that can be reached only by introspection. But introspection is rarely fruitful, and it is utterly unreliable. One must get "out" what is

[2] *Sämtliche Werke*, 33, p. 11: "*In Innere der Natur . . .*"; "Core or Skin": *Kern oder Schale.*

"inside" if one wants to see it, and the way to get it out is to talk, write, and act. To discover the mind—one's own no less than that of others—one must examine what one has done and said and written—and what one has not done and said, what one has failed to do. Understandably, it is more comfortable to look inside where it is dark and self-deception can proceed unchecked.

Freud taught people to write down their dreams and to talk to him and thus create a record that one could examine like any other record. In time, other therapists, notably including Fritz Perls, paid more attention to physical clues. But to discover one's own mind one does not necessarily need a psychotherapist, though it helps if one can talk to someone else who listens without passing judgment and who occasionally helps one to see in a new light what one has said and done or failed to do. Lacking a friend like that, one can write, but most people who keep diaries find it as unpleasant to read them as most people find it to listen for any length of time to their own voices. One talks or writes to get something out of one's system but is deeply reluctant to look at the record or to base one's self-image on the record.

To discover one's mind it helps to see whom one admires and whom one hates, what one loves and what makes one angry, and what one experiences as upsetting. Self-understanding can be self-transcendence. The self that is discovered can be seen as a childish self, as a photograph of the person one used to be. Understanding can emancipate us from the tyranny of tricks by which we are no longer taken in. Laughing at ourselves is sometimes liberating. Conversely, those who never feel "what fools these mortals be!"—emphatically including themselves—are still like children.

Among the things we can learn from the discovery and understanding of other minds is "what fools these mortals be!"—emphatically including ourselves. When we see their limitations we have good reason to ask ourselves whether we are essentially different. We can also ask ourselves why we admire or love this and become angry or upset about that. Understanding others and understanding ourselves are not totally different experiences. Not only is the method much the same, but understanding ourselves helps us to understand others, and vice versa.

Most interpreters of Hegel, Nietzsche, and Heidegger, Freud, Adler, and Jung have paid surprisingly little attention to the questions raised here. Hegel's, Nietzsche's, and Freud's immense admiration for Goethe has been considered as little as Heidegger's and Jung's attitudes toward Hitler when he first came to power; and Adler's and Jung's reactions to Freud as a human being have been ignored for the most part. It was assumed that it must have been theoretical differences that led to their break with Freud.

What I am suggesting goes straight against the microscopism that has spread through the academic world. One prefers to examine one concept or a single argument, or one devotes a whole seminar to a few consecutive pages. That way one is not likely to discover the author's mind; and as long as one fails to know that one is very likely to come up with wildly implausible interpretations that are, if not anachronistic and historically blind, psychologically quite impossible. To understand writers and artists one must have some sense of their oeuvre and see how it all hangs together and how a single person (or mind) finds expression in the whole of it.

Three objections come to mind immediately. First, the method here proposed is rather arduous and requires a great deal of reading, and rather careful reading at that.[3] This is true, but it would be surprising if the minds of

[3] For a detailed account of "The Art of Reading" see Chapter 2 of my *The Future of the Humanities* (1977).

Goethe, Kant, or Hegel, Nietzsche, Freud, or Jung could be discovered very easily without exertion. What is astonishing is surely that the minds of some great writers who are dead and who cannot be interrogated can be known at all. So-called empathy is unreliable if it is not based on documents and checked against them. But the discovery of a writer's mind does not have to wait until one has read the whole oeuvre. Reading involves conjectures about the author's mind, and some people read very perceptively and keep making conjectures that are soon borne out by further reading, including the author's letters and the testimonies of people who knew him. Few or even none of their hypotheses are contradicted as they read on, and eventually a lot of things fall into place and a coherent image of the author's mind emerges. If one's interest does not warrant further study, one may be content at that point to submit one's tentative results to others who have studied the same author, which can be a shortcut to discovering mistakes and thus advancing one's discovery.

The second objection is that most people don't write as much as the nine men on whom this trilogy has concentrated. Indeed, few people have written so much. How, then, can we discover their minds, especially if they are dead? In most cases the answer is plainly that it can't be done. We shall never know the minds of the parents or grandparents of these nine men as well as theirs. But I would much rather know Goethe's mind than his grandparents'.

As for our contemporaries, we saw at the beginning of the Epilogue to Volume II how Gilbert Murray thought that "many people now living have had closer and more intimate communion with the thoughts of Shakespeare, or Dante or Virgil or, it may be, Aeschylus, than with those of their next-door neighbours"; and we have discussed this view. To discover the mind of one's neighbor certainly requires some application, and one may well feel that one really does not desire to know it all that well.

Finally, what has here been said about people's minds may seem excessively intellectual. Many, if not most, people who do not write a great deal would consider it rather grandiloquent to speak of their "deeds," nor do they identify with their lives and works. What is likely to seem most personal to them and to define them as individuals is their feelings or emotions.

81 ▶▶▶ What is an emotion? A word for rather disparate phenomena, such as anger, fear, anxiety, and elation; resentment, hate, love, grief, and nostalgia; jealousy, depression, and despair. The first four can exist in a moment and can be induced by drugs. Depression can also have straightforward physiological causes, but the last eight emotions take time and consist largely of thoughts.

Emotions that take time, including the first four when they persist, are a mixture of sensations (such as pain, smells, tastes, sounds, tactile and proprioceptive sensations, and images)—and thoughts. Our experiences, including dreams, are also such mixtures. Typical patterns that recur and keep containing much the same or very similar thoughts are given names, like resentment, hate, and so forth.

When emotions recur often in the same person, they become habitual, and John Dewey remarked long ago that character is habits. When resentment or jealousy, anxiety or depression becomes habitual it becomes part of a person's character. The discovery of the mind clearly involves the discovery of a person's habits and habitual emotions. Habits can be observed, but how can emotions be discovered?

In the first place, they can be communicated verbally, as when one says: I feel depressed; or: I feel grief. Beyond such flat statements, which are not always true, emotions may seem to be ineffable; but they are not. Not only can the face and the rest of the body communicate emotions, not only do actions often speak louder than words, but emotions can be communicated verbally without recourse to naming. One can spell out the thoughts that make up such a large part of an emotion. In fact, attention to detail makes for a much more power-ful form of communication than a simple statement of the form: I feel x.

Some people think that depth of feeling or emotion rules out thought, and that anyone who thinks a great deal is likely or even bound to lack profound feelings. Yet many of the greatest poems and the most magnificent speeches in Shakespeare's plays move us by communi-cating emotions that are not simply labeled; they voice the thoughts that constitute most of the emotions. Nor does it require Shakespeare's genius, or gifts beyond the reach of ordinary mortals, to convey an emotion by observing and articulating its components.

It is a commonplace that one can change one's mind, but it is widely thought that one cannot change one's emotions. We are supposed to be in the grip of grief or jealousy, hate or love. Yet philosophers have long recog-nized that this widespread notion is false, and Socrates, the Stoics and Epicureans, and Spinoza are among those who have tried to teach humanity how to emancipate itself from this bondage. So did the Buddha, a hundred years before Socrates. The most common recipe has been to cultivate thoughtfulness and moderation while abjur-ing all passion. But it is arguable that this remedy is not much better than the disease it is meant to cure and that the price for it is too high. It seems to involve the sacrifice of most art and poetry. It is at least worth inquiring whether there are not other remedies. Freud should be seen also in this perspective: psychoanalysis was intended among other things to help us to break the grip of unwelcome emotions.

There are still other ways, such as writing poetry. Religions have prescribed rituals for grieving. For those who have no religion it is doubly difficult to cope with the loss of a parent, spouse, or child. There seems to be no space in which to grieve, no place to cry. One tries to wear a cheerful mask and exercises self-control. But one can also attend to one's thoughts and feelings, allowing oneself, or even pushing oneself, to dwell on the details of every passing thought and sensation until each has been realized fully. This need not be done in a spirit of self-pity. What is maudlin is usually the substitution of a cliché for honest observations of details. Writing poems, one can make it a rule to avoid sentimental approximations and try to record things in a lean style. Then the grief will prompt poem upon poem, and when the cycle is finished, the grieving will be done. Someone else might choose prose or paint or write music. Yet others may dispense with all that and simply concentrate on the experience until it has been completed.

Discovering one's mind is like discovering a continent: It changes one's life. One can ask oneself for a start: Am I free of fear? If not, what do I fear? What precisely? Am I free of resentment? And if not, what do I resent? What precisely? And how rational is it that I fear or resent this but not that? One can catechize oneself about hate, love, jealousy, and the rest. And one can ask oneself of which of these emotions one might be willing to let go. Never mind at that point whether you think that you can let go. Just ask yourself whether you might be better off if you did, and if you would like yourself better. Think of alternatives, using your imagination. You need no analyst to do that; *you* can do it though it is not at all easy. What is still harder, of course, is then going on to shed resentment or jealousy; but that, too, can be done even if it should take some time. Habits are hard to shake.

Some philosophers, notably Sartre in a short early book, *The Emotions* (1939), have generalized about the emotions without coming to grips with any one of them, and many of the generalizations do not really fit most emotions. They are, to repeat it, a rather disparate lot, and in German, for example, there is not even a word that means "emotions." *Gefühle* means "feelings"; *Stimmungen*, "moods." But philosophers have an inveterate tendency to stick to words, as Goethe's Mephistopheles remarked (line 1990), and from words they weave webs that obscure experience from them.

Not only philosophers and, of course, theologians and sociologists do this; the failing is much more widespread. All kinds of people have tried to catch the mind in a web of words instead of attending to details. Their battle cry has been: Long live labels! Yet labels allow for a great deal of latitude. Was Jung an "anti-Semite"? Such a question is almost stupid. For a start one would have to ask: When? Say, in 1934. If you would like to know, you must consider what he wrote in 1934—and that is the crux and not whether we choose to apply that label, which is, after all, far from precise.

It is the same with character traits described by words like cowardly, lazy, honest, or kind. Such labels are generalizations based on some instances, not on others; and they admit of degrees. To be even a little more precise one might have to say that an individual is sometimes more *x* and sometimes less, then not at all, and occasionally even the opposite. The same considerations apply to Jung's pair of terms: introvert and extravert. Even if he himself had given us better definitions than he did, such terms are not very helpful when one wants to discover Jung's mind, or Freud's or Adler's. But what I am rejecting here has been criticized at some length in Volume I. It is the Kantian approach that sticks to words and often spurious dichotomies, while Goethe realized that we are our deeds and that the mind needs to be understood in terms of development.

Rarely, a label does seem to fit beautifully. I could say that I know no man more honest than Freud. But such a flat statement has its drawbacks. It immediately makes many people bristle because it conflicts with their preconceptions or their associations with either the man or the epithet. The epithet, of course, can be defined carefully to show just what one means and does not mean. But the statement remains at most an abbreviation, and when it is challenged it must be spelled out. In this volume, I think, I have spelled it out.

82 ▶▶▶ One way of spelling out my objection to too much reliance on labels and dubious dichotomies is to give another example. Most people think of comic and tragic as opposites, yet they are in fact quiet asymmetrical. A picture of a grieving woman is quite apt to be experienced as tragic and will lead some people to cry, but a photograph of a joyous woman is not felt to be comic and cause for laughter.

Laughter, in turn, is rarely a reflex reaction to the perception of something comic. It can be aggressive or a way of showing off, and in many situations it is simply a way of saying that one has got the point, while failure to laugh would be a way of saying that either one has not got it or that one considers something not funny but in bad taste. Even when laughter is a reflex it is more often a response to embarrassment than a reaction to what is felt to be comical.

The asymmetry of the tragic and comic can be seen plainly by recalling how many photographs, paintings, and sculptures strike us as tragic, and how few, if any, as comical. What would make a photograph comical? Not that it shows us birth rather than death, or joy rather than grief, or someone laughing rather than crying. Rather, some incongruity, like a pigeon on the statue of a man who looks rather pompous—a gag of sorts that is far from being the opposite of a tragic picture.

Vulgar misinterpretations of Nietzsche's title *Beyond Good and Evil* abound, while few people have paid attention to Nietzsche's pronouncement in the second section of that book: "The fundamental faith of the metaphysician is *the faith in opposite values.*" I am suggesting that the manipulation of allegedly opposite concepts has obstructed the discovery of the mind, and I have tried to show this at length in the case of Kant. Jung's dichotomy of introvert and extravert still stands in this Kantian tradition.

This is not the place to inquire to what extent philosophy must be concept-oriented. Certainly, Nietzsche's "gay science" is in some sense more concrete, closer to life and the problems that confront us as we try to live meaningful lives. For that very reason, many philosophy professors have wondered whether it is really philosophy, and Heidegger and Sartre atoned for their partial absorption of Nietzsche's heritage by blending one part of Nietzsche with three parts of Kant and Husserl. This recipe was not original with them. Nicolai Hartmann, for example, had suggested in the preface of his influential *Ethik* (1926) that the task of ethics in our time consisted largely in achieving a synthesis of Nietzsche and Kant. And we have seen (in Section 30 of Volume II) how many others, from Hans Vaihinger to Martin Buber, felt more or less the same way.

Owing to Kant's influence, existentialism was an abortion, while it remained for Freud to develop the heritage of Goethe and Nietzsche. The point about existentialism is of sufficient importance to be developed here at least briefly.

83 ▶▶▶ One might think that the story that began with the juxtaposition of Goethe and Kant, and that included Hegel and Nietzsche among its protagonists, would find its culmination in existentialism. The so-called existentialists certainly thought it did; or rather, each of them thought ill of the others, had little respect for Freud's achievement, and saw himself as adding a crowning touch. Yet none of them made Goethe's legacy his own as Freud did, and none of them paid heed to Nietzsche's *psychology.* All of them were corrupted by Kant.

With Heidegger and Buber I have dealt at length in Volume II, with Sartre's critique of Freud in Section 28 above. I have also suggested (in Section 12) that Husserl's quest for absolute certainty, his attempt to establish "phenomenology as strict science," and Heidegger's attempt to lay a new foundation (*Grundlegung,* to use Kant's term) by creating a "fundamental ontology" hark back to Kant and neo-Kantianism. Jaspers and Heidegger, Buber and Sartre, tried to reconcile Nietzsche and Kant but failed to see how that was impossible. Existentialism could not survive because its central impulses were diametrically opposed to each other.

Heidegger and Sartre started out as phenomenologists; they were followers of Edmund Husserl. Heidegger's *Being and Time* appeared in Husserl's yearbook and was dedicated to him, and Sartre's early works contain many references to himself as a phenomenologist.[4] Yet Heidegger and Sartre tried to graft onto this heritage the altogether different legacy of Kierkegaard and Nietzsche, and the wide appeal of existentialism was

---

[4] In the Introduction to *The Emotions* (1939) he still said: "We . . . establish the essence of man *before* making a start in psychology." He called himself a phenomenologist and asked: "What must a consciousness be for emotion to be possible, perhaps even to be necessary?" This sounds like a parody of Kant.

due to that legacy. To show how different this legacy is from phenomenology it may help to put down a few characteristics in two columns:

Phenomenology	*Existentialism*
"Strict science"	Closer to literature than to science
Kant's unholy trinity of certainty, completeness, and necessity	Emphasis on uncertainty, caprice, absurdity, and opposition to systems
Intuition of essences ("Wesensschau")	Opposition to "essentialism"
Hyperacademic and scholastic	Antiacademic
Great appeal to Roman Catholic philosophy professors, including Pope John Paul II	Specifically condemned by Pope Pius XII in his encyclical *Humani Generis*, in 1950
Stresses cooperative research	Stresses the solitary individual
Stresses impersonal and objective knowledge	Stresses anxiety, despair, and decision

Nevertheless, it is easy enough to understand why these two philosophies, which stand diametrically opposed to each other, are so often lumped together as "Continental philosophy" and taught as if they were a single philosophy. Phenomenology is so barren that a course devoted to it alone would attract few students, while existentialism still seems suspect to many professors who feel unsure whether it is really respectable enough academically. Treating them together solves both problems. Nor is it in any way illegitimate as long as the basic differences are taken into account. What is unfortunate is that these differences have been ignored so often, and Heidegger and Sartre share some of the responsibility for that.

Heidegger, as we have seen, failed to understand himself very well and quite lacked what Nietzsche called "the courage for an attack on one's convictions." When Heidegger began *Sein und Zeit,* he still saw himself as a Christian theologian and a phenomenologist, but soon after the publication of that book, which was presented as the "First Half" of a larger work, he discovered Nietzsche, abandoned the project, and embarked on the second phase of his philosophy, in which Nietzsche, various poets, and the pre-Socratic philosophers are as prominent as Husserl, Kant, and Aristotle had been in the first. But instead of giving himself and his readers some account of the ways in which he had changed and developed, he considered it a point of honor to insist on the elements of continuity. As long as the fundamental conflict in his thought and intentions was repressed, it could never be worked out and solved. He was stuck.

Sartre did have the courage to change and develop without playing down the discontinuities of his thought. When he took up Marxism in 1960 and disparaged existentialism as "a parasitical system living on the margins of Knowledge,"[5] he made that clear enough; yet he, too, failed to understand clearly how phenomenology and existentialism stand opposed to each other. For this we can discern two reasons.

First, the author of *L'être et le néant* (1943) craved academic respectability almost as much as Heidegger did. He had published a novel and a volume of five shocking but splendid short stories; but as a philosopher he chose to write in the manner of

[5] *Critique de la raison dialectique,* p. 18.

"Hegel, Husserl, Heidegger" (to cite the title of one of his chapters) and played down the antiacademic heritage of Kierkegaard and Nietzsche. His celebrated play *Les mouches* (*The Flies*) is full of echoes of Nietzsche and based on Nietzsche's dictum: "To take upon oneself *guilt* and not punishment, that alone would be godlike."[6] But in his role as philosopher Sartre lacked the daring to follow Nietzsche very far.

His concern for academic respectability was a symptom of a more profound lack of courage. He was not prepared for the radical implications of the existentialist thrust. His remarkable lecture *L'existentialisme est un humanisme* (1946), which acquainted the world with "existentialism," shows this clearly. The ethic proposed here is not the Nietzschean ethic of *Les mouches* but an ill-considered version of Kant's ethic. The discussion after the lecture showed Sartre that this variant would not work, and the book on ethics that he had planned to write remained unwritten. Recoiling from the radical insecurity of his highly individualistic "existentialism," he then sought refuge in Marxism.

I have tried to show elsewhere how we find the same "existentialist pattern" in Kierkegaard, Heidegger, and Sartre, and how Marxism came to play much the same role for the later Sartre that Christianity had played for Kierkegaard. What they wrote about they endowed with authority, as when Sartre called Marxism "the one philosophy of our time which we cannot go beyond"; but the writer read his own ideas into Marxism (or Christianity—or in the case of Heidegger, into Hölderlin and the pre-Socratics), and got them back endowed with authority. This generally involved reinterpretations that strike many readers as very radical and exciting, though they

---

[6] *Ecce Homo,* I.5; cf. "The Adder's Bite" in *Zarathustra,* I. See "Nietzsche's Influence on *The Flies*" in Kaufmann, *Tragedy and Philosophy,* Section 51.

are philologically and historically quiet untenable; and it also involved a good deal of *mauvaise foi* or self-deception.[7]

In Heidegger's philosophy existentialism was merely one element with which he never chose to identify fully; in Sartre's development it was at most the second phase through which he passed on the way from phenomenology to Marxism, but in his philosophical books he never identified fully with this thrust, and he came close to working out its implications only in some of his literary works. Yet the excitement generated by Heidegger and Sartre was always due to this Nietzschean element in their work.

Neither of them ever came to grips with the fundamental conflict in his own thought. While Heidegger got stuck, Sartre turned to Marxism and naturally found himself involved in the very same conflict as before. While accepting it as "Knowledge" and "the one philosophy of our time which we cannot go beyond," he really never could accept it fully, and he remained an individualist despite himself.

There were other conflicts that he never managed to resolve, for example, his attitude toward words. He had been brought up to revere literature and the written word, but in his autobiographical book *Les mots* (1964) he railed against words, just like Hamlet, whose outburst undoubtedly inspired the title of the work: "I . . . Must (like a whore) unpack my heart with words."[8] With his enormous facility with words, Sartre felt that words were cheap compared to action. It seems as if he meant to punish himself as well as the flow of words without which he could not live when, being able to write beautifully and memorably, he cheapened words again and again in sloppily written journalistic pieces and even

[7] See Volume II, Section 35, note 16.
[8] In the final speech of Act II. See also line 194 of the same scene: "Words, words, words."

in philosophical works that he did not choose to revise with the loving care he devoted to his literary works. (See Section 34 of Volume I.)

Philosophy furnishes ample material for case studies, allowing us to discover the minds of philosophers and to show how an understanding of their mentality illuminates their work. Otherwise, twentieth-century philosophy, which is to say philosophy since Nietzsche, has contributed little to the discovery of the mind and does not provide a good foundation for it. Ironically, Nietzsche, who did contribute a great deal to it, is the only modern philosopher who has been approached as if he were of interest mainly as a psychological case, while his psychology has been ignored. So deep is the reluctance of most philosophers to face up to the subject of this trilogy.

84 ▶▶▶ Freud developed the legacy of Goethe and Nietzsche and contributed more to the discovery of the mind than anyone else in the twentieth century. I have tried to show that, but also that his therapy is dated like the great ocean liners that, in his time, provided the only means to reach the new world; and without stressing this fact, I have not found his contribution in his theories either. But what remains if one accepts neither his practice nor his theories? The question may seem to be rhetorical, but I have answered it at length in an attempt to show that a great deal remains; for example, the ten contributions discussed at length in the first chapter of this volume.

If I did not see Freud as well as Adler and Jung very differently from the ways in which their own disciples have seen them, there would have been no need to write this book. But one point on which I differ with Freud still needs to be spelled out. While he was not as deeply rooted in nineteenth-century science as has often been claimed, and Jung's talk of "Freud's soulless materialism" is laughable, Freud assumed as most people still do that the discovery of the mind calls for correct theories.

In fact, the people who contributed most to the discovery of the mind were poets and novelists, like Sophocles, Shakespeare, and Dostoevsky—and Goethe, Nietzsche, and Freud who developed a highly poetic science that was not really theory-oriented. Freud's discoveries of the importance of childhood experiences and of sex, and of the significance of dreams and mischievements help us to understand ourselves and other people better, even—and especially—if we do not accept the generalizations that he offered occasionally because he thought that he had to if he wanted to be scientific. Such generalizations can be proved wrong by counterexamples—even by a single exception—and Freud did not come close to showing that there were no counterexamples, nor have most of his followers tried to remedy this deficiency. Nor do Freud or Nietzsche command our admiration as methodologists. On that score they were not impressive. They taught us to ask illuminating questions.

That may sound like faint praise, but in fact no higher praise is possible when our concern is with discovering the mind. It is surely no cause for regret or recriminations that there are no universal laws that permit us to predict our own future or that of our fellow men. To understand ourselves and others better we need to ask fruitful questions and be alert to interesting possibilities. Once again an example may help.

Nietzsche spoke of "sublimated sexuality" and "sublimated sex impulse" and raised the question of what drives an artist sublimates and what drives scientists sublimate.[9] Freud developed this theme and sug-

[9] *Human, All Too Human*, Vol. II, Section 95; *Werke*, XI, p. 259; *The Will to Power* 677. For further references and detailed discussion see Kaufmann, *Nietzsche*, Chapters 7 and 8.

gested that art, writing, and science involve the sublimation of libido. Yet the sublimation of libido or the sex impulse is much more problematic than another kind of sublimation that Freud did not consider and that Nietzsche, who occasionally alluded to it, never explored at any length: the sublimation of aggression. In his late works, Freud postulated two basic drives, but he failed to note how much of art and literature, philosophy and psychology, involves the sublimation of aggression.

Freud and Nietzsche themselves furnish striking examples, and so does Goethe, whose Mephistopheles is among other things a vehicle for the poet's aggressiveness—"the spirit who always negates," criticizes, attacks, and takes pleasure in being destructive. Here one can truly speak of sublimation, because the writer who refines his aggressiveness and expresses it in civilized constructive ways in his works may actually get his aggressiveness out of his system that way. Goethe and Freud achieved a high measure of serenity because they managed to use their destructive impulses constructively.

Whether libido can be sublimated with equal success depends on how strong the sex impulse is in an individual. For some this strategy may work, while for many others libido is more like hunger that can indeed be forgotten totally while one is immersed in one's work though eventually it will claim its rights.

The sex lives of the nine men considered at length in this trilogy have not been explored in depth, but in most cases there is strong evidence that their sex impulse was relatively weak. Goethe, who wrote some of the most beautiful love poems in any language, is no exception; he probably was a virgin until he was almost forty. Like Leonardo, Michelangelo, and Beethoven, he seems to have channeled almost all of his vitality and libido into his work; and that was our good fortune.

One of the most remarkable features of the sex

impulse is that it obviously has a physical basis but is capable of assimilating other needs and desires; for example, the desires for security, reassurance, and conquests, and the need to fill a frightening void. Desires and needs of this kind are often mistaken for sexual needs although they can be satisfied nonsexually. Goethe and Beethoven, Leonardo and Michelangelo, Nietzsche and Freud did not have to satisfy needs of this kind through sexual intercourse. But even Freud and Nietzsche never fully understood this.

Neither Nietzsche nor Freud worked out a precise and tenable theory of sublimation, much less general laws that permit predictions; yet they taught us what kinds of questions we might ask. The suggestions just made here are clearly derived from their work and help us to understand the men studied in this trilogy as well as many others and ourselves. We need no universal law nor a full-fledged theory to ask: What part, if any, did aggression play in Freud's work? And then to recall how he compared himself to a conquistador (Section 50), or to realize how with his theories he struck back at the Vienna he hated, at its prudery and hypocrisy, at the dishonesty of mankind, at the morality and religion of his fellow citizens, and at the God of his fathers. Of course, the very same question is warranted in Jung's or Adler's case and always needs to be balanced by also asking what part love played.

Similarly, we need no universal law or precise theory to ask whether a man's relationship to his own mother influenced his character, or to note how Jung still fought his father in *Answer to Job.* One philosophical theory stipulates that every historical explanation implicitly invokes covering laws. In fact, I think, this is not what historians do, nor do we require such a model in the discovery of the mind. It is quite sufficient to note that men who feel that their mothers did not love them enough *often* overcompensate in later life and crave admiration and recognition. Eventually, of course, one will seek an answer to the question why there are exceptions to this rule, if there are, and what makes the difference. But even without knowing that, we have learned from Freud and Nietzsche what questions to ask. (See also Section 22 of Volume II.)

Freud's brief peripatetic analysis of Gustav Mahler provides a good illustration of this point. In 1908, the famous composer was persuaded to consult Freud, who was then on vacation. Although Freud generally would not see patients at such a time, he made an exception for Mahler who, however, sent a telegram breaking the appointment. This happened three times. Then Freud told him that he was about to leave for Sicily; Mahler went to Leyden to see Freud, and the two men walked through the streets for four hours. Mahler had no previous knowledge of psychoanalysis, but according to Jones (II, p. 80), Freud said he had never known anyone who understood it so quickly.

> Mahler was greatly impressed by a remark of Freud's: "I take it that your mother was called Marie. I should surmise it from various hints in your conversation. How comes it that you married someone with another name, Alma, since your mother evidently played a dominating part in your life?" Mahler then told him that his wife's name was Alma Maria, but that he called her Marie! . . . This analytic talk evidently produced an effect, since Mahler recovered his potency and the marriage was a happy one until his death, which unfortunately took place only a year later.

Apparently, Freud led Mahler to see his relationship to his wife in a new light. Mahler also said that he suddenly understood why the noblest and most emotional passages in his music had been "spoiled by the intrusion of some commonplace melody." After an unbearable scene between his parents, Mahler as a young boy had rushed out of the house in an emotional turmoil, and just then a hurdy-gurdy ground out *Ach, Du lieber Augustin*. Mahler felt that ever since then high tragedy and light amusement were associated in his mind, and "the one mood inevitably brought the other with it."

Work on associations had been done before Freud, and the point here is not to establish Freud's originality but rather the fact that our understanding of ourselves and others can be advanced without invoking universal laws or elaborate theories. What is crucial is asking fruitful questions.

We have seen that, according to Ernest Jones, "Freud several times said of Nietzsche that he had a more penetrating knowledge of himself than any other man who ever lived or was ever likely to live." In one way Nietzsche surely did understand himself better than Freud understood himself. Nietzsche recognized his own will to power much more clearly than Freud recognized *his*. Despite his immense emphasis on sex, Freud was anything but oversexed; he as able to channel most of his libido into his writing; and his sex impulse became very weak in his forties. His will to power, however, did not abate so early, and the fight he put up against his cancer for more than sixteen years is stunning. As a doctor, he could easily have put an end to his pain, but he underwent thirty-three operations, lived in pain much of the time, and kept writing until the end. He had no religious scruples about suicide and did not care as much about survival as he did about his work and the triumph of his ideas. As his system began to fight his as yet undiagnosed cancer, Freud realized that not all of human behavior could be explained in terms of the pleasure principle and the reality principle, but even then he never understood himself fully. If that can be said even of Freud, one might well say, with apologies to Shelley: Look on his works, ye Mighty, and despair!

85 ▶▶▶ That the discovery of the mind does not stand or fall with theories and that theories are often overvalued is no new idea. This insight has been central in Zen Buddhism from the start, many centuries ago, and something of the sort is also implicit in Buber's *I and Thou* and, again in very different form, in Werner Erhard's *est*.

If Freud's therapy is really dated like the great ocean liners, one must ask what has taken its place. No single method has, but the search for speedier and less expensive means has become more and more widespread since the Second World War. As far as therapy or self-understanding is concerned, the crucial choice is certainly not between Freud, Adler, and Jung. There are countless other alternatives, and most of them play down theory and look for quicker results.

Even if one did opt for an analysis, it would be far from irrational to consider the personality and wisdom of the analyst no less important than his theories. But many analysts, including some of the most renowned, are poor advertisements for their theories. Freud once discussed this point in his own inimitable manner:

> It is undeniable that the analysts have not in all cases attained in their own personalities the measure of psychic normality that they wish to help their patients to attain. Opponents of analysis like to point to this fact with scorn to use it as an argument for the uselessness of analytical exertions. On might reject this criticism as an unjust demand. Analysts are persons who have learned to practice a certain art and may be human beings on the side like anyone else. One does not claim, after all, that somebody cannot be a good internist if his own internal organs are not healthy.[10]

[10] *Werke*, XVI, p. 93f.

But Freud went on to admit that this analogy was improper because in some situations the analyst must "serve the patient as a model, in others as a teacher." Moreover, "the analytical relationship is founded on the love of truth, which means recognition of reality and precludes all illusion and deception." It is certainly legitimate to look at Freud, Adler, and Jung in this perspective. But there is also another consideration.

It is reasonable to judge a therapy by its results. One way of doing that is to try to amass statistics. The trouble with that procedure is that there are so many variables that are extremely difficult to take into account. One of these is the personality of the analyst. But it seems legitimate to look at the analysts themselves and ask what their theories have done for them. As one reads either the autobiography or the biography of Fritz Perls, the founder of Gestalt therapy, to give but one example, one can hardly help feeling that he never ceased to be a very sick individual.

His vivid sense of the limitations of words and theories was rooted in his own lack of any great literary or theoretical talent, but that in itself does not prove him wrong. Another point about Perls merits consideration here. In 1969, shortly before his death, he established a center at Cowichan in Canada and asked people to come to this quasi kibbutz, promising: "In three months there I can cure any neurosis." That was frankly a boast, and Perls himself could not know for sure whether he would be able to keep this promise. His biographer, Martin Shepard, who reported it (p. 183), explained: "Cowichan revolved around shared work, Gestalt therapy training sessions, and free-floating evening encounters in which appreciations and resentment were expressed. . . . And everything that happened there was grist for the thera- peutic mill." Why shouldn't such total immersion in a new enviroment make it possible to cut down the time required for a cure? Or for increased self-understanding? And for insight into the workings of the minds of others?

Naturally, others went on to seek ever shorter short-cuts, also involving groups rather than individual analytic sessions. One might suppose that the presence of a group is bound to become a diversion, and that much more can be accomplished when one has the undivided attention of the therapist or teacher. But as Woodrow Wilson recognized when he established the preceptorial system of instruction at Princeton University (he was president of the university before he became governor of New Jersey and then President of the United States), and as people who have participated in group therapy sessions have found again and again, this is false. Exposure to our peers and their confusions and complaints frequently allows us to see our own as in a mirror. The mirror is not always an ordinary fine mirror; often it is much more like a concave or convex funhouse mirror and gives us distorted images that are frightening or ridiculous. Theories have no monopoly on giving people insight about themselves and others; seeing oneself and others suddenly in new perspectives can achieve wonders.

While there is nothing wrong in principle with group sessions, it is worth asking, of course, whether any particular kind really produces more than a temporary lifting of the spirit, and whether it really results in any enduring self-understanding or insight about others. The answer does not hinge on whether the person in charge is a theorist of the caliber of Nietzsche or Freud.

Many people, including myself, have gained insight into themselves and others as a result of the *est* "training"; yet Werner Erhard, who designed it, is no theorist or writer at all. The present volume has dealt in some depth with Freud, Adler, and Jung and is not intended as a survey of dozens of alternatives. But let no one suppose that Freud marks the end of the road, or that only Jung and Adler have tried to go beyond him, or that what we need most urgently is yet another theory! Of course, we should ask eventually why something seems to work, and why something else does not, but insight does not have to wait until an elaborate theory has been established.

Plato insisted that reason can take us only so far, and that the last step to knowledge and insight has to be a vision. When he said this, his primary concern was no longer with Socrates' imperative: Know thyself! For those whose concern *is* with the discovery of the mind, no such neat sequence can be stipulated. But intellectual exertion is not enough.

Was all this research really necessary for an understanding of Freud, Adler, and Jung—or for self-discovery? Actually, much more reading would be needed to understand these three men thoroughly. I have merely provided some new perspectives and hope that from now on these men will not be seen quite as they used to be seen.

To ourselves there are many roads. One might even say what used to be said of Rome: All roads lead to ourselves. Yet all roads also lead away from ourselves and can become routes of escape. Nature can be a distraction and art a diversion, though it is also possible to discover oneself—or others—in a painting or sculpture, in a poem or a novel, in the sea or the woods.

Scholarship is often a form of escape. These pages, too, can be read as a diversion, perhaps even as a detective story. They could also enhance your self-understanding no less than writing them has increased mine.

Bibliography ▸▸▸

Adler, Alfred. A complete bibliography of his writings is included in *Superiority and Social Interest*. Edited by Heinz L. and Rowena R. Ansbacher. Evanston, Ill.: North-western University Press, 1964; 3rd ed., New York: W. W. Norton, in preparation.

———. *Co-operation Between the Sexes: Writings on Women, Love and Marriage, Sexuality, and Its Disorders*. Edited and translated by Heinz L. and Rowena R. Ansbacher, with an essay [pp. 248–421] by Heinz L. Ansbacher. Garden City, N.Y.: Anchor Books, 1978.

———. *The Individual Psychology of Alfred Adler: A Systematic Presentation in Selections from His Writings*. Edited and annotated by Heinz L. and Rowena R. Ansbacher. New York: Basic Books, 1956. Harper Torchbooks, 1964. Contains a bibliography of Adler's publications on pp. 465–70.

———. *Problems of Neurosis: A Book of Case Histories*. Edited by Philip Mairet. Introduction to the Torchbook Edition by Heinz L. Ansbacher. New York: Harper Torchbooks, 1964.

———. *The Science of Living*. New York: Garden City Publishing Co., 1929; Edited and with an Introduction by Heinz L. Ansbacher. Garden City, N.Y.: Anchor Books, 1969.

———. *Studie über Minderwertigkeit von Organen*. Berlin and Vienna: Urban & Schwarzenberg, 1907.

———. *Über den nervösen Charakter. Grundzüge einer vergleichenden Individualpsychologie und Psychotherapie.* Wiesbaden: J. F. Bergmann, 1912.

———. *Understanding Human Nature: A Key to Self-Knowledge.* Translated by W. Beran Wolfe. Greenwich, Conn.: Fawcett, 1961 (copyright 1927, 1954).

———. Andreas-Solomé, Lou. *In der Schule bei Freud: Tagebuch eines Jahres, 1912/1913.* Edited by Ernst Pfeiffer. Zurich: Max Niehans, 1958.

Ansbacher, H. L. "The Development in Psychoanalytic Theory toward a Humanistic Orientation." In A. S. Prangishvili, A. E. Sherozia, and F. V. Bassin, eds., *The Unconscious,* Vol. 4. Tbilisi, U.S.S.R.: Metsniereba Publishing House. In preparation.

———. See also under Adler and under Maslow. H.L.A. was for many years the editor of the *Journal of Individual Psychology* and contributed many articles to it.

Bergmann, Frithjof. "Epistemology and Social Science." Unpublished typescript.

Berlin, Isaiah. *The Hedgehog and the Fox.* London: Weidenfeld & Nicolson, 1953.

Billinsky, John M. "Jung and Freud (The End of a Romance)." *Andover Newton Quarterly,* November 1969, pp. 39–43.

Binswanger, Ludwig. *Erinnerungen an Sigmund Freud.* Bern: Francke, 1956.

Bloch, Jochanan. *Die Aporie des Du: Probleme der Dialogik Martin Bubers.* Heidelberg: Lambert Schneider, 1977.

Bottome, Phyllis. *Alfred Adler: A Biography.* New York: G. P. Putnam's Sons, 1939.

Brooks, Peter. Review of Sulloway (see below). *The New York Times Book Review,* February 10, 1980.

Buber, Martin. *Briefwechsel aus sieben Jahrzehnten,* edited by Grete Schaeder. 3 vols. Heidelberg: Lambert Schneider, 1972, 1973, 1975.

———. *Ich und Du.* Leipzig: Insel, 1923. *I and Thou: A New Translation with a Prologue 'I and You' and Notes by Walter Kaufmann.* New York: Scribner, 1970.

Eissler, K. R. *Talent and Genius: The Fictitious Case of Tausk contra Freud.* New York: Grove Press, 1971.

Ellenberger, Henri F. *The Discovery of the Unconscious: The*

History and Evolution of Dynamic Psychiatry. New York: Basic Books, 1970.

Erikson, Erik. *Gandhi's Truth.* New York: W. W. Norton, 1969.

Eysenck, H. J. "Astrology—Science or Superstition?" *Encounter,* December 1979.

Federn, Paul. "Sándor Ferenczi, . . . Gedenkrede, gehalten in der Trauersitzung der Wiener Psychoanalytischen Vereinigung am 14. Juni 1933, *Internationale Zeitschrift fur Psychoanalyse;* XIX (1933), 3.

———. See also under Maslow and under Nunberg.

Ferenczi, Sándor. *Bausteine zur Psychoanalyse.* 2 vols. Leipzig, Vienna, Zurich: Internationaler Psychoanalytischer Verlag, 1927.

Fisher, Seymour, and R. P. Greenberg. *The Scientific Credibility of Freud's Theories and Therapy.* New York: Basic Books, 1977.

———, Eds. *The Scientific Evaluation of Freud's Theories and Therapy: A Book of Readings.* New York: Basic Books, 1978.

Freud, Sigmund. *Sigmund Freud: Konkordanz und Gesamtbibliographie,* edited by Ingeborg Meyer-Palmedo. Frankfurt: Fischer, 1977. The concordance makes it easy to locate all references to the German *Werke* in the English *Standard Edition* or the German *Studienausgabe,* and vice versa. The bibliography of Freud's publications appears on pp. 79–103, an alphabetical list of his writings on pp. 104–14. A most helpful little book.

———. *Gesammelte Werke. Chronologisch Geordnet.* 18 vols. (Actually, Vol. II/III is one volume.) London: Imago, 1940–52. Vol. 18, *Gesamtregister* (Indices), Frankfurt: Fischer, 1968. Since 1960, the whole edition, Frankfurt: Fischer. *The Standard Edition of the Complete Psychological Works of Sigmund Freud.* 24 vols. London: Hogarth Press, 1953–74.

———. *Aus den Anfängen der Psychoanalyse. Briefe an Wilhelm Fliess, Abhandlungen und Notizen aus den Jahren 1887–1902.* [Edited by Marie Bonaparte, Anna Freud, and Ernst Kris]. London: Imago, 1950. *The Origins of Psychoanalysis.* Translated by Eric Mosbacher and James Strachey. New York: Basic Books, 1954.

———. *Briefe 1873–1939.* Edited by Ernst L. Freud [= Ernst and Lucie Freud]. Frankfurt: Fischer, 1960. *The Letters of*

Sigmund Freud. Translated by Tania and James Stern. New York: Basic Books, 1960.

———. *Neue Folge der Vorlesungen zur Einführung in die Psychoanalyse*. Vienna: Internationaler Psychoanalytischer Verlag, 1933 = *Werke*, Vol. XV. Listed here because in the text it is occasionally identified as Freud (1933).

———/Karl Abraham. *Briefe 1907–1926*. Edited by Hilda C. Abraham and Ernst L. Freud. Frankfurt: Fischer, 1965.

———/Lou Andreas-Salomé. *Briefwechsel*. Edited by Ernst Pfeiffer. Frankfurt: Fischer, 1966. *Letters*. Translated by William and Elaine Robson-Scott. New York: Harcourt Brace Jovanovich, 1972. The English version contains some material deleted in 1966.

———/Josef Breuer. *Studien über Hysterie*. 1895. Frankfurt: Fischer Taschenbuch, 1970.

———/C. G. Jung. *Briefwechsel*. Edited by William McGuire and Wolfgang Sauerländer. Frankfurt: Fischer, 1974. *The Freud/Jung Letters: The Correspondence between Sigmund Freud and C. G. Jung*. Edited by William McGuire. Freud letters translated by Ralph Manheim, Jung letters by R. F. C. Hull. Princeton: Princeton University Press, 1974.

———/Oskar Pfister. *Briefe 1909–1939*. Edited by Ernst L. Freud and Heinrich Meng. Frankfurt: Fischer, 1963.

———/Edoardo Weiss. *Briefe zur psychoanalytischen Praxis. Mit den Erinnerungen eines Pioniers der Psychoanalyse*. Frankfurt: Fischer, 1973. The letters in the original German, the memoirs translated by Martin and Etelka Grotjahn from the American edition, *Sigmund Freud as a Consultant: Recollections of a Pioneer in Psychoanalysis*. New York: Intercontinental Medical Book Corp., 1970.

———/Arnold Zweig. *Briefwechsel*. Edited by Ernst L. Freud. Frankfurt: Fischer, 1968.

———. *Protokolle* or *Minutes*. See Nunberg.

Friedenthal, Richard. *Goethe: His Life and Times*. Cleveland and New York: World Publishing, 1965.

Gay, Peter. *Freud, Jews and Other Germans*. New York: Oxford University Press, 1978.

Gerth and Mills. See Weber, Max.

Glatzer, N. N., ed. *The Dimensions of Job: A Study and Selected Readings*. New York: Schocken, 1969.

Goethe, J. W. *Sämtliche Werke. Propyläen-Ausgabe.* 45 vols., plus 4 supplementary vols. Munich: Georg Müller, and later Berlin: Propyläen Verlag, no dates.

Graf, Max. "Reminiscences of Professor Sigmund Freud." *Psychoanalytic Quarterly,* 1942, pp. 465–76. Translated by Gregory Zilboorg.

Grünbaum, Adolf. "Epistemological Liabilities of the Clinical Appraisal of Psychoanalytic Theory." *Nous,* XIV (1980).

———. "How Scientific is Psychoanalysis?" in *Science and Psychotherapy.* Edited by Raphael Stern, L. S. Horowitz, and J. Lynes. New York: Haven Publishing, 1977.

———. "Is Freudian Psychoanalytic Theory PseudoScientific by Karl Popper's Extension of Demarcation?" *American Philosophical Quarterly,* April 1979 (16.2), pp. 131–41.

Heidegger, Martin. *Sein und Zeit: Erste Hälfte.* Halle: Niemeyer, 1927.

Hesse, Hermann. *Gesammelte Werke,* Vol. XII. Frankfurt: Suhrkamp, 1970.

Holmes, D. S. "Investigations of Repression: Differential Recall of Material Experimentally or Naturally Associated with Ego Threat." *Psychoanalytic Bulletin,* 1974, pp. 632–53.

Husserl, Edmund. "Philosophie als strenge Wissenschaft." *Logos,* Vol. 1 (1900–1).

Jaffé, Aniela. *Aus Leben und Werkstatt von C. G. Jung.* Zürich: Rascher, 1968. *From the Life and Work of C. G. Jung.* Translated R. F. C. Hull. New York: Harper, 1971.

———. *C. G. Jung: Bild und Wort.* Olten: Walter, 1977. *C. G. Jung: Word and Image.* Translated by Krishna Winston. Princeton: Princeton University Press, 1979. The 205 illustrations include 47 in color, of which 11 show paintings by Jung.

Jaspers, Karl. *Allgemeine Psychopathologie.* Berlin: Springer, 1913. 7th ed., 1959.

———. *Vernunft und Widervernunft in unserer Zeit.* Munich: Piper, 1950.

Jones, Ernest. *Free Associations: Memories of a Psycho-Analyst.* New York: Basic Books, 1959.

———. *The Life and Work of Sigmund Freud.* 3 vols. New York: Basic Books, 1953, 1955, 1957.

Jung, C. G. *General Bibliography of C. G. Jung's Writings.*

Compiled by Lisa Ress with Collaborators = Vol. 19 of *The Collected Works*. Includes Original Works, translations into 19 languages, the German and English *Collected Works,* and Seminar Notes.

———. *Die gesammelten Werke von C. G. Jung.* 17 vols. so far. Zurich: Rascher, 1958–70. Olten: Walter, 1971– . *The Collected Works of C. G. Jung.* Translated mostly by R. F. C. Hull. New York: Pantheon Books for Bollingen Foundation, 1953–60; Bollingen Foundation (distributed by Pantheon Books, a Division of Random House), 1961–67. Since 1967, Princeton University Press. 20 vols. "Vol. 9" was published in 2 vols. as 9, i, and 9, ii. Vol. 19: *General Bibliography.* Vol. 20: *General Index.* The British and American editions have the same pagination, the German edition does not, but the marginal numbers of the paragraphs are the same and should therefore be cited instead of pages.

———. *Antwort auf Hiob.* Zurich: Rascher, 1952. Also in Vol. 11 of *Werke.*

———. *Briefe.* 3 vols.: 1906–45, 1946–55, 1956–61. Edited by Aniela Jaffé and Gerhard Adler. Olten: Walter, 1972–73. *Letters.* 2 vols.: 1906–50, 1951–61. Translated by R. F. C. Hull. Princeton: Princeton University Press, 1973–76.

———. *C. G. Jung Speaking: Interviews and Encounters.* Edited by William McGuire and R. F. C. Hull. Princeton: Princeton University Press, 1977. Not included in *Collected Works.*

———. *Erinnerungen, Träume, Gedanken.* Aufgezeichnet und herausgegeben von Aniela Jaffé. Zürich: Rascher, 1962, 4th ed., 1967. *Memories, Dreams, Reflections.* Translated by Richard and Clara Winston. New York: Random House, Pantheon, 1962. Not included in *Collected Works.*

———. *Notes on the Seminar in Analytical Psychology Conducted by Dr. C. G. Jung, Zurich March 23–July 6, 1925.* Arranged by Members of the Class. Zurich, 1926. Unpublished typescript, copyright 1926 by Dr. C. G. Jung.

———. *The Portable Jung.* Edited by Joseph Campbell. New York: Viking Press, 1971.

———. *"Wandlungen und Symbole der Libido. Beiträge zur Entwicklungsgeschichte des Denkens,"* in *Jahrbuch für Psychoanalytische und Psychopathologische Forschungen,*

1911–12 (III.1, pp. 120–227, and IV.1, pp. 162–464), and then in one volume, Leipzig and Vienna: Deuticke, 1912. This book, of which Jung later claimed falsely that it had precipitated the break with Freud, is not included in the *Collected Works;* only the extensively revised version of 1952 is included in Vol. 5. The original text of 1912 was translated by Beatrice M. Hinkle as *Psychology of the Unconscious: A Study of the Transformations and Symbolisms of the Libido. A Contribution to the History of the Evolution of Thought.* New York: Moffat, Yard; London: Kegan Paul, 1916.

Kaufmann, Walter. *Critique of Religion and Philosophy.* New York: Harper, 1958. With a new Preface, Princeton: Princeton University Press, 1978.

———. *The Faith of a Heretic.* Garden City, N.Y.: Doubleday, 1961. With a new Preface, New York: New American Library, 1978. Chapter XI: "Freud and the Tragic Virtues."

———. *From Shakespeare to Existentialism.* Boston: Beacon Press, 1959; rev. ed., Garden City, N.Y.: Doubleday, 1960. With a new Preface, Princeton: Princeton University Press, 1980. Chapter 16: "Freud."

———. *The Future of the Humanities.* New York: The Reader's Digest Press, 1977. With a new Preface, New York: McGraw-Hill, 1981.

———.*Nietzsche: Philosopher, Psychologist, Antichrist.* Princeton: Princeton University Press, 1950; 4th ed., revised and expanded, 1974.

———. Review of David Bakan, *Sigmund Freud and the Jewish Mystical Tradition. Judaism,* Spring 1959.

———. Review of Jones, Vol. 3. *Judaism,* Winter 1958.

———. *Tragedy and Philosophy.* Garden City, N.Y.: Doubleday, 1968. With a new Preface, Princeton: Princeton University Press, 1979.

———. *Without Guilt and Justice.* New York: Peter Wyden, 1973. New York: Dell, Delta Books, 1975.

———. See also under Nietzsche and Sartre.

Koestler, Arthur. *The Lotus and the Robot.* London: Hutchinson, 1960.

Kraus, Karl. "Traumstück." In *Dramen* (*Werke*, Vol. 14). Munich and Vienna: Albert Langen, Georg Müller, 1967.

Laplanche, J., and J. B. Pontalis. *Vocabulaire de la Psychanalyse*. Paris: Presses Universitaires de France, 1967. *The Language of Psychoanalysis*. Translated by Donald Nicholson-Smith. New York: W. W. Norton, 1973.

Lasch, Christopher, "Freud and Women." *New York Review of Books*. October 3, 1974.

Malcolm, Norman. *Ludwig Wittgenstein*. London: Oxford University Press, 1958.

Marcuse, Herbert. *Eros and Civilization*. Boston: Beacon Press, 1955.

Maslow, A. H. "Was Adler a Disciple of Freud? A Note." *Journal of Individual Psychology*, May 1962 (18.1), p. 125. Followed by "A Reply" by Heinz L. Ansbacher on pp. 126–35; "A Freudian View" by Ernst Federn, November 1963 (19.2), pp. 80–82; and "Reply" by H. L. Ansbacher, p. 82.

McGuire, William. Letter in *The Journal of Analytical Psychology*, January 1976 (21.1), pp. 94–5.

———. See also under Freud and Jung.

Minutes. See Nunberg.

Murray, Henry A., ed. *Explorations in Personality*. New York: Oxford University Press, 1938.

Neumann, Erich. *Ursprungsgeschichte des Bewusstseins*. Mit einem Vorwort von C. G. Jung. Zurich: Rascher, 1949. *The Origins and History of Consciousness*. Translated by R. F. C. Hull. New York: Pantheon, 1954. Harper Torchbooks, 1962. Princeton: Princeton University Press, 1970.

Nietzsche, Friedrich. *Gesammelte Werke, Musarionausgabe*, 23 vols. Munich: Musarion Verlag, 1920–29.

———. Between 1954 and 1974 all but three early works appeared in new translations by Walter Kaufmann. *The Portable Nietzsche*. New York: Viking, 1954, now Penguin, contains *Thus Spoke Zarathustra, Twilight of the Idols, The Antichrist*, and *Nietzsche contra Wagner. Beyond Good and Evil* (1966), *The Birth of Tragedy and The Case of Wagner* (1966), and *On the Genealogy of Morals and Ecce Homo* (1968)—all New York: Random House—were published in three volumes as Vintage Books and then also in one hardcover volume as *Basic Writings of Nietzsche*, a Modern Library Giant—all with commentaries. *The Will to Power*, with commentary, Random House, 1968. *The Gay Science,* with commentary, Random House, 1974.

Nunberg, Herman, and Ernst Federn, eds. *Protokolle der Wiener Psychoanalytischen Vereinigung,* 4 vols.: 1906–1908, 1908–1910, 1910–1911, 1912–1918. Frankfurt: Fischer, 1976, 1977, 1979, 1980? *Minutes of the Vienna Psychoanalytic Society,* Translated by M. Nunberg. New York: International Universities Press, 1962, 1967, 1974, 1975.

Orgler, Hertha. *Alfred Adler: The Man and His Work.* London: C. W. Daniel, 1939. New York: New American Library, 1972.

Perls, Frederick, S., Ralph Hefferline, and Paul Goodman. *Gestalt Therapy.* New York: Julian Press, 1951.

Perls, Fritz (= Frederick S.) *The Gestalt Approach and Eye Witness Therapy.* Science and Behavior Books, 1973. New York: Bantam Books, 1976.

———. *In and Out of the Garbage Pail.* Real People Press, 1969. New York: Bantam Books, 1972.

Popper, Karl R. *Conjectures and Refutations: The Growth of Scientific Knowledge.* New York: Basic Books, 1962. 2nd ed., revised, 1965. New York: Harper Torchbooks, 1965.

———. *The Open Society and Its Enemies.* London: Routledge, 1945. Revised ed., Princeton: Princeton University Press, 1950. "Addendum" in later editions, London: 1963; Princeton, 1966.

———. *The Philosophy of Karl Popper.* Edited by P. A. Schilpp. 2 vols. the Library of Living Philosophers. LaSalle, Ill.: Open Court, 1974.

Rank, Otto. *Das Inzest-Motiv in Dichtung und Sage.* Leipzig and Vienna: Deuticke, 1912.

———. *Das Trauma der Geburt und seine Bedeutung für die Psychoanalyse.* Leipzig, Vienna, Zurich: Internationaler Psychoanalytischer Verlag, 1924.

Reik, Theodor. *From Thirty Years with Freud.* Translated by Richard Winston from the German original of 1940. New York: International Universities Press, 1949.

Roazen, Paul. *Brother Animal: The Story of Freud and Tausk.* New York: Knopf, 1969.

———. *Freud and His Followers.* New York: Knopf, 1975.

Robinson, Paul. *The Freudian Left.* New York: Harper, 1969.

Rorty, Richard. *Philosophy and the Mirror of Nature.* Princeton: Princeton University Press, 1979.

Rosenberg, Samuel. *Why Freud Fainted.* Indianapolis and New York: Bobbs-Merrill, 1978.

Sachs, Hanns. *Freud: Master and Friend.* Cambridge: Harvard University Press, 1944.

Sartre, Jean-Paul. *Critique de la raison dialectique.* Paris: Gallimard, 1960. *Critique of Dialectical Reason.* Translated by Alan Sheridan-Smith. Edited by Jonathan Ree. London: NLB, 1976.

———. *Esquisse d'une théorie des émotions.* Paris: Hermann, 1939. *The Emotions: Outline of a Theory.* Translated by Bernard Frechtman. New York: Philosophical Library, 1948.

———. *L'être et le néant.* Paris: Gallimard, 1943. *Being and Nothingness.* Translated by Hazel E. Barnes. New York: Philosophical Library, 1956.

———. *L'existentialisme est un humanisme.* Paris: Les Editions Nagel, 1946. Philip Mairet's translation in Walter Kaufmann, ed., *Existentialism from Dostoevsky to Sartre.* New York: Meridian Books, 1956. Revised and expanded ed., New York: New American Library, 1975.

———. *Les mouches.* Paris: Gallimard, 1943. *No Exit and The Flies.* Translated by Stuart Gilbert. New York: Knopf, 1947.

Schönau, Walter. *Sigmund Freuds Prosa: Literarische Elemente seines Stils.* Stuttgart: J. B. Metzler, 1968.

Schorske, Carl E. *Fin-de-Siècle Vienna: Politics and Culture.* New York: Knopf, 1980.

Schur, Max. *Freud: Living and Dying.* New York: International Universities Press, 1972.

Shepard, Martin. *Fritz: An Intimate Portrait of Fritz Perls and Gestalt Therapy.* Saturday Review Press, 1975. New York: Bantam Books, 1976.

Simon, Ernst. "Sigmund Freud, the Jew." *Yearbook II of the Leo Baeck Institute of Jews from Germany.* London, 1957.

Smyser, William Leon. "The Czar of Psychoanalysis" *New York Herald Tribune,* Sunday, April 28, 1929.

Soyka, Otto. Review of Freud's *Drei Abhandlungen zur Sexualtheorie.* In *Die Fackel,* edited by Karl Kraus, Vienna, December 21, 1905 (VII. 191).

Sperber, Manes. *The Masks of Loneliness: Alfred Adler in Perspective*. (Translated by Krishna Winston from the German *Das Elend der Psychologie*, 1970.) New York: Macmillan, 1974.

Stern, Paul J. *C. G. Jung: The Haunted Prophet*. New York: Braziller, 1976. New York: Delta Books, 1977.

Storr, Anthony. *C. G. Jung*. New York: Viking Press, 1973.

Sulloway, Frank J. *Freud, Biologist of the Mind: Beyond the Psychoanalytic Legend*. New York: Basic Books, 1979.

Taft, Jessie. *Otto Rank: A Biographical Study Based on Notebooks, Letters, Collected Writings, Therapeutic Achievements and Personal Associations*. New York: Julian Press, 1958.

Viereck, George Sylvester. *Glimpses of the Great*. New York: Macaulay Co., 1930.

Weber, Marianne. *Max Weber: Ein Lebensbild*. Tübingen: J. C. B. Mohr, 1926.

Weber, Max. *Wissenschaft als Beruf*. Munich: Duncker & Humbolt, 1919. This is the source of *"die Entzauberung der Welt,"* cited in Section 22.

———. *From Max Weber: Essays in Sociology*. Translated, edited, and with an introduction by H. H. Gerth and C. Wright Mills. New York: Oxford University Press, 1946.

Wheelright, Joseph. Review of *The Freud/Jung Letters. Psychological Perspectives*, 2, pp. 171–76.

Wittels, Fritz, "Goethe und Freud." *Die psychoanalytische Bewegung*, II.5 (September–October 1930), pp. 431–66. Included in *Freud and His Time*. Translated by Louise Brink. New York: Liveright, 1931.

———. *Sigmund Freud: Der Mann, die Lehre, die Schule*. Leipzig, Vienna, Zurich: E. P. Tal & Co. Verlag, 1924.

Wollheim, Richard, ed. *Freud: A Collection of Critical Essays*. Garden City, N.J.: Anchor Books, 1974.

———. Review of Sulloway. In *The New York Review of Books*, November 8, 1979.

———. *Sigmund Freud*. New York: Viking Press, 1971.

Wortis, Joseph. *Fragments of an Analysis with Freud*. New York: McGraw-Hill, 1954.

Zaehner, R. C. *The Concise Encyclopedia of Living Faiths*.

New York: Hawthorne Books, 1959. Boston: Beacon Press, 1967.

Zweig, Stefan. *Die Welt von Gestern*. Stockholm: Bermann-Fischer, 1944. Frankfurt: Fischer Bibliothek, 1955. *The World of Yesterday*. (No translator is named, and the German edition is copyright 1944.) New York: Viking, 1943.

ADDENDA

Binion, Rudolph, *Frau Lou: Nietzsche's Wayward Disciple*, Princeton University Press, 1968.

Geertz, Clifford, "A Wary Reasoning: Humanities, Analogies, and Social Theory." Talk published under different title in *American Scholar*, Spring 1980; pp. 165–179.

Acknowledgments ▶▶▶

It has been my good fortune that William McGuire, executive editor of the *Collected Works of C. G. Jung*, and editor of *The Freud/Jung Letters* and *C. G. Jung Speaking*, works at the Princeton University Press and is a friend. He and W. W. Bartley III, a close friend who lives far away, have freely shared some of their knowledge and ideas with me and have commented critically on some of my material. This strikes me as doubly generous, considering that their views of Jung were very different from mine.

Indices ▶▶▶

All numbers refer to sections, not pages.
See also the elaborate tables of contents.

Index of Names for Volume I

Dürer, Albrecht, 30
Eckhart, Master, 21
Eckermann, J. P., 5
Eisler, R., 39n.
Elias, Julius, 18
Eliot, George, 14
Engelmann, Paul, 21
Engels, Friedrich, 45
Euclid, 22
Faust, 8, 9, 13, 16, 17
Feuerbach, Ludwig, 14
Fichte, J. G., 9, 19, 21, 22, 34, 35, 39, 43
Findlay, J. N., 40, 45
Freud, Sigmund, 1, 3, 5, 8, 9, 11, 13–16, 18, 20, 21, 26, 36, 40, 46
Friedenthal, Richard, 38n.
Fries, J. J., 21
Fulda, H. F., 39n
Garve, Christian, 34
Gast, Peter (Heinrich Köselitz), 34
Gide, André, 9
Glockner, Hermann, 12n., 37, 40
God, 5, 6, 22, 24, 32, 36, 38, 43, 46
Goethe, August, 6
Goethe, Cornelia, 38
Goethe, J. W., 2–20, 22, 23, 25, 26, 29–31, 34–43, 45, 46
Gogh, Vincent van, 7, 29
Gower, Lord Francis Leveson, 6
Haering, Theodor, 37, 39
Hamann, Johann Georg, 16, 25
Hamilton, Sir William, 39
Handel, G. F., 30
Hartmann, Eduard von, 39
Hartmann, Klaus, 45n.
Haydn, F. J., 30
Haym, Rudolf, 16n., 37, 40
Hegel, G. W. F., 2, 9–16, 18–22, 25, 28, 30, 34, 35, 36–46
Hegel, Karl, 44
Heidegger, Martin, 3, 15, 22, 26, 34, 35, 36, 39, 46
Heine, Heinrich, 26
Heisenberg, Werner, 13
Henrich, Dieter, 39n.
Herder, Johann Gottfried, 9, 16, 25, 34, 39
Herz, Marcus, 25, 34
Hesse, Hermann, 9, 43
Hilbert, David, 24n.
Hobbes, Thomas, 21, 34
Hoffer, Eric, 5
Hoffmeister, J., 39, 43n., 46n.
Hölderlin, Friedrich, 39, 42, 43
Homer, 14, 30, 46
Humboldt, Wilhelm von, 18
Hume, David, 21, 30, 34
Husserl, Edmund, 39
Iphigenia, 38
Ibsen, Henrik, 5
Irmischer, J. K., 24n.
Jachmann, R. B., 25, 30, 31, 34, 35
Jacobi, F. H., 4, 12, 16, 35
James, William, 8, 18
Jaspers, Karl, 35
Jesus, 15, 25, 26, 38, 43, 46
Jina, 21
Jung, C. G., 3, 14, 18, 36, 46
Kafka, Franz, 31

Kant, Immanuel, 2, 3, 5–16, 18–41, 43, 45, 46
Kantzenbach, F. W., 9n, 16
Kestner, Johann Christian, 4
Kierkegaard, S., 5, 15, 30, 34–36, 39, 40, 46
Klopstock, Friedrich Gottlieb, 16, 30
Knebel, Carl Ludwig von, 18
Knox, T. M., 38
Kuhn, Thomas, 12
Lambert, J. H., 39
Lao-tze, 21
Lasson, Georg, 40
Lazarus, Moritz, 39
Leibniz, G. W., 21, 22
Lessing, G. E., 17, 25, 26, 30, 32, 34–36, 38, 40
Lewes, George Henry, 14
Lewis, C. I., 22
Lichtenberg, Georg Christoph, 16
Lincoln, Abraham, 7
Lowenberg, J., 40
Luke, 25
Luther, Martin, 18, 20, 21, 24, 25, 27
Mach, Ernst, 39
MacIntyre, A., 38n.
Maimon, Salomon, 25
Malcolm, Norman, 45
Mann, Thomas, 9
Marcuse, Herbert, 40
Marius, Richard, 21n.
Mark, 38n.
Martini, Simone, 29
Marx, Karl, 18, 28, 38, 39, 43, 45, 46
Matthew, 25, 38
Mendelssohn, Moses, 17, 25, 34, 35
Mephistopheles, 6, 9, 10, 13, 17, 23, 46
Micah, 25
Michelangelo, 10
Moore, G. E., 46
Moses, 21, 24–27
Mozart, W. A., 30
Müller, G. E., 40
Müller, Max, 21
Napoleon, 7, 39, 40
Newton, Isaac, 11–13, 22, 35, 45
Nicolovius, Friedrich, 35
Niebuhr, Reinhold, 25
Niethammer, F. I., 39, 40n., 43
Nietzsche, Friedrich 2, 3, 5–7, 9, 11, 13–16, 18, 21, 22, 24, 26, 30, 34–38, 40, 42, 43, 45, 46
Nohl, Hermann, 37, 38, 43n.
Novalis, 39
Oedipus, 1, 7
Orestes, 38
Orwell, George, 31
Parmenides, 35
Pascal, B., 1
Paton, H. J., 22, 33
Paul, 25, 27, 38
Paulus, H. E. G., 46
Pindar, 4
Pitcher, George, 45
Plato, 2, 7, 8, 10, 21, 22, 30, 31, 35, 38, 40, 42, 46
Pniower, Otto, 10, 37
Pöggeler, Otto, 39, 43, 45
Popper, Karl, 45

Prometheus, 7
Purpus, W., 42n.
Rembrandt, 7, 10, 29, 30
Rilke, R. M., 14
Rousseau, Jean Jacques, 4, 24, 30
Samson, 7, 26
Sartre, Jean-Paul, 2, 5, 8, 34, 39
Saul, King, 7
Schelling, F. W. J., 9, 11, 18–20, 21, 22, 35, 37, 39, 43
Schiller, Friedrich, 2, 5, 8, 9, 12, 14, 18, 25, 30, 31, 35, 38, 42, 46
Schlick, Moritz, 21
Schmidt, Conrad, 45
Schopenhauer, Arthur, 9, 11, 14, 20–22, 30, 32, 34, 35, 37, 39, 46
Schopenhauer, Johanna, 6
Schultz, Uwe, 9n., 21n.
Servetus, Michael, 25
Shakespeare, William, 10, 14, 16, 18, 30
Shelley, P. B., 6, 14
Simmel, Georg, 14
Sinclair, Isaak, 43
Smith, Adam, 28
Smith, Norman Kemp, 22, 24, 33
Smith, Vincent A., 29
Socrates, 7, 31, 35
Solzhenitsyn, A., 35
Sophocles, 1, 7, 15, 30, 38
Soret, Frédéric Jacob, 9

Spiegelberg, H., 39n.
Spinoza, B., 4, 12, 22, 34, 35, 40, 46
Steinthal, H., 39
Stirling, J. H., 38
Strack, H. L., 25n.
Strauss, David Friedrich, 14
Strawson, P. F., 34n.
Taylor, Charles, 16
Tetens, J. N., 34
Thomson, William, 45
Vaihinger, Hans, 14, 33, 34n.
Virgil, 14
Vorländer, Karl, 14, 24ns., 25, 27, 30–32, 35ns.
Voss, Johann Heinrich, 30, 46
Vulpius, Christiane, 6
Wagner, Richard, 16, 37
Walch, Johann Georg, 24n.
Wasianski, E. A. Ch., 25, 34
Wilcox, John, 35n.
Wilhelm II, 25
Willoughby, L. A., 18
Wilkinson, E. M., 18
Wittgenstein, Ludwig, 21, 45
Wolff, Robert Paul, 23, 24
Wright, Georg Henrick von, 45
Zarathustra, 37
Zellman, C. G., 43
Zelter, K. F., 10, 14, 40

Index of Names for Volume II

Abraham, 48
Achilles, 14, 19
Adler, Alfred, 7, 17, 19, 21
Adorno, Theodor, 46
Aeschylus, 29, 41, 45, 53
Ajax, 14
Albert, Hans, 35n.
Alexander the Great, 14, 19
Allemann, Beda, 41n.
Andreas, Fred Charles, 27
Angel, Ernest, 33
Ansbacher, H. L., 19
Aristotle, 11, 16, 31, 35, 39, 43
Augustine, 40
Bacon, Francis, 29
Baeck, Leo, 44, 47, 50
Bakunin, M. A., 51
Baalshem, 46
Bäumler, Alfred, 17, 32
Beethoven, Ludwig van, 19
Behler, Ernst, 26
Bellini, Vincenzo, 28
Benjamin, Walter, 46
Bentham, Jeremy, 6
Berkeley, George, 17
Berne, Eric, 21
Bertram, Ernst, 27n.
Binswanger, Ludwig, 51n.
Bismarck, Otto von, 21
Bobynin, 20
Böhme, Jacob, 40
Borchardt, Rudolf, 46
Boswell, James, 20
Breazeale, Daniel, 15
Brod, Max, 46

Buber, Martin, 1–3, 5, 11, 15, 24, 30, 39, 41, 42, 44–55
Buber, Rafael, 45
Buddha, 23, 53
Bülow, Hans von, 27
Caesar, 19
Campbell, Joseph, 27
Camus, Albert, 21
Carus, Carl Gustav, 11
Cassirer, Ernst, 34
Chamfort, 27
Charlemagne, 23
Cicero, 26
Colli, Giorgio, 43
Confucius, 23
Contat, Michel, 26
Coupland, W. C., 11
Dante, 29, 53
Darwin, Charles, 15, 17, 18, 27
Descartes, René, 17, 31, 33, 35, 37, 51
Diemer, Alvin, 34n.
Dilthey, Wilhelm, 35, 36, 38, 50
Diomedes, 14
Dionysus, 17, 27
Divine, Father, 7
Dostoevsky, F. M., 10, 13, 21, 24
Dumas, Alexander, 22
Ebner, Friedrich, 49
Eckermann, J. P., 42
Eisen, Hal, 21n.
Eliot, T. S., 43
Ellenberger, Henri F., 7, 9, 11, 33
Emerson, R. W., 20
Engels, Friedrich, 51
Erhard, Werner, and *est*, 14, 21

Indices ▶ 489

Index of Names for Volume III

Buber, Martin, 11, 19, 24, 67, 69, 79, 80, 82, 83, 85
Buddha, 32, 81
Burckhardt, Jakob, 62
Burne-Jones, Edward, 52
Caesar, 28, 61, 62
Cain, 71
Calvin, J., 72
Campbell, Joseph, 70
Carus, C. G., 8
Charcot, J. M., 13, 15, 50
Chrobak, 50
Claparède, Edouard, 7
Clark, Vernon, 20
Cobb, Stanley, 76
Columbus, 17
Copernicus, 22
Dante, 80
Darwin, Charles, 8, 11, 22, 27
David, King, 71
Descartes, René, 11, 80
Deutsch, Helene, 40
Devatmananda, Swami, 56
Dewey, John 81
Dido, 28
Dilthey, Wilhelm, 11, 80
Dostoevsky, F. M., 24, 32, 37, 52, 84
Du Bois-Reymond, Emil Heinrich, 8
Einstein, Albert, 6, 13, 19, 20, 34, 70
Eissler, K. R., 36, 40
Eliade, Mircea, 61
Elijah, 62
Eliot, T. S., 64, 71
Ellenberger, Henri F., 35n., 36–38, 41, 75
Ellis, Havelock, 13, 25
Emerson, Ralph Waldo, 36
Erhard, Werner, and *est,* 30, 47, 48, 85
Erikson, Erik, 70, 76
Eve, 71
Eysenck, H. J., 20
Faust, 24, 63
Federn, Ernst, 39
Federn, Paul, 38, 39, 46
Féré, Charles, 49
Ferenczi, Sándor, 27, 30, 36–38, 46, 57, 58, 60, 66n.
Fichte, J. G., 8
Fisher, S., 26n.
Fliess, Wilhelm, 6–8, 15, 24, 36, 43, 46n., 50
France, Anatole, 61
Freud, Anna, 7, 40
Freud, Ernst, 44
Friedenthal, Richard, 5
Fromm, Erich, 48
Furtmüller, C., 39, 41, 60
Galdston, Iago, 8
Gandhi, Mahatma, 70
Gauquelin, Françoise, 20
Gauquelin, Michel, 20
Gay, Peter, 7, 52n.
Geertz, Clifford, 23n.
Gide, André, 16
Glatzer, Nahum, 71
Goethe, J. W., 4–12, 14, 15, 18, 19, 21, 23, 27, 33, 34, 37, 41, 42, 47, 53, 56, 60n., 62–64, 70, 72, 74, 78–82, 84

Gogh, Vincent van, 34, 47
Gomperz, Theodor, 13
Goodman, Paul, 30
Götz von Berlichingen, 63
Graf, Max, 41n., 52, 57
Greenberg, R. P., 26n.
Grünbaum, Adolf, 19, 29
Häberlin, Paul, 45
Habermas, Jürgen, 16
Haeckel, Ernst, 8
Hagen, 61, 62
Hamlet, 20, 51, 83
Hartmann, Eduard von, 12, 75
Hartmann, Nicolai, 82
Häutler, Adolf, 50
Heckel, Erich, 52
Hefferline, Ralph, 30
Hegel, 6, 8, 12, 18, 19, 23–25, 27, 28, 32, 33, 53, 55, 75, 79, 80, 83
Heidegger, Martin, 6, 11, 12, 15, 16, 18, 19, 23, 28, 44, 53, 60, 63, 68, 74, 76, 79, 80, 82, 83
Heine, Heinrich, 5–7, 12, 15, 37, 39, 42, 51, 52, 64
Helmholtz, H., 8, 10,
Hesse, Hermann, 22, 65n.
Hilbert, David, 80
Hinkle, Beatrice M., 58
Hirschfeld, Magnus, 25
Hitler, Adolf, 16, 56, 63, 68
Hitschmann, Eduard, 38, 39
Hofmannsthal, Hugo von, 36, 52
Hölderlin, 83
Holmes, D. S., 19n., 27
Homer, 37, 71
Hull, R. F. C., 7, 53, 54n., 55, 56, 68n.
Hume, David, 40
Husserl, Edmund, 12, 82, 83
Ibsen, Henrik, 12n., 36, 52
Jacobi, Max, 11
Jaffé, Aniela, 56, 62, 66, 68, 71
James, William, 32, 46, 54, 56, 69, 76
Janet, Pierre, 49
Januarius, Saint, 28
Jaspers, Karl, 6, 44, 49
Jekels, Ludwig, 39
Jeremiah, 32
Jesus, 62, 63, 72, 75, 77
Job, 71–73
Jocasta, 24
John the Divine, 72
John the Evangelist, 72
Jonah, 72
John Paul II, Pope, 83
Jones, Ernest, 6n., 7, 9–11, 14, 15, 17, 21n., 27, 30, 31, 33, 34, 36, 37, 41n., 42–44, 50, 52, 56–60, 49n., 60n., 84
Joseph, 26
Judas, 61, 62, 73
Jung, C. G., 1–4, 7, 8, 11, 12, 15, 17–19, 22, 23, 27, 34–37, 39–48, 52–82, 84, 85
Jung, Emma, 46n., 58–60, 64, 69
Kafka, Franz, 5, 6
Kahane, Max, 37
Kandinsky, Wassily, 52
Kant, 5–8, 11, 12, 15, 18, 24, 27, 28, 33, 40, 45, 53, 56, 61, 63, 64, 79, 80, 82, 83